Praise for *Waiting 'Til the Midnight Hour*

"Peniel E. Joseph, a talented young historian . . . has finally taken us beyond the politics of memory, mining virtually every available archive and printed source relevant to the Black Power saga. The result is an engaging . . . revisionist narrative that reveals a hidden world of black intellectual ferment and purposeful political organizing." —*The Washington Post*

"In his well-paced debut, Joseph gets beyond Black Power symbolism—afros, shades, black-gloved fists raised in the air—to examine the movement's origins, ideologies and key players. Vividly illuminates the personalities and politics of a turbulent time." —*Kirkus Reviews*

"*Waiting 'Til the Midnight Hour* marks the dawn of a new black narrative history; nuanced, deeply researched, and brilliantly insightful. [It] will become a new standard interpretation of black political culture in the 1960s."

—Manning Marable, professor of public affairs, history and African-American studies, Columbia University, and author, most recently, of *Living Black History*

"Peniel Joseph represents the best of a new generation of scholars whose work will substantially revise our understanding of the Black Freedom movement. Provocative and masterfully written, *Waiting 'Til the Midnight Hour* not only reveals the radical roots of Black Power but places the key activists and struggles within a global framework. It is one of those critically important books that will be read and debated for many years to come."

—Robin D.G. Kelley, author of *Freedom Dreams: The Black Radical Imagination*

"Joseph . . . surveys the full geographic and political panorama of the black power movement. . . . [He gives] a more complete overview of this era." —*Booklist*

"Peniel Joseph takes us beyond the simplistic and superficial treatments of the Black Power movement to present that movement in all its complexity, and in its historical context. It is a dramatic story, carefully researched, and deserving of our attention."

—Howard Zinn, professor emeritus of political science, Boston University, and author of *A People's History of the United States: 1492–Present*

"This fresh, powerful, and passionate history captures the complexity and reveals the often misunderstood character and impact of the Black Power movement."

—Ira Katznelson, Ruggles Professor of Political Science and History, Columbia University, and author of *When Affirmative Action Was White: An Untold History of Racial Inequality in Twentieth-Century America*

"The writing is nimble. . . . The author is often willing to face the more discreditable facts about the movement, giving the book a tough-mindedness necessary for coming to terms with the past."

—*New York Newsday*

"In writing this wise and dazzling display of literary elegance and expert excavation, Peniel Joseph has vaulted into the front ranks of interpreters of this nation's most explosive era: the 1960s."

—Gerald Horne, professor of history, University of North Carolina, Chapel Hill, and author of *Red Seas: Ferdinand Smith and Radical Black Sailors in the United States and Jamaica*

"Eloquent and scenic [with] just the sweep, force, and drama appropriate to its subject. Moves . . . easily and aptly back and forth between North and South, the local and the global, the political and the popular."

—David Roediger, Kendrick C. Babcock Professor of History, University of Illinois at Urbana-Champaign, and author of *Working Toward Whiteness: How America's Immigrants Became White*

"Joseph . . . brings to light less-known characters like the Rev. Albert Cleage Jr. of Detroit, who helped organize the 1963 Walk for Freedom a month before the March on Washington, as well as fresh judgments on figures like Malcolm X, 'black America's prosecuting attorney.' . . . [A] good introduction to the topic." —*Publishers Weekly*

"With rigorous scholarship, Joseph has done a great service toward the understanding of this complex history, enabling the spirit of those times to reach into the present through the voices of those who participated."
—Lewis R. Gordon, Laura H. Carnell Professor, Temple University, and coeditor of *Not Only the Master's Tools* and *A Companion to African-American Studies*

"The challenge in writing a history of Black Power rests in negotiating a maze of political, social, and economic forces, balancing the interplay of local, national, and international events, respecting the influence of big and small actors, and appreciating the rich intellectual inheritance that informed this movement. *Waiting 'Til the Midnight Hour* tells this story with sensitivity to the connection between the smallest historical detail and the broad sweep of black struggle."
—Craig Steven Wilder, professor of history, Dartmouth College, and author of *In the Company of Black Men*

"Informative and elegant . . . skillfully carries the reader across time and space . . . from Harlem to the rural South, Detroit to Los Angeles, Cuba to Ghana." —*Philadelphia Weekly*

Also by Peniel E. Joseph

*The Black Power Movement: Rethinking the
Civil Rights–Black Power Era* (editor)

WAITING 'TIL THE MIDNIGHT HOUR

WAITING 'TIL THE MIDNIGHT HOUR

A NARRATIVE HISTORY OF
BLACK POWER IN AMERICA

PENIEL E. JOSEPH

AN OWL BOOK

HENRY HOLT AND COMPANY ■ NEW YORK

Owl Books
Henry Holt and Company, LLC
Publishers since 1866
175 Fifth Avenue
New York, New York 10010
www.henryholt.com

An Owl Book® and 🅗® are registered trademarks
of Henry Holt and Company, LLC.

Distributed in Canada by H. B. Fenn and Company Ltd.

Library of Congress Cataloging-in-Publication Data

Joseph, Peniel E.
   Waiting 'til the midnight hour : a narrative history of
Black power in America / Peniel Joseph.—1st ed.
      p. cm.
Includes index.
   ISBN-13: 978-0-8050-8335-4
   ISBN-10: 0-8050-8335-9
   1. Black power—United States—History—20th century. 2. African Americans—
Civil rights—History—20th century. 3. Civil rights movements—United States—
History—20th century. 4. African Americans—Politics and government—
20th century. 5. African Americans—Intellectual life—20th century. 6. United
States—Race relations. I. Title: Waiting until the midnight hour. II. Title.

E185.615.J68 2006
323.1196'073—dc22   2005046765

Henry Holt books are available for special promotions and premiums.
For details contact: Director, Special Markets.

Originally published in hardcover in 2006 by Henry Holt and Company

First Owl Books Edition 2007

Designed by Victoria Hartman

Printed in the United States of America

D 12 13 14

For my Mother
and for Catarina

"We need to expand the civil-rights struggle to a higher level—to the level of human rights. Whenever you are in a civil-rights struggle, whether you know it or not, you are confining yourself to the jurisdiction of Uncle Sam. No one from the outside world can speak out in your behalf as long as your struggle is a civil-rights struggle."

Malcolm X, "The Ballot or the Bullet"

"So Black Power is now a part of the nomenclature of the national community. To some it is abhorrent, to others dynamic; to some it is repugnant, to others exhilarating; to some it is destructive, to others it is useful. . . . One must look beyond personal styles, verbal flourishes and the hysteria of the mass media to assess its values, its assets and liabilities honestly."

Martin Luther King Jr., *Where Do We Go from Here: Chaos or Community?*

CONTENTS

PREFACE

The Black Power movement remains an enigma. Historians trace its origins to Stokely Carmichael's defiant declaration during the June 1966 Meredith March, which would unleash a movement that would peak with the calls for armed struggle announced by the Black Panthers, and inspire the poetry and race consciousness of the Black Arts movement. In the popular mind, Black Power is most often remembered as a tragedy—a wrong turn from Martin Luther King Jr.'s hopeful rhetoric toward the polemics of black nationalists who blamed whites for the worsening urban crisis, on the one hand, and, on the other, gun-toting Black Panthers who vowed to lead a political revolution with an army of the black underclass.

Waiting 'Til the Midnight Hour reconsiders this story, arguing that understanding the history behind the iconic Black Power imagery—clenched fists, Black Panthers, racial upheavals, dashiki- and afrowearing militants—requires plumbing the murky depths of a movement that paralleled, and at times overlapped, the heroic civil rights era. Early Black Power activists were simultaneously inspired and repulsed by the civil rights struggles that served as a violent flashpoint for racial transformation. Occupying marginal arenas of black life that Ralph Ellison characterized as the "lower frequencies," radicals laid the groundwork for the racial militancy, cultural transformation, and political organizing of the late 1960s and early 1970s, the time in which Black Power occupied the national stage.

Black Power at the local, national, and international level would launch a radical political movement that while racially specific was nevertheless interpreted by a variety of multiracial groups as a template for restructuring society. Black Power, beginning with its revision of black identity, transformed America's racial, social, and political landscape. In a premulticultural age where race shaped hope, opportunity, and identity, Black Power provided new words, images, and politics. If the movement's confrontational posture quickened the pace of racial change, it also provoked a visceral reaction in white Americans who could more easily identify with civil rights activists than with Black Power militants. Ultimately, Black Power accelerated America's reckoning with its own uncomfortable, often ugly, racial past, and in the process spurred a debate over racial progress, citizenship, and democracy that would scandalize as much as it would change the nation.

WAITING 'TIL THE
MIDNIGHT HOUR

INTRODUCTION

TO SHAPE A NEW WORLD

Malcolm X arrived in Harlem in the early 1950s on the heels of the contentious departure of another of its adopted, if little-known, sons. As Malcolm was bounding into Harlem's local political arena, Harold Cruse was settling downtown, still clinging to wistful dreams that he had, temporarily at least, put on hold. As a young boy, Harold Cruse dreamed of becoming a writer. For a southern-born black boy coming of age in the Great Depression, this was an ambitious goal, with long odds. Born in Petersburg, Virginia, in 1916, Cruse moved as a young boy to New York City as part of the exodus to northern cities that would shortly transform African American life. The then-largest internal migration in American history sowed the seeds for Harlem's emergence as a cultural mecca that would become the headquarters for black political resistance, intellectual achievement, and cultural innovation. A second great migration, which started during the early 1940s, of southern-born blacks (which eventually eclipsed its earlier counterpart in both density and geographical breadth), extended to cities and regions recently buoyed by the movement for civil rights. Coalitions of civil rights activists, trade unionists, Communists, and

Pan-Africanists led strategic campaigns for racial justice and radical democracy that stretched from gritty Harlem neighborhoods through Detroit's industrial shop floors to Dixie's cradle, Birmingham, Alabama, and out west to Oakland's postwar boomtown.[1]

Cruse's favorite time was spent reading books at the local library. It was no ordinary public library. Harlem was home to the New York Public Library's Negro History Division, a repository of black history and culture founded by the Afro-Puerto Rican bibliophile, historian, and curator Arturo Schomburg. Schomburg's passion for African, Caribbean, and African American history provided the residents of Harlem's black community a window onto its past.[2]

In the 1950s, black nationalists stalked Harlem like itinerant Baptist preachers in search of wayward flocks, wistful for the heady post–World War I years, when "New Negroes" reshaped Afro-America with a dose of militancy as effervescent as it was unprecedented. Marcus Mosiah Garvey's dynamic presence had fueled this golden age, when the Universal African Legions (soldiers in Garvey's Universal Negro Improvement Association) held Harlem captive with precision marching, ornate uniforms, and defiantly proud stares.[3] No sooner had Garvey overcome what appeared to be insurmountable organizational, financial, and political obstacles than his movement collapsed, victimized by internal ineptitude, government surveillance, and jealous rivals. Garvey's arrest on charges of mail fraud, and subsequent incarceration during the mid-1920s, made room for other advocates of interracial class struggle who, during the height of the New Negro, could barely be heard above the din of nationalist fervor.

If Garvey's absence created space for radicals, the Great Depression invited another front in the war for racial equality: class-based political agitation. With organizing energies fueled by social crises, the Communist Party (CP) made small, but surprisingly robust, headway in Harlem. While Garvey stoked controversy through grand gestures aimed at coaxing dignity from Africa's descendants, the CP offered a Promethean vision of class struggle. As Cruse remembered, anyone who couldn't debate the finer points of Marx and Engels was "considered a goddamned dummy!"[4]

By the late 1930s, the Depression introduced the possibilities of social, cultural, and political revolution at home and abroad and reached Harlem's street corners, barbershops, churches, and other institutions. Much of Cruse's early political education took place at the Harlem YMCA, which served as a debating society, intellectual training ground, and incubator for what Cruse later described as a hotbed of political activity. The all-black neighborhood blurred class distinctions among Afro-Americans, where Harlemites rubbed shoulders with leading black literary lights.[5] Virtually every block of Harlem was up for grabs: nationalists exhorting on one corner, while Socialists and others set up their headquarters fifty yards away. Pamphlets on class struggle, Pan-Africanism, and trade unionism compressed decades of social history into easily digestible prose. Walking through parts of Harlem, you risked being bombarded by pamphleteers selling, or sometimes giving away, propaganda that recounted the history of Negro oppression and offered a blueprint for black liberation.

Fascism's triumphs in parts of Europe and Africa gave black Americans the opportunity to fight for freedoms abroad that they were denied at home. For blacks the fight against an overseas enemy lent urgency to domestic struggles for racial justice. Stationed in a supply company in Italy and North Africa, Cruse became friendly with Italian Communists. There were pragmatic reasons for such friendships. Preyed on by hijackers and other criminal elements, vulnerable black supply officers negotiated with the Italian Underground as a matter of professional survival and personal protection.[6]

Cruse returned home, more politically conscious and worldly, to a Harlem that had also matured. In fact, postwar New York City became a battleground for some of the most militant and cosmopolitan efforts to achieve racial equality in the United States, and Harlem was the movement's nerve center.[7] For instance, seizing opportunities created by postwar momentum for progressive politics, the National Association for the Advancement of Colored People—the NAACP—and the Council on African Affairs joined forces to promote a human rights platform for the nascent United Nations.[8] Groups such as the National Negro Labor Congress and the Civil Rights Congress, as well as leading black intellectuals (Paul Robeson, Richard Wright, and Langston Hughes among them), established relationships with Communists that ranged from dangerous flirtation to intimate association.[9] Communists, through support of black criminal defendants, sharecroppers, trade unionists, artists, and writers, also played an important, hotly debated role among black activists during this period. Black sympathizers, not to mention members, viewed the CP as a potential vehicle for liberation, while anti-Communists suspected the group of playing African Americans for dupes (a fear promoted by the federal government). The majority of black folk remained neutral, accepting the CP's support in certain instances of bald-faced racial injustice while never coming close to becoming professional members. In 1946, Cruse officially joined the Communist Party. Like many in his generation, he entered radical politics at the peak of its post–World War II popularity, only to come of age amid its steady decline during the Cold War.

From rural hamlets and small southern cities to giant urban metropolises, the black postwar generation challenged racial discrimination in industry, labor, housing, and domestic and foreign policy. Paul Robeson, the broad-shouldered Renaissance man who possessed the physique of a football player, the mind of an intellectual, and a sonorous bass voice that thrilled a global listening audience, emerged as the most popular spokesperson for black insurgency during the 1940s.[10]

Robeson's radicalism was rooted in his identification with underdogs of every race, color, and creed, an advocacy that found him proclaiming solidarity with indigenous people from Africa to the Soviet Union. Yet while leaders such as Robeson served as invaluable political mobilizers, a national black freedom movement was brokered, block by block, at the local level by far less glamorous figures.[11] Ella Baker (future founder of the Student Nonviolent Coordinating Committee), in her capacity as the NAACP's branch director, helped this process unfold in cities like New York through grassroots organizing efforts that stressed cooperation with trade unions affiliated with the left-wing Congress of Industrial Organizations (CIO).[12]

If the end of the war ushered in dramatic changes for black Americans, it also exposed enduring problems. Wartime race riots, most infamously Detroit's 1943 orgy of violence sparked by competition over jobs and housing, bared the enormity of the unresolved crisis. Rising expectations of black veterans met with racial violence, precarious employment opportunities, and a blatant defense of segregation that found local voice from Harlem to the Mississippi Delta to parts west and national representation among powerful Washington politicians.

International events paralleled, and at times intersected with, postwar black freedom struggles; events in Africa proved pivotal in this regard. The rapid decolonization of African states fostered domestic and international pan-African alliances, anchored by the stately presence of Afro-America's legendary intellectual propagandist W. E. B. Du Bois and the controversial outspokenness of Paul Robeson. Domestically, an assortment of militant organizations mirrored these developments, jointly promoting antiracism at home and human rights abroad.[13]

Postwar black activism heralded new hopes for racial justice in every facet of American life, though such hopes were offset by a presidential directive that established a hard peace through the threat of global war. The Truman Doctrine offered a picture of international, multiracial democracy that was, in theory, tantalizingly expansive. In practice, Truman's foreign policies created a domestic political order that sacrificed freedoms of speech and political association, not to mention agendas for racial and economic justice, at the altar of what he proclaimed to be a larger evil—Communist totalitarianism. Remnants of the black freedom struggle responded in different ways to the Cold War's assault on the civil liberties of black radicals. Robeson and Du Bois held steadfast in their commitment to Socialism and paid the price in legal troubles and tarnished reputations. Other, less stalwart, fellow travelers turned government collaborators, informing on ex-comrades. The NAACP navigated the political storms by turning inward, withdrawing from the postwar black liberal-left alliance and opting instead for a more narrow description of racial justice and domestic peace.[14]

Although after World War II black Americans would enjoy new rights, yet more freedoms remained to be claimed; it was the space between new rights and unclaimed freedoms that would fuel Black Power activists. In 1953, amid setbacks for radicals of all stripes and after less than a decade as a Communist, Harold Cruse left the CP. He was not alone. Like his more famous contemporaries, Richard Wright and Ralph Ellison, Cruse grew skeptical of the CP's capacity to lead a political revolution. Indeed, the Communist Party's Depression-era eloquence on race matters—exemplified by its vigorous attacks on segregation as well as the "black belt" thesis that allowed "Negro self-determination," or black nationalism, to penetrate Communist ideology—sagged in subsequent decades, weighed down by an almost evangelical sectarianism.[15] Ex-Communists and former radicals responded to the CP's ideological zigzags in different ways, with Ellison embracing American universalism, despite America's stubborn resistance to black inclusion, while Wright searched, until his premature death, for new revolutionary ideals. Cruse settled on a vision of black nationalism—self-determination, unity, and the cultural politics of race—that retained the international awareness he first witnessed on Harlem street corners, read about at the New York Public Library, and experienced through service in World War II and, ironically, the Communist Party. Cruse's disappointment with Communism could be seen in bitter personal relationships with Harlem's leading literary figures, such as Lorraine Hansberry, as well as in his own failures in the field of arts and letters. Operating in social and cultural arenas that claimed pride in an older style of black activism, while at the same time searching for new political horizons, Cruse would be both a participant and a critic of Black Power politics. In his 1967 manifesto, *The Crisis of the Negro Intellectual*, he charged white Communists and black radicals with failing to recognize that the key to African American liberation resided in the last place anybody cared to look: in the black community's indigenous, cultural, and artistic institutions.

The April 1955 Afro-Asian Conference, convened in Bandung, Indonesia, would provide hope for black radicals burned by the Cold War's scalding political climate. Paul Robeson, in his fifth year of domestic confinement after federal authorities stripped him of his passport, greeted the conference as a symbol of the kind of politics—of radical anticolonialism and self-determination—that furthered the commitment to human rights and freedom of expression that was his life's work.[16] Presided over by Indonesian president Sukarno and convened by the prime ministers of Indonesia, India, Burma, Ceylon, and Pakistan, the conference featured representatives of twenty-nine nonwhite nations whose populations together exceeded one billion. Bandung's declarations against racism, colonialism, and imperialism represented a watershed event: a "third bloc" opposing both capitalism and totalitarianism. The conference marked the birth of the Non-Aligned Movement, which defied the political requirement that even the tiniest country swear allegiance to the United States or to the Soviet Union. Neutrality, however, had its cost. Behind the scenes in Washington, the State Department observed the entire proceeding with keen interest, despite its public indifference to events in this far corner of the world.[17]

In the United States one modest, but powerful, act of political dissent coincided with the radicalism that Bandung expressed in bold strokes. In 1955, the same year as Bandung, Martin Luther King Jr. emerged as the young leader of the Montgomery, Alabama, bus boycott. Coupled with 1954's *Brown v. Board of Education* Supreme Court desegregation decision, the 1950s would then be christened as the start of the modern civil rights era.[18]

While black southern laborers, preachers, and college students stood poised on the edge of history (destined to be regarded, for the most part, as bit players in an unfolding historical drama; character actors overwhelmed by the glamorous star power and transcendent appeal of Martin Luther King Jr. and John F. Kennedy),[19] participants in the black freedom struggle reinvented themselves as political figures, cultural doyens, magazine editors, and, at times, reform-minded civil rights activists.

In the 1950s, many of the activists who had come of age during the war years, such as the members of the Harlem Writers Guild, formed relationships with Malcolm X. On the surface it was an unlikely alliance, since Malcolm represented a religious group—the Nation of Islam—that eschewed political involvement, going so far as to discourage its members from voting, marching on picket lines, or participating in boycotts. Yet Malcolm's personal biography and political history made him attractive to activists seeking renewed faith in radical politics. A former Pullman porter turned full-time hustler during the 1940s, Malcolm resided on the fringes of the postwar freedom surge. By the mid-1950s, however, he was an ex-convict turned local activist, an emerging national figure in a transformed political landscape. Malcolm's short stints as a laborer and longer residence in the bowels of black urban America shaped his political activism. In a relatively brief career that would be noted for its envelope-pushing militancy, Malcolm boldly confronted democracy's jagged edges, vociferously arguing that the goals of integration fell far short of complete equality for African Americans and that, ultimately, racial liberation required a political revolution. Malcolm's radicalism, most often recognized as the prophetic prelude to the fiery black awakening of the 1960s, took initial shape during the 1950s against the backdrop of southern civil rights insurgency and Bandung. For Malcolm, links between the local and the international were self-evident, only their programmatic implications remained frustratingly unclear. Over the course of the next decade, Malcolm X, the once-wayward son of a slain Garveyite preacher, would make it his mission to find—and institute—an unprecedented revolutionary politics as part of a quest for black power that would take him from jam-packed Harlem street corners and Los Angeles mosques to British universities, Middle East pilgrimages, and African kingdoms.[20]

1

FORERUNNERS

On a cold spring day in April 1957, Johnson X, a New York member of the Nation of Islam, interrupted police officers as they beat a black suspect.[1] "Why don't you carry the man on to jail?" Johnson asked officers before retreating back toward a growing crowd of spectators.[2] The police officers turned their nightsticks on Johnson, who shouted prayers to Allah as blood from a gaping head wound gushed over his clothes. Police handcuffed Johnson and took him to the local precinct, where the brutal assault continued out of sight of the crowd. Word of Johnson's beating inspired two thousand people to appear outside of Harlem's Twenty-eighth Precinct and demand that he be provided medical attention.[3] James Hicks, the *New York Amsterdam News*' crusading managing editor, contacted the one man he felt capable of preventing mob violence: Malcolm X, the thirty-one-year-old Muslim minister in charge of Harlem's local Mosque No. 7. Hicks asked Malcolm to mediate negotiations between law enforcement and community representatives in hopes of avoiding a riot.

Tall and intense in a camel-hair coat that accentuated the stripped-down elegance of the Nation of Islam (NOI), whose members took strict pride in their appearance, Malcolm agreed to participate in the clandestine meeting. From Hicks's fourth-floor office at the *Amsterdam News*, Malcolm X met with New York's deputy police commissioner and two other high-ranking department officials. After contentious talks, they agreed to let Malcolm see for himself if Johnson needed medical attention. Meanwhile, outside the 123rd Street police station, stone-faced rows of men from the Fruit of Islam (FOI), the NOI's security unit, lined up in formation, an all-black, unarmed, quasi-military regiment. Impeccably dressed and exhibiting discipline honed through a rigorous physical regimen that was rumored to include expertise in the martial arts, the FOI stood, arms folded, like a battalion awaiting orders. In the rear of this advanced guard were rows of neatly attired black women with white scarves covering their heads. Surrounding these separate gauntlets of Muslims were hundreds of locals, undisciplined and boisterous, who came to commiserate, vent personal rage against major and minor slights at the hands of the police, and see what would happen next. The air cracking with potential violence, the sight of the bloodied and badly beaten Johnson ended the debate over hospitalization. Johnson was transferred to Harlem Hospital, where a large crowd reassembled outside to await news of his fate. After treating him, frightened hospital officials released Johnson back into police custody and so resumed the tense standoff outside of the 123rd Street police station.[4]

For the second time, nervous department officials pleaded with Malcolm X to defuse the situation. Assured that Johnson would continue to receive medical attention, Malcolm walked outside the police station, whispered a few words to one of his lieutenants, and signaled for the Muslims to disperse. With military precision they—and the crowd—did just that, prompting one stunned police official to remark that what he had just witnessed was "too much power for one man to have."[5] The Johnson case became a part of Harlem folklore. Black newspapers turned the Nation of Islam into a household name in Harlem. "God's Angry Men Tangle with Police," proclaimed the *Amsterdam News* in a headline inspired by the title of Malcolm's syndicated news column, "God's Angry Men." Condemning the assault as "a flagrant display of police brutality," James Hicks denied police assertions that Johnson had resisted arrest.[6] Johnson survived: multiple brain surgeries and a metal plate in his head served as a permanent reminder of the ordeal. Awarded the then-largest police brutality settlement in New York City's history from an all-white jury, Johnson X won a rare victory in the war of attrition waged by black Americans on predominantly white institutions for full citizenship, equal rights, and racial justice.[7] As Malcolm later recalled, the "*Amsterdam News* made the whole story headline news, and for the first time the black man, woman, and child in the streets were discussing 'those Muslims.' "[8]

Even before the Johnson incident, the Nation of Islam had embarked on the long road from urban America's back streets to the center of racial discourse, a space it would claim for itself during the 1960s, as the Nation gradually downplayed religion and stressed economic uplift. Elijah Muhammad's attacks against "white devils" maintained the loyalty of the Nation's older, Depression-era disciples while Malcolm X brought in hungry new recruits. The political scene in postwar Harlem included openly Communist elected officials, Garveyites, trade unionists, and liberal integrationists. The Nation of Islam was, at least in the conventional sense, apolitical. Disputing the effectiveness of civil rights bills, picket lines, and standard protests, the Nation emphasized rebuilding black dignity and pride through bootstraps rather than ballots. Its militant rhetoric defined white supremacy as African Americans' punishment for defying religious prophecy. In the eyes of the Nation, white racism was the direct consequence of a wayward black people whose salvation lay in Allah's chosen messenger: Elijah Muhammad. Armed with religious knowledge that enhanced the more political solutions of its black nationalist predecessors, the Nation of Islam positioned itself as a new kind of truth teller.

In 1954, as the *Brown* decision triggered support for and opposition to racial segregation, Malcolm X took command of Harlem's 116th Street Mosque No. 7. Malcolm sought advice from Lewis Michaux, an activist who participated in Marcus Garvey's Universal Negro Improvement Association. Michaux's National Memorial bookstore (nicknamed the House of Common Sense and the Home of

Proper Propaganda) became the site of Malcolm's popular outdoor rallies.[9] Michaux and Malcolm's warm relationship contrasted with the bitingly friendly competition between Malcolm and sidewalk preachers, who pointedly questioned Malcolm's more outrageous claims even as they offered their own, equally colorful, beliefs as more historically accurate substitutes.[10] After he was promoted to Elijah Muhammad's national representative in 1957, Malcolm's eloquence became one of Harlem's star attractions. Faced with a choice between social marginalization and poverty and a national political arena that ignored that very fact, thousands of desperate black men and women opted for the Nation of Islam's promise of dignity, racial pride, and hope.

The rise of the southern civil rights movement paralleled these developments. Civil rights leadership's overt efforts for social integration and political inclusion for blacks contrasted with the Nation of Islam's vision of a separate black oasis within the searing American wilderness. For Harlemites, that wilderness was more than an eloquent metaphor. Crowded, substandard housing, high rates of unemployment, poor schools, high crime, and a scarcity of opportunity shadowed residents, who could spend a lifetime trapped in dangerous tenements, subject to police harassment, and preyed on by landlords, salesmen, and thieves. Black urban existence in the raw—here was the Nation of Islam's constituency.

Other groups presented black America's more polished face. Nationally, a burgeoning civil rights coalition projected Martin Luther King's vision of Gandhian nonviolence as the core of a new movement. King's celebrity coexisted with historic acceptance of black preachers as community leaders and the black church as the headquarters for African American social respectability. Local black militancy in the South existed alongside King's nonviolence, revealing a contested social landscape in which deep-seated traditions of self-defense found as much resonance with Malcolm X's blistering rhetoric as with King's eloquent pleas.[11] By the early 1960s, the Nation of Islam cultivated a cross-generational appeal that, in addition to rehabilitating ex-convicts and drug abusers, recruited sizable numbers of black intellectuals and middle-class professionals.[12]

New York—"colossal synthesis of urban hope and despair"—was the ideal city for Malcolm X and the Nation of Islam.[13] In Harlem, the competing forces of hope and despair engaged in open combat on every block. Intent on recruiting the thousands who doggedly held on to a quiet dignity as if it was their last possession, the Nation of Islam was in equal pursuit of the damned: the card sharks, pool hustlers, high rollers, and bottom feeders who made up an untapped reservoir of black political power. Outside the Optimal Cigar Store, the Broadway Bar, and the National Memorial Bookstore, speakers with stepladders, pamphlets, and megaphones stood as a testament to a tradition of soapbox sermonizing that dated back to the early twentieth century.[14] They provided more than local color; a promotion of racial uplift, cultural pride, and political propaganda was part education and part entertainment. While still noteworthy, their oratory fell short of what could be called radical, a designation reserved for blacks who sought to replace the existing social order.

Malcolm updated sacred and profane traditions of street speaking, turning old-fashioned rituals into state-of-the-art displays of rhetorical genius and political mobilization. Speaking outside churches, at black nationalist rallies, and on street corners in search of new recruits, Malcolm turned the technique he dubbed "fishing" into an organizational science. From street corners, stepladders, and Mosque pulpits, Malcolm recounted his personal history of crime and drug abuse, all the while extolling the redemptive teachings of the Honorable Elijah Muhammad and denouncing America as an unrepentantly racist and doomed land.[15]

Just as surely as activists like Malcolm X would transform the local black world, power brokers such as Congressman Adam Clayton Powell Jr. ruled it. Harlem's most senior and influential black politician, Powell was a formidable local leader even as his international carousing and rakish showmanship limited the time he spent with loyal constituents. Despite rumors to the contrary, Powell was more than just an absentee politician who worked the system to a degree that made his white colleagues blush. In truth, Powell represented the militant and pragmatic side of New York City's black freedom movement. The ultimate political survivor, he emerged from the radicalism of the late 1940s into the cautious Cold War liberalism of the 1950s with his reputation and prestige largely intact. Powell's controversial visit to the 1955 Bandung conference highlighted his brand of diplomacy, with the congressman (to the chagrin of some supporters and the delight of U.S. officials) extolling America's social progress and denouncing the Afro-Asian conference as merely playing politics with racial matters.[16]

Recognizing emerging talent, Powell invited Malcolm to speak at Abyssinian Baptist Church (where Powell presided as pastor), and he lavished praise on the young Muslim minister. During the early 1960s, Powell shared rallies with Malcolm in well-orchestrated displays of unity that masked their occasionally competing interests and clashing egos. Cultivating a pragmatic political alliance that introduced both men to new constituencies, Malcolm and Powell provided each other, respectively, with establishment legitimacy and street credibility.[17]

Law enforcement agencies, such as the Bureau of Special Services (nicknamed BOSS), an elite force of covert agents who served as New York City's counterintelligence unit, also took notice. In the late 1950s, as Malcolm's national profile soared, the FBI, which had been monitoring the Nation of Islam for years, designated him a "key figure."[18] Bureau officials expressed concern at the Nation of Islam's—and Malcolm's—ambitious plans to establish mosques on the West Coast and throughout the South.[19] At the same time, mainstream America discovered Malcolm X, who came to be understood as the sinister counterpart of Martin Luther King Jr. In an era when segregationists were labeling the NAACP and King as part of a Communist conspiracy, Malcolm's political rhetoric gave all sides pause. America's growing concern over the Nation of Islam's racial militancy benefited the respected liberal politics of the southern-based King even as it buttressed Malcolm's own claims to northern black leadership.

Malcolm's political integrity and personal charisma attracted some of New York City's most glamorous black artists and writers.[20] Through the actor Ossie Davis, he developed relationships with the black intelligentsia. Impressed by his brilliance and sharp wit, Davis and his wife, Ruby Dee, introduced Malcolm to a group of friends and associates that included the writers Lorraine Hansberry and Julian Mayfield.[21] Denied access to many of the entertainment industry's powerful stars, who were fearful that association with the Nation of Islam would hurt their careers, Malcolm instead brokered alliances with figures who, like himself, were tarnished by reports linking them to Communists and black extremists. Davis, along with John Killens and Mayfield, approximated the support King publicly received from Harry Belafonte and Sidney Poitier.[22] Davis and Dee formed this core group of second-tier celebrities who served as sounding boards, secret fund-raisers, and trusted confidants for much of Malcolm's career. Malcolm's high profile also propelled him beyond the Nation of Islam's cloistered world into a secular arena that included the era's leading black opinion makers. Since the national press reflected the stark color line of Jim Crow America, blacks looked beyond white media outlets for local, national, and international stories of interest. Years before white journalists noticed the Nation of Islam, Malcolm X cultivated black editors, publishers, and newspaper reporters. Nationally, the *Pittsburgh Courier, Chicago Defender, Baltimore-Washington Afro-American, New York Amsterdam News,* and *Los Angeles Herald Dispatch* shaped African American opinion, taking risks that their white counterparts did not by reporting news of the Nation of Islam. Journalists William Worthy, Louis Lomax, Alex Haley, and James Hicks would be particularly important in shaping Malcolm's public image. By 1958, a year after the Johnson X incident, Malcolm's notoriety grew, burnished by his column, "God's Angry Men." Eventually, Malcolm's media contacts would plant the seeds for one of the Nation's most profitable and important enterprises: *Muhammad Speaks.*[23]

Malcolm Little, born in Omaha, Nebraska, on May 19, 1925, raised in Michigan, schooled in the big-city underworlds of Detroit, Boston, and Harlem, and incarcerated for burglary in Massachusetts from 1946 to 1952, joined the Nation of Islam as a convict. Paroled in 1952, he was

by then a legend in the making—one who traced his political development to Elijah Muhammad, a most unusual mentor. The Nation of Islam was one of the dozens of groups organized during and after the
New Negro nationalism of the post–World War I era and its resurgence
during the Depression decade. Under Muhammad's leadership in the
1930s, the Nation of Islam preached a mélange of racial pride, personal discipline, and economic uplift as part of an unorthodox interpretation of the Islamic faith. While Marcus Garvey resurrected
ancient African kingdoms as proof that blacks were a people with a
proud history, Muhammad's religious doctrines declared that whites
were "devils," created by a renegade black scientist named Yacub. By
the early 1950s, the NOI had survived both the Messenger's (as
Muhammad was called by followers) temporary incarceration and the
internal squabbling that had destroyed similar groups. Spotting Malcolm's potential, Muhammad became a father figure who allowed his
younger protégé creative space to bring—up to a point—the NOI into
a world that had studiously ignored its presence, not to mention one
that Muhammad predicted was on the brink of destruction. Composed
of only several hundred true believers in the early 1950s, the Nation of
Islam gave little indication that, within a decade, it would become the
most controversial black organization in the United States, publish a
weekly newspaper with a circulation of over 500,000, and be regarded as
a violent, dangerously radical alternative to the civil rights mainstream.[24]

Malcolm X's aggressive recruiting strategies attracted tough, brilliant, and hard-working members. Malcolm's chief strength, his
charismatic speaking style, distilled social, political, and cultural issues
to their hard-boiled essence. This ability mesmerized supporters and
critics around the country and, in time, all over the world. His imposing physical presence—he stood six feet three inches, with broad
shoulders and oversized suits that draped his thin frame—lent an air of
undeniable authority to verbal pronouncements that even critics conceded possessed a brilliant flair.[25]

Behind grim sermons predicting America's impending destruction
were rituals meticulously practiced inside the Nation's storefront tem-
ples such as Mosque No. 7. Religious services conducted several times

a week revealed a world that combined elements of black nationalism, unorthodox Islam, and rigid discipline. Only blacks could enter the temple, and all persons were thoroughly searched for weapons. The Fruit of Islam confiscated sharp objects, which they placed in paper bags to be reclaimed after departing the mosque. Men and women sat on separate sides of the room. The FOI prowled the temple for troublemakers and stragglers while simultaneously leading the congregational call-and-response, punctuated by steady streams of "That's right" and "You tell it like it is."[26] No hymns were sung inside the mosque: a jukebox played jazz before services and occasionally a soloist sang "The White Man's Heaven Is the Black Man's Hell," written by Louis X (later Louis Farrakhan), a former calypso singer and one of Malcolm's most promising protégés.[27]

A large flag featuring a star next to a crescent served as a reminder that this was no conventional place of worship. A giant blackboard divided followers of the Islamic faith and Christianity under respective flags, plaintively asking which group would survive the coming apocalypse; words written under the Islamic flag—"Freedom, Justice, and Equality"—were worlds apart from those sprawled beneath the American flag—"Christianity, Slavery, Suffering, and Death."[28] The message and its deceptively simple presentation promoted the Nation of Islam's efforts to reveal hidden truths, to "make it plain," to all *Original Peoples* (the Nation of Islam's term for blacks). Stepping forward at the conclusion of each service, recruits were given a letter to copy as part of their initiation. Only after completing it, as well as undergoing a background check, could the individual be given an X—the Nation's surname for converts in lieu of "slave" names that evoked the legacy of America's slaveholding past.[29]

Muslim ministers relentlessly criticized what they described as Christianity's shortcomings. Describing his unsuccessful effort to convert a black Baptist, Malcolm liked to quip that after learning of the Nation's strict rules against gambling, alcohol, drugs, and extramarital affairs, the man promptly announced he would remain a Christian. Black Muslims belittled civil rights leaders as black men who historically failed to defend women and children. The Nation's promises of protection were reinforced by large signs declaring women to be the black nation's most "valuable property."[30] Well aware by this point that he had taken the congregation to the edge of their seats and the limits of their self-control, the Muslim minister would then pause. Like a shepherd steering his flock, as a test of faith, to the craggy edge of a cliff, the minister allowed the faithful to stop there to recognize the depths between themselves and Allah. Blistering rhetorical militancy would then retreat into the protective arms of civil society, and the minister would remind the congregation to always obey the law— within reason. As Malcolm put it, "We respect authority, but we are ready to fight and die in defense of our lives."[31]

Malcolm X and the Nation of Islam's militant black nationalism influenced and paralleled black America's interest in Africa during the late 1950s. Bandung's declaration of Third World political independence, coupled as it was with decolonization and Africa's entrance onto the global stage, excited black activists. American fears that Africa would turn into a Communist haven shaped the Eisenhower and Kennedy administrations' awkward courtship of Africa, including State Department–sponsored jazz tours of the Third World, recruitment of black diplomats, and civil rights reform guided as much by international implications as by domestic ones. Africa's new international stature made racial segregation more than the embarrassing vestige of an ancient regime; it threatened to compromise U.S. foreign policy's stated goal of containing Communism through the spread of international democracy. With national leaders failing to heed activists demanding an end to segregation, black Americans looked to Africa— and the larger Third World—as partners in exerting pressure on a country determined, in a single-minded effort, to win the Cold War.[32]

Black newspapers helped to fuel this pan-African surge. Africa's unfolding independence movements—both peaceful and violent— provided image makers with opportunities to shape history with their own renditions of dramatic political revolutions abroad. In turn, Ghana's prime minister, Kwame Nkrumah, educated at Lincoln University in Pennsylvania and tutored by radical thinkers from Europe, North America, and the Caribbean, held a special place in his heart for black Americans. Flush with the enthusiasm of independence, Nkrumah promised that Ghana would "show the world" that Africans could take the "lead in justice, tolerance, liberty, individual freedom and social progress."[33]

Ghanaian independence attracted American diplomatic recognition and a visit from Vice President Richard Nixon. The March 1957 celebrations in Accra, the capital, also drew important black figures including the labor leader A. Philip Randolph; the twenty-eight-year-old activist Martin Luther King Jr., still basking in the glow of the Montgomery bus boycott; and Shirley Graham Du Bois, W. E. B. Du Bois's wife. For black moderates, Africa's renaissance provided political leverage for domestic civil rights struggles. In the minds of black radicals from the United States, Ghanaian independence signaled a more distant possibility: an international political revolution. For vastly different reasons, then, black militants and moderates celebrated Africa's arrival on the world stage. Nkrumah's public call for skilled African Americans to aid Ghana's development tapped into pan-African impulses simmering since Marcus Garvey, and would ultimately lead to a small but significant black American expatriate community whose decade in Ghana would be marked by the euphoric highs of hosting Malcolm X in their ancestral homeland and the discouraging lows of corruption, Cold War repression, and political coups.[34] The *Amsterdam News* welcomed the surge in black protest, declaring 1957 as the "year Negroes fought back." Managing editor James Hicks singled out King's visit to Ghana as a gesture that "captured" black America's collective imagination.[35]

If King's trip to Ghana inspired hope, Nkrumah's tour of America triggered action. On Sunday, July 27, 1958, Nkrumah arrived in New York City for the first time as prime minister.[36] The visit culminated a weeklong domestic tour that included stops at the White House and Howard University. Riding in an open car, Nkrumah waved to a crowd of twenty-five thousand locals who lined the route of his thirty-four-block Harlem tour.[37]

The 1958 publication of Paul Robeson's *Here I Stand* helped dramatize Africa's importance in world affairs. "I am a Negro. The house I live in is in Harlem—this city within a city, Negro metropolis of America. And now as I write of things that are urgent in my mind and heart, I feel the press of all that is around me here where I live, at home among my people," read the first paragraph of Robeson's memoir. Combining autobiography and political essays detailing how historic efforts for black equality faced dangers from Cold War liberalism, *Here I Stand* signaled a modest coup for one of the world's most well-known figures. Ignored by the white press, *Here I Stand* received favorable coverage in black newspapers including the *Baltimore-Washington Afro-American* and the *Pittsburgh Courier*. Despite personal setbacks caused by his commitment to Socialism and freedom of speech and expression, Robeson held on to a defiant optimism. "The time is now," Robeson declared, for black Americans to agitate for freedom. "Negro power"—mass action backed by courageous, independent leadership devoted to self-determination for sixteen million African Americans—summed up Robeson's prescription and prophecy for the coming decade.[38]

In 1959, recent news from the civil rights front buoyed Robeson's optimism. Political and legal victories gained in the South had established it as the movement's most important beachhead. While King continued to grab headlines with his activism in Alabama and other southern states, Robert F. Williams provided direction for the freedom struggle through his words and actions in the South and the North. A tall, broad-shouldered veteran, Williams was a well-traveled former industrial laborer who dabbled in poetry, consorted with radicals, and remained defiant in the face of racial terror in Monroe, North Carolina. Williams's call for armed self-defense in the South sent shockwaves through America, galvanizing activists as far away as New York. Although a southerner, Williams had several things in common with prominent New York radicals, including military experience and literary ambitions. In 1955, Williams returned home to North Carolina and assumed leadership of the local NAACP chapter. Events in Monroe took on national significance when chapter members fought a series of pitched battles with the Ku Klux Klan. By 1959, Williams inspired radical activists in his resistance to white supremacy, establishing himself as a potentially more effective alternative to the apostle of nonviolence, Martin Luther King Jr. Comfortable with racial moderates and militants, Williams would soon be recruited by a laundry list of competing progressive forces. His supporters found themselves in the unenviable position of sharing him with groups they despised. Socialists, black nationalists, Communists, and militant liberals all vied for the man they affectionately called Rob.

Williams's national appeal was based on a combination of factors that included personal charisma, political ideology, and timing.[39] His harsh words in the aftermath of a violent assault by a white man on a black Monroe woman marked his break from the NAACP. "We must be willing to kill if necessary," he told a group of reporters, amplifying the kind of brutal realities that could turn a man to intemperate words and reckless public strategy.[40] The outburst brought swift punishment from the white press—and the national NAACP (which suspended him for six months)—vilifying him as an advocate of racial violence, just as black radicals greeted his statement with cheers.[41]

Williams's notoriety coincided with growing public controversy surrounding the Nation of Islam. Tipped off to a potential news story by the veteran black reporter and colleague Louis Lomax, Mike Wallace became the first white journalist to feature an exposé of the Black Muslims. The five-part documentary aired on Wallace's *News Beat* the week of July 13, 1959.[42] *News Beat* reporter Louis Lomax, accompanied by two white cameramen, received unprecedented access to the Nation of Islam's inner workings. Rare footage of the NOI and James Lawson's United African Nationalist Movement cast black nationalists as obscure counterparts to the racist southern White Citizens Council. From the studio, Wallace set the tone for the evening, chiding "soberminded Negroes" for failing to oppose the group. Wallace asked

Manhattan borough president Hulan Jack and NAACP chairman Roy Wilkins why they hadn't done more to forestall the growing Muslim menace. Booed off the stage by Muslims at an earlier NAACP rally, Jack knew better than to attack one of Harlem's most powerful groups. Wilkins claimed to have no knowledge of Elijah Muhammad or his syndicated newspaper column. He expertly deflected questions regarding the group, noting that while he never attended their street rallies, he supported the right to free speech. Photographs of Wilkins shaking hands with Malcolm X were offered by *News Beat* as evidence that the head of the NAACP was consorting with a black hate group, behavior that contradicted his outstanding personal and professional commitment to civil rights.[43]

The program boiled down the Nation of Islam's mix of religious evangelism and racial militancy to hate mongering. Descending into the homes of white Americans via a new medium, television, whose power was largely untested, the Nation of Islam received a dramatic if not entirely unflattering debut. More than simply putting the NOI and other black militants on the radar of ordinary Americans, the documentary ushered in the first intraracial political controversy of the civil rights era, pitting black separatists against integrationists. *News Beat*'s coverage also served as a coronation of sorts—marking Malcolm X as a new breed of black militant. The documentary's first glimpse of the Nation came via footage of the climax of the popular play *The Trial*, which featured a Muslim prosecutor seeking a collective indictment against the white race for black oppression. Images of thousands of Muslims voicing their approval at the mock court proceedings were followed by footage of an enormous Muslim rally in Washington D.C.'s cavernous Uline Arena; these images were accompanied by Wallace's clipped voice-over narration, which repeated the group's exaggerated estimates of a quarter of a million acolytes and provided details about Elijah Muhammad's personal history. Malcolm's subsequent appearance overshadowed Lomax's exclusive interview with Muhammad. Whereas Muhammad answered questions stiffly, Malcolm's eloquence focused on the Nation of Islam's collective indictment of white America. After Malcolm's defense of the Nation of Islam's philosophy and criticism of the NAACP, footage of Malcolm addressing an African Freedom Day rally in Harlem strengthened *News Beat's* claims that the Muslim movement had penetrated black America's foremost citadel.[44]

Elijah Muhammad arrived at St. Nicholas Arena for a major speech on the heels of the show's airing. Inside, six thousand turned out to hear him reject charges of hate mongering. Outside, almost one thousand Harlemites, many still dressed in their Sunday best, lined up against police barriers and listened to Muhammad through speakers set up to accommodate the overflow. Groups of white reporters and cameramen bantered with Muslim security officers who announced that no whites would be allowed inside. Refused entrance into the arena twice, Mike Wallace threatened to press his case to a higher authority; bewildered black journalists marveled at the clamoring white media desperate to attend the same closed-door religious meetings the black media had covered for years. Malcolm X and the Messenger's son, Wallace, shared the speakers' platform with Elijah Muhammad. Wallace Muhammad sketched a brief history of the Muslim movement while Malcolm X (recently back from the Middle East) spoke of Elijah's growing international reputation. Uncertain of the documentary's impact on his movement, Muhammad delivered a forceful speech, exhibiting the energy and stamina that, in later years, would elude him. He described himself as a divine messenger entrusted to redeem the lost souls of a proud but wayward people. His was a mission of cosmic origins, legitimated by Black Muslim orthodoxy, dutifully believed by growing numbers of converts. Muhammad challenged his critics to offer proof of the NOI's racial demagoguery and singled out Jackie Robinson as an Uncle Tom tricked into attacking him. Muhammad also hinted that he might be forced to retire over the recent furor.[45] The white press, which had excitedly reported the group's activities, now sought information attainable only with the help of black reporters. The publicity made Black Muslims part of the debate over America's civil rights struggle. But the NOI's iconoclastic religious and political practices would, from their first airing in the national media, remain on the fringes of respectable civil rights discourse. Martin Luther King Jr., Roy Wilkins, and Thurgood Marshall publicly chastised the Muslims as a "hate group" that had failed the litmus test for responsible leadership; blatantly one-sided, *News Beat*'s airing of "The Hate That Hate Produced" left the Nation of Islam open to ridicule and worse.[46]

"The Hate That Hate Produced" was broadcast just as Malcolm was visiting Africa. His 1959 tour amplified his interest in the larger world. As Muhammad's advance man in the Middle East, Malcolm had served as a liaison with Muslim officials in preparation for the Messenger's visit to Mecca.[47] As the FBI monitored his foray into Africa, Malcolm published his letters from Saudi Arabia and the Sudan in black newspapers. From Khartoum's Grand Hotel, he announced that "racial disturbances in faraway New York City" received front-page coverage in the Sudan. African concern for black suffering in America, he observed, was growing. Penetrating what Malcolm described as a "veil of global diplomatic art" were "hordes of intelligent Africans" unmoved by American propaganda extolling domestic racial progress.[48] Meanwhile, the national media ignored Malcolm's tour. Malcolm claimed that Elijah Muhammad's achievements were respected overseas; however, the Black Muslim movement had an ambiguous relationship with the larger Islamic world (which followed orthodox interpretations of the faith and did not recognize Elijah Muhammad as divine); in fact, rumors swirled that contemptuous Saudi officials barred him from Mecca.[49]

But Muhammad did make it to Mecca. With his sons Herbert and Akbar, Muhammad arrived in Turkey on November 23, 1959, three months after Malcolm, and toured the Islamic Middle East over the next six weeks. In Cairo, Muhammad received an audience with Egyptian president Gamal Abdel Nasser; in the process, the NOI leader solidified his claims of international religious and political legitimacy.[50] From Jeddah, Muhammad traveled to Mecca to complete the hajj. Led by a guide and draped in the garb of hajj pilgrims, two white sheets called the *ihram*, Muhammad recited Arabic prayers amid thousands of Muslims, successfully completing the holy pilgrimage.[51] Muhammad's visit made the front page of the *Amsterdam News*, providing public vindication for Black Muslims in Harlem sensitive to criticism of their unorthodox religious practices. Muhammad returned to the States confident that he had brokered international alliances. For Malcolm, Muhammad's hajj was bittersweet. The previous summer, within miles of the holy city, he was forced to return without making the pilgrimage, offering several excuses, including illness, scheduling conflicts, and fear of upstaging Muhammad. The Nation of Islam's rapid ascent was already taking its toll.

The Nation of Islam had, in fact, expanded to three interconnected kingdoms. In Harlem, Malcolm X presided over a local empire whose breadth was expanding daily. From his Phoenix mansion, Muhammad assumed the role of an aging king, the movement's unquestioned ruler who remained distant from all but the most vital internal affairs. Chicago, where Muhammad had established Mosque No. 2 after fleeing Detroit in the 1930s, was the Nation's financial headquarters. With the movement's unprecedented growth during the 1950s came increased credibility, and the resources to establish permanent facilities unimagined during most of the group's existence. Financial mismanagement, personal profiteering, and graft shadowed the NOI's expansion.

Privately, Muhammad feared that Malcolm might grow too powerful. Publicly, Muhammad proclaimed Malcolm his most faithful and outstanding convert.[52] Behind the scenes, Chicago officials, in an internal coup, wrested control of the group's flourishing newspaper, *Muhammad Speaks,* from Malcolm.[53] Malcolm, after several false starts, had started the newspaper from his basement in East Elmhurst, in Queens. Notwithstanding several pages dutifully exalting Muhammad as God's messenger, whose presence unlocked the key to black liberation and eternal salvation, *Muhammad Speaks* provided coverage of local and national civil rights struggles, black militancy and corresponding white resistance, and African and Third World liberation movements, explaining how all the elements figured into the international politics of the Cold War era. Editorial offices in New York and Los Angeles served as training grounds that helped Malcolm give *Muhammad Speaks* the intelligence and polish of a professional paper. The newspaper that Malcolm had established for the purpose of spreading Muhammad's teachings grew in popularity just as Malcolm's star within the Nation diminished. *Muhammad Speaks* became the Nation of Islam's key tool for harnessing the militant passions that gripped the black movement. Colorful ads in its back pages trumpeted the breadth of its news coverage, which spanned racial rebellions in "Greenwood, Angola, and Los Angeles."[54] Worldly and proudly partisan, *Muhammad Speaks* defied the expectations of black readers, NOI members or not.[55]

The Black Muslim phenomenon coincided with the staging on Broadway of Lorraine Hansberry's *A Raisin in the Sun,* which deployed conspicuous tropes (generational conflicts between mother and son, racial combat between blacks and whites, and economic clashes between haves and have-nots) that, in other hands, might have made for condescending, if well meaning, racial melodrama. It was a testament to Hansberry's precocious genius that the opposite effect was achieved, tucking Afro-America's historic global awareness, burgeoning racial militancy, and budding feminism into a quintessentially American tale of uplift.

The daughter of a prosperous Chicago family, Hansberry became a political protégé of Paul Robeson at the influential, although short-lived, periodical *Freedom.* At *Freedom,* Hansberry detailed the lives of black women fighting against racism in the United States, and the struggles of female peace activists in Asia, Africa, South America, and the Caribbean.[56] Hansberry's work placed her in the orbit of New York City cultural radicals that included the novelist John Oliver Killens and other members of the Harlem Writers Guild, as well as political luminaries such as W. E. B Du Bois and Robeson, whose Council on African Affairs shared offices with *Freedom* in a 125th Street brownstone. Hansberry's education in Harlem's "university of the streets" supplemented a bittersweet experience with the black bourgeoisie that most of her contemporaries could only imagine. Hansberry's unusual biography—an upper-middle-class black woman who abandoned a comfortable existence for identification with the racially and politically oppressed—would lead Killens to describe her as "a black nationalist with a socialist perspective."[57] Others were less kind. Harold Cruse's criticism, in *The Crisis of the Negro Intellectual* (1967), proved, even by his own caustic standards, particularly harsh, smearing Hansberry as a dilettante who worshipped white gods of integration and as a mediocre talent to boot.[58]

Ironically, *A Raisin in the Sun* left room for Killens's superlatives and Cruse's denunciations. In Hansberry's evocative depiction of a black family on Chicago's South Side, race and class confrontations play a part in the passionate temperament of characters whose angst over relationships, insurance policies, and upward mobility are detailed. With a title inspired by a nugget of Langston Hughes's poetic brilliance, *A Raisin in the Sun* tugged at white America's heartstrings, providing enough of a comfort zone for critics and fans to deflect Hansberry's radical forays into Pan-Africanism, cultural nationalism, and women's rights. Walter Lee Younger, the play's brooding yet optimistic thirty-five-year-old man-child, and the wise but stern matriarch Mama Younger enact a conflict that is neatly resolved by the play's end. Against considerable odds, the Younger family overcomes black swindlers and white racists to begin a daunting journey as residents of an otherwise all-white neighborhood.

Conventional interpretations ended here, however. *A Raisin in the Sun*'s young black women, from the prematurely aging Ruth Younger to the impishly rebellious Beneatha, broke the mold. These were black women with rich, complex, and painful interior lives. If Ruth's tenacious love for the sometimes self-delusional Walter Lee illustrated one generation's limited options, Beneatha's fierce precocity spoke of another. Socially ambitious, politically conscious, and intellectually gifted, Beneatha represented groups of black women who were, as in the title of Hansberry's posthumously published autobiography, young, gifted, and black. A combination of modern misfits and Old Testament prophets, such women seemed destined for the kind of heartbreak reserved for individuals born ahead of their time.[59]

Hailed by critics as a masterpiece and successfully staged on Broadway (and as a 1961 Hollywood film) starring Sidney Poitier, *A Raisin in the Sun* concealed renegade racial politics, subterranean class struggle, and more. Articulate Pan-Africanists, college students sporting afros scarcely in vogue, unemployed hustlers, and their burdened mothers all found something of themselves in a drama that wrung pathos out of the mundane: in Hansberry's prose, the experience of racial oppression reached new levels of emotional depth, literary eloquence, and political power. Even more striking, *A Raisin in the Sun* trumpeted the arrival of a cultural nationalism destined to be associated almost exclusively with Black Power militants.[60] Buried beneath the play's integrationist odyssey were Pan-Africanist visions of a freedom struggle spanning generations and continents. Ultimately, *A Raisin in the Sun*'s crossover appeal muffled its subversive dimensions, notably the character Beneatha's agile combination of feminism, nationalism, and international awareness. A watershed analysis of black life in Cold War America, *A Raisin in the Sun* captured the complexity of black existence that went beyond integrationist and nationalist poles, transcending Cold War–era racial fictions and social fantasies to reveal the grotesque, beautiful, and unintended consequences of American society at war with its founding ideals of freedom and democracy.[61]

In 1959, Robert F. Williams visited a New York City political landscape marked by a resurgent black nationalism. He also found kindred spirits. Mae Mallory, a hard-nosed local activist who would face a stiff prison sentence for aiding Williams's escape to Cuba two years later, was one of the first to offer help. Mallory organized an ad hoc group of supporters called Crusader Families. Williams's mimeographed *Crusader* newsletter, published to provide to the public his version of events in Monroe, inspired the group's name. Between 1959 and 1960, Williams formed alliances with activists associated with the Harlem Writers Guild and Malcolm X. Malcolm invited Williams to speak at New York's Mosque No. 7, giving the civil rights militant his personal stamp of approval while also helping raise funds for his activities in Monroe.[62] Taking careful note of this potential synergy, the FBI stepped up surveillance of Williams's activities, documenting his solidarity with the NOI's New York temple.[63] While Williams and Malcolm X loomed as significant domestic figures in America's civil rights drama, international events soon overshadowed them.

The Cuban revolution reverberated from Havana to Harlem. Internationally, Cuba threatened to upset American interests in Africa, Latin America, and beyond. Closer to home, Cuba's new regime effectively moved anticolonial struggles to within a stone's throw of American shores. Tall, burly, and gregarious, Fidel Castro lent the Cuban revolution an air of romance and intrigue that captivated American radicals. Castro's rejection of a comfortable, middle-class future in favor of the unproven promise of political revolution struck a chord among Americans, from downtown bohemians and beatniks to Harlem nationalists. As the Eisenhower administration's response to the new Cuban regime turned from nervous anticipation to overt hostility, black and white progressives mobilized on behalf of the tiny island. The Fair Play for Cuba Committee (FPCC) grew out of such efforts. Its support for Havana echoed radical sentiments in the black press, with the *Amsterdam News* declaring that black people's interest in Cuba offered "further proof" of the importance of the "international arena."[64] Leading black literary and intellectual figures joined Fair Play, including the writers Julian Mayfield, John Oliver Killens, John Henrik Clarke, and James Baldwin; the journalists Richard "Dick" Gibson and William Worthy; and Robert F. Williams. Collectively, Fair Play's African American supporters combined the internationalism of the Second World War era with a resurgent, cosmopolitan black nationalism.[65] Fair Play held rallies, distributed leaflets, and sounded a national alarm in hopes of "setting the story straight" about events in Cuba. In June 1960, Fair Play organizers offered Williams the chance to tour the island.[66]

Williams's trip echoed through two contrasting centers of power and influence: Harlem and Washington, D.C. In Havana, Williams consulted with Cuban officials, walking the streets in a straw hat, a holstered pistol on his hip, and sporting a wide grin. His imposing physique made these strolls a sort of traveling circus, with Williams trailed by children, intellectuals, government officials, and reporters. The government extended him every courtesy, which he repaid by taping a two-hour television interview and putting together a special issue of *Lunes de Revolución,* featuring artists and writers analyzing the connection between Jim Crow and the Cuban revolution. Cuba's well-publicized antiracist policies excited Williams the most, and after his visit he fondly remembered being "very much impressed" with Cuba's treatment of its black citizens. At a time when race seemed to confound politicians and institutions in the United States, Cuba offered hope to black Americans fed up with generations of delay on the road to racial justice.[67]

Fair Play organized a second tour of Cuba the next month. This time Williams led the group. Several of New York's notable black activists, including Cruse, Clarke, and LeRoi Jones, joined him. Mayfield and his wife, Ana Cordero, both served as interpreters. For Mayfield, Cuba amplified the international political awareness that he had maintained since his break with the Communist Party and through experiences in Puerto Rico.

Government officials feted the group of black writers and artists for their entire stay. The Casa de las Americas (House of the Americas)— the Cuban Cultural Ministry—sponsored the tour and arranged for reporters and photojournalists to greet the visitors alongside tables filled with colorful drinks, while a band lent the event the feel of a political celebration for visiting dignitaries.[68] The group stayed in the Hotel Presidente, a vestige of prerevolutionary Cuba.[69] Nevertheless, with Cuban guides at their disposal and itineraries packed with tours, interviews, and meetings, the delegation was awed by the human drama unfurling before their eyes.

Harold Cruse was impressed with Cuba, though years later he claimed to have outwardly concealed his enthusiasm for the revolution and Castro.[70] One of the tour's oldest participants, the middle-aged Cruse, having abandoned Harlem and the Communist Party for the

Lower East Side, was also a fugitive from the fertile political soil that had shaped him. He carried to Cuba the pain associated with missed opportunities and unfulfilled ambition. "A Negro Looks at Cuba," his account of the trip, reveals that despite his natural wariness, his time on the island had a lasting influence. "The two weeks that I spent in Cuba were one of the most inspiring experiences I have ever had," he wrote shortly afterward.[71] Within two years of this trip, he published an influential essay, "Revolutionary Nationalism and the Afro-American," in the journal *Studies on the Left*. More important than this modest professional coup was the essay's impact on a new generation of black radicals. Reflecting his evolving philosophy, as well as his recent visit to Cuba, Cruse suggested that black activists in America were in need of an indigenous political orientation, similar to what was occurring in Cuba yet unique to black American history and culture. He called this philosophy "revolutionary nationalism." Rejecting sectarianism, Cruse proposed an international political movement that would serve as a bridge between black nationalism and Marxism. There was a crucial twist to Cruse's thinking. The Third World, ignored by Marx and the contemporary American Left, could be the vanguard for the modern age of revolution; Cuba, in Cruse's estimation, was the new movement's most precious jewel. For young black activists in New York, Chicago, Oakland, Detroit, and Philadelphia, Cruse's words were momentous.[72]

While Cruse's earthy profile was no match for Williams's, the Cubans gave him the attention, respect, and dignity that he craved. Consorting with Cuba's leading writers, artists, and literary lights was a far cry from the lonely margins of his life in New York. The government placed ministers, undersecretaries, and apparatchiks of Cuba's infrastructure at the delegation's disposal. Taking advantage of the opportunity, Cruse eagerly participated in meetings with the heads of education, labor, agriculture, and housing in order to gain a view of the nuts and bolts of revolution. Cruse, Mayfield, and others conducted personal interviews with the island's large population of campesinos (peasants). Even if bitter experience with Communists had placed limits on their revolutionary sympathies, the skeptical Americans were persuaded by the positive support for the revolution and for Fidel Castro. Access to the inner workings of the government made Cruse uncharacteristically effusive. "These Cuban leaders are social pioneers of the first order," Cruse wrote, "for they are social engineers who have unleashed the dam of human energy that has been pent up for generations and they are channeling this energy into constructive projects which would amaze any American."[73]

On July 26, 1960, the American contingent participated in an "event of epic proportions."[74] Invited to celebrate the anniversary of Castro's daring but unsuccessful military raid seven years earlier, which marked the Cuban revolution's origins, Cruse and his comrades witnessed the unfurling of huge banners promoting the revolution and its hero, Fidel Castro. Cruse marveled at how it was possible for them to place banners at what seemed to be an impossibly high altitude. LeRoi Jones stood next to Cruse, and on all sides was surrounded by groups of Cubans hanging on to whatever they could find.[75] Rebel soldiers, whose full beards covered youthful faces, restlessly milled about. Thousands of Cubans walked alongside an endless line of trucks traveling toward Las Mercedes, the city in the Sierra Maestre where the celebrations would take place. When they arrived in Las Mercedes, Cruse and his companions were directed toward the speakers' dais. Commandante Juan Almeida, the rebel army's Afro-Cuban chief, greeted them. Charismatic, dark-skinned, and good humored, Almeida seemed to represent living proof of the revolution's ambitious racial agenda. After greeting the delegation, Almeida alerted Castro, who bolted from his seat to meet them. Castro greeted each member of the Fair Play delegation, who began taking their places of honor on the platform directly behind where he would speak.[76] LeRoi Jones strode past Castro's throng of admirers and shook his hand. Through an interpreter Jones asked Castro what he intended to do with the revolution. "A poet's question," replied an amused Castro, before embarking on a two-hour speech.[77]

In Cuba, LeRoi Jones found another métier: politics. Born Everett LeRoy Jones in Newark, New Jersey, he arrived in New York an aspiring poet and quickly established himself as a new kind of literary provocateur. His three years at Howard University had made him chafe at the conventions of the black middle class. He responded with provocative actions, such as sitting on Howard's esteemed campus eating a watermelon.[78] Dropping out of Howard in the mid-1950s, Jones embarked on a doomed stint in the Air Force that ended in a dishonorable discharge. In Puerto Rico, the Air Force's discovery of Jones's wide range of reading materials, which included a subscription to the Communist *Daily Worker,* revealed a budding intellectual whose political interest was piqued, although not entirely satisfied, by Marxist literature. Jones's literary flirtation with Marxism—one that included membership in the red-tinged National Negro Congress at Howard, sporadic attendance at Communist Party meetings, and future membership in the Fair Play for Cuba Committee—would remain unconsummated for almost two decades.[79] Fresh from the Air Force, in 1957, Jones landed a job at the Gotham Book Mart on 47th Street, rented a three-bedroom apartment in the East Village, and set out to establish himself in the city's world of arts and letters.[80] His timing was serendipitous. Jones's arrival in New York coincided with the advent of a literary movement. Poetry readings, scruffy beards, coffee shops, and hip language made the beats an avant-garde that questioned intellectual heroes while crafting an image of rebelliousness that captured the imagination of American youth searching for a cultural way out of the Cold War. A smattering of black poets, artists, and writers jammed the sidewalks of Greenwich Village, enjoying downtown New York's interracial bonhomie and unbridled creativity. Artist Ted Joans was the ubiquitous black beat, a former jazz musician who, according to legend, had thrown his trumpet into the East River to pursue his passion for painting.[81] With work accepted in small literary journals and a growing list of contacts who instantly recognized his promise, LeRoi Jones emerged as a rarity: a black writer on the cusp of mainstream success.

Cuba transformed Jones, who considered civil rights activism unimpressive, and as a result he became one of Robert Williams's chief advocates and fund-raisers. Beyond Jones, Williams's bold machismo inspired thousands of young people—including founders of key Black Power organizations—who first looked to Chairman Rob as an exiled political leader. For Cruse, Mayfield, and Jones, the Cuban revolution obliterated conventional political perspectives. Cruse, noting that revolutions in Africa and Latin America were at least partially shaped by culture, correctly predicted the power of independence movements among black nationalists. Mayfield would make his mark not just by analyzing revolutions in the Third World but by participating in them, first as a journalist in Nkrumah's Ghana and, later, as a political activist in Guyana. Jones came back to the States, overwhelmed by the sight of a revolution whose participants included politicians and poets.[82]

2

AT HOME IN THE WORLD

In the waning days of the summer of 1960, the Cuban revolution came to Harlem. On Monday, September 19, Fidel Castro and Cuba's diplomatic delegation abruptly left the Shelbourne Hotel in midtown Manhattan and moved to Harlem's historic Theresa Hotel. The relocation was highlighted by mutual recriminations: hotel management accused the Cubans of boorish behavior, and Castro countered with charges of racial discrimination.[1] Well past its heyday, when celebrities like Joe Louis and Josephine Baker stayed there, the Theresa became ground zero in the American storm caused by Castro's stay.

Malcolm X was the first local African American leader to greet Castro. James Hicks, head of Harlem's powerful Twenty-eighth Precinct Community Council, had tapped Malcolm to lead a welcoming committee for visiting dignitaries.[2] By 1960, Malcolm, and with him the Nation of Islam's local profile, had become national and cosmopolitan. A visit to Saudi Arabia and the Egyptian Nile Valley a year earlier had whetted Malcolm's appetite for international diplomacy. In Africa, Malcolm glossed over the presence of white Arabs, observing that "99 per cent of them would be Jim-Crowed in the United States of

America."[3] Malcolm also ignored Castro's alabaster complexion, claiming the white-skinned *Cubano* as his own, just as he had the pale-faced Arabs who called black Americans "brothers of color."[4] Shortly after midnight, the *Amsterdam News* reported Castro's first impressions of Harlem in an exclusive interview from the Hotel Theresa. "I had always wanted to come to Harlem," claimed Castro, "but I was not sure what kind of welcome I would get."[5] Surrounded by security forces and various aides-de-camp, Malcolm and Fidel communicated through a translator. A photographer snapped pictures as Castro chatted with Malcolm and his two Muslim aides, the two men sitting at the edge of a bed conversing intently. "I think you will find the people in Harlem are not so addicted to the propaganda they put out downtown," said Malcolm.[6] The two discussed a range of issues, including the status of embattled Congolese prime minister Patrice Lumumba, racial discrimination in Cuba and the United States, and relations between Havana and Washington. Castro hinted that his scheduled speech before the UN General Assembly would address these matters to Malcolm's satisfaction.[7] Described by Malcolm X as the "only white person he ever liked," Castro was quickly turning into a political icon in Harlem and Cuba, where William Worthy reported that Havana's twenty-story Riviera Hotel had been renamed Havana Theresa.[8] Malcolm deflected the Communist taint associated with Castro, even though he felt that American anti-Castro rhetoric was reason enough to support Cuba. Maintaining tight vigilance against Communist infiltration in Harlem's vast political and religious nooks, FBI surveillance took comfort in the fact that Malcolm steadfastly denied any red romance and resigned from the welcoming committee.[9] Malcolm X's meeting with Castro, his trip to Africa, and ties with Harlem radicals marked him as a polyglot—a black nationalist who, guided by pan-African impulses, nevertheless analyzed the world from an international perspective.

Coverage of Malcolm and Castro's meeting broke along the racial fault lines of the segregated national press.[10] The *New York Times*, while providing front-page coverage of Castro's visit, belittled Malcolm as "a leader of the so-called Muslim movement among United States Negroes."[11] Subsequent reports couched the incident as a public relations stunt orchestrated by Castro in an effort to gain black support and embarrass American officials.[12] The *Citizen-Call*, the other newspaper allowed access to the meeting, featured a front-page photo of Fidel and Malcolm.[13] The city's largest black newspaper, the *Amsterdam News*, trumpeted its exclusive interview with Castro and touted the leader's unscheduled visit as the unofficial start to presidential election-year tours from the "greatest array of national political candidates and their supporters" in Harlem's history.[14] Sara Wright broke the news of Castro's presence in Harlem to John Henrik Clarke and the rest of her Harlem Writers Guild colleagues. A few moments later, the group left Wright's house to welcome the Cuban delegation but didn't get close. By eleven in the evening, the Theresa was surrounded by thousands of Harlem residents waiting to catch a glimpse of Castro. The police cordoned off intersections as spectators filled up central Harlem's main arteries and side streets. On the fringes of the crowd, members of the Harlem Writers Guild, several of whom had just returned from Cuba, listened to Spanish songs and chants of "Viva Castro."[15]

Castro made race relations the focus of his visit; he walked arm in arm through Harlem with Commandante Juan Almeida, the dark-skinned Afro-Cuban military leader who was flown in by Castro from Cuba to remind Harlem of his personal commitment to racial equality. In interviews offered exclusively to handpicked black journalists, Castro praised Harlem and its residents. "My impression of Harlem is that it's wonderful," he said. "We are very happy here. I think this is a big lesson to people who practice discrimination."[16] Trailed by journalists, photographers, and a large entourage, Castro charmed the neighborhood with his wide smile and effusive demeanor. On Tuesday, September 25, Castro received Soviet premier Nikita Khrushchev. During a visit to New York a year earlier, Khrushchev had disappointed many by speeding through Harlem in a motorcade without stopping to greet local residents.[17] This time Khrushchev did no such thing. Theresa manager Love B. Woods received hundreds of telegrams for Castro from well-wishers around the world, and direct lines to Havana were added to the hotel's switchboard. Castro's visit energized Harlem, including those who ran the rackets. One newspaper reported that numbers runners were being deluged with "929," the address of Castro's personal suite.[18] Black nationalists conducted daily rallies outside the National Memorial Bookstore, and anti-Castro activists held competing demonstrations a block away. Several local politicians stayed above the fray; Adam Clayton Powell denounced the entire event.[19] *The Afro-American* provided a double dose of Castro coverage via William Worthy's latest Havana correspondence.[20] Worthy's accounts of the Cuban revolution were based on firsthand experience; during the revolution's earliest days, Worthy spent perhaps more time on the island than any other black American journalist.

Impeccably dressed in a light blue suit that matched his azure eyes, the dashing Egyptian president, Gamal Abdel Nasser, ventured into Harlem near the end of Castro's stay. Three thousand people, including a Black Muslim contingent estimated at one thousand, greeted him; many were carrying signs that evoked an appropriately complex pan-African impulse. Nasser's appearance in Harlem provided an exclamation point for Castro's visit.[21] A week of assorted intrigues, demonstrations, and debates over Cuba's role in international affairs culminated with Castro delivering a combative, four-and-a-half-hour speech at the United Nations that inspired anticolonial internationalists and offended Cold War liberals.[22]

Malcolm X and the Nation of Islam, the political activism of Robert Williams, and the Cuban revolution helped create a new generation of black nationalists who studied local organizing, the politics of armed self-defense, and global upheavals with equal fervor. But the 1961 assassination of Congo leader Patrice Lumumba transformed them into radicals. Eloquent, handsome, and bespectacled, Lumumba emerged, in July of 1960, as the Congo's most powerful leader. A former beer salesman turned political activist, Lumumba became the first African prime minister in a country with an almost completely uneducated native population. Lumumba was appointed after his release from a dingy jail cell, and his spectacular rise and fall illustrated the hopes and impediments confronting African nation building. In an international arena unfamiliar with African autonomy in foreign affairs, Lumumba's brazen confidence—punctuated by a groundbreaking, combative speech that outraged the former colonial power, Belgium—was viewed as politically unacceptable. His assassination at the hands of political enemies captured the imagination of scores of American blacks only recently introduced to African independence movements.

The previous year's events had primed Harlem for organized political rebellion; 1960 had been declared the Year of Africa by the United Nations. Lumumba's controversial political ascendance catalyzed black militancy.[23] On February 15, 1961, less than five months after Castro's visit, a group of black nationalists took over the United Nations. Outside, demonstrators picketed the organization's Forty-second Street headquarters, and, inside, things turned ugly. The root of the protest was Lumumba's assassination at the hands of those who, black radicals correctly observed, received covert support from Belgium and (through more ambiguous diplomatic and intelligence back channels) American forces.[24] The ensuing protests, fistfights, and arrests inside the Congo, around the world, and at the UN made international headlines and turned Lumumba into an icon of African independence. Organized by some of Harlem's leading activists, the protest was a bold gamble that paid off. Maya Angelou was among those who made their way inside the Security Council meeting. Abandoning California for a new life in the big city, Angelou had found a warm refuge in the Harlem Writers Guild. A single mother whose deep voice matched her imposing frame, Angelou was a struggling poet, writer, and singer. Her friend and fellow protester Rosa Guy had broken the news of Lumumba's death to her. A native of Trinidad, Guy had a bold demeanor and quick temper. Both attributes had been instrumental in her easy friendships with a number of African diplomats, and now her passionate temper was urging her to act.[25]

The Lumumba demonstration partially originated from meetings held at the penthouse apartment of jazz singer Abbey Lincoln and jazz drummer Max Roach. Lincoln was the most prominent member of the recently formed Cultural Association for Women of African Heritage. Engaged to Roach, Lincoln was politically outspoken, fiercely intelligent, an independent spirit. Groomed as a sex symbol in the mid-1950s, she rejected stardom's gilded cage in favor of radical political engagement.[26] Roach, in releasing the classic album *We Insist! Max Roach's Freedom Now Suite* (which featured Lincoln), placed jazz at the center of civil rights struggles. Lincoln's natural hairstyle, at a time when most black women took pains to straighten their hair, represented only the most visible testament of her commitment.[27] Movie-star handsome, Roach and the equally glamorous Lincoln lent an air of elegance to Harlem's political and cultural scene. The couple's penthouse served as a salon, the upscale counterpart of the brownstones and tiny flats where Harlem writers usually gathered. Together they formed one—actors Ossie Davis and Ruby Dee made up the other—of the era's two black radical celebrity power couples. Roach and Lincoln's artistic engagement and political commitment—they counted members of the Harlem Writers Guild and Malcolm X among their friends and acquaintances—anticipated LeRoi Jones's pioneering *Blues People* and Black Power activists' contention that jazz was "black" music expressed in the words of Malcolm X and the tenor saxophone of John Coltrane.[28] Artists who could have easily described themselves, in the radical vernacular of the day as borrowed from the French, as engagé, Roach and Lincoln made radical politics simultaneously look and sound good.[29]

Part protest demonstration and part funeral procession (including protesters in black arm bands and veils), the scene inside the United Nations was volcanic. Dozens of enraged activists united against a political assassination that took place half a world away.[30] Representatives from a number of groups showed up, including the Liberation Committee for Africa, On Guard, the African Nationalist Pioneer Movement, and the Cultural Association for Women of African Heritage.[31] From the balcony, the screaming voices of protesters could be heard. "Killers!" shouted one. "Murderers!" yelled another. "Lumumba! Lumumba!" they chanted in unison. Adlai Stevenson, two-time Democratic presidential candidate and U.S. representative to the United Nations, stood to address the meeting. Leaning toward the microphone, Stevenson removed his glasses and searched for the source of the rapidly escalating commotion.[32]

At 11:35 in the morning, protesters had entered the Security Council meeting where a melee broke out between security guards and demonstrators. Frantic crowds hustled out in a stampede of departing spectators and incoming security guards. LeRoi Jones and Mae Mallory huddled together and, in an instant, were cordoned off by security. Mallory engaged in a heated struggle that required the intervention of several guards. Police officers snatched Jones into a packed police van, banging his head against the paddy wagon's metal frame doors while other protesters were dragged outside and charged with disorderly conduct.[33]

The west side of First Avenue turned into a public rally for the remainder of the day, as Communists, reportedly banned by nationalists from joining the march, staged a sympathy picket across the street.[34] That evening, despite bone-chilling temperatures, more than two hundred protesters gathered on First Avenue at Forty-third Street. Demonstrators who assembled at Times Square turned midtown Manhattan briefly into a protest spectacle featuring virtually every black militant group in the city. Flanked by a phalanx of mounted police, demonstrators were forcibly halted at the Avenue of Americas.[35] Regrouping in Harlem, protesters met en masse to replay the day's events and discuss plans for the future. Defiantly telling reporters that "Negroes" were now "Afro-Americans," a small group of nationalists, Muslims, and community activists, surrounded by more than one hundred police officers, stood in the bitter cold the next day, chanting: "Who died for the black man?" "Lumumba!" they shouted, "Lumumba!" "Who died for freedom?" "Lumumba!" came back the ferocious reply.[36]

A picture of Calvin Hicks (being arrested before scandalized UN Security Council representatives) appeared on the front page of the next day's *New York Times*. A writer for the *New York Age*, Hicks, taken under the wing of the Harlem Writers Guild, was one of the Lower East Side's leading organizers. Stanley's Bar on Twelfth Street

and Avenue B served as a headquarters for black radicals living downtown. "It was," Hicks recalled decades later, "a comfort zone." A popular hangout for jazz singers, poets, and writers, Stanley's doubled as a
way station for would-be politicians, civil rights burnouts, and future
Black Power revolutionaries. Political debates often outpaced the consumption of beer, wine, and liquor. Regulars discussed the latest happenings in Cuba, prospects for armed self-defense, the incompetence of
white liberals, the naiveté of Martin Luther King Jr., the frightening
power of Malcolm X and the Black Muslims, and the hopeful promise
of African liberation. Harold Cruse, Maya Angelou, Archie Shepp,
Brenda Walcott, Ishmael Reed, and Aisha Rahman were part of this
circle of artists—some destined for fame, others for obscurity.[37]

Calling the protest an "invasion," the New York Times characterized the incident as the "worst day of violence" in UN history. The
Amsterdam News countered by portraying Lumumba's death as an
"international lynching" carried out "on the altar of white supremacy."[38] Lumumba's assassination unleashed global tremors of
anger and resolve, triggering protests in the Soviet Union, Paris, London, Ghana, and Tokyo.[39] In the counteroffensive that followed, Ralph
Bunche, the legendary African American intellectual and UN diplomat,
personally apologized for black participation in the fiasco.[40] City officials tried to connect the disturbances to a maze of Communist conspiracies and Black Muslim revenge plots. Malcolm X threatened to
sue Adlai Stevenson, New York City police commissioner Stephen
Kennedy, and any newspaper that tied the Nation of Islam to the
demonstrations. But Malcolm stopped short of denouncing the entire
event. "I refuse to condemn the demonstrations," he said, "and I will
permit no one to use me against the nationalists."[41]

James Baldwin went further. Baldwin, whose participation in the
civil rights movement seemed to grow with each crisis, published an article in the New York Times a few weeks after the UN disturbance.
The essay was inspired by guilt as much as by outrage. En route to the
demonstration, Baldwin was delayed—at a cocktail party.[42] "A Negro
Assays the Negro Mood" offered the Congo crisis as the starting point
for an analysis of black rage attributed to Communist subversives.[43]

According to Baldwin, red baiting provided no shelter for the gathering storm of black discontent. Violence at the United Nations was a surprise only to the many Americans who preferred not to visit Harlem and witness the community's growing despair. Characterizing sit-in demonstrations as just one of the "two most significant" movements among blacks, Baldwin argued that the goals behind these tactics went beyond "the consumption of overcooked hamburgers and tasteless coffee at various sleazy lunch counters." New waves of black militancy suggested something greater. Black people, he said, were forcing America to wrestle with its soul, and if the country refused, there were other, less genteel demonstrators—the Nation of Islam, the UN protesters—waiting in line for their turn.

Next he turned to the international arena. Baldwin pointed to Africa's emergence in world affairs as a promising sign of a black cultural awakening. In prose that foreshadowed both the eloquent tone of Martin Luther King Jr.'s "Letter from Birmingham Jail" and the fierce temper of Black Arts advocates, Baldwin recalled the shame he experienced growing up in Harlem and the pain he still felt knowing that black women continued to straighten their hair in a desperate effort to fit in. Baldwin ended his essay with a warning cloaked inside a plea. African Americans "who rioted in the United Nations" were, Baldwin wrote, "but a small echo of the black discontent now abroad." His last words referred to the nation's Cold War–driven foreign policy: "If we are not able, and quickly, to face and begin to eliminate the sources of discontent in our own country, we will never be able to do it in the world at large."[44]

While James Baldwin wrestled with national racial and political demons in public, in private Malcolm X confronted the limits of Muslim sectarianism. Shortly after the UN demonstration, Maya Angelou, Abbey Lincoln, and Rosa Guy met with Malcolm at the Shabazz Restaurant adjacent to Mosque No. 7. Over tea and bean pies, the women probed Malcolm for his reaction to their recent exploits. Malcolm informed them that he was very proud of what they had accomplished, adding that he had just finished squelching rumors of Communist conspiracies.[45] Malcolm's public denials of Black Muslim involvement in the UN demonstration, while technically correct, glossed over the obvious: he supported the demonstrators in both spirit and practice and, furthermore, he preached a political message that local militants took as a call to arms. On a more personal note, Malcolm genuinely admired the black women who had helped organize the type of muscular protest that fell outside the bounds of the Nation of Islam's agenda. Through their organizing, activists who looked to Malcolm as a political teacher and symbol of racial militancy outpaced their mentor, who continued to be hamstrung by the Nation of Islam. Forbidden from joining public demonstrations, Malcolm, like the devout Muslim he was, dutifully obeyed. For a man with immense intellectual gifts, supple political skills, and growing national ambitions, this was a difficult task. Soon, it would prove impossible.

3

WAGING WAR AMID SHADOWS

William Worthy first encountered the Nation of Islam in 1955 during an unscheduled New Year's Eve haircut at Boston's Shabazz Tonsorial Parlor. Worthy enjoyed the banter of the barbershop staff, quickly developing a warm relationship with them, a group of freshly converted Black Muslims who, soon afterward, gave him a calendar featuring Marilyn Monroe. With the Muslim neophytes' minor indiscretion, Worthy's professional association with the Nation of Islam began, leading to the occasional interview with Elijah Muhammad and a more personal relationship with Malcolm X.[1] Worthy's civil rights contacts also placed him at the scene during the early days of the Montgomery bus boycott.[2] A foreign correspondent for the *Baltimore-Washington Afro-American*, Worthy traveled freely between the front lines of some of the Cold War's most embattled countries and the then-equally dangerous domestic civil rights frontier. Professionally, he was the outstanding black foreign correspondent of his generation, attracted to stories taking place in the far reaches of the world. In an era when Cold War politics made black participation in foreign affairs dangerous, Worthy reported from Korea, Indochina, and Malaysia.[3] In 1956, Worthy toured Africa, covering bloody conflicts in Algeria and the Belgian Congo before sneaking into Johannesburg, where he witnessed the ugly face of South Africa's apartheid system, observing a government "living completely in a world of fantasy, unmoved and even unconscious of the liberation movements all over Africa."[4]

Worthy's byline was underwritten by his personal boldness, for he routinely ventured into perilous territory and just as often came away with an exclusive interview. In 1955, he became the first American reporter in seven years to perform a live radio broadcast from the Soviet Union. Within twenty-four hours of reaching Moscow, he was shaking hands with Nikita Khrushchev.[5] Worthy's professional assertiveness contrasted with his quiet personal demeanor. To look at him, one would never imagine that he set off a string of minor and major international incidents. Slightly built, with sad, deep-set eyes, Worthy grew up in a home in which defending personal convictions was considered a virtue. In fact, his political activism emanated from a deep-seated belief in human rights for all people. Born and raised in Boston, Worthy inherited his physician father's shyness while channeling his mother's gregariousness when necessary. Despite his natural reserve, Worthy received his share of attention. Recalling this irony decades later, Worthy noted that although unsolicited, much of his fame derived from his "articles, indictments," and prodigious political activism.[6] Worthy attended Bates College in Maine, avidly listening to Socialists who trekked north preaching the gospel of class struggle and social equality. A voracious reader and excellent student, Worthy began, at Bates, to question America's foreign and domestic policies. He wrote articles for the campus weekly and in his spare time delivered antiwar speeches that foreshadowed his refusal to serve in the Second World War. Days spent walking through the crisp air of the New England campus marked the beginning of a lifelong commitment to pacifism and social justice.[7]

Worthy found a kindred spirit in Carl Murphy, the *Afro-American*'s maverick publisher, who allowed the headstrong reporter considerable leeway. Worthy's extensive time abroad helped him build a network of contacts around the world. He was one of the few reporters who could boast of meeting or personally interviewing leaders from China, the Soviet Union, Africa, and India. These relationships helped Worthy's career, enabling him to become one of the era's few black journalists to operate comfortably in both the black and the white media. Considering Worthy's radical politics and the Jim Crow–era press, this was no small feat. Like Louis Lomax, who had parlayed his knowledge of the Black Muslims and their refusal to speak with white reporters into an exclusive interview, Worthy broke news stories that turned his skin color into a strategic advantage.

Worthy reported one such story in Christmas 1957, when, on break from Harvard University's prestigious Nieman Fellowship, he traveled to the other side of the world—China—while his colleagues enjoyed the holidays.[8] On the day he entered China, the State Department issued a statement expressing the government's displeasure. Returning home, Worthy was a fugitive, playing a game of cat and mouse with customs agents intent on confiscating his passport. Narrowly evading officials in Vienna and Budapest, Worthy arrived in New York, where CBS News, eager for his China exclusive (which included an interview with Premier Chou En-lai), provided a limousine for his appearance on Eric Severeid's *World News Round-Up*.[9] One month later, accompanied by the civil liberties lawyer William Kunstler, he turned in his expired passport and applied for a new one. The State Department denied his application in late March, after Worthy rejected its offer to renew his passport on the condition that he stay out of restricted countries.[10]

Three years after the China affair, federal officials arrested Worthy and indicted him, after he returned home from Cuba in 1961, for failing to travel with a valid passport. As a result, Worthy became the first American tried under the McCarran-Walter Immigration and Nationality Act. The Cold War–inspired measure gave the federal government broad powers over individual travel and targeted suspected Communists. Worthy's race, as well as escapades in China, Africa, and Cuba, made him an ideal target.[11] While the government's efforts to prosecute Worthy because of his political beliefs approximated a turkey shoot, the State Department's aggressive plans for payback enraged the soft-spoken journalist, intensifying his personal resolve. "Bobby and Jack Kennedy," proclaimed Worthy, "wouldn't know a civil liberty if it hit them in the face."[12] Worthy's criticism of the Kennedy administration found receptive audiences. Scores of colleges pursued him for the lectures that provided him with needed financial support.[13] In February 1961, Worthy embarked on one such engagement, a sixteen-day southern speaking tour sponsored by Tuskegee University in Alabama. On the last leg of his tour, Worthy, in an address to over two thousand Tuskegee students, decried U.S. coverage of Fidel Castro as a "hatchet job." Castro was "there to stay," he told his audience, adding that any hope for a Cuban-American rapprochement rested on Washington's coming to terms with the permanence of the Cuban revolution.[14]

Worthy's writing displayed both critical analysis and biting wit—two qualities that further embittered him to the State Department—especially after he snuck into Cuba via Mexico in 1961, thumbing his nose at newly imposed travel restrictions. Worthy did little to hide the ruse. "Due to the United States travel ban, I didn't expect to be able to see this island again for a long time," he wrote. "But after becoming ill en route to Mexico I got off the ship to consult a doctor here."[15] Federal authorities suspicious of Worthy's intentions had almost derailed his ploy while customs agents grilled him as he ate lunch aboard the SS *Guadalupe*.[16] In Cuba, Worthy wrote a series of news reports analyzing the island's social and political progress, its relationship to black Americans, and the revolution's impact on foreign affairs. He considered America's Cold War–driven foreign policy immoral, crippling to domestic and foreign affairs, and in need of serious change.

In October 1961, Worthy scored an exclusive on one of the year's biggest stories, scooping the national press by interviewing Robert Williams in Havana. Pursued by the FBI and North Carolina officials on trumped-up kidnapping charges, Williams fled to Cuba. Political acquaintances in the United States, Williams and Worthy now met under excruciating circumstances. Williams was wanted by federal and state authorities, and once again Worthy was violating State Department travel restrictions. There was poetic symmetry to their reunion: both the itinerant journalist and the maverick civil rights leader seemed destined to find peace only on foreign soil.

The *Afro-American*'s front page bared the enormity of Williams's escape from an American dragnet in bold print: "WILLIAMS FLEES U.S. BY NEW UNDERGROUND R.R." Headlines describing him as a modern-day fugitive slave evoked images of an antebellum America in which a grim fate awaited captured blacks. Worthy conducted an all-night interview with the exiled activist, reporting that Williams appeared relaxed and "unworried" after a harrowing ordeal that resembled a "fast moving thriller."[17] Carefully and obliquely, Worthy described the dozens of contacts in the United States and Canada that facilitated Williams's successful escape. Williams's miraculous reappearance in Cuba was the stuff of legend. His travails influenced black radicals from Monroe, North Carolina, to Accra, Ghana.

The Monroe Defendants—most notably the Harlem activist Mae Mallory, who helped Williams—would spend the next several years embroiled in legal trouble, accused of false kidnapping charges. Julian Mayfield, who personally aided Williams's escape, fled the States for Ghana with federal officials in hot pursuit. Worthy's interview poignantly revealed the man behind the outrageous sound bites that would frighten white Americans and also sell newspapers. Confident that Williams's reemergence would be "a turning point in our civil rights struggle," Worthy reveled in showcasing Williams's artistic soul. "Robert F. Williams is going to be known to the listening world by a theme song. When he begins his series of broadcasts over Radio Havana, the programs will open and close with a very moving song, 'Look At My Chains.' It describes the pains and emotions of a people still in bondage."[18] Williams's flight to Cuba, Worthy concluded, signaled an advance by retreat for the black freedom movement: a radicalization that would enlarge the struggle. After hours of discussion, Robert Williams, along with his Cuban bodyguards, left Worthy's hotel room. Williams, whose grace under pressure was remarkable, told Worthy that he was making plans to return to the United States. After Williams departed, Worthy found himself asking not if he would accomplish such a task but "what he will go back with and who will be at his side."[19]

Nine months after this interview, William Worthy stood trial in Miami, with both his professional career and his personal freedom in jeopardy.[20] Worthy's individual plight triggered collective acts of defiance.[21] Events surrounding his trial on charges of violating the McCarran Act inspired widespread support, including the satirical "Ballad of William Worthy" by the folk singer Phil Ochs.[22] Worthy turned his legal troubles into a political struggle that embarrassed the attorney general and pushed black protest into uncharted waters. Failing to receive a change of venue despite pleas from his lawyers, he was found guilty of violating the McCarran Act. At a time when leading civil rights groups were at odds with one another over the movement's political direction, Worthy's case provided a rare moment of unity.[23] It also helped open the Cold War's Pandora's box, hurling America's racial hypocrisy in the face of a government already anxious about its interests in the Third World. Convicted after a bench trial in August 1962, he offered no apologies. "Travel control is thought control and intellectual control. Free men, thinking men, concerned men want none of it."[24]

No name was given to William Worthy's political battles or the pockets of well-organized resistance that extended him aid and comfort. Many of them were northern militants who, while sympathetic to the civil rights movement, viewed their own struggles through different eyes. Mutual antagonisms cut off these invisible activists from white liberals and traditional civil rights leaders. On the fringes of the movement or, more often, an afterthought, black radicals during the age of civil rights walked a tightrope between conventional political protest and creative militancy. The black freedom movement in the North contained the grand passion, calamitous drama, and Shakespearean pathos that marked its southern counterpart. However, before the racial upheavals that would focus attention on urban areas across the nation, northern crises served as temporary distractions from the region that was largely considered America's civil rights front: the South. The blunt speaking, rough-hewn, at times riotously vulgar cadences of northern black activists and race leaders—populated with storefront churches, street speakers, Black Muslims, and outspoken black politicians—failed to resonate with a national media enthralled by the dignified, frequently mesmerizing oratory of southern black preachers. "Our war against oppression in the North is often like a battle against evanescent shadows," wrote Detroit activist Richard Henry in 1962.[25]

They were more than just shadows. White resistance in the North took shape as de facto segregation, a euphemism for a type of American apartheid that, while not sanctioned by law, like the South's de jure system of Jim Crow, proved—in its opaqueness—perhaps even more insidious. Though plagued by separate and unequal housing, schools, and life chances, blacks outside the South seemed incapable of convincing local and national media, politicians, or even civil rights leaders that their concerns were as compelling as sharecroppers registering to vote for the first time in a century or as inspiring as college students sitting in at coffee shops and lunch counters. Free to use public accommodations and exercise their voting rights, northern black struggles seemed both less urgent and farther removed from the Deep South's civil rights battlefields. Ironically, the stark gap in white America's perceptions of black life in the North and the South during the early 1960s was reflected in increasing support from northern liberals for southern civil rights organizations—activism that included financial contributions, support from prominent intellectuals and artists, and the active participation of hundreds of white volunteers from far-flung parts of the nation who traveled south to join the movement.

Down south the face of white resistance to waves of civil rights demonstrations, boycotts, and sit-ins could be seen in the frowning expressions of men and women, children and teenagers, the middle-aged and the elderly who wished to make the increasingly regular spectacles of black protest disappear. Some did more than just hope. Working-class vigilantes—sometimes formalized in the secret brotherhood of the Ku Klux Klan, more often culled together by shared skin color and rage against Negroes—beat up demonstrators in raw displays of physical violence that received cooperation from local authorities.[26] The South's white middle class resorted to tactics that were less overtly brutal but no less vicious. In the aftermath of the *Brown* desegregation decision, these southerners formed White Citizens Councils, which put an officious civic face on the politics of white supremacy; they preferred to think of it as a way of life rather than as racial oppression. Politicians and business executives topped this hierarchy of resistance, with elected officials openly defying court orders and even the threat of federal intervention while corporate leaders looked the other way, incurring the kind of substantial economic expense that retarded prospects for a technologically efficient, socially tolerant, and economically modern south. In 1962, southern resistance to racial integration stiffened. In Albany, Georgia, Martin Luther King's campaign for integration ran into a wall of official tolerance, stymied by a police chief, Laurie Pritchett, who steadfastly refused to provide King with the kind of public confrontation that would force federal intervention into what was still regarded as a regional issue. That same year, whites in Oxford, Mississippi, took a different approach, as thousands of demonstrators rioted on campus in shock and disgust at the enrollment of the University of Mississippi's first Negro student, James Meredith.

Racial politics outside the South took on not just a different character but also different ends. While southern blacks faced the humiliations of a Jim Crow system whose signs cheerfully announced they were unwelcome at restaurants, movie theaters, diners, and swimming pools reserved for whites, northern cities took unearned pride in their veneer of tolerance. Racism's effects in cities such as New York (including Harlem), Detroit, Chicago, Los Angeles, and Oakland could be measured by poor public schools, overcrowded housing projects, and high rates of unemployment rather than by Jim Crow in public accommodations and the lack of voting rights. In northern metropolises, the authorities, rather than goon squads, meted out antiblack violence while naked aggression characterized police attitudes toward the black community. In 1962, the brute force that too often substituted for effective crime fighting took the form of a melee outside a Los Angeles mosque that resulted in the death of Nation of Islam member Ronald Stokes.

Northern blacks tried a number of tactics aimed at securing good jobs, schools, housing, and equal opportunity. In New York and

Chicago, militants staged successful boycotts to protest segregation and unequal resources in the public schools. In Boston and Los Angeles, community organizers focused on public education, trumpeting educational opportunity as a constitutional and human rights imperative. In Philadelphia, community activists organized against racist employment practices with strategies that ranged from selective patronage campaigns to more bruising protests against the City of Brotherly Love's virtually all-white construction industry. While these activists stressed bread-and-butter issues, others around the country made plans for a revolution. In 1962, radical black college students in Ohio formed the Revolutionary Action Movement (RAM), a group committed to a brand of the revolutionary nationalism that Harold Cruse wrote about that same year. In California, activists associated with RAM founded *Soulbook*, a radical cultural magazine whose staff included future Black Power activists Ernie Allen and Bobby Seale. The Bay Area–based Afro-American Association represented one of the earliest expressions of Black Power on the West Coast. Organized by a charismatic young lawyer named Donald Warden, the association's blend of black history, study sessions, and street rallies attracted restless young militants, including Huey P. Newton and Ron Karenga. While these groups expressed, to varying degrees, Black Power activism at the local level, five periodicals reflected the movement's burgeoning intellectual, literary, and political ambitions. In the early 1960s, *Liberator, Soulbook, Negro Digest, Muhammad Speaks,* and *Freedomways* published political essays, literary criticism, and poetry that provided the foundation for the movement's political thrust and the Black Arts' cultural and literary nationalism. While Black Power activists admired civil rights insurgency, and even joined civil rights groups in hopes of pushing them further to the Left, black militants across the country laid the groundwork for turning local initiatives into an alternative national movement. These local forces would find a measure of unity and a national spokesman in Malcolm X.[27]

Civil rights–era Detroit reflected Richard Henry's description of racial warfare as a stealth conflict. Between the Second World War and the late 1960s, Detroit experienced dramatic changes in its racial, social, economic, and geographic boundaries. Increasing black migration to Detroit heightened tensions over jobs, housing, public schools, and political patronage. These transformations were book-ended by race riots in 1943 and 1967.[28] Racial peace in the aftermath of the 1943 riot was threatened by de facto segregation, police brutality, and bitter fights between blacks and whites over employment. Detroit's landscape included the combustible mix of a white population heading to the suburbs, waves of black migrants, and activists eager to turn civil unrest into community power. Black control of City Hall, for the first time in memory, appeared possible through proper timing, ambition, and militancy. The rising black population led to community, political, and corporate anxiety among whites that was only partially obscured by growing calls for urban renewal—a thinly disguised effort to clear African Americans from Detroit's darkening downtown. In the early 1960s, the city's tensions created a nexus of religious, political, and cultural activity that highlighted the possibilities of Black Power. Ultimately, postwar economic stagnation threatened both black and white progress. Reeling by the 1960s from the decline in heavy industry that had once made it the arsenal of democracy, Detroit was a city in which white ethnic enclaves and burgeoning black neighborhoods engaged in open conflict with one another.[29]

A powerful challenge to the status quo in Detroit emerged through a network of black organizations with one common denominator: racial militancy as a means of social and political progress. Reverend Albert Cleage Jr. (pronounced *Clague,* with a long *a*), Richard and Milton Henry, Jimmy and Grace Lee Boggs, and Luke Tripp made up the core of this self-described New Guard. Albert Cleage, who would become the principal leader behind the Black Theology movement during the late 1960s, served as the New Guard's spokesman. Renaming his Central Congregational Church the Shrine of the Black Madonna, Cleage conducted services underneath the watchful eye of an ebony Mary and caramel-colored baby Jesus who gazed down from a towering mural.[30] With dreams of establishing a separate nation in the Black Belt South, brothers Richard and Milton Henry would change their names to Imari and Gaidi Obadele and found the Republic of New Afrika. The Boggses shunned national celebrity in favor of local organizing and became obscure theorists who left an indelible imprint on Black Power radicalism. Some of Detroit's youngest activists formed Uhuru (Swahili for "freedom"), a militant collective led by Luke Tripp. Many of these youthful militants emerged as the organizers behind the wildcat strikes, against Detroit's automotive industry, that led to the League of Revolutionary Black Workers. The fluidity of the relationships within the organizations and among the leaders allowed a measure of intimacy in Detroit unencumbered by sectarian loyalties.

In a city filled with colorful political activists, Albert Cleage cut a larger-than-life figure. Possessing limited connections to "responsible Negro Leadership," the good reverend became the Pied Piper of the city's scoundrels—an assorted collection of militant youth, veteran activists, and the simply disgruntled. "It's very hard to lead an oppressed people, because they are always looking for a messiah," Cleage would dramatically intone, distilling the often unspoken pitfalls of charismatic race leadership. He frequently leveled scathing criticism against apathy and indifference, noting "how good blacks were at tearing things up," yet how "difficult it was to get them to build" institutions.[31]

Cleage's sermons were masterful exhortations to organize and protest that deployed images of both the sacred and the profane. This blending of the practical and the prophetic was no accident. Cleage believed that black oppression was both political and psychological. For him there was no better example of the enduring myth of black inferiority than biblical images. White supremacy was so powerful that even the religious figures blacks looked to for eternal salvation were white. The antidote would be a Black Christian Nationalist reinterpretation of the Bible—one that soothed wounded black souls while it inspired them to grab more earthly power than they had ever imagined. According to Cleage, power, not morality, stood between black Americans and the promise of freedom. But first black people had to believe that they were worthy of such awesome responsibility.

Cleage's oratorical gifts transformed Scripture into images of resistance and struggle, capturing the imagination of spellbound congregations.[32] Reimagining biblical tales as contemporary allegories of race, rebellion, and redemption, Cleage preached that bits of heaven should be fought for, and enjoyed, while people toiled on God's green earth. Rejecting "slave Christianity," Cleage sought to make the church "relevant to the Black Revolution."[33] From the pulpit he cast Jesus as the Black Messiah, who, with his apostles, battled the forces of evil at great personal cost. Cleage's sermons were published as *Black Messiah* in 1968. Envisioning Jesus as a proud and radical black prophet who raged against political and economic oppression enabled Cleage to turn his church into a headquarters for political activism.

In November 1961, Cleage and other blacks in the city formed the Group on Advanced Leadership (GOAL), an organization made up of militants who cloaked themselves in the rhetoric of the civil rights struggle to enjoy the respectability of a movement that they nonetheless criticized as too cautious.[34] GOAL specifically opposed black participation in machine politics. Black leaders anointed by City Hall enjoyed special privileges that conferred few if any benefits on most African Americans—circumstances that made the politically well connected vulnerable to charges of selling out.[35]

Malcolm X, whose high profile and electrifying oratory made him the rare speaker who could overshadow Cleage, frequented Detroit on personal and professional visits. The Motor City, the birthplace of the Black Muslim movement, housed its original temple. Almost a decade earlier, Wilfred X, Detroit's leading Muslim minister, had played a small but vital role in transforming the Nation of Islam by sponsoring Malcolm's parole. Within a year of securing a job in the furniture store Wilfred managed, Malcolm was promoted to assistant minister of Detroit's mosque and soon established his headquarters in Harlem.

During the summer of 1957, Malcolm made a triumphant return to Detroit. For four weeks he lectured to standing-room-only audiences on topics ranging from the Johnson X case to the civil rights crisis in

Little Rock, Arkansas. Local black newspapers hailed Malcolm as a new voice on the scene. His presence attracted attention to the NOI and, with it, increased membership and organizational changes, with Malcolm successfully lobbying behind the scenes for Elijah Muhammad to name Wilfred as head minister of the Nation of Islam's Detroit mosque.[36] More significant, Malcolm's triumph in Detroit continued the NOI's transformation from a small religious sect into a force whose influence reverberated on both coasts. Locally, Malcolm recognized the city's dense network of radicals as political comrades who, even if unwilling to pledge loyalty to Elijah Muhammad, might still accept Malcolm's tough talk of self-determination, community control, and self-defense. Thus Malcolm practiced his own brand of coalition politics in Detroit as he would in cities around the nation. After Malcolm's ties to the NOI dissolved, Detroit remained a personal and political haven during what would be the last year of his life.

Detroit's storied tradition of labor, political, and religious radicalism helped GOAL forge strong relationships with Black Muslims, nationalists, trade unionists, civil rights leaders, and Socialists, who made Malcolm feel at home. Milton and Richard Henry were instrumental in strengthening these ties. Younger brother Richard was a technical manuals writer at the U.S. Tank-Automotive Center in Warren, Michigan. As president of GOAL, he served as the group's publicist.[37] One of Malcolm X's closest political allies, Milton Henry was a lawyer, political strategist, and businessman.[38] A lieutenant in the Air Force, Milton was dismissed from the military in 1944 for absenteeism and insubordination. At his court-martial, he vowed that "some day I too will be in a position to dictate."[39] In Milton, Malcolm X found a friend with connections to local militants and broadcast media (Milton ran his own media company and would later found the glossy magazine *Now!*) and the person who would broker GOAL's alliance with the nation's most alluring black radical.

Jimmy Boggs and his wife, Grace Lee Boggs, were two of Cleage's most important allies. Writers for the journal *Correspondence*, the Boggses had been colleagues of the legendary Trinidadian Marxist C. L. R. James. By the early 1960s, they had broken with the Socialist

Workers Party in order to establish themselves as freewheeling Marxist theoreticians. Jimmy had become admired in radical circles with the 1963 publication of *The American Revolution*. Completed while he worked full-time in Chrysler's auto factory and published by Monthly Review Press as a one-dollar pamphlet, Boggs's analysis of race, class, and revolution influenced young activists increasingly committed to both black nationalism and anticapitalist struggles. Written in plain language free of Marxist jargon, *The American Revolution* argued that class struggle had reached a turning point where black workers would take the lead in creating a new society. Well acquainted with his neighbors whom he assisted when they were in need, Boggs became a folk hero in and around the Detroit area. Active in radical politics since the 1940s, Grace Boggs edited *Correspondence*, held a Ph.D. in philosophy, and was a frequent enough presence in black politics that the FBI mistakenly referred to her as an "Afro-Chinese."[40] By any measure, the Boggses were unusual both personally and politically. They were an interracial couple at a time when such unions were scarce. There were other distinctions as well. Jimmy was neat, orderly, and efficient, a proud man who meticulously completed household chores. Grace was an intellectual of Chinese ancestry who committed herself to the cause of black freedom with a skill and integrity that won over skeptics. Activists meeting the couple were impressed by Grace's intellect and Jimmy's warmth; the affable Jimmy and the more prickly Grace complemented each other, and young people found surrogate parents in the childless couple.[41]

The Boggses were both exemplars and organizers, their modestly furnished living room serving as an informal training ground for aspiring activists. Luke Tripp, who founded Uhuru, frequented the couple's home. Occasionally he would attend the Friday night meeting of the Socialist Workers Party, which, under the direction of George Breitman, openly embraced black nationalist sentiments associated with the Nation of Islam and other radical groups.[42] Attending these forums with Tripp were Mike Hamlin, John Watson, and General Baker, students who, in a few short years, would virtually paralyze the city's automobile industry through their organizing efforts. An undergraduate at Wayne State University studying politics and history, the twenty-one-year-old Tripp exemplified the broad experiences affecting local young people, whether listening to an Albert Cleage speech, attending a local Muslim mosque, or concluding the evening among a group of Socialists. Tripp could be something of a hothead, prone to providing outrageous, apocalyptic quotes to eager local reporters in search of sensationalistic headlines: "UHURU Leader Says That Whites Must Be Crushed!"[43] Engaging in daily physical exercise and a steady diet of black history, social movement literature, and Marxism, Tripp became the most visible face of the city's young militants determined to organize the ghetto.

Frequently, activists from other parts of the country would stop by the Boggses', report their activities, and engage in extensive political debates and strategy sessions. Max Stanford, energetic, brash, and only twenty-two years old, was one of the Boggses' "adopted" kids. Often dressed in jeans and white gym shoes, Stanford was a Philadelphia native who had been involved in militant civil rights activism since he was a teenager. Stanford and his friends would stay up all night in the Boggses' living room plotting rebellion. Their more experienced mentors challenged Stanford's and Tripp's youthful, at times fanciful, polemics. More often than not, the discussions turned into seminars in which the veteran activists demanded sharp analysis and concrete facts. Jimmy would ask questions that were difficult to answer: If the revolution was to succeed, how would the new society look? What would black people's place in it be, and what kinds of jobs, government, and society would exist?[44]

A bright student and a voracious reader, Stanford had dropped out of college and, with the Cleveland activist Donald Freeman, a university student turned radical, started RAM. Stanford cut an oddly impressive figure and at times a disconcertingly intense one, his black framed glasses becoming a kind of trademark. On more than one occasion he was rescued from the local police station by Grace Boggs after being picked up for "suspicious" behavior based more on racial profiling than the investigative prowess of the police. Such minor harassments did little to dampen Stanford's organizing ambitions. Inspired by Robert F. Williams and Malcolm X, RAM considered itself the infantry of the African American freedom struggle, promoting revolutionary nationalism in pamphlets, newsletters, and journals. RAM developed an ideology that the writer Phillip Abbott Luce described as "Marxism as interpreted by Elijah Muhammad."[45] The reality was more complicated. RAM's ideology encompassed Cruse's idiosyncratic internationalism, a nuts-and-bolts approach to class struggle, and a blueprint for political revolution drawn from Chinese Marxists, black radicals, and guerrilla struggles. In Detroit, Black Muslims, civil rights renegades, and aspiring revolutionaries were embarking on a political odyssey that would lay the framework for revolutionary nationalist strains of Black Power radicalism that would erupt before the end of the decade. In an era before the Black Panthers emerged, RAM was considered by the FBI to be among the nation's most dangerous black militants.

While RAM operated beneath the radar, GOAL basked in the local spotlight.[46] Its first significant victory, in 1961, was to help Democrat Jerome Cavanagh defeat the incumbent Democratic mayor Louis Miriani. The upset victory by a political neophyte, the thirty-three-year-old Cavanagh, was aided by a grassroots campaign orchestrated by Cleage and his allies. Disgusted with the Democratic machine, Cleage threw his support to the liberal Cavanagh in a move that reflected his growing political muscle and the black community's dissatisfaction with the status quo. His support of Cavanagh was evidence that black political strength could be wielded in the city. A year later, GOAL was Detroit's leading black radical organization and through its publication, the *Illustrated News*, announced that it would make the pursuit of political power its top priority; Cleage asserted that Detroit would "elect three Negro congressman in 1962 or not at all!"[47] Driving through the city in a convertible draped with a white sheet that read "3 plus 1," GOAL supporters spread the word with a zeal that made the most of the group's slim resources. Cleage was an optimist but no fool. Efforts to elect a member of Congress may have served as dress rehearsals for organized black power, but they also functioned in the here and now to give residents hope. Independent politics had become an increasingly attractive option in light of black leaders' weakened political muscles, atrophied by loyalty to the Democratic Party. Challenging what some came to feel was a parasitic relationship between Detroit's Democratic Party and their loyal black base, GOAL sponsored an independent slate of progressive black candidates with close ties to Detroit's grassroots movement, the idea being that the city's racial inequality would be, according to Cleage, best challenged at its supposed roots, City Hall.[48] While unsuccessful, the "3 plus 1" campaign proved that blacks could run candidates for office. The Reverend Cleage's unorthodox style did obscure, at times, his sophisticated attempts to groom a class of progressive black leaders who would control a major city. Wary of Uncle Toms, Cleage selected allies who had repudiated the city's political machine. His master plan depended on the development and coordination of a local movement supported by community organizers, churches, and educators. Metropolitan Detroit, almost a third of which was black and growing, would eventually validate Cleage, who was cultivating the political leverage to usher in black control of the city. Accordingly, black power would be established when and where African Americans were organized and savvy enough to elect black city council members, congressional representatives, prosecutors, and mayors.

The new mayor quickly ran afoul of black supporters with his failure to invite an African American minister to participate in his televised inauguration.[49] Regaining his footing after this political misstep, Cavanagh appointed Albert Pelham as the city's first black comptroller and also named blacks to important positions at the Department of Public Works and the Mayor's Commission on Children and Youth. Between 1962 and the riots of July 1967, Cavanagh was portrayed in the national press as "America's Mayor," a young, energetic liberal who had managed to solve the city's racial unrest and also harbored national ambitions. Detroit's image as a "model city" was burnished by a steady flow of federal antipoverty funds.[50] The majestic sounds of Motown, located in the Twelfth Street District, contributed to Detroit's growing reputation as a cultural mecca, replete with some of the earliest black recording stars, including the Temptations, Marvin Gaye, and the Supremes.

While Motown successfully created a new sound in the cultural arena, Detroit's white politicians continued to march to their own tune. Cavanagh's carefully crafted image as a liberal reached its high point during the Great Walk to Freedom, in June 1963. Organized in a fury of righteous indignation against racial violence in Birmingham, Alabama, the march featured Martin Luther King Jr. as its keynote speaker. While most cities looked forward to King's arrival as they would a plague of locusts, Cavanagh rolled out the red carpet. Welcoming King as Detroit's "distinguished guest of honor," the mayor locked arms with King and marched down Woodward Avenue in a maneuver that bolstered his profile as one of America's most daringly progressive politicians.[51]

Beneath Detroit's facade of progress were major problems, chief among them the fact that the Cavanagh administration turned a deaf ear toward its harshest critics. The mayor's steadfast support for the police department and urban renewal ignited grassroots black opposition against his administration, especially in neighborhoods threatened with displacement by the city's downtown redevelopment plans. Urban renewal cut both ways, bringing much-needed jobs, but in the process displacing longtime residents and permanently changing the character of entire neighborhoods while at the same time eliminating others. Federal poverty programs, while receiving heavy publicity, failed to deliver on their lofty promises. The Cavanagh administration also failed to keep in close touch with the streets; the mayor admitted as much only after the 1967 riot.[52]

Radicals organized against the mayor's lack of vision with a confidence that suggested that black power in Detroit was inevitable and would be accomplished sooner rather than later. While maintaining tenuous ties with established black leaders, Cleage charted a course that would lead to open conflict with black and white officials. Tension between what he described as the "New Negro vs. the Old Guard" was drawn into sharp relief during the 1962 congressional elections.[53] For GOAL, the election served as an opportunity to educate a black community unaccustomed to having real electoral options. The defeat of the GOAL-sponsored black candidate, Frederick Yates, proved that machine politics trumped pleas for race solidarity.[54] Yates's failure, perhaps preordained when the Democratic machine and Big Labor backed another candidate, underscored the competing loyalties of black leaders. A black candidate without the backing of prominent African American and Democratic constituencies, such as labor, stood no chance of being elected. In most cases, the whims of the city's machine, not progressive politics, would decide the fate of black progress. Patronage ties rendered Detroit's black officials incapable of forestalling short-term benefits for a long-term future still considered a risky proposition. The fear of reprisals from Detroit's white political establishment led many black leaders to an open alliance with a Democratic Party that thumbed its nose at complaints from below. Those willing to accept scraps from the table of the city's political and business elite could scarcely imagine that a black man—in this case onetime GOAL supporter and trade unionist Coleman Young—would be elected mayor in 1973. Black nationalist appeals to race pride and loyalty, which would catapult black office seekers to undreamed-of success a few years later, were, at this point, rendered moot in the city's ruthlessly efficient world of machine politics.

As militants in Detroit contemplated turning the city upside down in pursuit of black political power, Black Muslims quietly thrived. Although Elijah Muhammad presented himself as a spiritual leader above the fray of politics, the Nation of Islam nonetheless established itself as a formidable secular presence through the popularity of *Muhammad Speaks*, the speeches of Malcolm X, and the highly publicized killing of Los Angeles member Ronald Stokes.[55] Stokes's death at the hands of the police placed Malcolm X in the middle of a national controversy over police brutality, civil rights, and black militancy. Taking Stokes's death as an omen, hundreds of Muslims from around the country readied themselves for the long-predicted War of Armageddon, as disciples from New York and Arizona informed Los Angeles of their imminent arrival.[56] As preparations mounted for a day of reckoning, something unexpected occurred: Malcolm X, who awaited word on when to unleash Old Testament–style retribution on the city streets, was ordered to retreat. Elijah's instructions to "play dead on everything" mystified Malcolm, because they sapped the energies of the Black Muslim movement's most militant wing, who looked at Stokes's death as a sign that a racial showdown was imminent.[57]

The retreat was also a source of personal embarrassment. Malcolm's identification with the Muslims' militant wing made him ill suited to carry out Muhammad's orders to cool things down. Malcolm unleashed verbal polemics that compared Mayor Yorty and his police department to racist sheriffs in the rural South. Meanwhile, local mosque members formed vigilante squads, who pummeled defenseless white vagrants in Los Angeles's skid row area as revenge against the Stokes killing. Warned against practicing freelance retribution, some NOI members bitterly complained, others simply dropped out, while true believers followed the edict from headquarters to sell huge quantities of *Muhammad Speaks* in memory of their slain brother.[58] Hamstrung by Muhammad's orders, Malcolm lost face with Los Angeles Muslims. Hakim Jamal, a rough-cut ex–drug addict, was among those appalled by the behavior of Black Muslims after Stokes's shooting. Related to Malcolm by marriage, Jamal departed the Nation shortly after the Stokes incident, rejecting the group but maintaining his belief in Islam and Malcolm X until he was murdered in 1973.[59]

Stokes's unavenged death proved that, despite its rhetoric to the contrary, the Nation of Islam would not engage in open race war— even to avenge one of its "originals."[60] Within days of arriving in Los Angeles, Malcolm returned to New York to practice damage control, quelling further eruptions that local Los Angeles authorities claimed were increased by his presence.[61] Humbled but tenacious, an unrepentant Malcolm achieved a victory of sorts by publicizing the Stokes murder as the latest example that blacks outside the South were just as imperiled as the freedom riders and sit-in participants. Malcolm found solace in the provocative statement, touting an air disaster that killed scores of white passengers—120 from Georgia alone—as Allah's divine retribution. In the wake of this outburst, disbelieving journalists pilloried Malcolm.[62] News of the Black Muslim "riot" that took

Stokes's life dominated Los Angeles's typically segregated press. The *Los Angeles Sentinel* described Malcolm's voice as "cold and precise" when discussing the April 27, 1962, confrontation.[63] The *Los Angeles Times* headline "Muslim Cultist Killed, 6 Hurt in Police Battle" competed with front-page news of anti-Castro demonstrations in Havana.[64] Los Angeles's oldest black newspaper, the *California Eagle*, eulogized Stokes as the first Muslim martyr and offered extensive coverage of his death, including a guardedly sympathetic editorial that, quoting James Baldwin, viewed the melee as a virtual fait accompli, given the tortured state of relations between the police and the community.[65] In scores of interviews, Malcolm accused the Los Angeles Police Department of murder, meticulously outlining inconsistencies in police versions of events while emphasizing the physical abuse—including the fact that one victim had been shot in the genitals—experienced by Muslim defendants. "There was police brutality and atrocity and the press was just as atrocious as the police," he told one reporter, adding that the "blazing gun battle" that made national headlines was actually a one-sided massacre.[66] The Stokes killing raised the stakes for Malcolm's militant rhetoric, even while it led to a spectacular rise in the sales of *Muhammad Speaks*, which showcased the NOI's version of events.[67]

William Worthy's legal troubles and Malcolm X's simmering rage over the Stokes murder were highlighted at a forum in New York City on May 1, 1962. Malcolm and Worthy were featured speakers at a Tuesday evening symposium entitled "The Crisis of Racism." Proceeds from the event benefited the legal struggle of the Monroe defendants, who faced a politically charged criminal prosecution for aiding Robert Williams. An enthusiastic crowd packed the Palm Gardens to hear the featured speakers.[68] Murray Kempton, the *New York Post* reporter who had sympathetically documented civil rights struggles since the astonishing lynching of Emmett Till, moderated the panel.[69] The symposium illustrated bridges built between Worthy's internationalism and Malcolm's blunt attacks against racial oppression.

Worthy strode to the podium amid the thunderous applause that greeted Kempton's observation that he had spent more time in Cuba than any other American journalist. Recalling a 1956 interview with Kwame Nkrumah, Worthy spoke of internationalizing the civil rights struggle. He challenged the NAACP and CORE (Congress of Racial Equality) to support African independence and indicted the United States for arming Portugal against Angolan revolutionaries engaged in a guerrilla war for independence. After predicting revolutionary uprisings throughout Latin America, Worthy wondered whether America "required a tragedy" to comprehend the sweeping changes that were taking place around the world. He criticized Attorney General Robert Kennedy for not intervening in the Stokes case, and he followed this public rebuke with a gentle criticism of the Black Muslims, noting that African Americans had to distinguish between whites who were ignorant and those who were exploiters. Worthy, whose speech was interrupted several times by applause, concluded by vowing to take on the head of the FBI, J. Edgar Hoover, whom he suspected of engineering his legal troubles. Then, before ceding the microphone, he asked Malcolm X to provide him with "twenty to thirty" Black Muslims to serve as bodyguards during his upcoming Miami trial.[70]

Three days before conducting Ronald Stokes's funeral services, Malcolm relayed the particulars of the shooting to an unsuspecting midtown audience.[71] Malcolm, who arrived in New York emotionally exhausted, apologized for the tone and temper of his speech. Visibly upset, Malcolm cited the previous speakers' criticisms (James Farmer, of CORE, had preceded Worthy) as proof that America was a hopeless, irredeemable nation. He would rather be dead than integrate into a society that had been found guilty of brutal crimes such as the Stokes killing. Malcolm would later respond to feelings of guilt and political paralysis by crisscrossing the country giving speeches attempting to convince himself, as much as his audiences, that Stokes had not died in vain, taking careful steps to distance himself from the media's assertion that the Stokes affair was a tawdry shootout between the police and the Black Muslims. Employing the kind of grandiose language that the Black Panthers would adopt within a few years, Malcolm argued that Stokes was a victim of a modern-day Gestapo. The police, he asserted, were a marauding gang who terrorized unarmed black men and women. Malcolm's description of the Stokes incident as an example of American fascism was no accident. James Farmer had, earlier that evening, poignantly recalled his coming of age in the Jim Crow South, while Worthy's vivid description of America's colonial legacy was essentially the warm-up act for Malcolm's allegations. Anticipating the verdict of justifiable homicide that would be delivered by an all-white Los Angeles grand jury less than two weeks later, Malcolm issued words of fire that turned the Palm Gardens into a public memorial service for a man most participants had never even met.[72] In one breath he asked to be excused for unfurling his anger upon his largely receptive audience, while in another he launched into a frenzied description of the shooting's grim details. Malcolm curtly interrupted the audience's applause, reminding chastened onlookers that enthusiastic handclapping, head nodding, and the intermittent "Preach, brother" fell short of the resolution he sought. According to Malcolm, the Stokes incident was simply the latest addition to a mountain of evidence that revealed America's cruelty, desperation, and hypocrisy.[73]

Malcolm X, William Worthy, and Detroit's activists reflected the black freedom movement's overlapping circles, with GOAL representing radicals in local struggles, Malcolm expressing the national face of a militant movement for self-determination, and Worthy's globe-trotting internationalism rounding out black militancy's rich political, intellectual, and cultural landscape. It was within these radical networks, where optimists and cynics intersected, that Malcolm, GOAL, and Worthy operated. Collectively, their political struggles placed them at the forefront of an informal coalition of militants whose intellectual thought, political manifestos, and community organizing were early examples of Black Power.

4

LIBERATORS

Liberator magazine described 1963 as a "Year of Violence." The new year would see the emergence of independent black political organizing and also the murder of civil rights activist Medgar Evers and the church bombing that prematurely ended the lives of Denise McNair, Cynthia Wesley, Addie Mae Collins, and Carole Robertson—four young black girls in Birmingham, Alabama. *Liberator*, founded by the architect turned full-time activist Dan Watts, belonged to a new generation of publications showcasing the black movement's growing nationalism and race consciousness.[1] The focus of *Liberator* magazine was the relationship between black America and the Third World. Founding the Liberation Committee on Africa, in Harlem and several other cities, Watts was a key organizer of the 1961 United Nations protests in the wake of the Congo crisis. *Liberator* placed Watts in the unique position of being one of the few radical critics of Martin Luther King Jr. with the means and determination to harass the civil rights leader. *Liberator*'s sharp criticism of King placed Watts's wide-ranging allies—including Albert Cleage—in the precarious position of maintaining ties both to important national civil rights leaders and to local militants. Watts enjoyed a cordial, if at times testy, relationship with Harlem's militants. His autocratic style and political independence rubbed some the wrong way, yet his ownership of *Liberator* made him an attractive ally to political and literary figures who sought an outlet in which to publish their work.[2]

James Baldwin was the magazine's most accomplished contributing writer. Baldwin had traveled a lifetime since his days as a student at P.S.139 in Harlem, the alma mater of Harold Cruse, who served on *Liberator*'s editorial board.[3] A writer of rare genius, Baldwin grew up in poverty, defying the odds to emerge as one of his generation's most eloquent voices. Baldwin was a protégé-turned-critic of Richard Wright, the brilliant writer whose early literary promise gave way to professional disappointment, self-imposed exile, and premature death. During the early 1960s, Baldwin became the freedom movement's most revered public intellectual, his political militancy having struck a chord with white liberals who had awakened to the sounds of a political revolution too loud to ignore.

In 1963, James Baldwin emerged as America's most respected black writer.[4] The searing eloquence of his widely read essays on race, democracy, and civil rights, many of them published in major newspapers and magazines, made the black freedom struggle come alive for white and black readers. Baldwin's high profile and passionate writings in leading liberal political and literary journals inspired intense debates among black radicals regarding his new role as America's most renowned interpreter of race relations. The writer Sylvester Leaks accused Baldwin of collaborating with the white literary establishment by focusing on black oppression rather than on political resistance.[5] Partially fueling such detractors was Baldwin's rising literary star, an ascent that eclipsed scores of talented black contemporaries operating in virtual anonymity.[6] From Ghana, Julian Mayfield wrote an impassioned defense of Baldwin, arguing that Baldwin's years of exile in Europe made him uniquely suited to write about America's racial crises from a fresh perspective.[7] According to Mayfield, Leaks confused Baldwin's fierce compassion with surrender; mistook vivid, grim depictions of Harlem as stereotyping; and regarded the writer's celebrity as the undeserved spoils of a dilettante. Mayfield concluded his discussion of the "Baldwin phenomenon" by comparing America to a house that needed to accept its black occupants or be burnt asunder. James Baldwin, "almost alone," negotiated these rising tensions by continuing a feverish dialogue with whites, "offering them a way out, if only they will listen." If Mayfield's words failed to forge a consensus in the black community regarding Baldwin's stature, they illustrated the breadth of his appeal. Baldwin was being read by everyone from black nationalists in Harlem and Ghana to white liberals who pored over his graceful *New Yorker* essays and pungent *New York Times* opinion pieces.[8] Overshadowing talented social critics like John Henrik Clarke, Mayfield, and John Oliver Killens, Baldwin—perhaps more so than any other postwar writer—came to represent the literary voice of an entire movement. Baldwin's political maturity was marked by his decision, on his return to the United States after a number of years living in Europe, to aid civil rights efforts. What's more, Baldwin's involvement in the movement included friendships with some of the era's most visible black leaders— among them, Martin Luther King, Malcolm X, and Elijah Muhammad.

At the beginning of 1963, Baldwin caustically assessed the centennial of the Emancipation Proclamation. Recalling the racial violence that accompanied James Meredith's enrollment at the University of Mississippi the previous fall, he wrote of the "awful connection between the fact of Cuba and the fact of Mississippi which no one appears to recognize" as exemplifying a larger failure of American democracy, one that was global in its scope.[9] Released in May 1963, *The Fire Next Time* contained two essays, the second of which, "Down at the Cross," had received considerable attention the previous winter as "A Letter from a Region in My Mind" in the *New Yorker*. In the essay, Baldwin defended the Nation of Islam's harsh assessment— if not its apocalyptical vision—of American society, while recounting his Sunday afternoon visit with Elijah Muhammad during the summer of 1962.

A religious skeptic, political cynic, and literary maverick, Baldwin found himself surprisingly receptive to Muhammad's, and by extension Malcolm's, otherworldly visions of political Armageddon. Seated at Elijah Muhammad's impressive dining table, Baldwin became a dinner guest whose defense of white humanity against the litany of crimes alleged by the Nation of Islam diminished as the evening progressed.[10] To liberal *New Yorker* readers, Baldwin's retreat was akin to an abolitionist's slow conversion by a host of charmingly persuasive white supremacists. Sitting to the left of Muhammad, who was at the head of the huge rectangular table, Baldwin discussed religion, politics, race, and the possibility of redemption. Muhammad expressed delight at meeting a non-Muslim who hadn't been "brainwashed." Baldwin took the compliment in stride, noting that he "had left the church twenty years ago" and refused to join anything since. "And what are you now?" Muhammad asked. Responding that he was simply a writer, Baldwin spent the rest of the evening wondering exactly what, in fact, he was.

Assessing America's history of racial violence, Baldwin cast himself as a modern-day Jeremiah in a desperate struggle against impending disaster. "Time catches up with kingdoms and crushes them," he warned.[11] Striding in half an hour late, Elijah Muhammad kept Baldwin waiting before making a fittingly suspenseful entrance. Impressed by Baldwin's recent television appearance with Malcolm X, Muhammad warmly received the apprehensive writer. Baldwin had also served as radio moderator for a discussion between Malcolm and a student representative of the sit-in movement. During the latter event, Baldwin had found Malcolm to be unexpectedly gentle, more of a caring teacher than a racial demagogue.[12] Baldwin had grown up around Harlem street speakers and Baptist preachers and had decided, early on, that he had little use for either. Thus it came as something of a surprise to everyone, including Baldwin, that he agreed with much of what Malcolm said that day. That Baldwin, the atheist homosexual writer comfortable in the company of white elites, would provide a passionately conflicted defense of Black Muslims—an all-black, religious group whose racial cosmology held no hope for interracial brotherhood—was less of a stretch than many would have imagined. Although they operated in starkly different social spheres, the gap that separated Baldwin from the Black Muslims' racial militancy and Malcolm X's bristling rage would be measured in degrees that were growing smaller.

The Fire Next Time found Baldwin at the pinnacle of an American literary establishment that proudly claimed him as its own, although his flirtation with Black Muslims defined him as a political heretic and his acceptance of Muhammad's dinner invitation branded him an intellectual provocateur. Even its detractors hailed *The Fire Next Time* as an important piece of social criticism. More than that, the book established Baldwin as black America's "public witness," the official transcriber of a blues people.[13]

While radicals in Harlem and Ghana debated the relative merits of Baldwin's understanding of black life, the attorney general of the United States tapped Baldwin for his own exercise in racial diplomacy. In an effort to gauge the pulse of the black community, Robert Kennedy asked Baldwin to organize a meeting with leading cultural and literary figures. Baldwin dutifully rounded up a guest list that included Harry Belafonte, Lena Horne, Lorraine Hansberry, Professor Kenneth Clark, and Clarence Jones, King's personal attorney.

Designed as a discreet way for Kennedy to assess the collective black psyche through Baldwin's celebrity proxies, the May 24, 1963, encounter devolved into a raucous shouting match over the progress of the Kennedy administration's civil rights policies and the limits of black patience that was leaked to the *New York Times* and earned many in the room Robert Kennedy's lasting enmity.[14] Baldwin's role as Kennedy's personal, if also uncontrollable, emissary raised Baldwin's stature at the expense of the attorney general, whom one critic chided as "the little man who wasn't there."[15]

Baldwin basked in his status as America's premier oracle of race relations. In a live interview with Professor Kenneth Clark, the noted psychologist whose scholarship on segregation's effect on black self-esteem influenced the *Brown* Supreme Court decision, Baldwin recounted Kennedy's naiveté in a discussion that ranged from Cuba and racial violence in Alabama to urban renewal. FBI surveillance noted that the program, "Conversation with James Baldwin," was characterized as "Doctor Kenneth Clark of CCNY Interviews James Baldwin After Meeting Attorney General Robert Kennedy."[16] Baldwin's growing list of admirers now included Malcolm X, who in his denunciation of the March on Washington would observe that Baldwin was prevented from speaking at the event because he was "liable to say anything."[17]

Around the same time that Baldwin became the civil rights movement's first literary celebrity, Albert Cleage claimed the political spotlight by organizing black power in Detroit. As usual, Cleage's ambition made established black and white leaders alike uncomfortable. He described the former as so "identified with the white community that they would die if it collapsed" and warned the latter that the new year would showcase blacks engaged in a "struggle for power."[18] The struggles extended beyond the political realm into the cultural swamp that did so much to injure black self-image. Published by Grace Lee Boggs, *Correspondence*'s 1963 "Emancipation Proclamation" issue included a Black Art section. Highlighting African art and imagery, the supplement featured an essay by Max Roach on why jazz must benefit blacks and a profile of his wife, Abbey Lincoln, whose "natural Afro" hairstyle defined the beauty of black women as a statement of resistance.[19] Other stories covered traveling black beauty pageants, the brainchild of Harlem activists Cecil and Ronnie Brathwaite, who promoted the soon to be popular natural hairstyles.[20] The pageants attracted large audiences of nationalists, local activists, and curiosity seekers. In a few years, these spectacles of cultural pride would become the centerpiece of a political and cultural ethos; for now, they remained special-interest stories, even in black communities. Detroit's focus on black pride, while important, did little to quell feelings of bitterness and shame regarding the civil rights demonstrations taking place nationally.

One city loomed larger than any other in 1963. In the spring, Birmingham, Alabama, had become the site of open warfare between civil rights demonstrators, police officials, black locals, and white thugs who, while not official participants in the conflict, engaged in it nonetheless.[21] It was the first time that a major civil rights demonstration received extensive television coverage, with images of battered protesters—women and children included—shaking the country to its core. City authorities' unapologetic use of naked aggression against the marchers played out like a made-for-television morality tale. Birmingham's spring of racial tumult and grisly violence riveted America and attracted notice from the rest of the world.

In response, blacks throughout the nation held vigils, marches, meetings, and rallies in support of justice in Birmingham. For northern activists, Birmingham provoked more than militancy; it inspired action. Black newspapers echoed this determination. "Eyes of the World on Bitter Birmingham Struggle" read the headline of the *Baltimore-Washington Afro-American* in April.[22] The next month *Muhammad Speaks* proudly proclaimed that Birmingham's "determined" black community had "stepped up their struggle to end white supremacy."[23] On *Radio Free Dixie,* Robert F. Williams's program broadcast from Havana, Williams deliberated on the "disgraceful" government that allowed southern blacks to be oppressed by "white slave-masters." Exiled from the American political scene for over a year, Williams remained a formidable presence. *Negroes with Guns,* published in 1962, detailed his struggles in Monroe and quickly became required reading for young militants and students on both coasts, who also eagerly read the copies of the *Crusader* that survived shipment to the States. Shortwave radio operators tuned in to hear *Radio Free Dixie*'s unique blend of jazz, poetry, and politics. Describing Birmingham's white population as "savages," Williams's commentary "that the righteous must walk alone" would prove only partially true.[24]

America's racial crisis was more than a poignant synonym for violent white resistance to social progress. Inspired by Birmingham's days of rage, black Americans stepped up efforts to prove that demonstrators who walked through racist gauntlets in Alabama and throughout the South were not alone.[25] Photographs from Birmingham of police dogs attacking black children became a hot item, eagerly purchased by national and international press outlets. The most infamous showed a teenager unmoved as a German shepard bit his clothes and a police officer grabbed his shirt. The widely circulated image was published by *Muhammad Speaks* twice in one month, the second time on the cover, next to the body of Ronald Stokes—in a bid to connect Stokes's death to the wider civil rights struggle.[26]

While black activists in Birmingham confronted racial violence, Albert Cleage was being honored at a dinner by fellow freedom fighters.[27] Awards, fetes, and tributes were one of the movement's unspoken traditions. While they often reflected the self-important rituals of a black middle class that craved respect, they also provided well-deserved attention to local leaders. For militants like Cleage who resided on the movement's fringes, such recognition was rare. But Birmingham wasn't far from his thoughts. Accepting his plaque, Cleage discussed organizing a local sympathy march that would "show people how we feel about Birmingham but also about conditions here in Detroit."[28]

Two weeks after the dinner, Cleage participated in a citywide protest meeting. The idea was not new. In fact, local civil rights leaders had scheduled a similar planning meeting that had been poorly attended. After a frustrated audience demanded to hear him speak, Cleage took center stage. Judging Detroit's lack of an organized response to happenings in Birmingham as a "disgrace," Cleage proposed a demonstration so big that "the police would be afraid to show up."[29] Plans for a Great March began immediately. Led by Cleage and the Reverend C. L. Franklin, of the New Bethel Baptist Church, planners bypassed the local leadership (most notably the NAACP) to form the Detroit Council for Human Rights (DCHR).

The father of the future rhythm and blues legend Aretha Franklin, the Reverend Franklin's national profile had increased steadily during the early 1960s through the aid of powerful sermons that he recorded and sold locally. Franklin's local profile and national reach reflected a ministry that was, in almost every measure, more lucrative and popular than Cleage's. Dubbed the "Man with the Million Dollar Voice" and known as the Jitterbug Preacher for his sartorial flare, Franklin was an eloquent and dignified pastor, talented enough to preach before the National Baptist Convention by the age of thirty.[30] Cleage exploited Franklin's rift with the local NAACP, a conflict that was part of the national infighting between factions of the organization whose allegiance was split between Roy Wilkins and King. Propelled by a flurry of energy, the DCHR vowed to organize a mass demonstration in support of the Birmingham struggle, with King delivering the keynote address. Franklin's close friendship with King made him a formidable ally, capable of mobilizing a mass demonstration through the guaranteed participation of the man who, even militants admitted, was the most powerful black speaker in the nation. Cleage and Franklin's relationship was built on a precarious unity forged against common foes; yet behind the scenes, partisan tensions simmered. Cleage's grassroots connections, burnished by GOAL's rising profile, came close to but did not quite approach Franklin's proximity to King. If Black Power activists in Detroit longed for the national stage, it would take King to help them attain it.[31]

As Detroit activists plotted, Malcolm X raged. Barred by Elijah Muhammad from formal participation, Malcolm lent measured support to southern civil rights struggles while scrupulously hewing to the Muslim policy of nonengagement. Privately, Malcolm admitted feeling fatigued by a punishing schedule that intensified that spring.[32] Dispatched to the nation's capital at Muhammad's personal request, Malcolm juggled shifting personal loyalties and mounting professional responsibilities to the Nation of Islam with his own burning political ambitions. From Washington he addressed the Birmingham crisis as a militant statesman, announcing that blacks would be justified in killing attack dogs (whether two legged or four legged) that mauled innocents in Birmingham.[33]

The Los Angeles trial of fourteen Black Muslims in connection with the Ronald Stokes case exposed fresh wounds. "You usually," Malcolm deadpanned to reporters, "don't try men who were shot."[34] Los Angeles newspapers, he complained, had covered a fantasy world in lieu of the actual trial. "Anybody reading these papers," claimed Malcolm, would come to the conclusion that the Black Muslims lacked legal representation. "They print everything these policemen say as if it went unchallenged."[35] Jury deliberations extended for weeks and would culminate in a verdict convicting eleven of the fourteen defendants. As he had done a year earlier, Malcolm left retribution to a higher power.[36]

In Washington, Malcolm rubbed shoulders with Beltway politicians receptive to his tough talk against ghetto vice and moral decay. Democratic representative Edith Green met with Malcolm to discuss the District of Columbia's growing scourge of juvenile delinquency. At a press conference following this meeting, Malcolm segued to an examination of the national political scene. Responding to the president's recent comments that Birmingham opened the door to extremist elements such as the Black Muslims, he lambasted Kennedy for failing to send in federal troops before the city erupted into an all-out race war. Sporadic episodes of black militancy, observed Malcolm, had, in fact, forced the White House to act after weeks of stalling. Blasting Kennedy's concern for the nation's reputation abroad, Malcolm described the president as lacking the moral compass that the times required. Kennedy, he insisted, had acted out of naked political expediency. "Kennedy is wrong because his motivation is wrong."[37] Malcolm's attacks continued throughout the summer, highlighted by his remark that the jet-setting Kennedy simply "found no time to be president here."[38] Jarring as Malcolm's pointed comments about Kennedy's crusading foreign policy might have been, they remained largely ignored.[39]

On another occasion discussing Birmingham's racial violence, Malcolm excoriated the federal government, saving his most caustic remarks for black leaders he derided as little more than modern-day Uncle Toms.[40] Several days after this speech, the *New York Herald*

Tribune reported that Malcolm would personally visit Birmingham. After returning to Harlem, Malcolm backpedaled, describing the story—leaked by James X from the Nation's Birmingham mosque—as an unsubstantiated rumor.[41] Railing against nonviolent demonstrations they viewed as amateurish and ineffective, Atlanta's Jeremiah X and Birmingham's James X plotted to push the Nation of Islam into the thick of America's latest civil rights front. Right down to the press leak, Jeremiah and James's gambit had Malcolm's fingerprints all over it, just as Malcolm's denial was most likely a command performance by explicit request of Muhammad.[42] Barred from going to Birmingham, Malcolm launched attacks from the sidelines. "Martin Luther King," Malcolm said, was "a chump, not a champ. Any man who puts his women and children on the front line is a chump, not a champ."[43] Birmingham's lesson, warned Malcolm, scratched the surface of black rage that the nation ignored at its own peril.[44]

Malcolm placed Jackie Robinson in the same category as King: a race traitor. The reality was more complicated. Robinson was rightfully noted as a civil rights advocate and a strong "race man." A successful entrepreneur and newspaper columnist, Robinson quietly parlayed his historic role in breaking baseball's color line into a career as a respected business executive and influential political commentator. As a candidate for president in 1960, John F. Kennedy had unsuccessfully sought Robinson's endorsement.[45] A proud Republican, Robinson was complex enough to simultaneously denounce Castro's Harlem tour even as he admitted the controversial visit's positive impact on the black community.[46] An old-fashioned patriot and anti-Communist, Robinson parted company with black radicals, preferring to criticize segregation as a steadfast believer in the American Dream. Ralph Bunche, the distinguished UN undersecretary, exemplified the kind of high-level insider status Jackie Robinson admired.

After a youthful flirtation with radicalism in the 1930s, Bunche became the highest-ranking African American bureaucrat of the postwar era. In a speech at Mississippi's Tougaloo Southern Christian University, Bunche criticized Malcolm X and the Black Muslims. "Dr.

Bunche," responded Malcolm, "is saying just what he has to say in order to keep his job."[47] Adam Clayton Powell, targeted by Bunche in the same speech, mischievously welcomed Bunche "back into the Negro race" after what Powell caustically remarked had been a long absence. Robinson defended Bunche in his newspaper column. Describing Malcolm as a man who talked "one hell of a civil rights fight," Robinson targeted Malcolm where he was most vulnerable, criticizing him as an armchair warrior unwilling to dirty his hands participating in direct action. "Malcolm," wrote Robinson, "is very militant on Harlem street corners where militancy is not dangerous."[48]

Malcolm fought back in a scathing open letter published in the *New York Amsterdam News* accusing Robinson of being nothing more than a well-trained lackey of powerful white men. Robinson's support for New York's liberal Republican governor Nelson Rockefeller, Malcolm suggested, was simply the latest example of bootlicking patronage sought and received by Robinson from the likes of Los Angeles Dodgers executive Branch Rickey and former vice president Richard Nixon. The price for such influence, Malcolm argued, was too high, turning Robinson into an establishment puppet who could be used against high-profile black radicals. "It was you," Malcolm reminded him, "who let them sic you on Paul Robeson," invoking the Cold War's most prominent African American victim. For Malcolm, Robinson's political moderation smacked of racial disloyalty that, even more infuriatingly, was disguised as social activism. Malcolm concluded his letter by confronting Robinson's charge that he should have attended the funeral of the recently slain civil rights leader Medgar Evers: "When I go to a Mississippi funeral," responded an indignant Malcolm, "it won't be to attend the funeral of a black man!"[49]

Malcolm and Robinson's contretemps would prove to be a minor skirmish, a temporary distraction from a war of words between Malcolm and King, which would escalate in the months leading up to the March on Washington in late August. When a reporter interviewing Malcolm credited King with achieving a victory in Birmingham, Malcolm chafed. Interrupting his interviewer, Malcolm derided King as a poseur who defined freedom as drinking coffee next to whites. He downplayed the removal of Birmingham's violent city commissioner, Eugene "Bull" Connor, as fool's gold, noting that while Connor was a known "wolf," his replacement would be an equally treacherous "fox."[50] Malcolm's criticism of the Birmingham accord defied conventional wisdom: for instance, President Kennedy's decision to authorize Alabama's National Guard in the wake of a black uprising on Mother's Day eve was proof, Malcolm said, that King's civil rights strategy—beholden to the whims of white politicians who scarcely comprehended the breadth of black suffering or the depth of black anger—was intrinsically flawed. While this criticism seemed a bit peremptory, time would provide at least partial vindication for Malcolm, who predicted that Birmingham's little-discussed rebellion portended a coming black revolution.[51]

In the midst of Birmingham's violent spring, the *New York Times* identified Malcolm as the leader of a racial consciousness that the paper characterized as a "powerful force for change." Accordingly, Malcolm X, and not Elijah Muhammad, was named the movement's most influential catalyst. Malcolm, the story asserted, received grudging admiration from civil rights conservatives for his ascetic lifestyle and outstanding abilities.[52] The article suggested that black nationalism—heretofore considered the last refuge of racial arsonists—did indeed inspire the kind of broad social activism that included northern militancy, voter registration in the South, and Birmingham's desegregation campaign.[53] In the same story, civil rights leaders expressed resentment over increased racial anxieties while militant intellectuals fumed at the state of America's race relations. Roy Wilkins singled out the glacial pace of racial progress as the culprit behind the Black Muslim phenomenon, while CORE's James Farmer fretted about well-intentioned surges of racial pride creeping into reflexive antiwhite sentiment. Ignoring Wilkins's candid admission that race consciousness predated the arrival of Malcolm X and the Nation of Islam, the article claimed that black nationalism's influence in the civil rights arena was the secret behind proliferating racial unrest.[54] A subsequent report in *Life* magazine proclaimed Malcolm to be the Nation's de facto leader, prompting him to deploy frantic efforts at damage control that only increased tensions within the organization.[55] Conducting marathon interview sessions for two high-profile book contracts, Malcolm attracted the attention of universities, television cameras, newspapers, and, increasingly, publishing houses interested in his thoughts.[56] The publication of Louis Lomax's *When the Word Is Given*, which excerpted speeches from Muhammad and Malcolm, continued this trend. Demonstrating the gap in stature between Malcolm and Elijah Muhammad, *When the Word Is Given* featured a photo of Malcolm on its cover; inside, Lomax analyzed several of his speeches to Muhammad's one. The book's subtitle, *Elijah Muhammad, Malcolm X, and the Black Muslim World*, failed to hide the fact that, on the page and in the public imagination, Malcolm's intelligence and charisma dwarfed Elijah Muhammad's.[57]

As Malcolm X waged rhetorical battles in Washington, plans for Detroit's Walk for Freedom were in full swing. By early June, organizers had raised $20,000 of the $100,000 that would be donated to the Southern Christian Leadership Conference for civil rights organizing down south. Activists distributed five thousand bumper stickers and fifty thousand handbills throughout the city, while a building on Grand River and Columbus was designated as march headquarters. With the goal of one hundred thousand demonstrators, organizers reached out to more than one hundred local and national groups for support. Leading up to the event, weekly rallies were held at churches to discuss strategy and disseminate information. The *Illustrated News* brimmed with enthusiastic support, extending a special invitation to blacks living in poor neighborhoods and paying high rents.[58] The planned demonstration attracted national attention, some of it unwanted. Robert Kennedy dispatched FBI agents to investigate possible agitators and hate groups. Meanwhile, a hesitant but humbled NAACP endorsed the march, along with the AFL-CIO and local Democratic Party officials, wisely choosing public support over political irrelevance.[59] As Detroit's city fathers engaged in some serious stagecraft, Mayor Cavanagh took pains to claim the event's significance as his own, casting the city as a model of racial fairness and the march as a demonstration of interracial progress.[60] Local NAACP leaders were pleased to accept this olive branch, believing that Mayor Cavanagh, who provided City Hall's official seal and United Auto Workers president Walter Reuther's participation, lent the event the momentum needed to make it a success.[61] The march had become both grander and more moderate than its earliest architects could have imagined.

Two weeks before the march was scheduled, civil rights leader Medgar Evers was assassinated outside his home in Jackson, Mississippi. Evers, an NAACP field secretary and a leading figure behind James Meredith's bruising struggles to enter Ole Miss, had earned a reputation as a courageous, stubborn, and uncompromising local leader. In 1962, Evers had begun a voting rights direct-action campaign in Jackson.[62] Around the nation, the gruesomely poignant details of Evers's assassination, including how he had been gunned down in his own driveway, were replayed. Psychological scars awaited his wife and children, as well as the country itself, which would be forced to confront the creeping suspicion that no civil rights activists were safe. Evers's death haunted the Walk for Freedom. Hours before the march, bystanders lined up along the anticipated route, bearing footstools, lemonade, and folding chairs. Around three in the afternoon, large crowds met at Woodward Avenue and Vernor Highway and proceeded down Woodward, west on Jefferson to the arena. Thousands hoisted placards that ranged from the generic "Freedom Now" to the more confrontational "White Man Wake Up, or Wake Up Dead," along with numerous signs memorializing Medgar Evers. The mass of black marchers practically concealed the smattering of whites. Marchers teased bystanders for their lack of participation, at times running over and grabbing black spectators. "Come on, get out here," implored one man. "You ain't in Mississippi. You don't have to be afraid here. Let's walk."[63]

Frontline demonstrators were "swept along Woodward" by the surging crowd as thousands made their way to Cobo Arena to hear the speakers. Clasping hands with Mayor Cavanagh, C. L. Franklin, former governor John B. Swainson, Walter Reuther, and Martin Luther

King Jr. formed the head of a massive crowd that overwhelmed downtown Detroit.[64] The *Detroit News* described the picture of thousands of black bodies marching down Woodward "as if a huge dam had burst," which was indeed an appropriate metaphor.[65] A sea of humanity seized Detroit's downtown and temporarily claimed the city's conscience. Cobo Arena accommodated sixteen thousand people, and an additional ten thousand packed the adjoining Cobo Hall. With the exception of several hundred reserved seats, both sections were filled an hour before the arrival of the scheduled speakers.[66] Marchers stacked hundreds of signs at the arena's entrance and, inside, children waved miniature American flags.[67] An additional one hundred thousand people packed the Civic Center Arena area to listen to the proceedings through loudspeakers. Thousands nearby departed the area even as thousands more came to hear King. Inside, almost twenty speakers filled the platform and nervous city officials marveled at the large crowd's disciplined enthusiasm. Women fanned themselves with programs and sleepy children dozed off, unaware of the whooping and hollering that greeted virtually every speaker.

Mayor Cavanagh began the day by warmly welcoming Dr. King as a "symbol of intelligent, enlightened leadership."[68] Walter Reuther dismissed the "high-octane hypocrisy" sweeping the nation and expressed support for continued demonstrations. "Let's keep the freedom marches rolling all over America," he said. "We shall not rest until we have full freedom for every American."[69] Albert Cleage challenged the cozy rapprochement among the speakers. "Negroes are discriminated against on every hand, right here in Detroit." Standing on the speakers' platform amid various state and city officials, Cleage continued: "We have served notice on the state of Michigan and the City of Detroit that we are part of the freedom struggle."[70] Concluding his speech with repeated chants of "We must FIGHT and FIGHT and FIGHT," Cleage enjoyed the crowd's enthusiastic response which was evidence of his growing stature in Detroit and, soon, nationally.[71]

When Martin Luther King Jr. stepped to the podium, thousands greeted him with a "sudden burst of thunder" that throttled Cobo Arena's high rafters. Those in the crowd, most of whom had never seen him in person, shook "their heads in disbelief" and proud amazement at King's oratory. One usher called him "the Moses of the Twentieth Century."[72] While King spoke, "you could see the faces of some being literally transformed into the faces of free people."[73] King's speech was eloquent and, perhaps considering that the march represented what he approvingly described as a "new militancy," a bit combative. Proclaiming that the "hour is late and the clock of destiny" was winding down, King asserted that black oppression in America sowed the seeds for the nation's self-destruction.[74] That Sunday evening in Detroit, he concluded his speech with a more emotional version of the "I Have a Dream" oration that he would deliver two months later.

The Walk for Freedom epitomized what Cleage would later describe as an "epidemic of militant action" sweeping the nation.[75] Detroit basked in the afterglow produced by the demonstration. The press joined in the city's vigorous self-congratulation, with the *Detroit News* commenting that despite the enormous crowd, "not a police dog, water hose or shock stick was evident."[76] Yet in the wake of what would be the March on Washington's spectacular success, the Walk for Freedom was destined for obscurity. The significance of the Detroit event—as a mass demonstration cosponsored by northern militants and allies of Malcolm X, on the cutting edge of early Black Power militancy—was relegated to a footnote.

On August 28, 1963, unnoticed among the throngs of people, William Worthy passed out leaflets at the March on Washington to promote the idea of an all-black political party.[77] "The Declaration of Washington" urged blacks to take control of their destiny by providing one million votes for the Freedom Now Party (FNP) in 1964. Several months earlier in Cleveland, during a stop on his national speaking tour, Worthy had attempted to convince a skeptical audience that black political power "could change the world." In Cleveland, Worthy passionately described the limitations of the two-party system, highlighting the likely influence and power an independent black party could wield, in the North and in the South. Rejecting Uncle Tom diplomacy in Africa and "banana diplomacy" in Latin America, Worthy suggested a "clean break" from Cold War politics, offering a foreign policy based on human rights advocacy.[78] On the night of the March on Washington, Worthy and a group of black radicals hatched their follow-up plans to publicize the Freedom Now Party, including a sit-in the next morning at FBI headquarters. Informants immediately alerted the bureau's Washington Field Office, which sprang into action, applying "automobile, pocket receiver and foot surveillance coverage" to FNP members, including distributing photographs of Worthy to local agents. In the midst of preparing the FBI's seventy-five-page report on the March on Washington, the bureau made plans to quell any potential FNP mischief.

The day after the march, Worthy and seven Freedom Now Party representatives held an unscheduled meeting with J. Edgar Hoover. The impromptu summit took place following an early-morning news conference in which the FNP attorney Conrad Lynn announced plans for a "symbolic sit-in" at the FBI director's office to protest waves of antiblack violence in the South. In response, the FBI suggested a meeting to defuse what bureau files described as a "sudden and fast-developing" situation.[79]

Worthy and Lynn led their astonished fellow activists into Hoover's office just after nine o'clock. Hoover shook hands with each participant before the group sat at a conference table in the director's outer office. The unusual question-and-answer session found Hoover vigorously defending the bureau's civil rights record on matters of racial injustice against Lynn's allegations, delivered cross-examination style, which included citing one incident of racial violence after another—for example, the 1962 Black Muslim police shooting in Los Angeles that, Lynn argued, would expose the FBI as collaborators in an international scandal. A surprisingly patient Hoover interjected, explaining that the FBI did not have the authority to investigate that Freedom Now representatives presumed it did, disingenuously adding that such power would turn the bureau into a "national police force" with undemocratic powers. To charges that FBI agents were too chummy with southern law enforcement, Hoover detailed his personal efforts to assign impartial, northern-born agents to civil rights hot spots, point-ing out King's mistaken allegation that agents in Albany, Georgia, were southern-born, as proof of misstatements and extremism on both sides. Worthy broke through the temporary air of civility by discussing the hundreds of unsolved bombings and acts of violence then raging down south, noting that nothing less than the FBI's reputation as America's premier criminal investigative agency was on the line. "This is a fact and not fiction," Worthy told Hoover, raising his voice and slapping his hand on the conference table for added emphasis. Characterized by in-ternal FBI documents as a man with an "unsavory background," Wor-thy concluded by observing that since Hoover's tenure was nearing an end, recent civil rights mishaps might place his distinguished legacy in jeopardy.* Hoover countered this second line of charges by listing suc-cessful prosecutions in the South that belied the bureau's poor reputa-tion among black militants. Worthy, in turn, wondered why the FBI refused to publish or make available to the public facts about its civil rights investigations. Hoover responded to this question with one of his own, asking, perhaps facetiously, if any of the participants had seen his recent article, "The FBI's Role in the Field of Civil Rights," published by the bureau. Hearing no affirmative replies, he furnished all eight representatives with a copy, then confided that his hands were tied be-cause of the stalling tactics of big city police chiefs in Los Angeles, Boston, and New York. Hoover went on to praise the previous day's March on Washington as a positive step in race relations, optimistically predicting that the event would minimize further "unjustified violence against the Negro." Near the conclusion of the meeting, Worthy brought up the image of an FBI agent taking notes while protesters were being brutalized, adding that agents could at least "make citizen's arrests" in the face of blatant criminal acts. Hoover countered that agents were down south to gather evidence, not to serve as bodyguards for civil rights demonstrators. After an hour the meeting ended.

---

*Hoover would reach the mandatory retirement age on January 1, 1965. In 1964, President Lyndon Johnson waived this requirement, extending the director's tenure to the virtual lifetime appointment that, in fact, it was.

Outside, Freedom Now representatives met with local reporters, a scene that the FBI public relations guru Deke DeLoach would describe as having burnished the bureau's reputation at the expense of a group of slick-talking, slightly intimidated rabble rousers. Each side produced its own spin, with Worthy and Lynn highlighting the morning's dramatic exchanges and DeLoach chalking up the episode to a masterfully orchestrated bureaucratic exercise that blunted the force of a gathering storm of racial militancy.[80] The bureau followed up by sending letters to Freedom Now Party representatives providing point-by-point refutations regarding civil rights controversies (including Robert Williams's forced political exile) discussed during the August 29 meeting. Behind the scenes, Hoover ordered FBI field offices to provide FNP activists with minor courtesies (including more copies of Hoover's civil rights articles), in an effort to portray the FBI in a positive light and to guard against negative publicity from possible future sit-ins.[81]

As the FBI negotiated a peace with Freedom Now activists, Albert Cleage worked to build Detroit's local FNP, an activity that compromised his role in the Northern Negro Leadership Conference. The NNLC was organized as a follow-up to the successful Walk for Freedom, but Cleage resigned from the planning committee three weeks before the scheduled conference in what was charitably described by participants as a difference in policy between Cleage and C. L. Franklin. In truth, the disagreement centered more on ideology than on policy. As head of the Conference Planning Committee, Cleage had invited groups of radical activists, including Dan Watts, whose penchant for criticizing King irritated Franklin. Planned attendance by Worthy and suspected Communists like Conrad Lynn also made Franklin, who feared that consorting with such elements would damage his national reputation, uneasy.[82] Following this logic, Franklin insisted on preventing the conference from being hijacked by "black nationalists and other radical groups."[83] While the Detroit Council for Human Rights had been founded by Franklin and Cleage the previous spring as an alternative to the NAACP, Cleage and his allies were, by the fall, once again outsiders.[84]

The Grassroots Leadership Conference was a response to Franklin's maneuvers. The conference featured notable civil rights renegades, including Milton Henry, who invited his friend Malcolm X to deliver the keynote address. Jimmy Boggs served as the group's chair and Grace Lee Boggs as its secretary. Held during the second week of November, the Grassroots Conference signaled changing times. Composed of local leaders who represented the crème de la crème of black militants nationally, the Grassroots Conference pledged support for the Freedom Now Party and the idea of running black candidates in local elections.

The Grassroots Conference attracted some civil rights leaders attending Franklin's Northern Negro Leadership Conference, including Gloria Richardson. Petite, intelligent, and tough, Richardson was the rare female civil rights leader with a national reputation. Known as the Lady General of the movement, Richardson headed a civil rights group in Cambridge, Maryland. Political violence in Cambridge during 1963 drew national attention and placed local and federal officials in the unusual position of negotiating with a black woman and eventually leading to a landmark desegregation agreement between Richardson and Robert F. Kennedy. A political maverick, Richardson was a Howard University–educated, middle-aged leader of the Cambridge Nonviolent Action Committee, an affiliate of the Student Nonviolent Coordinating Committee, or SNCC (pronounced "snick") whose rapport with the city's working-class and poor communities made her a threat to white officials and black middle-class powerbrokers alike. Richardson's militancy would facilitate her fall from grace shortly thereafter, when, fresh from Cambridge's landmark racial accord, she publicly boycotted black participation in a citywide integration referendum. For Richardson, black citizenship was nonnegotiable, and she viewed the idea of a referendum as antidemocratic and an insult. Increasingly out of place in the civil rights mainstream as her militancy grew, Richardson served as a mentor to future Black Power activists, including Stokely Carmichael, through her steadfast commitment to self-defense in the face of racial terror. While future histories would suggest that Richardson was ahead of her time, a more precise characterization of her militancy might be that it embodied a sentiment that existed below the surface of the national civil rights movement. At these lower frequencies, tenacious souls like Richardson expressed an uncompromising view of racial freedom that was often interpreted—by black moderates, white liberals, and federal officials—as belligerence. By the time of the Grassroots Conference, Richardson was a national leader in search of kindred political spirits. Upset over what she viewed as an aversion to black militants at the Northern Negro Leadership Conference, she arrived at the Grassroots Conference in time to listen to Malcolm X's keynote.[85]

Gloria Richardson was one of two thousand people who packed the Sunday night mass rally to hear Malcolm X deliver his "Message to the Grassroots." In what would become the most influential speech of his career, Malcolm addressed a capacity crowd from a podium in Motown.[86] Unbeknownst to the audience and to Malcolm himself, it would be one of his last speeches as a Black Muslim; Malcolm's nagging doubts about the group's failure to participate in historic civil rights struggles were by this time converging with substantiated whispers of the Messenger's womanizing and Chicago's financial mismanagement. Investigations into the Nation's affairs revealed corruption that tested Malcolm's personal loyalty and religious faith. Unaware of the inner turmoil inside the NOI, conference participants heard the sound of a man losing his religion.

In Detroit, Malcolm laid the ideological foundations for nothing less than a political revolution by blacks who sought to control their own destinies. His worldly speech, which plumbed the political, historical, and racial depths of American life, unleashed a secular ecstasy, a sentiment that grew the further Malcolm strayed from religious and political sectarianism.

That evening Malcolm X traveled very far. He began his address by suggesting that it was less of a speech than an extemporaneous chat between speaker and audience. Rather than discuss black people's differences—especially religious—he exhorted the audience to focus on resistance to racial oppression, which is what united them. Invoking the solidarity that guided the Afro-Asian Conference in Indonesia almost a decade before, Malcolm held up Bandung as an alternative model of governance for black leaders perpetually squabbling over petty differences.[87] Western colonialism necessitated the unity that Malcolm called for, and history revealed that only bloodshed would reverse the suffering of black people around the world. Like a district attorney making the case against a defendant being tried in absentia, Malcolm presented evidence to a jury that numbered in the thousands. A decade in the Nation of Islam had burnished Malcolm's role as black America's prosecuting attorney, and in fact Malcolm suspected that, in another life, he would have made an excellent lawyer.[88]

Malcolm used the Russian and American revolutions to explain the differences between "a black revolution and a Negro revolution." The former involved social upheaval while the latter did not. How could black people afford to be nonviolent, he asked, "when your churches are being bombed" and little girls are being murdered? As an alternative to nonviolence, Malcolm laid out a definition of revolution that went beyond marches on Washington, lunch counter sit-ins, and traditional civil rights tactics:

Whoever heard of a revolution where they lock arms, as Rev. Cleage was pointing out beautifully, singing "We Shall Overcome"? You don't do that in a revolution. You don't do any singing, you're too busy swinging.[89]

Interrupted by an explosion of laughter, he continued elevating black nationalism as the base for a sweeping global revolution. "If your [sic] afraid of black nationalism," Malcolm proclaimed, you were terrified of revolution. "And if you love black nationalism, you love revolution." Crafting the homespun allegories that enthralled ordinary black Americans, Malcolm discussed slavery, distilling four centuries of racial oppression into two simplistic composites: the Field Negro and the House Negro. Field Negroes worked in the hot boiling southern sun for no money. These slaves experienced ritualized brutality, were perpetually malnourished, and lived in shelter unfit for human beings. Intelligent and crafty, the Field Negro despised white masters and concocted plans to escape, committed acts of sabotage, and prayed for divine intervention to rid the world of slavery.

The House Negro had a starkly different experience. He ate the scraps from the Master's table, enjoyed a modicum of liberty, and identified so completely with whites that he used the pronoun "we" when discussing the Master's wants, needs, hopes, and fears. If something bad happened to his owner, the House Negro prayed for his deliverance and the perpetuation of white supremacy. Malcolm's allegory boiled America's wrenchingly complex history of slavery to two essences that explained the way in which class, integration, and black nationalism were rooted in the experiences of black Americans during centuries of oppression. Civil rights organizations such as the NAACP and preachers of nonviolence such as Martin Luther King Jr. were modern-day House Negroes. In contrast, Malcolm defined the black masses as contemporary Field Negroes: black people, like himself, who were catching hell every day.

Malcolm concluded his speech by discussing the recent, hugely successful, March on Washington. Ordinary blacks willing to risk their lives for change had supported the march. But its original focus had been to engineer a massive civil disobedience campaign aimed at shutting down the nation's capital. "That," Malcolm suggested, "was the black revolution." The White House had thwarted a potential scenario that "scared the white power structure in Washington, D.C. to death," he explained. Huge sums of money—nearly $1 million to start—distributed to a half dozen civil rights groups made the question of political revolt moot even before the march began. Malcolm accused the Kennedy administration and the civil rights establishment of brokering an unholy alliance that shortchanged those most vulnerable to corruption from above, turning the entire affair into a "farce on Washington."[90]

Malcolm's speech at the Grassroots Conference brought together two generations of activists gathered in Detroit to organize a national movement for Black Power.[91] "The Message to the Grassroots" was the conference's crown jewel. Over the next decade the speech became a quintessential example of Malcolm's rhetorical genius and political complexity and was widely distributed around the country. Mixing black nationalism, anticolonialism, and self-defense with the now-famous allegory of House Negroes and Field Negroes, the speech showcased Malcolm's global vision before his break from the Nation of Islam. The enduring legacy of Malcolm's speech would be reflected in the activism of a younger generation of Black Power militants who openly identified themselves as Field Negroes. In just a few years, the Black Panthers would go one step further than Malcolm, advocating the establishment of a revolutionary movement made up primarily of precisely those poor blacks whom Malcolm identified as modern-day Field Negroes. No gathering during the early 1960s better reflected early Black Power militancy than the Grassroots Conference, whose key participants (William Worthy, Dan Watts, Jimmy and Grace Boggs, Gloria Richardson, Albert Cleage, and Malcolm X) embodied nothing less than a genealogy of Black Power's local, national, and international character.

Three weeks after his Detroit appearance, Malcolm's association with the Nation of Islam took a dramatic turn. During an early December speech in New York, Malcolm, responding to a reporter's question about John Kennedy's assassination, answered with a statement about "chickens coming home to roost."[92] Elijah Muhammad had expressly forbidden comments against the slain Kennedy, and Muslim officials continued to monitor Malcolm's speeches to document any indiscretion. The words caused a furor, marking Malcolm—for the first time—as vulnerable to organizational punishment. His subsequent three-month suspension from the NOI, ordered by the Messenger, shocked Malcolm, the general public, and even the FBI, who the previous month had noted a lull in the Nation's internal conflicts even as agents reported Malcolm's suspected contacts with African diplomats.[93]

News of Malcolm's suspension competed with headlines touting

Kenya's impending nationhood and the new president Lyndon Johnson's recent White House meeting with Roy Wilkins.[94] Malcolm's punishment exposed tensions that had existed within the NOI since the late 1950s and were exacerbated by the Stokes case. But it also unleashed philosophical yearnings partially stifled by a decade of political servitude. While thousands in the Nation faithfully awaited God's will as defined by Elijah Muhammad, Malcolm found himself on the wrong end of the Messenger's personal judgment. Public relations savvy and survival instincts guided the Messenger's crafty rebuke, which was cloaked in expressions of public condolence over the untimely death of America's "white devil" in chief. Muhammad took advantage of public grief over the Kennedy assassination to neutralize Malcolm by stripping him of his global pulpit. More ominous, Muhammad's highly publicized censoring contained threatening edges intended for sectarian insiders. In *Muhammad Speaks*, the Messenger quietly planted seeds for Malcolm's permanent expulsion. "I do not classify Minister Malcolm X as a hypocrite," he asserted, but warned that even his top lieutenant was required to stay within certain bounds. Stopping short of denouncing Malcolm, Muhammad hovered within inches of sanctioning violence against his protégé, hinting that strict obedience to a chain of command was all that lay between those who rule and unspeakable heresy.[95] Malcolm X, who had spent much of the decade questioning the loyalty of black leaders, now faced similar charges.

At the end of 1963, Albert Cleage summarized the year's events as the "next step of the Black Revolution." According to Cleage, the Grassroots Conference unleashed the potential of a united front of black nationalists and militants.[96] Black impatience with oppression had produced a condition for which "there was no cure but action."[97] Cleage specifically cited the wave of mass demonstrations in Birmingham and Detroit as examples of the black movement's new temper. But while opening up public accommodations in certain areas, demonstrations had failed to increase black power across the nation.[98]

The Freedom Now Party contained a loose network of militants inspired by William Worthy's prodigious imagination. But local politics and scant resources kept the FNP from cohering as a national organization. New York representatives (most notably Harold Cruse) repudiated white involvement as a leftist conspiracy to take over the militant movement and destroy black nationalism. Nationally, the Freedom Now Party survived for the next two years, with the group showing modest strength in local and statewide elections in Michigan before dissolving by the mid-1960s. Meanwhile, Worthy's struggles against travel restrictions continued. In 1964, his indictment for traveling without a passport would be thrown out by a federal appeal's court and his name cleared. Later that year, after he regained his passport, he left for Vietnam, where he would remain for over a year.

Privately reeling from his suspension, Malcolm simmered while completing a book project that predated Muhammad's decree of silence. Dismissing talk in the *Amsterdam News* of internal strife, Malcolm emphatically denied rumors of organizational turmoil, describing himself as the Messenger's slave, servant, and son, before launching into an extemporaneous, revealing riff that would turn into one of 1964's biggest news stories.

> But I will tell you this: The Messenger has seen God . . . and was given divine patience with the devil. He is willing to wait for Allah to deal with this devil. Well, sir, the rest of us Black Muslims have not seen God, we don't have the gift of divine patience with the devil. The younger Black Muslims want to see some action.[99]

5

POLITICAL KINGDOMS

Malcolm X's suspension continued into the new year, 1964, out-lasting the national period of mourning for President Kennedy that ended the third week of December. Elijah Muhammad's public silencing had turned into a prolonged political limbo for Malcolm, with his prospects for reinstatement dimming each day.[1]

Banished from public speaking, Malcolm maintained his high profile through a friendship with the boxer Cassius Clay, who had been associated with the Black Muslims since 1962. Clay invited Malcolm and his family to Miami for his upcoming title fight with the heavyweight champion Sonny Liston. Pictures of a beaming Malcolm, surrounded by his wife, Betty, their three daughters, and Clay appeared on the front page of the *Amsterdam News*, a pointed reminder to the Nation of Islam of the banned New York minister's enduring appeal and political savvy.[2]

In the middle of February, Muslim officials leaked news that Malcolm would not attend the annual Savior's Day meeting in Chicago and that his suspension from the NOI remained indefinite.[3] Malcolm responded by announcing his intention to return to action in March regardless of the consequences.[4] Anticipating a tense confrontation during Savior's Day, the *Baltimore-Washington Afro-American* described the meeting as an afterthought to the main event: "Elijah vs. Malcolm: Showdown Set Feb. 26."[5] Through press leaks, the two sides played a game of cat and mouse. The *New York Times* noted the absence of New York leaders during Savior's Day at the same time that it published reports that suggested that Muhammad had bypassed Malcolm in favor of Dr. Lonnie X, former head of Atlanta University's Math Department and Washington D.C.'s new head minister. The *Amsterdam News*—whose relationship with Malcolm stretched back almost a decade—countered that Malcolm would return to "the thick of things" in March.[6]

The war for the Nation's soul turned out to be little more than a skirmish, with Muhammad banishing his most able general far away from Malcolm's thousands of prospective troops. Publicly, even as word came from Muhammad that Malcolm's suspension was indefinite, Malcolm maintained otherwise. His relationship with Cassius Clay stoked Malcolm's hope that he could restore his position among Black Muslims.[7] Several newspapers reported an imagined coup: Clay would be an integral part of Malcolm's political future outside the Nation.[8] The African American press trumpeted rumors of Malcolm's exit from the Black Muslims, buffered by Clay's financial backing, alongside cryptic remarks from Harlem activists suggesting to Muhammad that he reconsider the suspension.[9] Where Malcolm saw Clay as potential leverage for restoring his status, the Messenger and Chicago officials envisioned Clay as a pliable gold mine and powerful drawing card. Moving decisively to end this potentially dangerous friendship, Muhammad rewarded the young boxer with a new name—Muhammad Ali—thereby successfully reclaiming Malcolm's protégé.

Muhammad spoiled what had been a spectacular few days. Fresh from Ali's victory over Liston, Malcolm and the new champ had taken a splashy tour of the United Nations. Surrounded by swarms of admirers in the world's peacekeeping headquarters, the two men generated palpable excitement.[10] At the New York offices of the *Amsterdam News*, Ali described his growing admiration for Malcolm X. "I fell in love with him," remarked Ali, "after watching him on television with those educators—leaving them with their mouths wide open."[11]

Shortly after his public appearances with Ali in February and March 1964, Malcolm X declared his political independence.[12] For practical reasons, Malcolm declined to discuss the specifics of his departure with Muhammad, instead sending an emotional, two-page telegram to the Messenger. "I have never spoken one word of criticism to the press about your family. You are still my leader and teacher, even though those around you won't let me be one of your active followers or helpers."[13] As a private plea for calm before the storm of recriminations to come, Malcolm's gambit was destined to failure. There would be no graceful exit from the Nation of Islam.

Four months after the speech at Detroit's Grassroots Conference, where he roasted the civil rights establishment as feeble-minded Uncle Toms, Malcolm announced his willingness to work with mainstream leaders. There were other changes as well. "Brother Malcolm X," as he now wanted to be known, described the broad outlines of a new organization, Muslim Mosque Inc., with its own political direction. At a press conference at New York's Park-Sheraton Hotel on March 12, Malcolm answered questions about the upcoming political elections and the role he would play in shaping black activism. Close to sixty members of the press and at least two FBI agents filled the Conventioneer's Conference Room of the hotel's mezzanine level.[14] Former Fruit of Islam member James 67X and Lewis Michaux distributed handouts to the press that sketched Malcolm's new political course, along with a copy of the telegram he had sent to Muhammad the day before.[15]

Malcolm's prepared statement at the Park-Sheraton revealed political transformations small and large. He predicted that the year 1964 threatened to be "an explosive one," and he was determined to actively engage in what he called a human rights struggle. He remained a Muslim, but in a veiled jab at Elijah Muhammad, claimed no otherworldly powers. In an effort to bury the hatchet with civil rights leaders, he offered amnesty over long-standing disagreements. Malcolm explained that whites could offer financial support but not join the Muslim Mosque; black unity, he hinted, had priority over interracial alliances. He concluded with tough talk about self-defense and an ominous note about the future. Since it was legal for blacks to "own a shotgun or a rifle," said Malcolm, law-abiding African Americans should form rifle clubs in places where the government was "unable or unwilling" to offer them protection. Preemptively defending himself against his critics, he recited a brief checklist of cities that had recently exploded in racial violence: Cambridge, Maryland; Danville, Virginia; Plaquemine, Louisiana; and Birmingham, Alabama. Malcolm concluded his statement with a single sentence that was at once a public plea and a subtle threat: "If the government thinks that I am wrong for saying this then let the government start doing its job."[16]

Months of political turmoil did little to dampen Malcolm's trademark grace and wit. He made it a point to call many of the journalists by name and managed polite, well-thought-out answers, even to the most absurd questions.[17] He sidestepped Dan Watts's question about whether he would run for political office, instead explaining that he would not publicly endorse any candidate or party: "We will keep our 1964 election plans a secret until a later date, but we don't intend for our people to be the victims of a political sell-out again."[18]

The name Malcolm chose for his own organization, Muslim Mosque Inc., obscured rather than clarified its proposed secular mission. Attempts to secularize Muslim Mosque meetings by jettisoning conventional Muslim prayers would prove to antagonize dozens of stalwarts who, while abandoning the NOI, still clung to tenets of its faith. Recognizing the confusion elicited by the uninspired name, Malcolm, a few months later, announced the founding of a second group. This time, inspired by African politics overseas, Malcolm called the new group the Organization of Afro-American Unity (OAAU) and, at the announcement of its formation, hinted at plans to form powerful, unexpected, alliances.[19] Among them was a tentative coalition with ACT, whose name reflected its intended modus operandi rather than an acronym. ACT featured notable local and national figures whose militancy placed them on the margins of the civil rights mainstream: Gloria Richardson, fresh from listening to Malcolm's riveting "Message to the Grassroots" speech; Lawrence Landry, leader of the Chicago school boycotts that paralyzed the Windy City; Harlem rent strike leader Jesse Gray; Washington, D.C., CORE activist Julius Hobson; and the veteran activist Milton Galamison. Two days after his Park-Sheraton press conference, Malcolm met with many of these activists in Chester, Pennsylvania, where he received loud applause from the sixty-odd delegates representing over forty-five civil rights groups, assuring the slightly awed group of militants that he would aid their efforts in any way possible.[20]

As if to verify his sudden willingness to engage in direct action, Malcolm paid a surprise visit to the Reverend Galamison's Brooklyn church, Siloam Presbyterian, two days later. Involved in a nasty fight to integrate New York City's public schools, Galamison had staged a series of boycotts and marches on the Board of Education. The previous year Malcolm and Galamison had been on opposite sides of a local television debate over school integration.[21] Then, Malcolm had emphatically rejected the idea of integration. Now, while still unconvinced of Galamison's strategy, Malcolm's presence signaled qualified support for protest tactics that he had previously denounced as pointless. His appearance at Siloam Presbyterian Church, the boycott's headquarters, created a buzz among the gathered press corps and activists alike. Declining to march to the school board for fear of inciting needless controversy, Malcolm served notice to New York's civil rights leaders that he was ready for action.[22]

Elijah Muhammad doubted his protégé's foray into politics, stating that there were no earthly solutions to racial oppression.[23] The Messenger's disappointment, as described by newspapers to have included weeping upon hearing news of Malcolm's defection, quickly turned into righteous indignation.[24] Muhammad's savvy performance as a

rejected mentor guaranteed that the thousands of Black Muslims unaware of the group's inner turmoil would remain loyal. Muhammad
reiterated his declaration that he was a man of peace, praised Malcolm
as being too intelligent to incite a violent war with the Nation, and preemptively announced—as he was certain Malcolm was ready to—his
willingness to work with major civil rights groups.[25] In telephone conversations with Chicago officials, Muhammad predicted that Malcolm
would come crawling back to the NOI once his individual adventures
proved fruitless. Muhammad explained that he would give Malcolm
more incentive to do so by ordering him stripped of all possessions,
which included Malcolm's home in Queens.[26] In short order, accounts
of Malcolm's treachery flooded *Muhammad Speaks*, as well as urban
newspapers from New York to Chicago. Passages carefully chosen by
NOI officials from the Qur'an revealed Malcolm to be a false prophet
who deserved nothing less than the full wrath of Allah.[27]

Well-attended rallies in Harlem proved that even though Malcolm
lacked a functioning organizational apparatus, he had lost little of his
drawing power. Before a cheering crowd of one thousand supporters at
Rockland Palace on 155th Street, he announced plans for a voter registration drive and for a convention at which the participants could decide whether to form a political party or a "black nationalist army."
"If they don't let us have Madison Square Garden," said Malcolm,
"maybe we can have it in Times Square."[28] In the days following his
split from the NOI, Malcolm coordinated a number of interviews and
sketched out future plans, sometimes simultaneously. He suggested to
one reporter that squadrons of black intellectuals and professionals
were ready to join him now that he was free of the religious orthodoxy
that made some of his more worldly admirers cringe. While sipping
ginger ale, Malcolm characterized civil rights boycotts as passé
demonstrations that distorted the true meaning of revolution. As he
did in the "Message to the Grassroots," Malcolm promised to explain
the meaning of black revolution and black nationalism to wider audiences than he had reached during his time in the Nation of Islam.
Black Americans "were getting angrier," Malcolm said. "And I'm the
angriest."[29]

A week after Malcolm's declaration of political independence, the jazz critic A. B. Spelman sat with him for a lengthy interview. Simultaneously published in the radical journals *Monthly Review** and *Revolution*, the interview found Malcolm overtly courting divergent constituencies—young people, civil rights leaders, and black radicals—in an effort to realize his ambitious plans. Malcolm touted his recent alliance with ACT, calling the black revolution a forest fire razing everything in its path. Describing the civil rights movement as a white-dominated diversion, he predicted that the coming year would produce unprecedented violence. As an aside, Malcolm would, only half jokingly, regret his public candor.[30]

Malcolm's burgeoning ties with the most radical elements of the freedom struggle contrasted with his foray into mainstream politics. At the end of March, he traveled to Washington to hear the "climactic session of the Senate debate" on the civil rights bill. Nearly upstaging Martin Luther King Jr., who was also present, Malcolm's surprise appearance seemed both an exercise in showmanship and a test of hard-won independence. Having secured a visitor's pass, Malcolm proceeded to observe the inner workings of government that most Americans left to politicians and lobbyists. In between watching the debate from the Senate gallery, Malcolm periodically stalked the corridors of Washington, holding impromptu press conferences in which he reasserted his skepticism toward the political process. "You can't legislate goodwill," he said, predicting that strict enforcement of the proposed bill would "bring a civil war to the South and a race war to the North."[31] Accompanied by a small group that included Benjamin 2X, Malcolm claimed to possess countless reserve troops prepared to

---

*The same issue of *Monthly Review* featured excerpts from the Revolutionary Action Movement's manifesto, written by Max Stanford, that first appeared in the March issue of *Correspondence*. In an editorial entitled "The Colonial War at Home," *Monthly Review*'s editors presented RAM's tract as an example of "a New Negro radicalism" light years ahead of "Black Muslimism," a movement credited as a "forerunner" of black radicalism. Undoubtedly, RAM's deep appreciation for class struggle impressed the publishers of a journal that touted itself as "an independent socialist magazine."

swarm the entire capital city. "When word got out in New York that I was coming down it was all I could do to keep a great crowd from coming with me to demonstrate right now. They're ready."[32] Malcolm X and Martin Luther King Jr.'s only joint appearance provided a historic photo op for the press, as well as a brief moment of exchanged pleasantries.[33]

Barely a month after his remarkable press conference, Malcolm left for a five-week tour of Africa. Pressure from the NOI made Harlem a claustrophobic, not to mention potentially deadly, political environment. Before leaving New York, however, Malcolm made quiet inroads with local and national political leaders, community activists, and intellectuals.[34] Growing conflicts with the Nation of Islam pushed Malcolm to define his independent political orientation, the specifics of which would be revealed in one of his most famous speeches, "The Ballot or the Bullet," which he would deliver in Cleveland, Detroit, and other cities. Braiding an analysis of self-defense, electoral politics, and Pan-Africanism with an assertion that America's civil rights struggles were part of a global movement, in this speech Malcolm defined his new political direction.[35] "We need to expand the civil rights struggle to a higher level—the level of human rights," Malcolm told his audiences. Malcolm's search for racial justice outside "the jurisdiction of Uncle Sam" was exemplified by the efforts of early Black Power radicals—from Detroit and Harlem to the Deep South and the West Coast—to expand freedom's frontiers. "The Ballot or the Bullet" chronicled the political journey of both Malcolm and his generation of black radicals who gave the speech its shape and meaning through their political activism. Malcolm summed up the radicals' demands succinctly: "Civil rights for those of us whose philosophy is black nationalism, means: 'Give it to us now. Don't wait for next year. Give it to us yesterday, and that's not fast enough.'"

In the "Ballot or the Bullet," Malcolm defined black nationalism as more than a simple call for unity or promotion of racial pride. Instead, black nationalism was part and parcel of the radical black self-determination, even in the face of ideological heresy, that Malcolm had been preaching for some time. Having been ousted from the Nation of

Islam, Malcolm conjured no new dogmas to replace the old. "We want to hear new ideas and new solutions and new answers," he said. This openness to the unfamiliar was not as remarkable as it appeared on the surface, since even during his stint with the Nation of Islam, Malcolm's intellectual curiosity existed in tandem with Black Muslim orthodoxy. More extraordinary during his last year was the breadth of his intellectual appetite. Circumspectly dialoguing with white Socialists, gingerly consorting with civil rights activists, and delving headlong into pan-African politics and international diplomacy with zeal, Malcolm continued to capture the imagination of supporters and stoke the suspicions of critics.[36]

In April, Malcolm gave another version of "The Ballot or the Bullet" speech before two thousand people at Detroit's King Solomon Baptist Church. This time he contrasted visions of imminent race war with a final, fading opportunity to win black freedom through political power.[37] Malcolm found good company among fellow apostates in the Motor City, where lapsed Christians, black Socialists, teenage revolutionaries, recovering Uncle Toms, and exiled members of the black bourgeoisie formed the vanguard of the city's radicals. Malcolm's constituency included ex-Muslims, radical intellectuals, cosmopolitan gadflies, and young people. Max Stanford, who had graduated from chatting about political revolution in the Boggses' living room to being field chairman of the Revolutionary Action Movement, was among those who rallied around Malcolm. Donald Freeman, RAM's cofounder, had been present at the Park-Sheraton press conference. Through these contacts, Malcolm forged ties with young militants across the nation who sought to transform Malcolm's talk of rifle clubs and self-defense groups into action. Malcolm's politics drew him closer to Detroit even as it irrevocably distanced him from his older brother, Wilfred X.[38]

Having arrived in Africa, Malcolm spent his second night in Ghana at the home of Julian Mayfield, who, after helping Robert Williams escape from North Carolina, left the United States for Africa, where he and his wife, Dr. Ana Livia Cordero, made a life for themselves. The visit was the final leg of a breathless five-week tour of Africa and the Middle East that took Malcolm to Cairo, the United Arab Republic, Beirut, Saudi Arabia, and Nigeria.[39] His seven-day stay in Ghana was the first of two extended trips to the continent in 1964. On both tours he addressed capacity crowds, debated students until dawn, and lectured at prestigious African universities.[40] In Accra, the Ghanaian capital, a group of writers and artists, including Maya Angelou, Vicki Garvin, Les Lacy, and Mayfield, welcomed Malcolm. Mayfield led the contingent of black expatriates who organized Malcolm's itinerary, keeping him apprised of local politics and gossip and arranging a brief meeting with President Kwame Nkrumah. In West Africa, Mayfield served as Nkrumah's personal advisor and speechwriter and achieved the stature that, despite his near celebrity status in certain circles, had eluded him in the United States.[41] Mayfield's biggest thrill was living next door to W. E. B. Du Bois and his wife, Shirley Graham Du Bois. The close proximity allowed a warm friendship to develop as Mayfield's wife provided the aging Du Bois with medical assistance until the living legend's death, on the eve of the March on Washington.[42]

Angelou abandoned her life in Harlem after a whirlwind romance led to an impetuous marriage to an African diplomat, and a new name—Maya Angelou Make. In Ghana, the outgoing Angelou made friends, including Garvin, whose attractive appearance and petite frame evoked popular images of a dignified suburban housewife rather than the radical trade unionist that she was. The scion of a middle-class family, Lacy had first embraced race consciousness via jaw-dropping encounters with black nationalist street speakers while a student at Berkeley. Leaving behind interracial comrades and white lovers, Lacy set out for Africa in search of a deeper understanding of his heritage and personal identity. This collection of talented, if cynical, writers, activists, and trade unionists formed the Malcolm X Welcoming Committee. Adding to their day-to-day duties as teachers, speechwriters, and journalists, they arranged Malcolm's schedule, packing his itinerary with a daunting array of tours, lectures, press conferences, and dinners. Having arrived at the doorstep of Ghana's revolutionary Pan-Africanism by way of the revolving ideological doors of postwar black radicalism, the black expatriates he met carried baggage from membership in other organizations and bitter experience with various political sects. Nonetheless, they longed for leaders worthy of their respect, and Malcolm gained their confidence and personal trust. During quiet times he lectured against smoking, encouraged them to stay in good health, and reminded them that long-term struggle requires sacrifice.[43] Malcolm's presence was like a breath of fresh air for the homesick Americans who were too proud or embarrassed to admit that they missed certain things about home such as easy access to goods and services, accessible public transportation, and even pork sausages.[44]

FBI surveillance confidently noted that Malcolm did not meet with Nkrumah "nor did the government hold any official reception for him."[45] The first count was incorrect, and the second matter was more complicated. While the government didn't officially welcome Malcolm, his allies extended him an unofficial welcome nearly equal to a more formal recognition of his visit. Malcolm's reception in Ghana illustrated just how far the group that hosted him had come. Ghanaians celebrated Malcolm X as "the symbol of the militant American black man," who had traveled across distant lands to visit the "very fountainhead of Pan-Africanism."[46] Privately, Malcolm laid out a bold course of action. Over dinner, exiles peppered him with questions about his split with Elijah Muhammad, his tour of Africa, and future plans.[47] Ghana was a natural place to cultivate historic alliances. The *Osagyefo* (the "redeemer" of his native land), Kwame Nkrumah, had been educated in the United States and admired Marcus Garvey. While American expatriates found refuge in the continent's liberated territory, Malcolm sought to harness the power present in Ghana for political leverage back home. He tested out his idea of carrying the freedom struggle into the international arena, listening to writers, students, intellectuals, and ambassadors, quietly making plans to shake up the civil rights movement in the late spring. He ignited controversy in Ghana as he did everywhere else. The explicitly racial tint to Malcolm's speech at

Ghana's Marxist Forum unleashed vigorous debate between orthodox Marxists and more cosmopolitan radicals; in the *Ghanaian Times,* the writer H. M. Basner chastised Malcolm for ignoring class struggle, while Julian Mayfield offered a sharp rebuttal.[48]

Near the end of his stay, Malcolm met with Nkrumah at Christianborg Castle, the presidential palace, in Accra. The meeting was orchestrated by one of the *Osagyefo's* most influential American advisors, Shirley Graham Du Bois who, after judging Malcolm to be "brilliant," hastily arranged a meeting with Nkrumah. She also gave Malcolm an extensive tour of the Ghanaian television studios she supervised, and arranged for her son, David Du Bois (W. E. B. Du Bois's stepson), to serve as his future host in Cairo.[49]

Malcolm met with Nkrumah on a Friday morning at the president's office. From behind his large desk Nkrumah greeted Malcolm with a warm smile and firm handshake. Retreating to a couch, they discussed civil rights, the connections between Africans and their ancestors in America, and Pan-Africanism.[50] That the encounter was brief did not surprise Julian Mayfield, who understood that divergent political fortunes compounded the lack of personal connection between the two men. Nkrumah, two years away from the defeat that would inspire him to forge an alliance with the Black Power activist Stokely Carmichael, knew that he was navigating a position for Ghana in world affairs dominated by American interests. Disappointed by his reception, Malcolm privately reeled over the sight of white secretaries and apparatchiks who stalked the halls of Ghana's Socialist government.[51]

Malcolm's brief exit from the stage of America's racial drama would, over time, pay dividends.[52] Returning to the States aware of his global appeal yet uncertain how to translate it into political power, Malcolm cast about for a way to fill his days. Successfully "securing scholarships for African American students at Cairo's Al Azhar University" was a symbolic start, illustrating his groping efforts at creating genuine relationships between domestic and international freedom fighters.[53] Vowing to cut through the thicket of intrigues that threatened his personal and political survival, Malcolm returned to Harlem as black America's unofficial prime minister. His conversations with expatriates pursuing revolutionary internationalism had produced crucial pieces of the puzzle that he had, for many years, been attempting to complete. For a man who was uncertain of his ultimate political destination, Ghana provided snapshots of a revolutionary work in progress.

Malcolm returned from Ghana on May 21, 1964, and walked into the biggest press conference that he had ever seen.[54] Dozens of reporters treated Malcolm's new name, El-Hajj Malik El-Shabazz, and the news of his hajj pilgrimage, with shock and surprise. Another press conference, at the Hotel Theresa's Skyline Ballroom, would follow. Television cameras, newspaper reporters, photographers, and freelance writers packed the eleventh floor of the venerable hotel to greet Malcolm. Dressed in a blue seersucker suit and in need of a haircut, Malcolm looked rakishly handsome, with his reddish beard and a broad smile.

Malcolm's letters from Africa had reveled in the Middle East's racial diversity. Five years earlier, Malcolm had confidently reported to the *Amsterdam News* that the Arab world was filled with dark-skinned Africans who closely resembled their American counterparts. So perhaps naturally, newspapers speculated that Malcolm's spiritual rebirth in Mecca had moderated his political philosophy.[55] Reporters tried to confirm rumors that he had abandoned the Black Muslims' racial separatism in favor of a new ideology. Malcolm hedged but answered affirmatively. Acknowledging that he no longer condemned whites solely because of their skin color, he issued a collective indictment against white supremacy based on historic crimes against blacks.[56]

Malcolm's homecoming coincided with new talk of revolution coming out of Detroit. The day after Malcolm's return, Milton Henry, whose radicalism now outpaced many of his colleagues', gave a lecture to the Friday Night Socialist Forum that simultaneously captured the interest of the FBI and the imagination of local militants. Henry's address, "Proportioned Underground Warfare," evoked fantastic images of daring raids hatched by urban guerrillas engaged in a type of war that could be won by a limited number of combatants fighting a superior force. Even a book of matches could create major damage, Henry argued; such havoc would perhaps provide greater leverage than conventional civil rights tactics. Henry's visceral description of urban guerrillas plotting acts of industrial sabotage presaged Black Power activists' talk of race war that would consume U.S. politics several years later. According to FBI informants, Henry's speech attracted enthusiasm from an interracial audience of about one hundred: "It was the most intense group of people the writer has ever witnessed from one of these affairs."[57] In a memorandum to director J. Edgar Hoover, Detroit's special agent in charge wrote:

> A summary of Milton Henry's speech would be that he is trying to show that a well disciplined underground of all black guerillas [sic] could cause pandemonium and in this way let everyone know that the Negro aims to gain his absolute, complete freedom. The sabotage of buildings, gas tanks, grain storage, elevators, etc. would be for the purpose of waking everyone up to the fact that Negroes want to be heard. The group would be all black, well disciplined, and dedicated. It was repeated often that there is no desire to kill people for the sake of killing, but the aim would be property.[58]

Henry's rhetorical nuance and legal expertise saved him from being arrested. His talk, Detroit's special agent in charge lamented, had been merely hypothetical. Since there was no "direct call" for guerrilla warfare, Henry was guilty only of provocative polemics.[59] Down south, members of the Revolutionary Action Movement, echoing Henry's call to take the movement to a higher level, embarked on a two-pronged strategy of publicly disparaging civil rights groups for not resorting to self-defense techniques while infiltrating these groups in hopes of spreading their radical influence.[60]

In June, political events pressed Malcolm forward at a frenetic pace.[61] Malcolm's creation of the Organization of Afro-American Unity implicitly acknowledged the limitations of the Muslim Mosque's unsuccessful combination of the religious and the secular. Members of the black intelligentsia, including John Oliver Killens and John Henrik

Clarke, were invited to serve as advisors to a planning group for the OAAU that featured members of the Muslim Mosque. The organization also invited a broad section of black radicals to a reception in advance of the group's founding rally at the end of June. Intended to be an umbrella organization flexible enough to include black nationalists, liberals, and Socialists, the OAAU represented Malcolm's most systematic attempt to gather black American support for an international pan-African perspective.[62] Still basking in the glow of his African tour, Malcolm argued, hyperbolically, that there were "more Africans in Harlem" than in any city in Africa.[63] His opening address outlined the OAAU's ambitions, including involvement in local political clubs, rent strikes, and electoral campaigns. Liberation from the "bonds of white supremacy," however, required more than just good jobs, decent housing, and a sense of identity. Malcolm also proposed a "cultural revolution" that would use the restorative power of black art to transform Harlem and the rest of the black world, all for a membership fee of $2 a year.[64]

But the OAAU proved to be a hard sell, with fewer than a hundred people registering for membership.[65] Despite strong personal appeal and charisma, Malcolm lacked the time and patience to build a solid organization. There were, as well, other concerns. Peacefully resolving unfinished business with the Nation was now impossible, in light of the avalanche of publicity that had accompanied Malcolm's allegations of Muhammad's marital infidelities. Instead of providing Malcolm with new leverage in his war to gain a greater share of public sympathy than Muhammad, in some quarters Muhammad's profile had only been strengthened at the expense of Malcolm's reputation. Efforts at brokering a truce also failed.[66] Cornered, Malcolm made plans, once again, to leave the country.[67]

Malcolm's latest travel plans coincided with new revelations published in the *Chicago Defender* that leveled detailed charges against Elijah Muhammad. In exclusive interviews, Wallace Muhammad and the Messenger's grandson Hasan Sharief, recounted the heavy price they paid for "deviating" from Muhammad's teachings. To stunned *Defender* readers, Wallace revealed a sordid world where threats and intimidation shadowed his every move. Publicly unburdening himself of secrets he had revealed to Malcolm more than a year earlier, Wallace justified his actions as penance for his conversion of countless souls into what he now viewed as a corrupt organization. Dispensing with his uncle's measured tone, Hasan Sharief denounced Muhammad as a "fake and a fraud," accusing his grandfather of betraying his most faithful followers while opportunistically recruiting celebrities like Muhammad Ali.[68] Ignoring the barrage of accusations from the Messenger's relatives, Chicago officials released a statement attacking the credibility of one of Muhammad's former secretaries and characterizing Malcolm as the mastermind behind Wallace's and Hasan Sharief's confessions.[69]

Harlem exploded less than two weeks after Malcolm left for his second African tour. The July 16 shooting death of fifteen-year-old James Powell by off-duty police officer Thomas Gilligan triggered ten days of violence whose implications extended far beyond uptown Manhattan. Transformed into a domestic battleground, Harlem raged as bottle-throwing residents and helmeted riot control officers clashed. The day of Powell's funeral, further conflict erupted on 133rd Street, as cops pummeled bystanders and fired shots into a crowd filled with bitter mourners and spectators.[70] Youthful protesters waged fierce battles with police officers from rooftops, abandoned buildings, and burned-out cars. On Sunday, July 19, Jesse Gray, the Harlem rent strike organizer, addressed a packed audience filled with local militants eager for payback. The meeting's theme, "Is Harlem Mississippi?," left little to the imagination. Beaten to a pulp by police officers the previous night, the heavily bandaged Gray climbed the podium at Mount Morris Presbyterian Church and urged the crowd to organize for a black takeover of the city. "There is only one thing that can correct the situation," said Gray, "and that's guerrilla warfare." Declaring that such a task required "100 skilled revolutionaries who are ready to die," Gray whipped an already charged audience into a frenzy.

Boos greeted local CORE leader Marshal England's pleas for calm and drove him offstage.[71] Veteran street speaker Eddie "Porkchop"

Davis momentarily restored order by diplomatically calling for black men with military training to step forward. Wise enough to understand the futility of war talk, a resigned Davis—perhaps remembering Harlem Renaissance poet Claude McKay's New Negro anthem "If We Must Die"—explained that "if we must die, let us die scientifically." James Farmer and Bayard Rustin, two aging lions of nonviolence, offered sanguine words that nonetheless left them heckled, embarrassed, and eager to leave. With the city poised for further eruptions, municipal authorities pleaded for federal intervention. On Monday, July 20, in the wake of more than one hundred police and civilian injuries, fifteen confirmed shootings, and two hundred arrests, President Lyndon Johnson—against the counsel of his advisors—sent the FBI into Harlem, where agents investigated connections between the riot and what wire services referred to as "the Black Muslims and other extremist groups." Meanwhile, Harlem militants distributed thousands of fliers that read, "Wanted for Murder—Gilligan the cop."[72]

Martin Luther King Jr. arrived in New York City on July 27 to broker a peace treaty between City Hall and Harlem residents. As King's entreaties for a civilian review board fell on deaf ears, Harlem nationalists planned rallies to organize the desperate energy left in the riot's wake. Within days, newspaper reports described the unrest as red, not black, painting a portrait of Communist conspiracy that warranted official investigation. Local media debated the role that outside agitators had played in the conflict. The arrests of William Epton and Conrad Lynn were touted as providing two smoking guns. Blacks with strong ties to the radical Left, Epton and Lynn had organized a protest demonstration, in defiance of a police ban, under the auspices of the Progressive Labor Movement.[73]

Harlem burned first, and then St. Louis, and the violence soon spread through Rochester, New Jersey, and Philadelphia, some of the worst urban areas in America, within a few weeks of each other. From Detroit, Albert Cleage characterized the riots as reflecting the "depth of the Negro's discontent and frustration, but also the total bankruptcy of 'responsible' Negro leadership." *Muhammad Speaks* published a photo of police beating Harlem residents underneath a headline that was an admonition cloaked in outrage: "With Messenger Muhammad—THIS WOULD NOT HAPPEN!"[74]

On the first full day of rioting in New York, the OAAU issued a press release detailing Malcolm's most recent activities. "During the midst of the racial turmoil here in America," the statement read, "the most militant of the militant Negroes—Malcolm X—was in Cairo, Egypt, where he was the only American allowed into the Organization of African Unity."[75] The press release outlined a new kind of international politics. The freelance diplomacy Malcolm was currently practicing was firmly rooted in a radical Pan-Africanist impulse that highlighted shared interest in the common cause of a global human rights revolution. "Our problem is your problem," read the statement. "It is not a Negro problem, nor an American problem." This last line—honed in dozens of speeches around the world—resonated in the hearts and minds of a generation of black activists. "This is a world problem; a problem for humanity. It is not a problem of civil rights, but a problem of humanity."[76] Langston Hughes, whose literary genius and radical sympathies stretched back to the Harlem Renaissance, was one of the few commentators to note the historical significance of Malcolm's journey. Old enough to remember attempts by black activists to petition the United Nations following the Second World War, Hughes hoped that Malcolm's maverick diplomacy could recruit the "Afro-Asian" block to the struggle for black equality.[77]

In Cairo, a global city he breathlessly described as "revolutionary," Malcolm reunited with old friends and made new enemies.[78] Julian Mayfield stopped by to visit, as did Shirley Graham Du Bois, whose son David lived in Cairo. The New York Journal American writer Victor Riesel interpreted Malcolm's visits in Cairo as smokescreens for Communist conspiracies that stretched from Havana to Beijing, singling out Du Bois as proof of Malcolm's nefarious intentions.[79] In Africa, Riesel took personal offense at Malcolm's vivid descriptions of racial oppression, arguing that the militant leader depicted America as a "vast national torture chamber."[80] Malcolm's time in Cairo inspired inquiries from State Department officials who worried about the long-term effects his interventions might have on American foreign policy, while also fretting over rumors that the Saudis bankrolled him.[81] In a back-page story that excerpted chunks of his OAAU manifesto, the *New York Times* dryly reported the Justice Department's interest in Malcolm's human rights campaign.[82] More comfortable with Malcolm as a saber rattler than as a diplomat, U.S. journalists cautiously covered what on the surface appeared to be Malcolm's improvisational plunge into the murky depths of foreign policy. Indeed, at times it was. In Kenya, Malcolm sauntered over to a surprised group of SNCC activists on a three-week tour underwritten by Harry Belafonte to discuss his Pan-Africanist inclinations.[83]

During the second half of his stay in Africa, he returned to Ghana for a bittersweet reunion. Mayfield, Angelou, and Lacy all noticed the difference in his behavior. A restless irritability had replaced the energetic demeanor of his spring tour; this time he spoke in hushed tones of conspiracies and impending violence that awaited him back home.[84]

Malcolm X returned to New York from Africa on a chilly evening during the last Tuesday in November 1964. At Kennedy Airport more than fifty supporters greeted him, waving placards that read "Welcome back Brother Malcolm," as he reunited with Betty and three of their children.[85] Not everyone celebrated his return, however. Two former protégés, recently promoted to Malcolm's former Harlem mosque, denounced his activities abroad, expressing concern over reports that Malcolm had not only received an endorsement from the World Muslim Council but also slandered the Messenger as a "religious faker." While acknowledging Malcolm's "undeniable oratorical and organizing talent," Muslim officials branded him a usurper cut off from the group that had nurtured him. "He now stands alone" was their quote.[86]

Political isolation once again inspired Malcolm's bold plans. During an interview with the *Amsterdam News,* Malcolm announced he would tour Mississippi, Alabama, Georgia, and other southern states to promote voter registration and education.[87] In late December, Fannie Lou Hamer, the southern-born sharecropper turned civil rights activist, would share the stage with Malcolm in New York. Inspired by the SNCC Freedom Singers' stirring tribute to Kenyan vice president Oginga Odinga, Malcolm reiterated his support for Kenya's Mau Mau uprising, noting that Odinga was a fierce warrior who rejected nonviolence yet won his freedom. Malcolm also held up Hamer's endurance in the face of beatings that left her permanently injured as evidence that black freedom necessitated the adoption of self-defense.[88]

Malcolm began 1965 shadowed by death threats and planning for the future.[89] His response was to accentuate the fruits of his international travel, taking credit for African criticism of the United States in UN debates over civil war in the Congo—political unrest that, in fact, could be traced to Patrice Lumumba's 1961 assassination.[90]

Twice in the next two months he made good on his vow to venture into the South. While he never made it to Mississippi, Malcolm did visit Alabama. Addressing a capacity crowd at Tuskegee Institute, Malcolm received an unexpected invitation to speak in Selma the next day, where King was in the middle of organizing a nonviolent showdown in an effort to secure black voting rights.[91] Malcolm's appearance in Selma annoyed Southern Christian Leadership Conference staffers, who pleaded with him to limit his comments to the situation at hand. From the pulpit at Brown's Chapel A.M.E. Church, Malcolm pursued his agenda, exploring themes—internationalism and the House Negro and Field Negro analogy—that were less familiar in the South. Sitting down to enthusiastic applause, he chatted with Coretta Scott King before heading for the airport.[92] Malcolm was shuttled to Europe for a series of speaking engagements and returned to the States just in time for a torrent of harassment from the Nation of Islam.

The verbal assaults on Malcolm in *Muhammad Speaks* reached a fever pitch that February.[93] On Valentine's Day morning, Malcolm's home was firebombed, an attack that rattled his composure and ended his legal dispute with the NOI. A judge ruled that Malcolm had no claims on the rubble, forcing him to recover his belongings under the cover of night. Publicly Malcolm remained defiant. "It doesn't frighten me," he said, adding that the latest attempt on his life would not prevent him from speaking out.[94]

The next week played out like a surreal dream as Malcolm engaged in a series of forlorn press conferences, interviews, and speeches in which he predicted his own death, condemning those who would be held responsible. Malcolm charged the Nation of Islam with firebombing his home and denounced the group for resorting to tactics typically associated with white supremacists. Muslim officials countered that Malcolm had set fire to his own home as a publicity stunt.[95] Within the hidden bowels of the Nation of Islam, officials and soldiers anxiously awaited word of Malcolm's fate, which would come on February 21 in the form of a premeditated diversion followed by deafening gunshots. The ghastly sight of Malcolm's bullet-ridden body was juxtaposed with images of fleeing assassins, frightened bystanders, and bewildered bodyguards, in what started out as an OAAU rally at the Audubon Ballroom in Harlem.[96] Talmadge X Hayer was apprehended on the spot as one of five killers. Within a year, two others were tried and convicted, along with Hayer, of Malcolm's murder. The convictions ended legal wrangling but not speculation that, except for Hayer, several more of his assassins remained on the loose.[97]

After Malcolm X's assassination, Harlem became a battleground between disciples of Muhammad and the scattered remains of the Muslim Mosque and the OAAU. In the middle were thousands of residents braving freezing temperatures to view Malcolm's body in a glass-covered copper coffin at the Unity Funeral Home, a two-story brick building accented by a green canopy, between West 126th and 127th Streets.[98] Despite Muslim partisans' warnings that those who paid their respects were risking their lives, over ten thousand visitors poured into the modest funeral home. Mourners crossed generational, political, and religious lines, their presence acknowledging Malcolm as a bold prophet cut down in his prime.[99] Word that the New York Police Department's clandestine Bureau of Special Services had been present at the Audubon the day Malcolm was gunned down fueled conspiracy theories that also counted Black Muslims, local authorities, white supremacists, foreign governments, the CIA, and international spies among the growing list of suspects.[100]

The day after Malcolm's assassination, a fire gutted Mosque No. 7.[101] Police immediately declared the blaze suspicious, at the same time that rumors of Muhammad's imminent assassination prompted Chicago authorities to establish round-the-clock protection outside his gated mansion.[102] Protected by legions of security, Muhammad denied any involvement in either Malcolm's murder or the fire, adding that "Malcolm died according to his preaching."[103] Seeking to avert open warfare in Harlem, the NYPD dispatched hundreds of officers to neighborhood streets, setting up a special command center. Under police floodlights, activist Jesse Gray called for stores to shut down in Malcolm's memory, while grief-stricken supporters gathered outside Lewis Michaux's bookstore to commemorate his death.[104]

Nationally, Malcolm's death rocked a cross-section of activists. CORE leader James Farmer, whose public jousting with Malcolm disguised a cordial private relationship, correctly predicted that he would become a hero to black militants.[105] Although journalists disagreed over Malcolm's legacy, a grudging admiration marked the words of both supporters and detractors. The *New York Times* described him as "an extraordinary and twisted man" who wasted his "many true gifts to evil purpose." Elsewhere the paper claimed that "World Pays Little Attention to Malcolm Slaying," pointing to tepid reaction in the Middle East, Africa, and parts of Europe as proof that Malcolm was no international martyr.[106] The black conservative journalist Carl Rowan refuted the *Times* report, admitting that African and Asian countries were eulogizing Malcolm as a hero. Reading excerpts from pro-Malcolm editorials at a Foreign Service Association speech in Washington, the unsympathetic Rowan asserted that "misinformation" had caused Africans to condemn Malcolm's death as a critical blow to the civil rights struggle.[107] Black newspapers claimed Malcolm as the necessary black sheep of a race still largely under siege. Reporter Jimmy Booker's declaration that "no one knew Malcolm X better than the

Amsterdam News staff" reflected a decade-long association that began shortly after Malcolm arrived in Harlem. Within a month of Malcolm's death, the *Amsterdam News* ran a series of articles that examined "the man, his philosophies, his life and death" as the opening salvo in a posthumous effort to reveal the "Real Malcolm X."[108]

6

"BLACK" IS A COUNTRY

On February 22, 1965, the day after Malcolm X's assassination, LeRoi Jones announced, at a press conference in New York, plans to create the Black Arts Repertory Theater and School (BARTS). Five years after his Cuban tour, Jones formally embraced Harlem. Like many of his peers, Jones found himself increasingly drawn to Malcolm's rhetoric, machismo, and ideology during the early 1960s. Jones's award-winning play *Dutchman* reflected the bitter realities of his dual existence as a downtown bohemian and a budding black nationalist. Dubbed the King of the Lower East Side, Jones was on the verge of a new kind of literary superstardom. He refused, however, to be merely the latest black writer whose jabs stirred slumbering liberal souls. Unlike the more compassionate James Baldwin, Jones offered white liberals little hope of redemption, instead lashing out in personal confrontations that left his victims gasping for air. Malcolm's death rendered whatever temptations of fame and fortune offered moot. Feeling "stupid, ugly," and "useless" after hearing the news, Jones stopped pretending to be a black revolutionary and become one.[1]

Like a drunk regaining consciousness after a long stupor, Jones fled

Greenwich Village. When he arrived in Harlem looking to establish a headquarters for political revolution, his decision seemed as daring as it was improbable. Harlem was full of seasoned activists, would-be revolutionaries, hard cases, and crack pots who knew the landscape much better, having organized, worked, and lived in it. None, however, matched Jones's obsessive drive, determination, or the sheer confidence that made him bold enough to think that an avant-garde African American poet, the boy wonder of the literary elite married to a white woman, could lead a black revolution. Deploying black art as a vehicle for political expression was not new. The Harlem Renaissance had produced a groundbreaking movement for black culture; the Communist Party, for a time, had nurtured Richard Wright and other luminaries; and the Harlem Writers Guild had kept creative engagement alive during the 1950s, while Jones was enjoying the good life in the Village. Jones's foray into Harlem coincided with the black nationalist resurgence that Malcolm X set in motion on the national level, which on the local level would take the form of militant political groups and arts collectives in urban centers across the country that found international inspiration in icons such as Patrice Lumumba, Kwame Nkrumah, and Fidel Castro. For Jones, black art required a political commitment that would open the doors to a new way of life, for him, for Harlem, and for blacks around the nation.

"To a growing list of 'dirty words' that make Americans squirm," wrote Jones in 1962, "add the word *Nationalism*." Jones's poetry and prose during the 1960s would help transform black culture, antagonize mainstream sensibilities, and turn him into a literary and political phenomenon. Published the year after Malcolm's death, Jones's collection of essays, *Home,* traced his initially awkward, then strident embrace of black nationalism. Suffering creative setbacks from "having been taught that art was 'what white men did,' " Jones examined black life from the inside out. Poignant, angry, and wistful, *Home* found Jones ruminating on the quality of black literature, the strategy of nonviolence, and his complicity in the racial strife gripping the nation. A masterpiece of social, political, and literary criticism, *Home* documents the influence of the race consciousness that had expanded beyond Harlem street speakers and long marchers from across the country into the intellectual regions where Jones resided. Claiming that blacks constituted a nation within a nation, Jones, in the essay " 'Black' Is a Country," argued that African Americans should draw strength and inspiration from seeming marginality. "The struggle is for *independence,* not separation—or assimilation," he wrote. "And we must now, in what I see as an extreme 'nationalism,' " recognize the true face of a nation bound together by skin color, tradition, and a cultural heritage—"i.e., in the best interest of our own country, the name of which the rest of America has pounded into our heads for four hundred years, *Black.*"[2]

The Black Arts Repertory Theater and School represented Jones's attempt to achieve his mandate. BARTS drew young writers and artists into an experiment that combined literary pursuits and community activism. Sonia Sanchez, whose poetry would galvanize Black Power activists, joined the Black Arts project. So did Larry Neal, a clandestine activist whose essays helped define the emerging movement. Rolland Snellings, whose pugnaciousness and artistic talent made him comfortable around picketers and poets, was also on hand. A grant from a Harlem antipoverty agency supported jazz performances, poetry readings, outdoor plays, and summer concerts. Recruiting a "young intelligentsia who could not find self-respect except in opposition to black oppression," BARTS signaled a major, though largely unrecognized, shift in the black freedom struggle. Through BARTS, Jones used creative expression to educate and politicize Harlem's poor. Harold Cruse taught a course on cultural philosophy, which was attended by Harlem activists, including Yuri Kochiyama, a Japanese American internment camp survivor involved in Malcolm X's OAAU and other causes.[3] Classes in music, dance, and playwriting supplemented remedial education and job training, traveling exhibits, a bookmobile, and a theater that attracted hundreds of Harlem residents. Weekend musical performances featuring Sun Ra, an eclectic jazz performer and prodigious talent, highlighted the summer concert series. Jones's strategy was as successful as it was short-lived. Alerted to BARTS's use of public funds for a political agenda deemed suspicious at best, panicked antipoverty officials redirected money to other programs.

Over time, BARTS was transformed from an abstract concept into a political and cultural movement. Catalyzed by Harlem's experiment, cultural centers, theater groups, and organizations formed beachheads in dozens of cities across the country. Cultural festivals and conventions popularized the concept, strengthening the infrastructure for community organizing and the creation of new institutions. By 1966, Black Arts represented a movement that envisioned itself as much political as cultural: a collaborator with Black Power that combined creative innovation and political improvisation.[4]

While the establishment of the Black Arts Theater marked the first anniversary of 1964's Harlem uprising, violent jolts shook California, touching off a second consecutive summer of civil disorder. On August 11, a routine traffic stop in the Watts section of South Central Los Angeles triggered a week of upheaval. Occurring only a few days after the triumphant passage of the Voting Rights Act, the devastation in Watts dwarfed the Harlem riot. Burning stores, sniper fire, and National Guard soldiers, as well as a curfew, made sections of the city resemble a war zone.[5] Interrupting his vacation in Puerto Rico, Martin Luther King Jr. rushed to Los Angeles to offer his assistance. King's meeting with Mayor Sam Yorty and police chief William Parker turned acrimonious; in the end, the police chief angrily rejected King's suggestion of a civilian review board, and King called for Parker's resignation. Putting the best face on Los Angeles' history of racial division, California governor Pat Brown stressed an imagined preriot era of peace and goodwill. The mayor and police chief offered alternative explanations. Parker praised fearful white residents who purchased guns to "protect" their communities, while Yorty dismissed black residents' charges of police brutality as a Communist conspiracy.[6]

King's meetings in Watts's black community took on a similarly hostile edge. Heckled by angry residents and horrified by the ravaged landscape of the riot's epicenter, King left Los Angeles, aware of the limits of legal equality without parallel economic strides.[7]

For government officials, Watts provided a different lesson. From his Austin, Texas, ranch, Lyndon Johnson condemned the violence and implored blacks to live up to the responsibilities of full citizenship.[8] On the heels of the president's Howard University commencement speech two months earlier, Watts represented a domestic political crisis. Then, a triumphant Johnson had laid the groundwork for social and political equality across racial lines. "In far too many ways," admitted Johnson, "American Negroes have been another nation deprived of freedom, crippled by hatred, the doors of opportunity closed to hope." At Howard, Johnson cited a litany of social and economic indicators that reflected a widening opportunity gulf based on skin color that the president described as "solely and simply the consequence of ancient brutality, past injustice, and present prejudice." Howard University students applauded Johnson's soaring eloquence twenty-six times that day.[9] Now, Watts exposed the bitter reality behind Johnson's plea to end black isolation in urban ghettoes by waging war on the poverty that stifled dreams.

"We've just got so much to do," Johnson confided to King, "that I don't know how we'll ever do it, but we've got to get ahead with it." During a mostly one-sided telephone conversation in August, amid the Watts crisis, Johnson gave King an insider account of the difficulties his poverty bill faced in the Senate. Returning to the business of Watts, Johnson relayed Mayor Yorty's charges against civil rights leaders in Los Angeles before asking for King's assessment of the situation. King advised the president that the situation in Los Angeles was grim, but held out hope that the federal response could avert future eruptions. To Johnson's request for policy recommendations, King suggested that accelerated antipoverty measures be immediately deployed to the riot area. Johnson urged King to increase pressure on recalcitrant Washington politicians by highlighting Johnson's leadership on racial issues, and in return King praised the president's Howard speech as the most eloquent summation of the civil rights issue ever made by a politician. The conversation concluded with Johnson issuing a delicate, if distinct, warning over an issue that would ultimately destroy his relationship with King. After submitting to King a furious roll call of the numerous programs that comprised his ambitious domestic agenda, Johnson turned momentarily defensive, noting how Congress—despite his having won all but five states the previous November—thought him vulnerable on the issue of Vietnam. The president told King, "They all got the impression that you're against me in Vietnam." "You don't leave that impression," Johnson pressed. "I want peace as much as you do and more so cuz I'm the fella that had to wake up this morning with fifty marines killed." Johnson signed off by telling King that he could call the White House (collect if necessary) anytime.[10]

The October 1965 publication of *The Autobiography of Malcolm X*, written by Alex Haley, followed on the heels of Watts.[11] Malcolm's posthumously published autobiography was praised in leading journals and newspapers around the country, its success marking black radicalism as a new, relatively unexplored, literary topic, able to offer the uninitiated an intimate and unvarnished portrait of black militancy. Advertised as the story of a "hoodlum, dope peddler," and "pimp" who became "the most dynamic leader of the Black Revolution," *The Autobiography of Malcolm X* successfully packaged Malcolm's story as an important, slightly sentimental, personal odyssey whose narrative style substituted personal redemption for Malcolm's political rage.[12]

In the wake of Malcolm's assassination and the uprising in Watts, the Student Nonviolent Coordinating Committee's organizing efforts in Atlanta and Lowndes County, Alabama, took on a new edge. SNCC's ambitious urban projects pushed the group into uncharted territory. By the early 1960s, SNCC had emerged as the freedom movement's wild card, small, brash, and agile enough to take chances that its larger counterparts could not. Founded in conjunction with the spontaneous sit-ins that originated in Greensboro, North Carolina, on February 1, 1960, SNCC activists practiced the slow, tedious, and patient voter registration drives in the most dangerous parts of the South, receiving little national credit for its efforts—although the bravado, precocious-ness, and idealism of its activists managed to annoy both white federal officials and black civil rights leaders. SNCC attracted radicals from the Revolutionary Action Movement, black nationalists from the North, and a host of other mavericks. Wary of ideological blinders, SNCC would chart its own course, one that would place Black Power activism at the center of a new movement for local, national, and inter-national liberation.

From its humble beginnings, SNCC eschewed both the pragmatism of movement elders and the cautiousness of federal officials, preferring to confront what Stokely Carmichael described as "raw terror" in the rural South. Their experiences, witnessing small acts of courage by semi-literate sharecroppers, and, at times, saving lives and mourning senseless deaths, accelerated SNCC's expectations for racial justice and height-ened its disappointments at the failures of the federal government, civil rights leaders, and American citizens to achieve racial equality, leading to increased militancy, factionalism, and recklessness.[13] During SNCC's efforts to organize a political party in rural Alabama, the black panther was chosen as the symbol for a local group of grassroots activists: the Lowndes County Freedom Organization (LCFO). Thousands of young activists around the country would later adopt the symbol, including the Oakland-based Black Panther Party for Self-Defense, in October 1966.

Stokely Carmichael, who had been a strong presence in SNCC since his undergraduate days at Howard University, embodied the group's new direction. After graduating in 1964 with a degree in phi-losophy, Carmichael became project director for its voter registration efforts in that year's Freedom Summer. Carmichael thrived in rural Mississippi, establishing a reputation as a brilliant organizer, expert raconteur, and fearless driver—whose nickname, the Delta Devil, re-flected his skill at the high-speed driving that kept him one step ahead of local authorities and vigilantes.[14]

Stokely Carmichael was born on June 29, 1941, in Port of Spain, Trinidad, and grew up in the house that his carpenter father had built.

Migrating to the United States in the 1940s, Adolph and May Charles Carmichael left their middle child, Stokely, and his two sisters in the care of their doting grandmother and several aunts. Raised in the port city with its lush trees, colorful festivals, and blue seas, Stokely Standiford Churchill Carmichael—called "little man" because of his dapper clothes from the States—spent a happy early childhood. Though he was born and raised in the Caribbean, Carmichael's relationship with the region would remain star-crossed. For most of his adult life, Carmichael's radical politics would cause him to be officially banned from entering the island of his birth as well as other parts of the West Indies.[15]

In 1952, Stokely, age ten, and his sisters joined their parents in a cramped Bronx apartment, where the children experienced the booming sounds of urban living and their first winter.[16] A skilled craftsman who dreamed that Stokely would become a physician, Adolph moved the family from the predominantly black South Bronx to the mostly Italian Morris Park neighborhood. Transplanted to a middle-class area, Carmichael negotiated two worlds—one black and one white—during much of his youth. His status as a minority during the school day gave way to all-black family gatherings at night. On frequent trips to Harlem's historic 125th Street, Carmichael encountered African American oral traditions, local customs, and political culture.[17] Carmichael became one of the few black students at the prestigious Bronx High School of Science. His four years at Bronx Science—where his classmates included Eugene Dennis Jr., the son of a high-ranking Communist official imprisoned under the Smith Act—grounded his future political activism.[18] Carmichael's association with red diaper babies and the scions of New York liberals led him to Bayard Rustin. An itinerant pacifist and vagabond philosopher born in the Caribbean, Rustin was perhaps the best-known black Socialist in the civil rights movement. While Carmichael and Rustin would find themselves on opposite ends of ideological questions in the next decade, the veteran activist served as one of Carmichael's earliest political mentors.

The National Memorial Bookstore and the Schomburg Library introduced Carmichael, as it had Harold Cruse, to pan-African writers and revolutionaries who inspired community activists and sidewalk historians. Carmichael's trips to Harlem coincided with historic changes in Africa that made movements such as Mau Mau and names like Nkrumah roll off the tongue of politically conscious black New Yorkers.[19] During Carmichael's senior year at Bronx Science, revolutions rippled from Africa to the Deep South.

After graduating from Bronx Science in 1960, Carmichael entered Howard University. At the nation's premier historically black university, the nineteen-year-old found himself in an atmosphere filled with contradictions: a campus where student appetites for mixers and fraternity parties competed with the latest news from the civil rights front.[20] Howard, which took pride in training generations of black professionals, inevitably sought to distance itself from student militancy. Having a sizable portion of African and Caribbean students put the university in a precarious position: its reliance on federal funding controlled by Dixiecrats in Congress conflicted with the student body's pan-African impulses. In an atmosphere abuzz with tales of dashing students engaged in civil rights struggles down south, Carmichael joined the Nonviolent Action Group—Howard's SNCC affiliate. In NAG, Carmichael met Cleveland Sellers, Mike Thelwell, and Charlie Cobb, all of whom would become friends and political comrades.[21] Washington, with its unique mix of rural and urban geography and northern and southern populations, politicians, and institutions, ensured that NAG's efforts to combat segregation would be flexible, creative, and worldly. Although its membership was overwhelmingly black, NAG included eight whites, as well as students from the Caribbean, the Deep South, and the urban North.[22]

In 1961, Carmichael joined a group of Freedom Riders headed for Mississippi, gently telling his mother not to worry, that he was "going to jail" and to be "proud," not ashamed. May Carmichael spent a tense evening listening to the radio before learning of her son's arrest. Responding to neighbors who asked, "Is that your boy Stokely they've got down there?" she responded as her son had instructed. "Yes, that's my boy and I'm so proud of him I don't know what to do!"[23] Carmichael spent forty-nine days in jail, mostly at the Mississippi State

Penitentiary in Parchman, a sobering introduction to the high stakes of civil disobedience that only solidified his resolve.[24] He would spend subsequent summers down south, as NAG brought the civil rights movement to Howard.[25]

In 1964, after receiving his degree, Carmichael devoted his energies to full-time organizing, a job that depended on his communication skills and easy rapport with rural southern blacks—both of which would become legendary.[26] So too would his confidence, quick mind, and sharp wit. Even among the outstanding young men and women who constituted SNCC's cadre of organizers, Carmichael stood out. Tall, handsome, and charismatic, he charmed the elderly with his graciousness and captivated the young with an energetic spirit that was as playful as it was political. Friends teasingly called him "Stokely Starmichael." Perhaps the result of his uncanny ability to instill confidence in others, Carmichael could make fun of anyone, even Baptist preachers, whom he would expertly imitate performing off-color sermons.[27] Fearless, willingly venturing into unsavory places as if they were no more or less dangerous than a local black church, Carmichael was more politically driven than many of his counterparts in SNCC. Joining a Nashville sit-in soon after his release from Parchman, Carmichael upset participants trained under the nonviolent guru Jim Lawson, who told him in no uncertain terms to cool it. Carmichael's reluctant compliance with the request was an example of his belief that local people should set the pace of their struggles and dovetailed with his expert ability to explain philosophical issues to both the educated and the unlettered.[28]

Called Bloody Lowndes because of the violence directed at civil rights workers there, this small rural county between Selma and Montgomery became an unlikely incubator for Black Power politics. Blacks in the county outnumbered whites four to one; yet as late as 1965, it had registered only two courageous voters, including John Hulett, who became president of the county's civil rights group.[29] Carmichael helped organize the Lowndes County Freedom Organization, to circumvent the racist Democratic Party machine.

In November 1965, *Look* magazine profiled these efforts, in a story whose captions described Carmichael as "a young revolutionary" engaged in the arduous task of organizing rural people against a backdrop of fear.[30] Carmichael arrived in Lowndes County fresh from the momentum of the late winter's Selma-to-Montgomery demonstrations.

Photographs of marchers being beaten at the Edmund Pettus Bridge in Selma had galvanized the nation's outrage, culminating in the passage of the Voting Rights Act in August. The Selma march and the legislation that followed, however, only stiffened white resistance in Lowndes County. Viola Liuzzo, a white supporter from Detroit, was killed during the Selma-to-Montgomery march in the early spring, and Jonathan Daniels, a white volunteer whose intelligence and commitment had earned him Carmichael's respect, was murdered shortly after Liuzzo.[31] At the height of the conflict between demonstrators and police and yet away from the cameras, Carmichael suffered a breakdown after being trapped in a Montgomery hotel while mayhem reigned a few feet away. "I was by my window and I looked down and saw the cops beating and I couldn't get out. I was completely helpless. There was no release. I kept watching and then I began screaming and I didn't stop screaming."[32] At that moment, Carmichael remembered, "I knew I could never be hit again without hitting back."[33]

Against Selma's backdrop, Carmichael, Hulett, and the rest of a SNCC contingent that included Judy Richardson, Scott Smith, Willie Vaughn, and Bob Mants quietly organized blacks in Lowndes.[34] Taking advantage of an obscure state law that facilitated the creation of independent political parties, Carmichael managed, in one stroke, to defy both the civil rights establishment and the Democratic Party while promoting two of the movement's major goals: black voter registration and political participation. Assuring locals that the all-black party was open to whites, Carmichael and LCFO members began an intensive education mission for first-time voters that included classes in African history and literacy. In addition, SNCC organizers played tapes of

Malcolm X and produced pamphlets that broke down the intricacies of local politics, offering simple directions to new voters. In the midst of organizing Alabama's only black-led political party*—known in the press and by locals as the Black Panther Party—Carmichael outlined SNCC's plans. "It's very simple," he said. "We intend to take over Lowndes County."[35]

SNCC's earlier, failed efforts to infiltrate the national Democratic Party partially inspired Carmichael's strategy in Alabama. In 1964, SNCC wanted to replace the all-white Mississippi delegation with one that represented the state's interracial population; however, a compromise, brokered at the last minute, left the insurgent Mississippi Freedom Democratic Party humiliated and robbed of the franchise in the middle of the presidential nominating convention. For Carmichael, the Atlantic City ambush provided clarity: raw political power, not social integration, would purchase black freedom, and until then, local people would shoulder the cost because no northern armies of white liberals would descend upon the likes of Lowndes County. This left blacks to organize, finance, and control the movement. Aware that such thinking bordered on blasphemy in an interracial movement that depended on white financial assistance, Carmichael was unapologetic. "SNCC has to become less popular because it's going to have to say the things I'm talking about."[36] In Lowndes, long-standing traditions of southern black community organizing collided with SNCC's new militancy. Since its inception, SNCC had successfully blended old and new traditions, providing a creative tension that accounted for the group's stubbornness, political commitment, and physical courage.[37] SNCC's new plans for black self-reliance in Alabama involved downgrading interracial organizing as a means of gaining white liberal support in service of elusive dreams of integration. Black nationalism, long viewed as the opposite of racial integration, now promised to hold the key to building urban power bases across the nation.

---

*There were at least two other black-led political parties in America at this time: the Mississippi Freedom Democratic Party and the Freedom Now Party.

Alabama provided cover for SNCC's more radical plans. State law required a new party's nominating convention to take place near a public polling facility—in the case of Lowndes, the courthouse, which also served as Democratic Party headquarters. After the county sheriff informed the LCFO that its convention would receive no police protection, Carmichael contacted the Justice Department's John Doar, who dispatched a federal official to huddle with local organizer John Hulett. Cautioned by Doar's emissary "not to start any trouble," Hulett responded with his usual directness. "We don't intend to" start any trouble. "We are within our rights. We will come armed. You tell the crackers not to start any trouble, because if they start something we're going to finish it."[38] These were no idle threats. Armed guards, including members of the Deacons for Defense and Justice, a self-defense group from Bogalusa, Louisiana, protected local rallies.[39] After an all-night meeting, the Justice Department lawyer produced documents signed by Alabama attorney general Richmond Flowers and the Lowndes County Probate Court judge on behalf of the LCFO. The decision included one important compromise. The LCFO would hold its nominating convention at the First Baptist Church of Hayneville, a half mile from the county courthouse.[40] Nine hundred African Americans attended the nominating convention, on May 3, 1966, to place the black panther on the ballot for the upcoming November election. LCFO's use of the coiled animal as the party's symbol would prove to be more than a creative inducement against local disfranchisement.

Five days after this minor miracle in Lowndes, Carmichael became SNCC chairman during the group's annual election, at Kingston Springs, Tennessee. In truth it was a symbolic position, since SNCC's decentralized structure ensured that important decisions required the approval of an executive body. But Carmichael's election over the more moderate John Lewis served as the capstone for SNCC's radical orientation. A series of debates, internal criticisms, and policy proposals found veteran activists reflecting on the lessons they had learned in six short years. Among the most profound was the admission that SNCC's earlier calls for an interracial democracy, absent the corrupting values of political power, had been hopelessly naive. Member Ivanhoe Donaldson argued that SNCC should acknowledge the role of black nationalism in community organizing, establish closer ties to Third World revolutionaries, and help white supporters organize within their own communities. The last suggestion had been the subject of an aggressively written "black position paper," authored months earlier by SNCC activists in Atlanta.[41] Donaldson's presentation mixed SNCC's grassroots approach to organizing with a knowing recognition of what he described as the group's "radical mystique."[42]

In his role as chairman, Carmichael immediately sparked controversy by rejecting an invitation to attend the civil rights conference to be held at the White House; he publicly described integration as "an insidious subterfuge for white supremacy." This remark brought swift rebuke from King, who regretted SNCC's overt flirtation with black nationalism.[43] The press, which had greeted news of Carmichael's election as a triumph for black militants, positioned Carmichael and King on opposite poles of the movement's growing political and generational divide. In this sense, Carmichael assumed Malcolm X's role as King's most visible adversary. King's criticism of Carmichael's brash statements belied what would, in spite of tactical disagreements, develop into a cordial friendship. In fact, shortly after his election, King called Carmichael to offer congratulatory words and advice.[44] Over the next two years, their relationship would constitute an ideological and generational dialogue. Sparked by a one-man political crusade, King, the template for an era, and Carmichael—soon to become one himself—found themselves at the center of the last great march of the civil rights movement and the nation's first recognition of Black Power.

7

"WHAT WE GONNA START SAYIN'
NOW IS BLACK POWER!"

Black Power echoed through America in the summer of 1966 all the way to the Mississippi Delta, a region that had done its best to remain deaf. In a late spring heat wave, hundreds descended upon Mississippi in a march that was as much about outrage as it was civil rights. The demonstrators, led by Martin Luther King Jr. and Stokely Carmichael, marched through the Magnolia State in defiance of white terror. The hastily planned event continued James Meredith's solo March Against Fear, which had begun on Sunday, June 5. Four years earlier, Meredith had become a household name as days of rioting intended to keep him from enrolling at the University of Mississippi pushed the Kennedy administration into the civil rights front. In that earlier confrontation, the former governor Ross Barnett emerged as Meredith's main foil, a "proud Mississippi segregationist" in public who privately engaged in tense negotiating sessions with the White House to enroll Meredith at Ole Miss.[1]

Four years later, there were no made-for-television antagonists eager to fulfill pre-scripted roles to forward the nation's racial progress. This time America's entire social system was the villain—an unapologetic harbinger of racial segregation, poverty, and white supremacy. In 1966, a determined Meredith challenged this system with his feet. While his supporters scratched their heads, Meredith vowed to walk alone from Memphis, Tennessee, to Jackson, Mississippi, to combat "the pervasive fear" of the state's black residents to exercise their constitutional rights. The idea of a one-man march was unusual, to say the least. Feisty, temperamental, and unpredictable, Meredith was something of a mystery to friends and foes alike. Dressed in a pith hat, sunglasses, and an ivory-tipped walking cane, he cut an impressive figure on a journey that would be a homecoming of sorts. Since graduating from Ole Miss in 1963, Meredith had visited the state just once, after the death of his father. A small group of reporters, photographers, and curiosity-seekers trailed after him as Meredith began his solitary walk in Memphis, at the Peabody Hotel, twelve miles north of the Mississippi state border.[2] On the second day of Meredith's planned 220-mile trek, Aubrey James Norvell, an unemployed Memphis contractor, ambushed him, firing multiple shots. Pictures of a wounded Meredith dragging himself along the highway made front-page news.[3] A stream of distinguished visitors descended on Meredith's bedside at Bowld Hospital, seeking proof for themselves that initial wire reports announcing his death were false. They also sought permission to continue what became known as the Meredith March. King, accompanied by the newly elected head of the Congress of Racial Equality, Floyd McKissick, promised his support. Carmichael, with his colleague Cleveland Sellers, arrived shortly after, turning Meredith's hospital room into a movement planning session.[4]

Struck in the neck, back, and both legs by buckshot, Meredith was seriously injured but would recover. A furious Meredith proclaimed that he had been shot down like "a goddamn rabbit" and publicly regretted having carried no arms.[5] What started as a local story of limited interest, described by *Newsweek* as "Meredith's little march," now exploded into "the biggest parade since Selma."[6] From his Texas ranch, President Johnson issued a statement ordering Attorney General Nicholas Katzenbach "to spare no effort" in bringing Meredith's assailants to justice.[7] The shooting provided fresh momentum for civil rights legislation, offering proponents of the president's new civil rights bill with an unexpected opportunity to argue that the federal government was responsible for the safety of civil rights workers in the Deep South. But supporters of the bill also saw new dangers. House Judiciary chair Emanuel Celler, a Brooklyn congressman and a cosponsor of the bill, warned against the influence of black nationalists, identifying Carmichael, James Baldwin, and LeRoi Jones as provocateurs behind a growing trend of racial militancy.[8]

Marchers experienced blistering ninety-degree temperatures along Federal Highway 51, through the red clay roads of the backwater towns of Midnight, Coldwater, and Philadelphia.[9] They walked south, from the state's northernmost regions, destined for Jackson, the capital. Clashes over armed self-defense, interracial cooperation, and political tactics marked the walk through Mississippi. On June 7, two sets of marchers gathered in Hernando. The activist and comedian Dick Gregory headed a small contingent that retraced Meredith's twenty-six miles back to Memphis. King, Carmichael, and McKissick led a larger group, continuing the 194 miles remaining to Jackson. The drama continued to unfold as King, Carmichael, and others marched south away from Hernando. Three Mississippi state troopers forced demonstrators from the main road. "Get off this highway!" yelled one. The group could march on the side of the road but not on the highway. "We walked" on the highway from "Selma to Montgomery," objected a surprised King. They could march to "China," a trooper replied, as long as they stayed on the side of the road.[10] Following this exchange, troopers pushed members of the group to the side of the road. Cleveland Sellers was shoved into the mud while Carmichael braced himself on one knee and fell to the ground; King tumbled over him. Reporters scribbled notes and photographers snapped pictures as demonstrators rolled around the highway. At one point, King restrained a visibly angry Carmichael.[11] Most of those assembled had experienced, and seen, far worse. Yet during a minor scuffle, the troopers' comparatively tame act of indecency would catalyze those proposing a new militancy in black freedom struggles.[12] Plans to stretch the limits of accepted protest tactics, already quietly under way, were accelerated as organizers encountered early resistance.

Meredith's shooting briefly created a broad coalition among movement factions, with Whitney Young of the Urban League and Roy Wilkins of the NAACP arriving in Memphis from New York to participate. Two days after Meredith was shot, Wilkins called on local NAACP chapters to hold rallies both to protest the shooting and to commemorate the assassination of Medgar Evers.[13] There were also practical considerations. As one observer noted, the NAACP had flown into town to "see that the march didn't go nationalist as it went national."[14] The meeting started off promisingly. Carmichael, Sellers, and Stanley Wise represented SNCC. The Meredith shooting propelled Carmichael into crisis mode. After visiting Meredith, he flew to Atlanta to pitch the idea of SNCC's participation in the march to a sympathetic but skeptical executive committee. Granted permission, Carmichael and his colleagues planned to make the march an example of SNCC's commitment to the empowerment of local blacks in the Mississippi Delta.[15]

King and Bernard Lee, representing the Southern Christian Leadership Conference, and McKissick of CORE were already at the meeting when Carmichael and his two associates walked in. Wilkins and Young were the last to arrive. Two of America's most prominent civil rights leaders, they possessed tremendous influence, their range of contacts stretching from business and civic groups all the way to the White House. Conservatively attired in suits and carrying imperious-looking briefcases, they commanded the presence and authority of elected officials. Meeting Carmichael for the first time to hammer out delicate negotiations, Wilkins and Young questioned the presence of Sellers and Wise. "Martin, you know we talk with generals," Wilkins insisted, "not with rank and file."[16] After a brief debate, Carmichael's associates stayed—but with the understanding that SNCC retained only one vote. Then Wilkins laid out the NAACP's plans, assuring those present that money, press coverage, and national support were guaranteed as long as all agreed to forgo vigorous criticism of the Johnson administration.

Carmichael offered a different vision. Carmichael's plan favored local involvement over northern troops, unlettered activists over visiting dignitaries, and a permanent community-based movement over a media-driven spectacle. Recalling this meeting three decades later, Carmichael summed up SNCC's perspective: "Our folk would be doing the marching. SNCC projects would be doing the organizing. We could turn it into a moving freedom day."[17] McKissick voiced support for SNCC's ideas, but Wilkins objected to Carmichael's call that the march be limited to local blacks. SNCC's willingness to accept the support of the Deacons for Defense and Justice also spurred contention. King moderated the evening's debates, but his stately presence did not quell heated exchanges between Carmichael and Wilkins. Several issues, including the level of militancy, criticism of the Johnson administration's civil rights record, and the presence of the Deacons for Defense, made the unity of purpose that all sought difficult to attain. Debate over the march's political direction turned into an all-night discussion over the march's proposed statement of principles. Wilkins and Young argued that marchers should work to strengthen the pending civil rights bill, while Carmichael backed a more comprehensive statement, to be issued by march leaders, focusing on the federal government's failure to enforce existing civil rights laws.[18] After all sides agreed to moderate the language of the "march manifesto," a temporary détente was reached; the next morning Young and Wilkins refused to sign it. They objected to, among other things, the description of the document as a "manifesto," for fear that it would link them to Communists; King's signature on the "manifesto" would undermine Wilkins and Young's line of argument.[19] Having lost a test of wills with youngsters they considered rabble-rousers, Wilkins and Young departed for New York, but not before telling anyone who would listen that the march would be a disaster.[20] With the most conservative leadership banished north, Carmichael set out to make Mississippi a test case for SNCC's radical ideas. "We decided," he would recall, "to use the march for an education purpose."[21] Recent experiences in Lowndes County would prove key.

Even with the departure of the Big Two, debates between King and Carmichael over the march's direction continued.[22] More than a decade into his public career, King had been awarded a Nobel Peace Prize in recognition of his civil rights activism. In his capacity as the broker of the historic, albeit tortured, alliance between the federal government and the civil rights movement, King lent the occasion credibility and vital resources. As a young political activist who had spent the past five years engaged in the thankless but crucial task of door-to-door organizing in the rural South, Carmichael lacked King's impressive portfolio. Reporters enthusiastically played up the generational differences between the two, casting the soon-to-be-twenty-five-year-old Carmichael as the latest foil of King, twelve and a half years his senior. In the words of one periodical, King was the movement's "main-liner," while the youthful Carmichael was its "hard-liner."[23] Carmichael refused to shrink at the wide gulf between himself and King, choosing instead to regard King as a cherished colleague and personal equal. If King was rightfully considered the movement's public face, Carmichael reflected the movement's private pain, youthful buoyancy, and hidden passions. The Meredith March bound Carmichael and King as close comrades even as it drew stark tactical lines between them. Behind closed doors, the two men enjoyed an easy familiarity. King admired Carmichael's commitment to struggle, and Carmichael appreciated King's unassuming demeanor and earthy sense of humor. Organizing the march allowed Carmichael to see a different, less formal, side of King. "During those sweltering Delta days Dr. King became to many of us no longer a symbol or an icon," he remembered, "but a warm, funny, likeable, unpretentious human being who shared many of our values."[24]

The divergent perspectives of the organizations they headed, however, magnified their tactical differences. SNCC harnessed the energies of black students who fashioned a take-no-prisoners approach to political struggle. Overshadowed by civil rights leaders who remained at the center of crises only long enough for well-timed photo ops, SNCC members considered themselves the movement's shock troops, unglamorous organizers who risked their lives for principle. Founded in the aftermath of the Montgomery bus boycott, the Southern Christian Leadership Conference waged high-profile political campaigns in major cities across the South. In the late 1950s, SCLC's political chutzpah and penchant for grabbing headlines created friction with the venerable NAACP, which viewed King's operation as publicity-seeking upstarts. SCLC flourished despite these tensions, attracting skilled organizers and helping to frame local struggles for national consumption.

Each day of the march, awkward situations arose, inviting a tug-of-war between moderates and radicals that could be seen in the demeanor and attitude of marchers. Movement chants and slogans that in the past had reflected unity of purpose now revealed widening political and ideological gulfs. When King and SCLC workers shouted "Freedom!" to blacks along the march, SNCC workers countered with "Uhuru!," the Swahili word for "freedom."[25] Tensions flared when King, sporting dark shades and a straw hat, and Carmichael, hands nonchalantly in the back of his blue overalls, were interviewed walking at the head of the march. Asked whether the Meredith incident would shake the movement's resolve, King dutifully professed his unwavering commitment to nonviolence, while Carmichael casually proclaimed his tactical rather than philosophical support.[26]

Protected by the Deacons for Defense and recruiting black volunteers along the way, the Meredith March quickly became something different from what Meredith himself had envisioned.[27] The Deacons represented an ever-present but hidden feature of the civil rights era: armed self-defense. Memories of Robert Williams's escapades, while fading in the minds of most Americans, remained a powerful, if also ignored, part of the black freedom movement. Few observers knew, for instance, that even the apostle of nonviolence—Martin Luther King Jr.—had, for a time at least, been under armed guard, during the watershed Montgomery bus boycott.[28] Like a band of southern guerrillas, the Deacons offered protection that local and federal authorities seemed unable or unwilling to provide. Organized in 1964 to safeguard parts of Louisiana and Mississippi against the sharp uptick in Klan activity precipitated by the passage of the Civil Rights Act, the Deacons were a group of hard-edged working-class black men whose very presence magnified issues of self-defense and violence. By the march's end, the specter of armed self-defense that haunted the movement like a fitful dream would emerge in the public witness of Stokely Carmichael.[29]

The march's first days featured a mixture of small crowds, newspaper reporters, and curiosity-seekers. Leaders hashed out logistical details and conferred with local organizers: Would voter registration facilities be available in each town? Specific distances were meant to be covered during the day, followed by evening church meetings and planning sessions.[30] Demonstrators experienced multiple sources of harassment: speeding cars zoomed within inches of marchers; at night, white mobs shouted racial slurs and brandished guns as activists set up tents; and hoodlums chased roving voter registration teams down Mississippi highways, attacking them with bottles and rocks.[31] The character of the march seemed to change shape from town to town, with the Delta's deepest recesses offering much-needed support and enthusiasm.

Three days after being shot, Meredith left the hospital amid reports that warring civil rights groups taking part in the march had "patched up their differences" and agreed to focus on strengthening the president's impending civil rights legislation. In the town of Coldwater, organizers released a manifesto signed by representatives of SCLC, SNCC, CORE, the National Council of Churches, and Charles Evers, Mississippi's NAACP field director and the brother of slain activist Medgar Evers.[32] Some 150 demonstrators were joined by about 400 local supporters as they passed through Coldwater's hilly countryside.[33]

In a sudden about-face, Charles Evers publicly charged that the march was exploiting Mississippi at the expense of local blacks and the NAACP. His statement brought renewed focus on internal conflicts just as the march, now in the town of Sardis, faced new restrictions from local officials. An order banning journalists, organizers, and demonstrators from parking within a mile of the march met with reports of state troopers calling marchers "niggers." For the first time, demonstrators spent the night along the march route, and more than three dozen white supporters joined the main column.[34] On Saturday, June 11, marchers stopped at the Batesville County Courthouse and registered fifty black voters. While El Fondren, a retired farmer who claimed to be 106 years old, was the most notable registrant, applause greeted all those brave enough to register.[35]

In the town of Oakland, marchers encountered rain, intimidation, and apathy as scattered groups of organizers canvassed the region, sometimes traveling as far as fifty miles away from the march route, in hopes of registering rural voters. Revelations that the Deacons provided armed escorts and carried guns in their cars stirred heated exchanges among certain demonstrators that were reported in the press as proof that the movement was in danger of collapse.[36]

Small miracles greeted demonstrators in Grenada. On Tuesday, June 14, Flag Day, jubilant men and women crossed the Yalobusha River Bridge singing and imploring spectators to "Come on over." The appeals proved irresistible to locals who joined the march en masse.[37] Grenada officials proved unusually accommodating. King, back from Chicago after a two-day absence, and McKissick met with town officials to hammer out details of the appointment of black voter registration officials as demonstrators tentatively used washrooms to test equal access to public facilities.[38] Beneath a hot sun, one group of protesters surrounded a monument of Confederate president Jefferson Davis and placed an American flag atop it.[39] White residents, arms impassively folded, glumly watched the scene as they listened to the SCLC's Robert Green crow, "We're tired of seeing rebel flags. Give me the flag of the United States, the flag of freedom."[40] Grenada's remarkable turnaround was the feel-good story of a march lacking the clear-cut drama associated with past campaigns in Selma and Birmingham.[41]

But the promise of racial integration in Grenada proved to be short-lived. During Green's impromptu "desecration" of Davis's statue, one man had fumed that he recognized "two" of his "niggers" in the crowd. "They won't have any jobs tomorrow," he promised.[42] After the demonstrators left, the black registrars lost their jobs and public facilities were quickly resegregated.[43]

Meanwhile, Carmichael's aide Willie Ricks continued to lead advance teams of organizers throughout the Delta. A rakish pied piper in charge of crowd preparation, Ricks led sharecroppers from plantation cotton fields into marching lines with evangelical fervor.[44] Plans were afoot to unveil SNCC's new slogan in Greenwood. Black residents of Greenwood felt an affinity for Carmichael; they believed he was one of them. Two years earlier, during the Freedom Summer drive, Carmichael had served as SNCC's project director there, so he knew the area and its activists. He also knew Greenwood's jails, having been arrested so frequently that virtually the "whole town," including the police chief, recognized him.[45]

On June 15, demonstrators traveling on the shoulder of Federal Highway 51 walked on freshly cut grass, courtesy of state maintenance workers. State troopers acted as an advance security force, fanning out miles ahead of human columns, preparing towns for the arrival of the demonstrators. John Doar, of the Department of Justice, praised the patrolmen while one journalist extolled the dramatic "new mood" that had taken over white Mississippians.[46] King, headed back to Chicago for two days, was more skeptical of the state's change of heart, characterizing Mississippi's attitude as "a more sophisticated form of resistance to racial desegregation."[47]

On Thursday, June 16, Governor Paul B. Johnson Jr. reversed his policy of heavy protection, telling reporters that he refused to "wet nurse a bunch of showmen." The governor's actions had serious consequences. White vigilantes took note of the state's shifting mood; one gun-toting spectator heckled, harassed, and threatened marchers with impunity.[48] Local officials added to the day's surprises, rescinding approval of Stone Street Negro Elementary School as an evening campsite—the type of arbitrary justice that made the idea of law and order in parts of the South seem like some sort of cosmic joke. After a confrontation with the city's public safety commissioner over the campsite, Carmichael and two colleagues were arrested for trespassing. "Let them arrest you," Ricks told Carmichael. "We'll get you out of jail, and you come out and make the speech tonight." And with those words, Ricks vanished.[49]

Released after spending several hours in jail, an agitated Carmichael made his way to Broad Street Park (where marchers had been given be-lated permission to set up a campsite) and into history.[50] With a tractor-trailer as a stage and Ricks, who had been prepping the crowd, by his side, Carmichael began speaking. Slowly, he discussed his past work in Greenwood and his personal relationship with its residents, before introducing the slogan "Black Power." "This is the twenty-seventh time that I've been arrested. I ain't going to jail no more. The only way we gonna stop them white men from whuppin' us is to take over. What we gonna start sayin' now is Black Power!" He was just be-ginning. "The white folks in the state of Mississippi ain't nothing but a bunch of racists," proclaimed a visibly angry Carmichael. As he pep-pered the members of the crowd with the question "What do we want?" they enthusiastically responded, "Black Power!" The day's events had turned the assembly into a kind of an outdoor church meet-ing with Carmichael starring in the role of country preacher. "Every courthouse in Mississippi," he said, "ought to be burned down to get rid of the dirt."[51]

After years in the Delta, Carmichael favored plain, deceptively sim-ple language. The softest remnant of his Caribbean accent inflected his speech, punctuating his words with an urgent lyricism. The clipped speaking style that mesmerized the crowd drew from both his Bronx childhood and the more recent time he spent in the Deep South.[52] Though Carmichael's language lacked King's controlled cadences and rhetorical polish, he borrowed the rhythms and flourishes of the Harlem street speakers he listened to as a young boy, introducing to civil rights a new brand of rhetorical militancy. Yet Carmichael's defi-ant, in-your-face posture suggested a younger Malcolm X, as did his quick wit and obvious intelligence. To the untrained eye, the gangly speaker appeared neither in control of his emotions nor body. Carmichael's unpredictable body language fueled the moment's raw intensity, flaming passions and building a rapport between him and the audience that electrified some, frightened others, and marked a public turning point for the black freedom movement. For the rest of the march, Carmichael would raise the slogan "Black Power" to excited crowds while Ricks and Sellers distributed Black Power pamphlets and posters courtesy of SNCC's printing offices in Atlanta.[53]

King arrived in Greenwood the day after Carmichael's "Black Power" speech, the second consecutive day of high tension. At a mass rally at Greenwood's Leflore County Courthouse, leaders in command of columns that each approached one thousand people ran a bizarre gauntlet, including a service attendant who water-hosed demonstrators, sheriff's deputies who assaulted one of King's top aides, and the frightening figure of Byron de la Beckwith, Medgar Evers's unconvicted assassin. From the courthouse steps, Carmichael repeated his call for self-determination: "The only way we can change things in Mississippi is with the ballot. That's black power."[54] Carmichael's and King's respective aides, Ricks and Hosea Williams, led the evening rally with parallel chants of "Black Power" and "Freedom Now," a development that caused King private anguish, since it smacked more of competition than friendly humor.[55]

On June 19, the thirteenth day of the march, its ranks increased to twelve hundred in the farm town of Belzoni, an area "rich in cotton and racial hate" deep in the Delta.[56] Sharecroppers from surrounding plantations, a landless peasantry that toiled in anonymity, walked outside the town limits, forming a parallel column that swelled the demonstration when the two groups converged.[57] For most of their lives, Belzoni locals had experienced the kind of poverty that was unimaginable to many Americans. Yet many still dared to hope; two years earlier, the Mississippi Freedom Summer had cut through generations of illiteracy, fear, and violence to register black voters. The price had been steep, and included the violent deaths of Michael Schwerner, James Chaney, and Andrew Goodman. Now the Meredith March roused the humblest to their feet. For a demonstration that had seen as few as three dozen participants along some stretches of highway, this showing represented a remarkable upswing.[58]

As the march moved through the Delta, Carmichael took time off to appear on the news program *Face the Nation*.[59] Dressed in a suit and tie that reflected his deliberative intellect, often overshadowed by his provocative words, Carmichael was asked whether Black Power could be equated with violence. As he had done many times before, but never in front of a national audience, Carmichael asserted his qualified support for nonviolence—at which point the interview, conducted by Martin Agronsky, went downhill.[60]

> AGRONSKY: But you seem to be arguing that wherever the Negroes cannot get what they wish they are entitled to use violent methods to achieve it.
>
> CARMICHAEL: On the contrary. I have never said that.
>
> AGRONSKY: You are not saying it?
>
> CARMICHAEL: I am not saying that. I have never said that. When I talk about black power I talk about black people in the counties where they out-number them to get together, to organize themselves politically and to take over those counties from white racists who now run it.[61]

According to Carmichael, Black Power emanated from the hopes and dreams of people in rural communities, a view that reflected his experiences as an activist. Pressed by James Doyle about Alabama's "Black Panther Party," Carmichael interjected, "The name of the organization in Lowndes County is not the Black Panther Party," reminding his audience that the panther was only a symbol of the local black political group.[62] Yet within a year, the black panther would emerge as the defining symbol for an entire generation.

The march's final days were equal parts anger, delirium, and resignation.[63] On Saturday, June 25, Meredith returned to the walk he had started more than two weeks earlier, and promptly initiated his own march, from Canton to Tougaloo, after being inadvertently left behind by the march's coordinators.[64] King, Carmichael, and one thousand other demonstrators converged near the Tougaloo College campus in preparation for the final eight-mile leg to Jackson.[65] The school became the site for a reunion of sorts, with the appearance of movement veterans including King's former aide Wyatt Tee Walker and former SNCC executive director James Forman. Behind the scenes, officials haggled over the next day's program. Charles Evers and Whitney Young now wanted to participate. Young agreed to endorse the previously controversial "march manifesto" and in exchange received a place on the program. Evers, whose support for the march had been marred by inconsistencies, was not offered a place.[66] SNCC workers passed out bumper stickers featuring a black panther; young women hawked buttons. A star-studded rally featuring the entertainers Sammy Davis Jr., Burt Lancaster, and Dick Gregory capped off the evening.[67]

The Meredith March concluded on Sunday, June 26, 1966, as a crowd estimated at between twelve thousand and fifteen thousand people assembled in front of the Mississippi State Capitol Building. Thousands poured into columns toward the capitol grounds, marching in step with a four-piece band. Sharply dressed men and women, fresh from church in their Sunday best, were joined by the more casually attired as they all headed toward the capitol. National Guardsmen armed with riot guns and tear gas and hundreds of state and local law enforcement officers provided security in case of potential violence in the aftermath of what Governor Johnson labeled as "weeks of provocation."[68] The burning of the Confederate flag on the capitol grounds by a SNCC member drew large applause and, in spite of a few arguments with police officers, a festive mood filled the the air.[69] Meredith dismissed reports of internal squabbling among the demonstrators. "From what you've seen on television and what you have read in the newspapers," he quipped, "you might assume that I have been shot by a Negro, since all you've been hearing is about the Negroes being divided."[70] Struggling with the reality of a national political landscape that might not keep up with the pace of black militancy, King confessed to cheering thousands that his dream "had turned into a nightmare."[71] Riffing on his "I Have a Dream" speech, King defiantly proclaimed "that even in Mississippi justice will come to all of God's children."[72]

Carmichael sounded an alternative note. The movement, he said, had to build a political base so powerful that blacks would "bring them [whites] to their knees every time they mess with us."[73] An earlier afternoon scene between SNCC activists and an elderly black woman illustrated in miniature the world that Carmichael invoked in his speech. As the march drew to a close, a car full of SNCC activists passed Mollie Gray, a sixty-one-year-old domestic. They implored her to join in their jubilant chants. Sipping ice water under a mimosa tree, Mrs. Gray, amused by the audaciousness of it all, chuckled and cried out "Black Power."[74]

Black Power would scandalize American politics. The national media seized upon Carmichael's declaration of "Black Power" as the signpost of a new militancy. Following the Meredith March, *Time* judged the slogan to be "a racist philosophy" that preached segregation in reverse. *Newsweek* called it a "distorted cry" that frightened whites. In a similar vein, the *Saturday Evening Post,* editorializing that the phrase would precipitate "a new white backlash," confessed its own prejudices: "We are all, let us face it, Mississippians. We all fervently wish that the Negro problem did not exist, or that, if it must exist, it could be ignored." *U.S. News and World Report* agonized over the term, looking toward "Negro moderates" to allay fears that the words promoted reverse discrimination.[75] King distanced himself from the slogan but refused to censure the meaning behind the message or the messenger. Triumphant and slightly bewildered by his notoriety, Carmichael emerged from Mississippi as the spokesman for a generation of black radicals. If King and the SCLC represented a movement that expressed, with quiet dignity and social reserve, an unwillingness to wait for racial justice, Carmichael and SNCC portrayed the impatient face of political anger.

SNCC underwent significant changes as well. John Lewis resigned from the group shortly after the march. A deeply spiritual man who had been among the first students attracted to King's interpretation of the philosophy of nonviolent direct action, Lewis took issue with the group's new political emphasis and was hurt and angry that Carmichael had replaced him as SNCC chairman.[76]

In its aftermath, critics characterized the incident as the rude behavior of the movement's enfants terribles. The truth was far more complicated. For several years, SNCC made slow, painstaking inroads into dismantling white supremacy through voter registration and education. SNCC's critics targeted even these reforms; for example, SNCC's call for black voters in Alabama to boycott the Democratic primary was described as "destructive mischief-making."[77] SNCC's attempt to establish a black political base in Lowndes County, which Carmichael had spearheaded, was attacked as the "rule or ruin" strategy of "extremists" out to "sabotage" racial reform in Alabama.[78] The criticism hurt SNCC, which—unlike the mainstream civil rights organizations—enjoyed no more than a grudging tolerance from the federal government and the media. At the same time, six years of tireless organizing had taken its toll. Frayed nerves led to heated arguments; contributions dried up. Factionalism, which SNCC's decentralized structure had been intended to discourage, developed as individuals followed divergent political paths, including black nationalism, which many within SNCC had once casually dismissed.[79] Escalating pressures led to health problems and a transformation in the physical appearance of SNCC members, whose "haggard" faces reflected a particular kind of combat experience.[80]

But still Stokely Carmichael emerged as the undisputed leader of Black Power. Carmichael himself admitted that the movement had "grown out of the ferment of agitation and activity by different people and organizations in many black communities over the years."[81] Paul Robeson, Richard Wright, and Adam Clayton Powell had used the term, just as the activism of Malcolm X, Robert Williams, and Gloria Richardson had embodied the phrase, even before its widespread use. The writings of Lorraine Hansberry and Harold Cruse, the music of Nina Simone, Abbey Lincoln, and Max Roach, and the traveling urban pageants of the African Jazz Arts Society also reflected the movement's diverse cultural forebears. Yet the movement's complex pre-history would quickly fade. Almost as soon as it was uttered, a new wave of black aspirations, dreams, and dissent became encapsulated within one powerful slogan—Black Power—that would become as hard to define as it would remain controversial.

The bitter antagonisms that were barely contained by the Meredith shooting erupted the next month, at the twenty-third annual convention of the Congress of Racial Equality, in Baltimore in July 1966. Founded as an interracial civil rights organization in the 1940s and energized by the well-publicized Freedom Rides in the early 1960s, CORE was in the process of embracing Black Power. Fannie Lou Hamer, the middle-aged former sharecropper whose public witness against Mississippi's racial violence earned her Malcolm X's respect as well as the awe and admiration of militants and moderates, blasted "chickeny black preachers" and "the Negro bourgeoisie and Ph.D.'s" for selling out the masses of blacks intent on pursuing power.[82] Carmichael, arriving in place of King, said that blacks needed to "define" their own "tactics," whether whites approved or not, going on to criticize America's escalating war in Vietnam.[83] Lyndon Johnson's recent decision to bomb oil depots in Hanoi and Haiphong dramatized Carmichael's insistence that discussion of nonviolence in the movement be tabled as long as "the United States continues to commit violence in Vietnam."[84] Although King maintained that his pastoral duties in Atlanta had kept him away from Baltimore, his aides told another story. Convinced that SNCC's Black Power slogan had been launched at the expense of the larger movement—in the process harming King's reputation—SCLC staff members charged that CORE was "yelling 'black power' louder than SNCC" and advised King against appearing at the convention.[85] Even absent the prestige that King's attendance would have conferred, the meeting made national headlines. While not explicitly rejecting the slogan, James Farmer, the former CORE leader, warned delegates of their responsibility to explain the phrase to a skeptical public. Farmer's assertion that "the rule of 'black and white together' is still our guide" would be contradicted by convention proceedings during which former CORE allies were attacked, while stunned white supporters were hesitant to speak in open sessions.[86] On July 4, CORE announced its declaration of independence from the civil rights movement, stating that Black Power was official organizational policy. Four contentious days of debate defined the expression as a combination of race pride, economic independence, and political power. Reversing a decision that Farmer had made the previous year, CORE adopted a resolution opposing the war in Vietnam and offering support for draft resisters. McKissick, who, on the final day of the Meredith March, had heralded the evolution of "Negroes" to "black men," criticized President Johnson's approach to civil rights as paternalistic, while Harlem activist Jesse Gray predicted that the war for racial equality would be a street fight.[87]

The NAACP's fifty-seventh annual convention began in Los Angeles the day after CORE's ended. There, Roy Wilkins described CORE as an emerging threat to the NAACP's historic vision of a multiracial America. Efforts to discredit Black Power escalated during the second day, when Vice President Hubert Humphrey, without using the term, announced on the convention floor his support for civil rights, issuing words of caution to unnamed opponents: "Yes, racism is racism—and there is no room in America for racism of any color. And we must reject calls for racism, whether they come from a throat that is white or one that is black."[88] Fifteen hundred delegates greeted Humphrey's speech, which promised renewed federal commitment to civil rights and antipoverty programs, with a standing ovation.

On the last day of its convention, the NAACP issued a call for a sweeping reassessment of its relationship with other civil rights groups. The resolution proposed that the organization no longer cooperate with groups that duplicated its own work, that were financially unstable, or sought money from the same sources that gave to the national organization.[89] This was payback, in the form of reduced financial support, for CORE's declaration of war, SNCC's takeover of the Meredith March, and a host of recent slights, both real and imagined, against the NAACP and Wilkins.

Meanwhile, like an itinerant evangelist delivering sermons on black pride, self-determination, and political power, Carmichael continued to preach the gospel of Black Power around the country. While his charisma had been previously confined to the denizens of small backwater towns in the southern Delta, Carmichael now commanded the attention and adulation of a celebrity, having refined that impression thanks to his recent decision to trade in his overalls and dungarees for dark slacks, sunglasses, and leather jackets. Television and print media found a fascinating persona in the handsome activist. The legendary photojournalist Gordon Parks, who traveled with Carmichael for four months shortly after the Meredith March, came away impressed by his intellectual and social dexterity.[90] *Ebony* magazine credited Carmichael as the "architect" of Black Power while describing him as a leader who "walks like Sidney Poitier, talks like Harry Belafonte and thinks like the post-Muslim Malcolm X."[91]

The media wasn't the only group fascinated by Carmichael. The FBI, which had stepped up its surveillance of Carmichael since the Meredith March, was intensely interested in his public utterances. The first paragraph of a bureau memo describing one of his June television appearances noted that "Carmichael made no reference to the Director or the FBI."[92] Sensitive to the faintest whiff of public scrutiny, the bureau kept secret files noting that, during a CBS appearance two years earlier, Carmichael had criticized the FBI.[93] Carmichael's previous charges that investigators had not done "a damn thing" in the arena of civil rights now kept agents' eyes glued to *Face the Nation*.[94]

Nationally, Carmichael began to inspire a mixture of admiration and revulsion that rivaled the memory of Malcolm X. Unbeknownst to Carmichael, his career as a local organizer was coming to an end, curtailed by endless speaking engagements, media requests, opportunities and dangers undreamed of several months earlier.[95] Discussing his newfound fame, he sounded overwhelmed. "I'm an organizer. I want to go back to what I can do best. I'm too young for this job. I don't know enough about the outside world. I need time to read, learn, reflect. I think, perhaps, that more than anything else I'd like to be a college professor."[96]

If Carmichael's private side gravitated toward bookish introspection, his public charisma indisputably lent Black Power its wide appeal among a new generation of activists. Aspects of Black Power consciously sought to restore black male assertiveness through political organizing, something for which historical precedent existed. Carmichael's particular kind of male attractiveness recalled early-twentieth-century black leaders. The post–World War I New Negro Manhood Movement included veterans who had expressed their rage against Jim Crow by fighting in Europe. The contrast between the terrible cost of preserving democracy abroad and America's unapologetic commitment to white privilege at home made domestic racial unrest inevitable. Now, with notable exceptions, Black Power activists continued to embrace an aggressive vision of manhood—one centered on black men's ability to deploy authority, violence, punishment, and power—that amplified postwar masculinist rhetoric as it also aped the larger society's blinders regarding women's roles in political struggles.[97]

Media coverage of Carmichael perpetuated the image of Black Power as an all-boys club; while, nationally, journalists touted him as America's new racial arsonist. In contrast, television's sympathetic portrayal of the epic battles in Birmingham and Selma had helped turn the tide of world opinion in favor of civil rights. Liberal newspapers, magazines, and journals contributed to the recognition of civil rights as a moral good. Proclaiming that the end of segregation was a fight for American democracy's very soul proved effective in recruiting thousands of white participants into the struggle, along with more passive sympathizers who bristled at the news of another incident of racial violence.

Black Power, on the whole, received little public acceptance, instead garnering negative media coverage and confusion, anger, and even rage on the part of whites. Outraged citizens wrote letters to the FBI inquiring about the legality of Carmichael's citizenship.[98] Network television coverage routinely featured Carmichael in outrageous news clips designed to scare white Americans out of their wits, fears Carmichael did nothing to mitigate. Speaking in Cleveland in the wake of a recent riot there, Carmichael spoke in bombastic tones: "When you talk of black power, you talk of bringing this country to its knees." Declaring that Black Power meant the destruction of "Western Civilization," he urged black men to refuse to serve in Vietnam. These widely reported comments led Ohio's Democratic congressman to seek Carmichael's prosecution for violation of draft laws. Although the effort was unsuccessful, it would not be the last time that Carmichael drew the wrath of elected officials.[99]

Carmichael refused to censor himself. During a speaking tour of riot-torn Chicago in July 1966, Carmichael continued his efforts to build support for Black Power, meeting with community leaders, holding press conferences, and appearing on local radio and television. At a union hall for a late-evening speech, he addressed young black gang members in attendance, trying to convince them that Black Power, rather than gang warfare, held the key to their future.[100] During the same tour, he laid out the political, cultural, and intellectual outlines of Black Power. "This is 1966 and it seems to me that it's 'time out' for nice words," he began.[101] He recalled that as a child in school, he was told that if he worked hard enough he would succeed, but bitter experience had destroyed his youthful optimism. The sit-in movement and student activism had successfully challenged perceptions of blacks as lazy and shiftless; yet, just as quickly, another scapegoat was introduced. Referring to Assistant Secretary of Labor Daniel Patrick Moynihan's controversial report, "The Negro Family: The Case for National Action," which linked the roots of black poverty to the fact that a higher percentage of black than white households were headed by women, Carmichael railed against blacks willing to engage in dialogue with Lyndon Johnson while the president "talked about their mammas." "I don't play the dozens with white folks," he continued. "To set the record straight, the reason we are in this bag isn't because of my mamma, it's because of what they did to my mamma."[102]

Black people, he said, needed to reject negative images that assaulted them daily, choosing instead to see their broad noses, kinky hair, and thick lips as beautiful. "We have to stop being ashamed of being black," he said. "We are not going to fry our hair anymore but they can start wearing their hair natural to look like us."[103] Yet Carmichael proposed more than a cultural transformation. Blacks had to move beyond writing poems in the aftermath of Malcolm X's assassination and start building institutions.[104] No matter what the cost, and despite increased white opposition, black people would define

Black Power. "We can't let them project Black Power because they can only project it from white power and we know what white power has done to us."[105] There was hypocrisy, Carmichael noted, to liberal commentators eager to embrace the civil rights cry of "Freedom Now" but uncomfortable with Black Power. Whites, Carmichael explained, opposed Black Power because it would cost them influence they didn't want to lose. Everything that African Americans controlled was thanks to white approval, a historic illness that Carmichael maintained Black Power would cure. He went on to predict that within a decade, blacks would control "all the major cities," the possibility of which, with careful planning and solidarity, would allow blacks to "smash any political machine in the country that's oppressing us and bring it to its knees."[106]

During this speaking tour, Carmichael briefly met with King, before traveling to Detroit. King's campaign for jobs, housing, and racial justice in Chicago, which predated the Meredith March, had shifted dramatically. Spasms of violence on the city's West Side had erupted into days of rioting and with them an escalating battle between the police and residents. King's personal efforts to quell disturbances in the wake of the riot were met with fresh bursts of violence. After three consecutive days of chaos, Illinois governor Otto Kerner deployed four thousand members of the National Guard to restore order.[107] During a visit to Chicago in July, Carmichael invited King to the Labor Day Black Power conference in Washington, sponsored by Adam Clayton Powell and organized to define "Black Power."[108]

The timing of the planned conference seemed appropriate. July 1966 was an entire month of unabated urban rioting that included violence in Omaha, Nebraska; Amityville, Long Island; and Baltimore. Top law enforcement professionals offered conflicting explanations for the spate of violence. In the *New York Times,* Attorney General Katzenbach asserted that the riots were based on complex social and political factors, while FBI director Hoover issued a warning, taken from a recently released Senate Internal Security Subcommittee document, that the Communist Party had spread its tentacles into a constellation of domestic social activist groups. Offering more scandal than proof, Hoover tied Communists to a conspiratorial web that touched the breadth of American political and civic institutions, including labor, civil rights, student, and peace groups.[109] Contrasting statements—the FBI director pointing to a shadowy conspiracy just as the attorney general suggested that no such evidence existed—reflected the distinct experiences of two men who interpreted the civil rights movement through starkly different prisms.

While Hoover and Katzenbach issued mixed messages on behalf of the government regarding the origins of the escalating urban crisis, liberals of all colors appealed to the public sector and the private sector for help. At the Urban League's fifty-ninth annual convention, Whitney Young called for federal programs focused on transforming America's ghettoes.[110] In Raleigh, North Carolina, King outlined a ten-year initiative, costing $100 billion, for urban renewal patterned after the postwar Marshall Plan.[111] Former national security advisor turned Ford Foundation president McGeorge Bundy echoed both ideas, describing the black freedom struggle as "the most urgent domestic concern of this country." Acknowledging government's central role in providing opportunities for African Americans, Bundy unveiled the Ford Foundation's latest programs—in research, leadership, communications, and justice—developed to bolster the diminishing returns of Great Society legislation.[112] Newspaper columnist Tom Wicker also weighed in on the riots with an editorial that compared the cost of inner-city reconstruction with the war in Vietnam. For Wicker, the question was whether or not America, "after the long years of neglect and discrimination," was ready to pay overdue debts.[113]

Organizers of the Black Power conference appealed to a cross-section of black activists looking for answers to these questions, including Elijah Muhammad and the Nation of Islam. Carmichael met with the Messenger in early August, with the two men trying, and failing, to recruit the other. Muhammad offered Carmichael the organizational backing of the Black Muslims only if the young activist joined the group and recognized him as a modern-day prophet. Carmichael politely refused, backing out of an invitation to attend a Black Muslim rally at the end of August in Chicago.[114] Likewise, Muhammad declined Carmichael's invitation to the Labor Day Black Power conference, holding to a prophet's prerogative that *his* leadership would end the nation's racial turmoil. Nevertheless, the two maintained a cordial relationship, and *Muhammad Speaks* continued to prominently cover Carmichael's political activities.[115]

Prospects of a formal alliance between SNCC and the Nation of Islam faded just as two new controversies began. On August 10, Mendel Rivers, Democratic congressman from South Carolina, wrote the attorney general regarding Carmichael's antiwar statements. Rivers specifically inquired as to whether Carmichael's public speeches decrying American involvement in Vietnam violated the Universal Military Training and Service Act, charges that had already been leveled at Carmichael by a fellow congressman from Ohio.[116] Rivers's inquiry coincided with a crisis in SNCC. On August 12, the Philadelphia police, in a series of spectacularly coordinated and highly publicized assaults, simultaneously raided four SNCC offices, recovering two and a half sticks of dynamite.[117] Headlines credited Frank Rizzo, the city's crusading deputy police commissioner and future mayor, with uncovering a "dynamite plot" and branded SNCC as national instigators of urban violence.[118] Dubbed the Cisco Kid, after the character of 1940s-era movie serials, and popular for his brutally effective policing, Rizzo was a folk hero to white ethnic Philadelphians who greeted his loquacious bravado—he vowed to personally arrest Carmichael if he violated any city laws—as exactly the kind of backbone missing from the faceless Washington bureaucrats who were more concerned with civil liberties than law and order.[119] City officials justified the overwhelming force (eighty police officers) used in the raids by linking the dynamite to an imminent campaign of terror masterminded by SNCC.[120] Lurid headlines obscured what was largely a fictional crisis. Of the four persons arrested, only one was a SNCC staff member. The next spring, with little fanfare, the police would release the remaining three defendants of the dynamite plot.[121]

The Philadelphia incident coincided with the attorney general's candid testimony, before a Senate subcommittee on domestic disorders, that "some unpredictable event" could lead to rioting in dozens of

American cities. The hearings turned contentious when Katzenbach's former boss, New York senator Robert F. Kennedy, accused the Johnson administration of lacking a program to confront urban misery. "We're looking at all this as a whole for the first time in a generation," pleaded Katzenbach. "I'm just not satisfied," Kennedy interrupted, demanding an explanation for the Justice Department's failure to offer a comprehensive solution to escalating urban violence. "You've made that quite clear, Senator," replied Katzenbach. Katzenbach's testimony contained a startling revelation: namely that "disease and despair, joblessness and hopelessness, rat-infested housing and long impacted cynicism" were behind the riots, rather than conspiracies led by Communists or Black Power militants.[122]

As Katzenbach testified, Assistant Attorney General Fred Vinson responded to Rivers's letter about Carmichael with a pro forma note thanking the congressman for his interest and assuring him that, if warranted, an investigation would begin. Perturbed by the perfunctory reply, Rivers fired off another letter the next day. In stark language, Rivers reminded the attorney general of his position as chair of the House Armed Services Committee while threatening Katzenbach with the prospect of testimony before a House hearing related to Carmichael. Katzenbach got the message, apologizing for any misunderstanding and noting that although the First Amendment protected Carmichael's speeches, his antiwar statements could be used in a future prosecution. Mollified but still puzzled by Katzenbach's equivocation, Rivers asked the attorney general why he seemed unwilling to prosecute Carmichael.[123]

On August 21, as Rivers and Katzenbach engaged in their Beltway maneuverings, Carmichael appeared on *Meet the Press*. Introduced by moderator Edwin Newman as one of "six of the nation's top Negro leaders in their first joint live broadcast," Carmichael was the youngest participant in a distinguished panel that also featured King, Wilkins, Young, McKissick, and Meredith.[124] Black Power was only part of the discussion, which covered a range of topics: fallout from the Meredith March; debates over self-defense; the growing white backlash; the

Vietnam War; black unemployment; and the recently leaked memo on the state of the black family by Daniel Patrick Moynihan. Surrounded by peers and mentors, Carmichael was dignified and deferential, at times taking a back seat as questions were fired at his movement elders. Lawrence Spivak, one of the show's permanent panelists, opened the special ninety-minute edition by asking King whether America's civil rights crisis was "growing worse."[125] Despite significant progress, noted King, "there is still a tragic gulf between promise and fulfillment" unmet amid a growing tide of expectations. Pressed by the black conservative journalist Carl Rowan about divisions among civil rights leaders, Wilkins downplayed any conflicts. Pointing to both King's and SNCC's reliance on the justice system, Wilkins, the consummate insider, took satisfaction in the fact that, in spite of strategic and ideological differences, "we all come to the courtroom and to the law eventually." Following King's early departure and a station break, Carmichael responded to questions regarding his allegations that the white press purposely distorted the Black Power slogan. SNCC, he explained, had just decided that it would no longer define the term for the press. Carmichael reiterated his opposition to the war and voiced support for McKissick's and Meredith's contention that self-defense was a necessary option for blacks.* Reporters twice asked Wilkins and Carmichael for comment on SNCC's recently leaked Black Power position paper. Excerpted in the *New York Times* and erroneously attributed to Carmichael (it was, in fact, written by renegade members of SNCC's Atlanta Project), portions of the paper disparaged the NAACP as an organization whose work was hopelessly compromised by unresponsive leadership. Both men refused to take the bait. Near the program's conclusion, the syndicated columnist Rowland Evans, with assistance from Newman, questioned Carmichael about his upcoming activity:

---

*While asserting that white supremacy had to be abolished, by force if necessary, Meredith—an Air Force veteran—publicly supported the war. "I think that if we lose Vietnam, this nation will go down," he said at one point.

MR. EVANS: Mr. Carmichael, were you invited by Bertrand Russell to that so-called "War Crimes Trials" in Europe?

MR. CARMICHAEL: It is not so-called. It is a war tribunal.

MR. EVANS: Are you going?

MR. CARMICHAEL: Yes, we, the Student Nonviolent Coordinating Committee, have certainly accepted—

MR. EVANS: You personally?

MR. CARMICHAEL: —the invitation.

MR. NEWMAN: Invitation to what, Mr. Carmichael? Let's make it clear.

MR. CARMICHAEL: To attend the war tribunal that is being convened by Mr. Russell and—

MR. EVANS: Bertrand Russell. Are you going yourself, Mr. Carmichael?

MR. CARMICHAEL: I am not sure, but I'd like to very much.

MR. EVANS: You think President Johnson is guilty. Is that fair?

MR. CARMICHAEL: I didn't say I did. That is why I am going to the war tribunal, to see the evidence.

MR. EVANS: You think he may be?

MR. CARMICHAEL: I certainly don't agree with the war in Vietnam. I think it is an immoral war. Yes, I think it is an immoral war.

FBI officials requested transcripts of the program. Like Representative Rivers, the bureau zeroed in, both before and after the show, on Carmichael's frequent calls for young people to refuse the draft. In addition, the FBI continued to supply the White House with detailed summaries of Carmichael's activities, further advising field agents of the "intensification" of efforts to investigate Carmichael and SNCC, cautioning that, since SNCC was "primarily a civil rights organization" news of such efforts could damage the bureau.[126] Sedition was one of several potential charges against Carmichael being pursued by the FBI.

The bureau's and the White House's interest in Carmichael were complementary.[127] On the same day that Rivers initially contacted the attorney general, assistant FBI director Deke DeLoach received a telephone call from Marvin Watson, special assistant to the president. White House advisors informed the FBI of Johnson's concern "about the activities of Stokely Carmichael" and SNCC. Specifically, Johnson requested "reassurance that the FBI" had Carmichael under tight surveillance and urged the bureau to scrutinize possible ties to Communist organizations and front groups. Despite DeLoach's assurances that the FBI had "excellent sources" inside SNCC, Watson requested updated reports on Carmichael's activities "at least several times a week."[128] Two days later, the bureau asked for telephonic surveillance on Carmichael and SNCC's Atlanta offices. Katzenbach balked at giving the bureau free reign, reasoning that Carmichael "might violate the law and be prosecuted" in the near future. A week after Johnson's request and Katzenbach's demurral, memos to FBI special agents in charge in Atlanta, Washington, and New York ordered increased surveillance of Carmichael and SNCC.[129]

In Philadelphia, SNCC went on the defensive in response to a crisis triggered in part by local law enforcement. In Atlanta, Carmichael and SNCC's efforts to use Black Power as an organizing tool would unleash unexpected consequences for law enforcement, who claimed that SNCC inspired citywide unrest. On a mildly warm Tuesday in September in Atlanta, a police officer shot a black man suspected of car theft. The shooting ignited long-simmering tensions between local Vine City residents and white authorities. Located in southeast Atlanta, Vine City housed some of the city's poorest blacks, making it the flashpoint for SNCC's organizing efforts. Plagued by rats, poor services, and dilapidated housing, the neighborhood's conspicuous blight contrasted sharply with the gleaming skyline of downtown Atlanta. Vine City attracted a militant and tenacious SNCC cadre, many from northern cities with strong ties to black nationalist groups. SNCC staffers in Atlanta published a local paper, *Nitty Gritty*, and were behind the collective authorship of the Black Power position paper, which had roiled SNCC in early 1966. Some of these members, such as Roland Snellings, also belonged to the Revolutionary Action Movement and were attempting to radicalize SNCC. Their hard-nosed tactics did little to endear them to SNCC officials, who considered them to be an inter-mittently effective band of racial separatists and adventurers.[130]

Following the shooting, Vine City activists drove a SNCC sound truck into the heart of the black community. By the afternoon, almost one thousand demonstrators were engaged in open rebellion. Mayor Ivan Allen Jr., considered a model of racial liberalism, began a speech that pleaded, unsuccessfully, with the crowd for order and ended in a humiliating spectacle as the surging throng knocked him down as po-lice officers stood by.[131] Unable to calm the crowd, the usually mild-mannered Allen ordered his officers to "tear all the houses down if necessary. I want the people dispersed. Tear the place up."[132] Police ar-rested more than two dozen people, chasing them down "side streets, hurling canisters at their heels."[133] Events deteriorated the next day as Allen blamed SNCC for the rioting, singling out Carmichael. "If Stokely Carmichael is looking for a battleground," said Allen, "he cre-ated one last night, and he'll be met in whatever situation he cares to create."[134] While Allen's tough rhetoric made him a hero to white resi-dents weary of racial friction, it also exposed the frayed nerves of liberal politicians in the face of Black Power. In 1963, Allen had taken the unprecedented step of endorsing the March on Washington; by the next year, he was among a handful of southern mayors to support the 1964 civil rights bill.[135] By 1966, Allen typified the ideological limits and political patience of the New South.

Police arrested Carmichael two days after the rebellion, on a Thurs-day night, on charges of "inciting to riot and disorderly conduct distur-bance."[136] His arrest came after SNCC members spent a day canvassing Atlanta with leaflets detailing their version of events. The next day, Carmichael was transferred from the city jail to county jail as the mayor, SNCC, and local civil rights groups issued bitter recriminations at one another. Through SNCC's Atlanta headquarters, Carmichael an-nounced his refusal to post the $10,000 bond, as well as his intention to stay in the county jail "indefinitely." Prison officials countered by placing Carmichael in isolation.[137] Atlanta experienced renewed vio-lence on Saturday night, after a car carrying four whites shot two black men. The attack left a sixteen-year-old boy dead, a police officer wounded, and a throng of new arrests, including that of SCLC aide Hosea Williams, for disobeying police orders.[138] On Sunday night, Allen returned to the scene of the latest shooting and watched as two hundred boisterous protesters marched around a four-block area in Atlanta's northeastern neighborhood. Angry descriptions of neighborhood living conditions and demands for Carmichael's release drowned out Allen's pleas to protesters, leaving Atlanta poised for yet more violence.[139]

King was left to wrestle with the collateral damage from Atlanta's uprising. Carmichael's arrest placed added pressures on King and, by extension, on the broader movement. As Carmichael and a growing number of militants defined it, Black Power complicated King's focus on northern inner cities. King's Chicago campaign stalled; the signing of an accord between movement leaders and city officials was more of a stalemate than a settlement and local militants charged that King had sold them out. Greeted with jeers at a Chicago church on the last day of August, King expressed his agreement with Carmichael's emphasis on black social and political power.[140] Carmichael's tactics, however, were another matter. SNCC's approach in Vine City, King argued, had undercut Carmichael's objectives by injecting violence into the political arena.[141] The defeat in Congress of the president's civil rights bill offered the capstone to what appeared to be the movement's slow death due to irresolvable ideological conflicts.[142]

By 1966, domestic race relations evoked parallels with the end of Reconstruction, when efforts to secure racial justice faltered in the face of national fatigue over escalating conflict. Dissent—whether in the form of urban rioting, black nationalism, SNCC's antiwar activism, or Black Power radicalism—gained strength as civil rights politics faltered. Complaints from white liberals, shrinking financial contributions, and President Johnson's preoccupation with Vietnam jeopardized the massive federal programs promoted and still hoped for by rights leaders. More important, Black Power had altered freedom's political calculus. With even reliably liberal northern politicians dodging fair housing laws and conservative hard-liners warning of urban anarchy, House Democrats stood poised to lose dozens of seats, which would even further undermine Johnson's ambitious social agenda.[143] If political fatigue over race relations threatened to hinder legislative breakthroughs, it also suggested "at least the possibility that the nation is moving into a vicious cycle in which Negroes riot because whites do not do enough and whites do not do enough because Negroes riot."[144]

SNCC's ability to bring the Black Power movement nationwide remained questionable. The group's field secretaries and organizers were in retreat or on the speaking circuit while its projects faltered, producing internal debates that yielded only short-lived ideological unity and no clear sense of political purpose. As chairman, Carmichael's undeniable political charisma was overwhelmed by his ability to alienate white liberals and mainstream rights leaders. Within SNCC, two views of organizing had developed. One side insisted that SNCC should be all black, its white organizers pushed into white neighborhoods. The other, while acknowledging the importance of purely racial appeals, held up past achievements by SNCC's white members as deserving of organizational loyalty that transcended race. A temporary compromise allowed a handful of white veterans to remain, even as rumors persisted that Carmichael had purged dozens of whites from SNCC. Looming largest in SNCC's transformation from idealistic young activists to cynical veterans was Carmichael: "If scaring whites is an art," wrote one reporter, "Carmichael seems well on his way to becoming a master."[145]

Bayard Rustin, whose seamless yet dramatic blend of social democratic politics and Gandhian nonviolence made him a living legend in the same civil rights and radical circles that nurtured Carmichael as a teenager, added his powerful voice to the chorus of criticism of the state of civil rights.[146] In an essay published in *Commentary*, " 'Black Power' and Coalition Politics," he dismissed Black Power as "simultaneously utopian and reactionary" and argued that black aims for political power outside the Democratic Party were hopeless, because of blacks' minority status as well as the fact that a rhetorical focus on race precluded any discussion of the economic roots of African American misery.[147] Rustin's essay was part of an exchange with the writer David Danzig, who defended Black Power.[148] Rustin also criticized Carmichael's "extravagant rhetoric" and what he characterized as Black Power's unwillingness to form political alliances.[149] For Rustin, black advancement was impossible without the aid of strong coalitions. In an earlier and influential *Commentary* article, Rustin had famously suggested that the civil rights movement had shifted from "protest to politics."[150] In that essay he had also outlined an ambitious agenda to place an interracial coalition of visionaries at the center of progressive politics.[151] Carmichael's call for blacks to organize a national Black Panther political party, in contrast, placed racial solidarity ahead of interracial alliances—he dared white and black liberals to "prove that coalition and integration are better alternatives."[152]

Carmichael's response to critics eulogizing the end of the civil rights movement's heroic period and, with it, the failure of Black Power, was an essay, "What We Want," that appeared in the September 22, 1966, issue of the *New York Review of Books*.[153] For Carmichael, pundits who blamed Black Power for "white backlash" missed the point. Black Power was an integral part of a continuous dialectic of black struggle against racial oppression—specifically, violent, organized white opposition. "One of the tragedies of the struggle against racism," wrote Carmichael, was the absence of a national group that spoke the language of urban militants. Carmichael traced the civil disturbances that federal officials called riots and that Black Power activists interpreted as rebellions to the spectacle of a civil rights struggle that consistently "demonstrated from a position of weakness." He blamed SNCC and other civil rights organizations for acting as disingenuous interpreters for poor blacks, rather than accurately and directly speaking in the voice of the dispossessed. "We cannot be expected any longer to march and have our heads broken in order to say to whites: come on, you're nice guys. For you are not nice guys. We have found you out." Here was both a charge and a confession, an acknowledgment of his own past political service that, in Carmichael's view, made him culpable (though hardly in the manner his critics suggested) for the racial violence plaguing the nation.

Cries of "Black Power" rose above the commotion of everyday politics because they reflected the contemporary mood among blacks and also because public controversy finally could not halt blacks from speaking out. "For once, black people are going to use the words they want to use—not just the words whites want to hear. And they will do this no matter how often the press tries to stop the use of the slogan by equating it with racism or separatism." The essay outlined SNCC's Black Power advocacy as a natural outgrowth of the group's organizing history, recalling victories and setbacks for voter registration and political participation as a unique education: a kind of tortured experience that revealed the cost of black citizenship in America. Lowndes County, Carmichael explained, had confronted deep-seated traditions of white terror, violence, and fear with a disciplined militancy that was at once historic and revelatory in its stubborn simplicity. "These men and women are up for election in November—if they live until then," he wrote. "Their ballot symbol is the black panther: a bold, beautiful animal, representing the strength and dignity of black demands today. A man needs a black panther on his side when he and his family must endure—as hundreds of Alabamians have endured—loss of job, eviction, starvation, and sometimes death, for political activity. He may also need a gun and SNCC reaffirms the right of black men everywhere to defend themselves when threatened or attacked." Carmichael's words stood on a razor's edge: a political program backed by a self-defense posture whose subtleties both law enforcement and the majority of Americans missed. Providing the clearest definition of Black Power to date, Carmichael described it as "the coming together of black people to elect representatives and to force those representatives to speak to their needs."[154]

While Carmichael publicly defended Black Power, federal officials continued their clandestine observation. The FBI's first request of acting Attorney General Ramsey Clark, in the fall of 1966, had been for microphone surveillance of Stokely Carmichael. In a move that surprised Washington insiders in September, President Johnson had appointed Nicholas Katzenbach as Under Secretary of State, naming Clark as his replacement.[155] On October 27, Deke DeLoach arrived in Clark's office for an afternoon meeting to discuss the use of wiretaps and microphones in a bureau investigation of organized crime in Las Vegas. Catering to one of J. Edgar Hoover's pet peeves, Clark criticized Justice Department attorneys for their lax security with microphone logs, even assuring DeLoach that Walter Yeagley, an FBI-trained assistant attorney general, would shore up Justice's security protocol. Clark also brought up the Carmichael wiretap request, telling DeLoach that he was "inclined to disapprove the request" for three reasons. Carmichael might be facing imminent criminal prosecution, he was a well-known civil rights leader, and the potential public fallout resulting from a leak would embarrass all concerned parties. Informed of Johnson's special interest in Carmichael, Clark told DeLoach that he would carefully consider the entire matter.[156]

Behind a veneer of bureaucratic policy, Clark's respect for civil liberties marked him as an enemy of Hoover's FBI. Clark's nomination and eventual confirmation placed the FBI under the nominal leadership of a man whose philosophy of "combating crime through an attack on poverty" Hoover considered reprehensible.[157] Clark's nomination also affected the makeup of the Supreme Court. The resignation of his father, Associate Justice Tom Clark (who had known Hoover since Clark's days as attorney general under Harry Truman), during the winter of 1967, paved the way for Thurgood Marshall's historic confirmation as the first African American to sit on the Court. A soft-spoken, thoughtful Texas liberal, Ramsey Clark decried the use of electronic surveillance except in the interest of national security and resisted presidential pressure to arrest Carmichael.[158]

While Clark tried to forge his own path in the Justice Department, Carmichael's speeches placed him under increased scrutiny. Carmichael's criticism of the Vietnam War marked him as an activist bold enough to announce his resistance to the draft a year before Muhammad Ali's controversial refusal, and creative enough to regard links between domestic and international fronts of Black Power as a source of strength where others saw potential disaster. In New York, Mendel Rivers, still smarting from the Justice Department's refusal to prosecute the SNCC chairman, attacked Carmichael in the same speech, before the Veterans of Foreign Wars convention, in which he scoffed at Ali's request for a service deferment as a Muslim minister.[159] Rivers's preoccupation with Carmichael mirrored President Johnson's own growing personal interest, rooted in Carmichael's vocal war opposition. In speeches and interviews, Carmichael repeatedly assailed the war, pointedly criticized Johnson, and vowed to "go to Leavenworth" before serving in the armed forces.[160] Off the record, Johnson blamed his inability to pass new civil rights legislation (despite an overwhelming Democratic legislative majority) on two intertwining phenomena—Black Power "and Stokely Carmichael." At a cabinet meeting in late September, the president described Carmichael as "a young man" who didn't know "his rear end from his elbow," who "defeated the civil rights bill."[161]

In a private conversation with advisor and Associate Supreme Court Justice Abe Fortas, the president went further, targeting Carmichael's militant rhetoric as costing him votes. After Johnson asked Fortas whether the Court would "do anything on law and order this session and tell these fellas that they've got to quit turning over cars and stuff," Fortas accused Justice Hugo Black of stalling efforts to reconfirm local antirioting decisions with the Court's official stamp. Citing dwindling approval ratings and polls that indicated riot politics resonated with voters more than Vietnam or the economy, the president identified white Americans as fed up and fearful, a lethal combination with potentially staggering political consequences. Johnson's private solution—to "do something to shake them up like convict that damn Carmichael and uphold it"—would preoccupy pundits, politicians, and government officials over much of the next two years.[162]

During the last week in October, Johnson toured South Vietnam on a secret, morale-boosting mission designed to counter fallout from the international conflict whose domestic political woes accrued daily. Johnson's surprise trip grabbed headlines in a manner that antiwar critics could only dream of. Wearing his trademark, and proudly ostentatious, ranch suit—tan jacket, presidential insignia over the right pocket, and matching pants, and short-sleeved shirt—Johnson joked with soldiers, presented medals, and pledged the nation's support for its troops.[163]

Johnson's assurances of U.S. resolve abroad figured into the assessments of civil rights advocates determined to recapture national attention and political momentum. On the day of Johnson's visit to South Vietnam, a coalition of civil rights, religious, and labor leaders unveiled an ambitious Freedom Budget—a $185 billion political gamble that would take ten years to implement and an act of Congress to pass. The Freedom Budget was the brainchild of A. Philip Randolph, the movement's elder statesman and founder of the Brotherhood of Sleeping Car Porters, as well as a onetime Socialist. At a two-hour press conference held at a Harlem church, Freedom Budget organizers announced an audacious plan to lift 34 million Americans out of poverty—three quarters of whom were white—through increases in federal benefits, a guaranteed annual income, and subsidies for health care, housing, and agricultural workers. Dr. Leon Keyserling, chairman of the Council of Economic Advisors under Harry Truman and a key drafter of New Deal legislation, claimed that the Freedom Budget would require no new taxes, nor would it siphon funds committed to Vietnam.[164]

The day after both events, Carmichael underwent a detailed physical (at the request of New York City's Selective Service director) as part of a draft status reevaluation. Reports of the exam created a feeding frenzy among news outlets, including the *David Susskind Show*, which preempted its regular programming in favor of a taped interview with Carmichael, originally scheduled for November.[165] Carmichael's current 1-Y classification meant that he failed to live up to the "mental, moral, or physical induction standards." Outside the induction center, Carmichael, en route to a brief reunion with relatives in Harlem before departing for a West Coast speaking engagement, joked with reporters that he wore tinted granny glasses because "they make me look nonviolent."[166]

Jimmy Garrett, head of San Francisco State College's newly organized Black Student Union (BSU) and a former SNCC activist, hosted

Carmichael in the Bay Area that October. The BSU illustrated the growing strength of black nationalism around the nation. On Saturday, October 29, Carmichael addressed ten thousand students in Berkeley's amphitheater.[167] Contentious public debate and private negotiations between university officials and campus organizers preceded his appearance. Berkeley's Black Power conference, "Black Power and Its Challenges," would embroil Carmichael in the increasingly vicious gubernatorial campaign between the liberal incumbent, Edmund "Pat" Brown, and the conservative upstart Ronald Reagan.[168] Two days before Carmichael's visit, Governor Brown, in a move dismissed by Reagan as a "stunt," interrupted his campaign appearances to huddle with Oakland officials to discuss possible rioting caused by the conference.[169] Carmichael began his speech with humor: "It is a privilege and an honor to be in the white intellectual ghetto of the west." Responding to critics who accused SNCC and Black Power of thwarting the civil rights bill, he described a domestic landscape poisoned by white supremacy and an international arena in which American military power threatened to run amok.[170] Carmichael's Berkeley address provided insight into the freedom struggle's evolution.[171] Carmichael posed what he described as a fundamental question: "How can white society move to see black people as human beings?"[172] Black Power radicalism, for Carmichael, offered the solution. "The failure of the civil rights bill," he argued, did not rest with Black Power or urban rebellions but suggested the failure of American democracy. Connecting black oppression with global wars and arguing that domestic civil rights setbacks should be placed at the feet of white citizens who refused to obey the law, Carmichael delivered a speech that defied journalistic clichés if only because its vision of radical Black Power was rooted in a rational critique of events.[173]

On October 31, two days after Carmichael's speech, Vice President Hubert Humphrey summoned Deke DeLoach for a briefing. The news was grim. The assistant director of the FBI informed Humphrey that the recent Black Power conference had been attended by nearly five thousand people and had "received a great deal of support" from Communists. During an hour-long meeting, DeLoach explained how

Carmichael had insulted top White House officials and "indicated his complete opposition to the draft." Humphrey's response was predictably fierce.[174] After telling DeLoach that he was "sick and tired" of hearing about Carmichael, Humphrey, having recently spoken to Pat Brown, predicted that the besieged California governor would "get the hell beat out of him" in the upcoming election. The vice president read California voters' anger over racial unrest, Black Power militants, student radicals, and antiwar protesters as a prelude to future electoral disaster. DeLoach understood Beltway politics and, sensing Humphrey's creeping panic over Brown's sagging fortunes, relayed the FBI's frustrating efforts to get Justice's approval for a wiretap. Although, according to DeLoach, Carmichael "was no longer an authentic civil rights leader," the assistant director said that, as far as he knew, the latest request was sitting on the attorney general's desk. "You tell Ramsey Clark," replied an agitated Humphrey, "that this would be a ridiculous thing to do and tell him I said this" before requesting from DeLoach up-to-date intelligence on Carmichael's political activities.[175]

Carmichael's notoriety placed internal pressures on SNCC at the same time that his high profile challenged the organization's aggressively democratic, collective approach to leadership and policy making. As Carmichael's stature grew, the lines between his personal political opinions and official SNCC policy were blurred. Since his assumption of the chairmanship in the spring and especially in the months following the Meredith March, the press increasingly portrayed SNCC as a hierarchical organization controlled exclusively by Carmichael. Frustrated by this, Carmichael found it increasingly difficult to modulate his visibility for the benefit of the group. Ruby Doris Robinson, who along with Carmichael and Cleveland Sellers formed SNCC's executive committee, questioned the chairman's political discipline, a criticism echoed by others in the group.[176] During a central committee meeting in October, tensions exploded and Carmichael reluctantly agreed to curtail his speaking engagements after December in order to focus on organizing concrete SNCC programs.[177]

Shortly before the first national elections since the passage of the Voting Rights Act, Carmichael was in Lowndes County, Alabama, which remained a special place for him. He spoke there at a rally on November 7, the day before the election. Over six hundred people packed a black church to hear Carmichael deliver his emotional address. "It is so good to be home," he began. "When we pull that lever we pull it for all the blood of Negroes that the whites have spilled. We will pull the lever to stop the beating of Negroes by whites. We will pull that lever for all the black people who have been killed. We are going to resurrect them tomorrow."[178]

All seven Lowndes County Freedom Organization candidates, represented on the ballot box by a black panther, lost. But it wasn't a fair fight. Plantation owners, who had evicted sharecroppers for registering, appeared to reverse course by trucking black workers to the polls. They did so, however, with ballots already marked for white candidates. Reports of stuffed ballot boxes and barred poll watchers also plagued the election.[179] While coordinated voting fraud and intimidation won the day, an important precedent would prevail. LCFO candidates for sheriff, coroner, tax assessor, tax collector, and three Board of Education slots tallied impressive voting blocks, providing a glimpse of New South politics. In the election's aftermath, the *Movement*, SNCC's monthly newsletter, delivered a postmortem that would prove prophetic: "LOWNDES COUNTY: Candidates Lose, but Black Panther Strong."[180]

Just as black candidates made history by losing an election in Lowndes County, Republicans made national headlines by winning. Historic gains in the overwhelmingly Democratic House and Senate threatened to reverse the Republican Party's minority party status, in both the upper and lower houses—a reality since the end of Reconstruction. Racial division within the Democratic Party formed the key to the Republican Party's renaissance, with many white Democrats breaking generations of familial custom and political tradition to cross party lines. Republican strength in key Senate contests, including the historic ascension of Edward Brooke of Massachusetts as the first black senator to win a 20th-century general election, surprised analysts who had predicted that sizable Republican gains would be limited to Congressional elections.[181] In addition, Republicans claimed six governorships, including Ronald Reagan's overwhelming victory in California. Richard Nixon, whose tireless campaigning on behalf of the Republican slate laid the groundwork for his astonishing comeback, emerged as one of a handful of frontrunners for the Republican Party's 1968 presidential nomination.[182]

While pundits sorted out a transformed electoral landscape, Carmichael continued to tour the Bay Area as part of a two-week fundraising effort.[183] His itinerary included inner-city campuses, suburban universities, high schools, and community centers. In front of packed houses of whites, Carmichael softened his public image by offering a lucid defense of Black Power from prepared texts that burnished his image as an intellectual provocateur equally adept at professorial lectures and angry polemics. For black audiences, he adopted a less formal, more militant style of speaking that mesmerized the grassroots from the Mississippi Delta to Oakland's inner city. Behind the scenes, Carmichael held private meetings with local activists. FBI informants alerted the bureau of Carmichael's intentions to direct the Bay Area's political energies "into one overall organization."[184] Dozens of Black Power activists and organizations had popped up all over California, with the Bay Area and Los Angeles emerging as centers of the new radicalism, which would also harbor deadly conflicts. As activists jockeyed for position in a climate that valued street credibility as much as political philosophy, confrontations over organizational names, personal status, and past histories erupted.

From northern California, Carmichael flew to Los Angeles to speak at a Black Power rally in Watts, sponsored by the Black Congress—a consortium of Los Angeles–based militants. Carmichael's scheduled appearance so alarmed city officials, who were aware of rumors that his visit might trigger violence, that they denied the rally's organizers a permit. Carmichael publicly proclaimed his intention to speak whether permission was granted or not, which he did at Will Rogers Park in South Central Los Angeles in a speech that concluded without incident. While Carmichael spoke, FBI informants milled about the crowd, local law enforcement taped the talk for a possible grand jury indictment, and an army division stood by in case of trouble.[185]

In December, Carmichael and Bayard Rustin met for a debate, "The Future of the Negro Movement for Civil Rights," at Hunter College, in New York. Used to friendly disagreements on the movement's front lines that nevertheless remained largely hidden from public view, Carmichael's and Rustin's competing, irreconcilable views on Black Power now turned them into public combatants. When it came to the subject of Black Power, Carmichael and Rustin talked past each other. Rustin's diverse identities as a radical pacifist, social democrat, homosexual, and movement philosopher made him regard Black Power as a tragic retreat from an optimistic universalism at the core of his personal and political history.[186] For Carmichael, Black Power did indeed promote universalism, but it did so in black. That is to say Black Power recognized power's ability to shape politics, identity, and civilization, and sought to extend these privileges to African Americans—a group that was too often excluded from even the broadest interpretations of whose interests constituted those of humanity. While critics feared that Black Power hinted at a perverse inversion of America's racial hierarchies, Carmichael envisioned something both more and less dangerous— a black community with the resources, will, and imagination to define the past, present, and future on its own terms.

At Hunter, Carmichael detailed the political legitimacy of Black Power while Rustin promoted and endorsed the A. Philip Randolph-sponsored Freedom Budget. Several years earlier, Rustin had been dispatched by Howard University students (including Carmichael) to debate the then-notorious Malcolm X. Now this meeting with Carmichael provided a déjà vu of sorts. At that time, although the seasoned Rustin had held his own, Malcolm won an emotional victory in the eyes of Howard's student body. Now, Carmichael played the fire-eater to Rustin's pragmatist and elder statesman. Riffing off his *Commentary* essay, Rustin spoke eloquently of coalition politics, the crushing effects of automation on black unemployment, and the limits of Black Power. "We cannot succeed alone," Rustin chided Carmichael, "for we are only 10 per cent of the population." Rustin dared Carmichael to provide a blueprint for racial uplift that went beyond slogans. After reminding Rustin of SNCC's formative role in mainstream politics during the fiasco of 1964's Mississippi Freedom Democratic Party, Carmichael challenged his opponent, the principled pacifist, to morally justify his support for Lyndon Johnson. Disappointed by Rustin's response that the president represented the lesser of two evils, Carmichael maintained that, in fact, Black Power offered a radical alternative that refused to compromise with corruption in public life.[187]

8

STORM WARNINGS

The racial uprisings and black protest that marked the previous
three years would continue into 1967. Yet as the decade proceeded,
Black Power, rather than civil rights, framed public perception of these
events. Racially charged civil disturbances in Newark and Detroit ignited political controversy, intellectual debates, and shifting national
priorities. Black Power activists—through antiwar activism, self-
defense organizations, and expressions of cultural pride and racial
solidarity—amplified the growing civil unrest in America at the same
time that they changed its very expression.

For Stokely Carmichael, 1967 unfolded at breakneck speed.
Carmichael's swashbuckling political internationalism continued in
the tradition of the equally daring, if also at times ill-fated, political
activism of Paul Robeson, W. E. B. Du Bois, and Malcolm X. After a
year spent concentrating on Black Power's domestic possibilities,
Carmichael embarked on a tour of outlaw nations that would expand
his political vision and personal notoriety.

At the start of the year, the House of Representatives' unprecedented refusal to seat Adam Clayton Powell spurred a tactical alliance

between black moderates and militants to save Powell's political career, one that blended personal scandal with racial militancy. Charged with misappropriating funds and other ethical violations, Powell, in addition to being barred from his seat, lost the chairmanship of the House's powerful Education and Labor Committee. One thousand supporters conducted a roaring vigil for the disgraced congressman on the morning of January 10, 1967, as chartered buses from New York City, Baltimore, and Philadelphia transported demonstrators calling for his immediate reinstatement and invoking protection of Powell as a point of black pride. Stokely Carmichael was one of Powell's most vocal supporters. Although their relationship had cooled since Powell made disparaging comments about him the previous fall, Carmichael's belief that racial unity trumped ideological squabbles buoyed Powell.[1] In the House, Powell's colleagues voted 364 to 64 against reinstatement, after denying an earlier motion to seat him pending an investigation on numerous allegations of corruption. For those outside, racial solidarity trumped the archaic rules used to bar Powell from the incoming congressional class. Powell's afternoon address masterfully played up black resentment against Beltway politics, urging voters in his district to withhold federal taxes until his seat was restored.[2] For Powell, the loss of his chairmanship effectively ended his career. Although he would return to Congress (without his seniority or chairmanship) for a final term in 1969, Powell's tenure as the consummate black political insider and agitator had by then come to an unceremonious end.[3]

While the sun set on Harlem's legendary lawmaker, Carmichael headed west.[4] He appeared at the three-day Survival of Black People Conference in the Bay Area in late January, which was notable for the heavy presence of Black Power radicals. Local activists, such as Huey P. Newton, a twenty-four-year-old part-time college student who had recently organized a group of armed militants called the Black Panther Party for Self-Defense (BPP), attended the conference. Speakers cited California governor Ronald Reagan's recent election as the latest example of a national conspiracy to stifle Black Power. When local militants approached Carmichael with the demand that his speech focus on Malcolm X's legacy, he balked at the suggestion, preferring instead to give his planned address on coalition politics. However, a Malcolm X tribute was independently organized the next month.[5]

The First Annual Malcolm X Grassroots Memorial Conference featured Betty Shabazz, Malcolm's widow, as well as a contingent of local militants who arrived at the San Francisco airport to provide her with an armed escort. With Shabazz in tow, the convoy descended upon the offices of *Ramparts* magazine. Staff writer Eldridge Cleaver was startled by the sound of a terrified white secretary declaring that men with guns were invading the building. Spectators gawked at a scene that shattered conventions in ways difficult to comprehend. The sight of young black men armed with guns seemed more a declaration of war than an organizational excursion. Outside the *Ramparts* offices, traffic stopped as reporters rushed the building, photographers snapped pictures, and the faint sound of police sirens whirred in the distance. Huey P. Newton, Black Panther minister of defense, led Shabazz's retinue of rough-looking reformed troublemakers, ex–hard cases, and amateur political activists into the *Ramparts* offices.

Newton, along with Black Panther Party chairman and cofounder Bobby Seale, had participated in a number of other local Bay Area political groups, eventually writing off their fellow participants as armchair revolutionaries more interested in philosophy than action. Founded in October 1966, the Black Panthers were a local group that, although not yet known nationally, had caught the interest of the radicals on the staff of *Ramparts*. Mao Tse-tung's *Little Red Book*, filled with pithy quotes that the Black Panthers believed contained the keys to political revolution, illustrated the party's creative interpretation of Marxist icons and ideology. They settled on selling Mao's book (as a way of raising operating funds for the Panthers) after noting that white college students were eager to purchase copies. Profits from selling books on Berkeley's campus were invested in the purchase of guns to defend the black community. The image of Black Panthers hawking copies of Mao's red book was part of Newton's personal formulation that black nationalism must be rooted in class struggle. Made up of maverick black nationalists and unconventional Marxists, the Black Panther Party for Self-Defense christened themselves (after Harold Cruse's terminology) "revolutionary nationalists," inspired by sweeping independence movements abroad yet committed to black self-determination at home, as articulated in their own, soon to be popular, ten-point program. The Black Panther Party's audacious vision of freedom demanded, among other things, an end to police brutality in black communities, social justice, economic equality, and peace.

Cleaver shuttled past the crowd in time to overhear *Ramparts* editor Warren Hinckle III assuring a police lieutenant that the Panthers were there for an interview. The Black Panthers' exit was even more fraught than their arrival. As a car carrying Betty Shabazz sped toward the highway, a group of Panthers lingered, sparking a face-off with the police, as both sides brandished guns. "Don't point that gun at me! Stop pointing that gun at me!" shouted one cop. Newton walked to within a few feet of the officer. "Let's split, let's split," Seale implored. Cleaver, like the rest of the magazine's staff as well as the crowd, stood frozen. By now, police officers had unstrapped their pistols, while the group of remaining Panthers stood their ground behind Newton. Tightly gripping his shotgun, Newton pumped a round into the chamber, sending chills down the collective spines of spectators and participants. After several tense moments, one police officer sighed and withdrew. With a shotgun still in his hand, Newton and the Panthers backed out of the building and moved across the street, into their car.[6]

The *Ramparts* confrontation was a local story with national significance. For Newton and the Black Panther Party, the incident, if chiefly symbolic, was the first in a series of confrontations that, with help from *Ramparts*, transformed a small band of armed militants into internationally respected revolutionaries.

Founded as a five-times-a-year journal for liberal Catholic intellectuals, *Ramparts*, by 1967, had all but willed itself into a glossy magazine with a reputation for high-profile muckraking that began to attract a sizable reading audience. A well-publicized exposé of the CIA's ties to the National Student Association reflected the marketing savvy and political commitment of its progressive editors, Warren

Hinckle III and Robert Scheer. The magazine featured antiestablishment writers who enjoyed stirring controversy; staff writer Eldridge Cleaver was one of them. A convicted felon who had spent almost a decade in California's penal system, Cleaver was also a promising literary talent who found in *Ramparts* a professional home that he could use to establish important political connections with the Bay Area New Left. Cleaver identified his wish to join the Black Panthers as the instant Newton stared down police officers outside the *Ramparts* offices; initially enrolling covertly, Cleaver's membership nonetheless constituted the most important recruit yet made by the group. In less than two years, the Black Panthers would reflect Cleaver's vision as much as, if not more than, Newton's.

As the Black Panthers gained strength organizing in the Bay Area, Carmichael worked to revitalize SNCC by touring historically black colleges in the South. Carmichael's latest speaking tour tapped directly into the growing racial consciousness among a cross section of the African American community. The mixture of black college students primed for political dissent and Carmichael's reputation for galvanizing large groups worked together to exaggerate local fears of violence. In the aftermath of Carmichael's controversial April 8 appearance at Vanderbilt University, suspicions that SNCC orchestrated a campaign to promote civil unrest throughout Nashville appeared to be confirmed. Carmichael departed before violence erupted there, but his presence only fueled the paranoia that seemed to surrounded his every move.[7] To thunderous applause, Tennessee's House of Representatives called for Carmichael's deportation from the United States; the legislators ignored a local politician who pointed out that Carmichael was a citizen.[8] Critics charged that Carmichael was a one-man army, traveling around the country leaving insurrection and disorder in his wake.[9]

Of course, no Black Power organization, let alone a single individual, had the power to direct festering racial resentments into widespread violence. This simple truth contradicted conspiracy theorists who saw Carmichael as a guerrilla general whose SNCC troops followed a precise chain of command. In fact, SNCC's financial woes reflected its deep organizational crisis. Setbacks, including project closings, staff defections, and an inability to effectively organize northern ghettoes, offset SNCC's success at promoting Black Power at the national level. Internal divisions over the group's ideological direction, as well as Carmichael's volatile public image, only added to these difficulties. Media depictions of Carmichael and SNCC as a group of proviolent "black racists" hampered its efforts to organize on a large scale around black consciousness, resulting in a sharp decline in financial contributions, which only further perpetuated the mythology of the pure, harmonious, pre–Black Power SNCC fast becoming the stuff of legend.[10]

Less than a week after the Nashville disturbance, Carmichael attended New York City's massive Spring Mobilization antiwar rally that featured Martin Luther King Jr. and noted author Dr. Benjamin Spock. On the subject of Vietnam, Carmichael and King had traveled different roads toward the same destination. Vocal opposition to American involvement and, especially, black participation in Vietnam was a highlight of Carmichael's tenure as SNCC chairman, drawing the attention of both the White House and the Justice Department. While Carmichael leapt into the escalating Vietnam debate, King took baby steps. In January 1967, *Ramparts*' illustrated report "The Children of Vietnam" helped nudge King from his fence straddling, though he continued to proceed cautiously. SCLC's agonizing deliberations over whether to publicly break with the Johnson administration over Vietnam involved calculating such a decision's political effect on the group. Speeches in Chicago and Los Angeles during the winter of 1967 prepared the way for King's address at New York's Riverside Church in April—his most forceful criticism, yet, of the war. Before three thousand people, King linked spiraling military expenditures abroad with America's faltering war on poverty, challenging the nation to transform its values from materialism to humanism, and going so far as to outline specific peace proposals. King's Riverside address was the start of a personal and political odyssey—characterized by unrelenting criticism from policy makers, prowar civil rights leaders, and many journalists—that would end one year later among striking sanitation workers in Memphis, Tennessee. Against a backdrop of condescension and ridicule from the press, furious FBI investigations, as well as the public admonition of less daring movement colleagues, King addressed the Spring Mobilization.[11]

Competing estimates from the mobilization's organizers and New York City officials placed attendance at between one hundred thousand and four hundred thousand; in addition, fifty thousand attended the mobilization's West Coast rally, at San Francisco's Kezar Stadium, featuring Coretta Scott King, *Ramparts* editor Bob Scheer, and—in a parole-jeopardizing appearance—Eldridge Cleaver.[12] New York's rally dwarfed San Francisco's in size and prestige, bringing remnants of the civil rights coalition into an alliance with peace groups who realized that their combined interests had the makings of a powerful movement. In the weeks leading up to the event, some moderate organizations dropped out, fearful of a takeover by radical sponsors and wary of the protest's national director, James Bevel, an SCLC aide who had a penchant for controversy. From Central Park, King, Spock, and Harry Belafonte led demonstrators through a four-hour march to the United Nations. An hour before the noon parade, dozens of young men gathered in the park to triumphantly burn their draft cards. New Yorkers mixed with daffodil-wearing flower children, Black Power militants, and student activists who arrived by chartered bus and train. Expressions of support and rage marked the trek from Central Park to the United Nations as three thousand police officers—the largest contingent since Nikita Khrushchev's visit seven years earlier—kept the small but vocal prowar demonstrators separate from the larger rally.[13] King's keynote urged students to organize peace demonstrations on campuses during the summer, and his closing refrain to "stop the bombing, stop the bombing" struck a responsive chord.[14]

Carmichael, who spoke after King, proved more combative. After leading groups of marchers waving Vietcong flags, Carmichael—amidst chants of "Black Power!"—starkly condemned the war:

> We maintain that America's cry of "preserve freedom in the world" is a hypocritical mask behind which it squashes liberation movements

which are not bound, and refuse to be bound, by the United States' cold war policies. We see no reason for black men, who are daily murdered physically and mentally in this country, to go and kill yellow people abroad, who have done nothing to us and are, in fact, victims of the same oppression. We will not support LBJ's racist war in Vietnam.[15]

If King's presence at the United Nations symbolized the peace movement's status in the highest echelons of protest, Carmichael represented its Janus face, the specter of uncontrollable and unforgiving dissent on the part of voiceless Americans of all colors. Despite these differences, Carmichael and King found common ground at a postrally meeting, sponsored by Harry Belafonte, featuring SCLC and SNCC activists.[16]

The gulf between the government's Vietnam policy and outspoken political dissent increased at the end of the month. On April 28, General William Westmoreland, head of American forces in Vietnam, delivered before Congress a speech designed to bolster sagging support for the war. The first commander to address Congress during wartime, Westmoreland spoke confidently of an American victory based on "unrelenting but discriminating military, political, and psychological" warfare. Interrupted by bipartisan applause nineteen times, Westmoreland cautioned against talk of cease-fire, highlighting the military's strategic capabilities and his own personal resolve. At the conclusion of his speech, the general, "trim, starched, and four starred," saluted members of Congress and received a standing ovation.[17]

In the second week of May, during SNCC's annual meeting in Atlanta, Carmichael officially stepped down as chair.[18] Hubert "Rap" Brown, the younger brother of the respected SNCC activist Ed Brown and a dynamic speaker in his own right, succeeded him. Brown's tenure as chairman marked SNCC's last year of national influence. During that time, the tough, self-assured Brown would emerge as the comet of the Black Power era, a bright burning star whose presence faded after one spectacular, streaking ascent. Carmichael's arrest just weeks later in Prattville, Alabama, for leading a "Black Power" chant, continued a pattern in which his actions thrust SNCC into the thick of racial unrest. An exchange of gunfire between police and militants in Prattville prompted the governor to call the National Guard, a response that Brown characterized as "a declaration of war" warranting retribution from the black community. Released from jail, Carmichael led a march to within a block of the state capitol (he was prevented by court order from coming any closer). Less than a week later, clashes once again broke out in Atlanta between police and locals, following another Carmichael speech.[19] Racial violence in Atlanta and Prattville took place against a backdrop of civil disorders in Cincinnati, Buffalo, and Tampa that Black Power militants described as an unfolding domestic revolution.[20] For the moment, Black Power remained a revolution whose spokesmen gave voice to—rather than inspired—the outrage of the masses from below.

Carmichael, free of the SNCC chairmanship, made plans to resume grassroots organizing. His Washington homecoming provoked a fierce response from pundits and politicians. "Stokely Carmichael says he's coming," warned the *Wall Street Journal*, "and the nation's capital is in a sweat."[21] As Vice President Hubert Humphrey dedicated swimming pools and Lady Bird Johnson planted flowers as part of the administration's efforts to beautify the capital, militants complained of apathy among the district's black residents, and local and federal officials held their breath. The FBI, meanwhile, channeled anxiety into action. Righteous indignation filled bureau memos quoting Carmichael's May 14 statement, during a Chicago speech, that he intended to "take over" the nation's capital "lock, stock, and barrel." The FBI warned the White House about SNCC's potentially toxic effect on local businesses, just as the bureau's Washington Field Office assured Hoover that blanket coverage of Carmichael's activities included the services of ten informants and the cooperation of the Park Police and the Metropolitan Police Department's intelligence division. On May 16, the FBI released excerpts from Hoover's testimony before the House Appropriations Subcommittee emphasizing Carmichael's close acquaintance with Max Stanford, leader of the Revolutionary Action Movement, which Hoover described as "a highly secret all-Negro, Marxist-Leninist, Chinese-Communist" group. While not specifically branding Carmichael a Communist, Hoover's testimony suggested guilt by association. In Grand Rapids, Michigan, for a speech, Carmichael sidestepped the controversy, challenging Hoover to prove the charge.[22]

Suspicions that Carmichael would serve as a pied piper to Washington's black militants proved premature. A July speaking appearance in London cut short Carmichael's personal declaration of "all-out war" in advance of SNCC's summer project.[23] Almost as if on cue, Rap Brown took temporary command of the stage. A passionate speaker whose folksy humor was inflected with a southern drawl, Brown would prove to be the most provocative Black Power spokesman.[24]

But violence was never far off. In Newark during the second week of July, rioting erupted one day after plans for a Black Power conference in the city were announced—another example of the growing disappointment over the failure of Great Society programs (in both scope and administration), as reflected in the contentious debates and open hearings before the Senate Subcommittee on Employment, Manpower, and Poverty.[25] Moved by an incident of police brutality against a local black cab driver, residents of Newark's ghetto engaged in an outburst of violence. Reports of sniper fire against law enforcement, the theft of dozens of guns from a department store, enforcement of a curfew, and armed National Guard members added to a mood already thick with racial tension.[26] Governor Richard Hughes and Newark mayor Hugh Addonizio drove through the heart of the city on the second day, watching in helpless anonymity as families snatched clothes, toys, appliances, and liquor from ruined stores.[27]

LeRoi Jones, who fled Harlem for his hometown of Newark shortly after the demise of the Black Arts Repertory Theater and School, responded to Newark's conflict by organizing. Jones's brutal beating at the hands of the Newark police at the height of the violence further accelerated his political radicalism. Arrested on the third day of unrest, Jones suffered a gaping head wound that authorities claimed was the result of an errant bottle thrown by looters. Held on a $25,000 bail, a record for the city of Newark, Jones became a unifying symbol for the city's black militants.

Indiscriminate shooting of suspected looters by the National Guard and state troopers led to widespread condemnation of Newark officials, which was backed by eyewitness accounts of the troopers' weekend reign of terror against residents.[28] In a report that would become required reading for urban police departments, New Left activist Tom Hayden documented Newark's official response, openly speculating that, having exhausted legal avenues to equality, black militants would resort to "organized violence."[29] Within three years, Newark's political and racial tensions would move to the ballot box, culminating in a struggle that would pit entrenched local politicians against Black Power militants.

The Second Annual Black Power Conference, held in the wake of the Newark riot, would feature a new face of black militancy, one in search of innovative political strategies. Attended by over one thousand participants, ranging from community organizers to businessmen, the conference proposed concrete strategies and tactics for economic empowerment, community control, armed self-defense, and black identity. Speaker after speaker, in workshops and plenary sessions, expressed a commitment to protecting the black community in future conflicts.

Jones's beating, subsequent arrest, and trial marked a crucial turning point in his personal transformation from poet to political activist. These changes, including the adoption of the name Amiri Baraka and marriage to a black woman, Sylvia Robinson, paralleled efforts to turn Black Power militants into grassroots organizers. Surrounded by Black Power activists Larry Neal, Ron Karenga, and Floyd McKissick, Jones held a press conference on the heels of Newark's violence. "We are over sixty percent of the population of Newark, New Jersey," said Jones, "and we will govern ourselves or no one will govern Newark, New Jersey." As militants applauded, Jones described the city's surreal week of violence as an urban rebellion and political insurrection rooted in racial prejudice, poverty, and bureaucratic corruption.[30]

Jones's predictions came true; Newark did spark a community-based movement with national ambitions. Between 1967 and 1974, Jones helped create and lead a series of local groups, national federations, and international conferences that used black nationalism as a template for community organizing. Jones's support of Kenneth Gibson's successful 1970 mayoral candidacy made him a power broker in Newark's local political landscape and represented the potential for a national movement for Black Power.[31]

The nation's worse race riot since Watts in 1965, Newark's violence triggered smaller disturbances in Plainfield, East Orange, Rahway, and Elizabeth. In Boston for its fifty-eighth annual convention, the NAACP denounced the rioting in Newark but blamed local officials for failing to move fast enough to redress Newark's high rates of poverty and slum conditions. The *New York Times* echoed this sentiment, challenging Governor Hughes's description of the riots as "plain and simple crime" while noting that the unrest resembled more of a political rebellion than racial pathology.[32]

Detroit exploded just as Newark's Black Power conference—which approved resolutions to boycott the upcoming Mexico City Olympics, investigate the possibility of creating a political party, and hold national and international political conventions—concluded, less than a week after National Guard troops left the city. As thousands of Detroit residents swept through seven square miles in a destructive fury, Michigan governor George Romney ordered 1,500 National Guardsmen, with tank support, to end the rioting. Initial waves of 700 troops and 800 state and local officers proved unable to break the rebellion's momentum.

From his headquarters at the Shrine of the Black Madonna, Albert Cleage, touting a black nationalist–themed spiritual awakening, would try to harness militant energies both before and after Detroit's historic episode of violence. While Cleage preached a revolution of values, the city's young Black Power activists targeted Detroit's automobile plants. Over the next several years, wildcat strikes organized by the Dodge Revolutionary Union Movement and the League of Revolutionary

Black Workers paralyzed much of the city. These strikes were emblematic of a style of Black Power radicalism that could be traced back to living-room chats where Jimmy and Grace Boggs and youthful militants traded war stories and plotted revolution.[33]

The Detroit riot's origins began when the raid of a "blind pig"—police parlance for an illegal after-hours spot—on Twelfth Street resulted in the arrests of more than seventy people, in turn sparking public outcry and citywide destruction. Billowing clouds of smoke emanated from burning West Side tenements, private homes, and businesses. Looters ravaged large chunks of one of the city's main streets, Woodward Avenue, as well as Grand River, where twenty square city blocks burned. Under threat of bricks, bottles, and sniper fire, firefighters in parts of the city abandoned their posts, leaving buildings ablaze and water hoses in the streets.[34] On a late-evening helicopter tour of the devastation, Governor Romney remarked that Detroit "looks like a city that has been bombed."[35] Behind the scenes, President Johnson delayed National Guard deployment to Michigan until Romney's pleas conformed to federal guidelines, a decision that the governor interpreted as a public humiliation that damaged his political ambitions. Johnson authorized the use of federal troops in a nationally televised address. "We will not endure violence," Johnson informed the nation. After describing most blacks as law-abiding citizens, the president stated that the violence witnessed in Detroit "had nothing to do with civil rights" and vowed to take necessary steps to punish the guilty.[36] Republicans reacted to the ten-minute address with scorn, touting the latest wave of urban violence as yet another crisis that Johnson had ignored in spite of the "mounting evidence" that the civil disorders of the past four years were actually the result of careful planning.

Johnson's public statesmanship masked private anxiety. During the grimmest days of urban violence, the president remained huddled with advisors, dispatching a civilian team (including Roger Wilkins, the thirty-five-year-old assistant attorney general and nephew of Roy Wilkins) to Detroit that barely escaped being shot at by nervous National Guard troops.[37] At a White House meeting the day after his national address, Johnson turned to J. Edgar Hoover for answers. The

FBI director encountered a White House under siege and a president certain that outside forces were orchestrating the crisis. Pressed to uncover evidence of a national conspiracy, Hoover admitted, with startling candor, that there was no organized element behind the rioting—not the most welcome conclusion, since it was the opposite of what Johnson wanted to hear (or what events suggested). Late-night reports of disorders in Philadelphia; Harlem; Cambridge, Maryland; and two cities in Michigan amplified Johnson's fears and provided Hoover with an opening to expand FBI power. One month after this meeting, Hoover would receive approval for the expansion of the bureau's Counter Intelligence Program (Cointelpro) to coordinate investigations of "black nationalist, hate-type organizations."

Originally deployed during the 1950s against Communists (including Martin Luther King Jr.'s suspected affiliation with subversives), Cointelpro, now charged with a broader scope, focused almost exclusively on Black Power militants, in the wake of government intelligence on racial rioting. Hoover's relationship with Attorney General Ramsey Clark continued to be acrimonious, as it had been with the two previous heads of the Justice Department, Nicholas Katzenbach and Robert F. Kennedy. Clark's sensitivity to potential abuses of power in the areas of surveillance surpassed that of both his predecessors. Hoover, whose first days of public service predated the Great Depression, would not be stopped by Clark—even if recent Supreme Court decisions affirming and expanding defendant rights made his job that much harder. The director publicly stated his belief that civil disobedience and legal loopholes had contributed to the decline of law and order; ironically, it was now Clark who would help restore some of this lost order. In September, Clark ordered the FBI chief to investigate whether the riots had in fact been planned, a request that would prove to be the seed for the bureau's Ghetto Informant Program, which, with the aid of four thousand nationwide associates, reported on the pulse of the black community to the FBI and the White House.[38]

By the winter of 1968, Cointelpro's primary mandate was to prevent the rise of an African American leader who could successfully knit together a national coalition—what the bureau referred to as a "black messiah." Cointelpro would eventually include 360 operations designed to disrupt black nationalist organizing and, ultimately, would represent a watershed event in American history as it curtailed the FBI's long-practiced policy of requiring a connection between domestic dissidents and foreign agents to justify bureau activity.[39] Its secret war against Black Power activists would be marked by unprecedented abuses of federal power that featured the systematic, illegal harassment, imprisonment, and, at times, death, of black militants.

With Carmichael (whom the bureau singled out as one of three potential "black messiahs," along with King and Elijah Muhammad) overseas, Rap Brown fit the description of a national urban guerrilla leader. While Detroit residents engaged in sniper fire, sabotage, and looting that required thousands of federal troops to quell, Brown appeared at the center of a civil disturbance in Cambridge, Maryland. In a fiery speech, Brown called for an escalation of black liberation politics, explicitly sanctioning guerrilla warfare as a political tactic. "If America don't come around," he warned, "we are going to burn it down!"[40] Several hours after Brown's speech, tensions between local blacks, the police department, and fire officials exploded. The final result—two square blocks in Cambridge's black ward burned to the ground, the National Guard recalled, and gunshot fire grazing Brown's head—further confirmed the popular notion that when Black Power came to town, so did trouble. Journalists only contributed to this perception, as did politicians, most notably Maryland's formerly moderate governor (and future vice president of the United States) Spiro Agnew, who rode the wave of public discontent to national prominence. Almost four decades later, federal reports describing Cambridge's riot as a "local level civil disturbance" challenged, too late, the mythology behind the contemporaneous accounts and subsequent histories.[41] The FBI launched a manhunt for Brown on the charge of inciting a riot, just as federal troops quelled the last bits of violence in Detroit. Arrested in Virginia on July 26, Brown shouted that "America has finally taken off the black robe and put on the white sheet," before being whisked away.[42] That same day, national civil rights leaders, including King, Roy Wilkins, Whitney Young, and A. Philip Randolph, called for an end to racial violence. Citing Newark and Detroit as examples of the national crisis, the joint statement pleaded with all citizens to oppose violence and lawlessness—as well as "joblessness, inadequate housing, poor schooling, insult, humiliation and attack."[43]

But politics hampered civil rights leaders' efforts to ameliorate violence through federal legislation. The latest setback for comprehensive antipoverty legislation included Congress's recent, contentious dismissal of a rat-control bill aimed at eliminating vermin in inner cities.[44] Meanwhile, journalists hailed the antiriot manifesto as civil rights leadership's sensible return to moderation. Editorialized as the "Voice of Negro Leadership," in reality King, Wilkins, Young, and Randolph constituted the nation's shifting political center.[45] The new middle ground, occupied by Democrats and Republicans alike, staked support for massive federal legislation in riot-torn cities as a last stand against civil disorder and race war, even in the face of more riots. In New York, disorder broke out in the predominantly Puerto Rican enclaves of East Harlem and the South Bronx. The city's worst rioting since 1964 spurred John Lindsay, the handsome, liberal Republican mayor with barely concealed national political aspirations, to tour potential trouble spots to talk to militants. Lindsay's dialogue led the police department to approve of the use of Spanish-speaking officers, in an effort to promote community understanding in the barrio.[46]

New York City's local innovations reflected the national inclination toward a pragmatic program to attack the roots of racial unrest. President Johnson's appointment of Illinois governor Otto Kerner to head an inquiry into urban rioting fit this description. Armed with the president's mandate, Kerner pledged that he and his eleven-member commission were up to the task. "We are being asked," Kerner said, "to probe into the soul of America."[47]

Near the end of July, national leaders continued their public soul-searching. King, joined by Roy Wilkins and Atlanta mayor Ivan Allen, called for massive programs aimed at achieving racial harmony through federal expenditures. At a panel in Washington, King addressed America's racial crisis. "White Americans and black Americans must realize the mutuality of their destinies," said King. "There can be no separate white path to power. We all need each other." Attacking Congress for loving "rats more than people," King's edgy remarks reflected frustration with the pace of racial progress, a mood echoed by fellow panelists. Invoking, respectively, the honor and accomplishment of civil rights politics as seen in the March on Washington and the shame and ignominy of Black Power as evidenced by Stokely Carmichael's rabble-rousing, Mayor Allen argued that the country could afford to support cities to the tune of $20 billion to $30 billion a year.[48]

For the moment, and in a maneuver that would become increasingly less exceptional for civil rights and Black Power activists, King deftly transformed himself from preacher to politician as he sought to renew faith in the commitment of secular institutions to social equality. Johnson would prove equally chameleon-like as he placed a new emphasis on the nation's spiritual health. The immediate response to escalating urban violence occurred on Sunday, July 30, as churches, synagogues, and other houses of worship observed President Johnson's call for a national day of prayer for racial peace. Accompanied by Lady Bird Johnson and their daughter Lynda, the president attended services at National City Christian Church, in downtown Washington, where the Reverend Dr. George David led the congregation in a prayer for "the reconciliation of this nation, for the binding of wounds, and the healing of hurts."[49]

As the nation prayed and the Kerner commissioners convened, Rap Brown urged blacks to arm themselves in preparation for a political revolution.[50] At a press conference before a packed audience in Washington, Brown stated that "violence is necessary, it is as American as cherry pie." Denouncing civil rights leaders' recent appeal to end violence, Brown described Johnson as an "outlaw from Texas."[51] Released on bond from the Alexandria, Virginia, city jail, he cut a daring figure as a contemporary Black Power revolutionary. In dark sunglasses and wearing a bandage on his forehead from his earlier skirmish in Cambridge, Maryland, he warned that national unrest revealed the first step in an imminent revolution. Local and federal authorities would pursue numerous charges against Brown, ensuring that someone else would lead the revolution he confidently predicted. During the next year, the periods of incarceration, travel restrictions, and extradition battles that grew in proportion to Brown's ever-bolder rhetoric had the effect of limiting his ability both to organize at the local level and to serve as a national spokesman.

American cities burned as Carmichael tossed rhetorical Molotov cocktails from Europe, Latin America, and Africa as part of a life-altering five-month tour around the world. In London, Carmichael gave a series of speeches on Black Power, met with local militants, and outraged British authorities.[52] The main draw of the Congress on the Dialectics of Liberation, which featured a lineup of speakers including the influential radical intellectual Herbert Marcuse, was Carmichael's address, which impressed participants as theoretically sophisticated and topically rich. Among those who came away energized from the event was Angela Davis, Marcuse's student whose future political activities would also spark an international furor. In fact, Carmichael's London visit inspired enough controversy to make future trips there impossible. On July 27, the House of Commons banned him from returning to Britain, asserting that his presence was "not conducive to the public good."[53] From London, he traveled to Cuba by way of Prague, a fugitive from both State Department and SNCC directives. His presence in Havana, for different reasons, angered both the U.S. government and SNCC—perhaps the first time since the early 1960s that these two groups saw eye to eye. Washington viewed the trip as a high-level embarrassment that eroded America's international prestige.[54] Carmichael's increasingly maverick political maneuvers also alienated SNCC leaders, who, disapproving of the trip, chose instead to send an official delegation to Cuba for a meeting of the Organization of Latin American Solidarity (OLAS). The *Washington Post,* noting this strange synergy in a story that covered SNCC's public rebuke of Carmichael's speeches in Cuba, cheerfully observed that the FBI was "quietly" amassing evidence against him.[55]

Despite the critical eye of the FBI and the disaffection of SNCC leaders, Carmichael, a new kind of political ambassador, arrived in Havana just in time for the island's July 26 independence celebrations.[56] Unlike Malcolm X's international tours, which gained little attention from mainstream journalists, a hostile and disbelieving American press documented Carmichael's every move; in fact, his attendance at the OLAS conference coincided with massive civil unrest in the United States.[57] The *National Guardian* tallied up four months of urban uprisings with the headline: "Black Rebellion in 56 U.S. Cities." Casualties neared one hundred, and property damages surpassed half a billion dollars.[58] A Harris poll indicated that a majority of whites expressed support for substantial federal aid to blacks in the wake of rioting while also revealing the prejudice of its ranks, evident in the suggestion that "outside agitators" orchestrated much of the ghetto violence.[59] *Newsweek* touted the "hard-core ghetto mood" to the nation as a parallel universe bereft of law and order. Noting that nearly half the rioters had had no criminal records, the magazine interviewed psychologists, inner-city residents, and demonstrators as a way of making sense of four years of civil unrest.[60]

At the opening of the OLAS conference, Carmichael held a press conference that excluded American reporters for what one SNCC activist described as "past services rendered."[61] For more than two hours, Carmichael fleshed out Black Power's position on international struggles. "Communism can be many things—Russian, Czech, Yugoslav, Cuban," he said. "The system we like best is the Cuban."[62] Commenting on the urban rebellion in the United States, he remarked that "40 percent of the troops in Vietnam are Negro and some good may come of it because when they come back they will be trained to kill in the streets."[63] Back home, Carmichael's perceived threats against American leaders carried the most weight. Following his comments that "vengeance must be taken against the leaders of the United States" for the murder of black radicals, critics charged treason. Arkansas senator John McClellan explored legal ways to make Carmichael's international travels permanent. Informed by the Justice Department that Carmichael had broken no laws, one Mississippi representative suggested creating one that would bar his return. In July, the House overwhelmingly passed what even supporters acknowledged as an "anti-Carmichael" bill, making it a federal crime to cross state lines to incite a riot.[64]

OLAS debates on the future of Third World revolutionary struggles reflected factional disputes between those who advocated radical reform in Latin America and those who believed in armed resistance.

American diplomats had anticipated such splits, planning contingencies in case leftist guerrillas wrestled power from the mainline Communists, who adhered to Moscow's policy of peaceful coexistence.[65] In Cuba, Carmichael aligned himself with those taking up armed struggle, applying to the United States Che Guevara's revolutionary mandate to create "many Vietnams." "We must internationalize our struggle, and if we are going to turn into reality the words of Che to create two, three or more Vietnams, we must recognize that Detroit and New York are also Vietnam."[66] Carmichael's greatest indulgence came courtesy of Fidel Castro, who served as a tour guide through Cuba's Sierra Maestre, ensuring that the young activist would remember his experience as "eye-opening, inspiring, and mind-blowing."[67]

Surrounded by Latin American guerrilla fighters and dignitaries, Carmichael became the unexpected center of attention, hailed in the Cuban press as a harbinger of an African American revolution.[68] Arriving in no official capacity, he was nonetheless made an honorary delegate and granted permission to address the six-thousand-person convention. An enormous portrait of Che Guevara, the Argentinean-born hero of the Cuban revolution, draped the back of the convention hall.[69] The words next to Che served as a slogan and a summation: *"El deber de todo revolucionario es hacer la revolución"* ("The duty of each revolutionary is to make the revolution"). In his speech, "Black Power and the Third World," Carmichael referred to the "intertwined" destinies of black and Third World peoples.[70] Tailoring his words to his international, overwhelmingly pro-Socialist audience, Carmichael spoke in leftist language he would later reject. Cuba, Carmichael said, served as a "shining example of hope" to blacks in the Western Hemisphere.[71] Black Power was an anticolonial struggle within American borders, similar to Cuba's revolution and also to the struggles being fought around the world.[72] The bulk of the speech bolstered Carmichael's claim that, global in scope, Black Power sought to reclaim a cultural heritage denied by white supremacy. The speech represented a bold, even brazen maneuver by Carmichael, who, almost overnight, became an international political figure comfortably sharing foreign stages with professional revolutionaries.

After a year of clandestine White House and FBI inquiries regarding his draft status, Carmichael did in fact end up in Vietnam, but not in the manner (through the draft) his most ardent enemies hoped. Cuban officials' arrangements for Carmichael's tour through off-limits Asian and African countries paralleled the State Department's plans to confiscate his passport. Amid reports from Cuban intelligence that American officials had laid a trap for Carmichael at his Madrid connection, he was rerouted to an Aeroflot plane carrying a Soviet delegation back to Moscow. En route to Hanoi, Carmichael briefly stopped in Beijing, where he met Shirley Graham Du Bois. In Hanoi, Carmichael rendezvoused with Ho Chi Minh, leader of North Vietnam and revolutionary icon, who reminisced about listening to Marcus Garvey as a young man visiting Harlem.[73] From Vietnam, Carmichael traveled to Algeria. His itinerary in Africa highlighted countries that had successfully engaged in armed liberation struggles. Black radicals viewed Algeria's successful guerrilla campaign against French colonial occupation as Africa's Vietnam. A veteran of America's civil rights battlefield, Carmichael arrived in Africa eager to learn at the feet of revolutionaries.[74] "For me, the international struggle became tangible, a human reality, names, faces, stories, no longer an abstraction," Carmichael recalled decades later. "And our struggle in Mississippi or Harlem was part and parcel of this great international and historic motion. It was both humbling and inspiring."[75]

Carmichael's six-week stay in Algeria, which occurred against the backdrop of the June 1967 Arab-Israeli War, placed him in the center of a firestorm between Middle East partisans and proxies. That summer, the publication of a pro-Palestinian article in *SNCC Newsletter* led to charges of anti-Semitism, which were successful in driving off the last of SNCC's Jewish supporters. SNCC's position, that Palestinians were victims of colonialism and that Zionism abandoned principles of human rights for imperial power, proved consistent with its evolving philosophy. Even as it faced withering domestic criticism leveled by the still powerful, if also shrinking, remains of the civil rights coalition, SNCC held firm, brandishing its independence as a sign of uncompromising commitment to the rights of indigenous people to freedom, even if doing so meant alienating former allies. If SNCC's political irreverence damaged its reputation in the United States, it impressed Third World partisans, including Algerian officials, who welcomed Carmichael as a courageous freedom fighter. In the long term, charges of anti-Semitism would continue to dog Carmichael, who vigorously denied them at the same time that he energetically denounced Zionism.[76]

From Algeria, Carmichael went to Conakry, the capital of Guinea, on the Atlantic coast, where he met President Ahmed Sékou Touré, an outspoken, charismatic proponent of Pan-Africanism. Touré admired Carmichael, and the two developed a close rapport.[77] Ghana's deposed president Kwame Nkrumah also lived in Guinea. Ousted in a coup eighteen months earlier, Nkrumah remained, in spite of his misfortunes, a legend among Pan-Africanists. Amilcar Cabral, a native of Guinea-Bissau, whose robust guerrilla war against the Portuguese was planned out of Conakry, rounded out Guinea's prominent trio of African revolutionaries. The staging point for the most successful military campaign in Portuguese Africa, Guinea housed one of the many locations of Cold War–driven intrigues engulfing the continent. As secretary general of the Partido Africano da Independencia da Guine e Cabo Verde (PAIGC),* Cabral commanded the respect of the Guinean government, received Cuban military and technical assistance, and in the early 1970s introduced a pragmatic blend of Marxism and African cultural nationalism that would inspire Black Power activists.[78] Having left Cuba amid pledges to support guerrilla fighters in Latin America and with news from the United States hinting of domestic insurrection, Carmichael secretly requested that Cabral train a small force of African American guerrilla fighters. Ultimately, Carmichael abandoned these impulsive plans, a decision influenced by his growing attachment to Nkrumah.

Meetings with Nkrumah and Touré affected Carmichael's belief that

---

*The Party for African Independence to liberate Guinea-Bissau and Cape Verde.

Pan-Africanism would one day liberate black Americans. Nkrumah and Touré sought to pass the torch of revolutionary Pan-Africanism to Carmichael, whom they recognized not only as a gifted orator but also as a natural leader and a curious student. Still clinging to his dream of a unified Africa, Nkrumah saw Carmichael as a chance to regain political power in Ghana.[79] Guinea's capital, with its coastal surroundings, low-rise buildings, and arid climate dotted with mango trees and coconut palms, reminded Carmichael of his native Port of Spain. Nkrumah's scenic coastal villa provided an ironic contrast to the reality of political exile. During their initial meeting, Carmichael searched for words while Nkrumah lectured on pan-African linkages across the Atlantic.[80]

Privately, the two engaged in "almost daily" discussions during which Carmichael dutifully listened as Nkrumah linked his personal hopes for political restoration to African American freedom struggles.[81] Carmichael found a mentor just as the deposed African ruler needed a protégé. Nkrumah's victorious campaign against British colonialism and less successful battle against internal corruption and external enemies provided historic lessons for Carmichael. Equally important, in Guinea, Carmichael enjoyed unprecedented access to the pan-African legend and African statesman who had time on his hands. Indeed, Nkrumah spent the rest of his life plotting his return to Ghana, corresponding with supporters around the world, writing several books about Ghanaian politics and the future of Africa, and burnishing his reputation as a pan-African visionary. He also fiercely held onto the accoutrements—if not the power—of his past position, receiving gifts from Socialist-bloc countries, expert medical care, security, and other courtesies (most notably being named copresident) from Guinea's graciously authoritarian president, Sékou Touré.[82] Having been mentored by a roster of pan-African giants that included W. E. B. Du Bois, George Padmore, and C. L. R. James, Nkrumah pointedly criticized Carmichael's Cuban speech for virtually ignoring Africa. Africa, Nkrumah argued, held the key to both men's political fortunes. "The concept of Black Power will be fulfilled," wrote Nkrumah, "only when Africa is free and united."[83] Carmichael took these words to heart and before leaving for Tanzania, he promised the *Osagyefo* he would return to Guinea. In Africa, Carmichael also met his future wife. At a reception in Conakry, he reintroduced himself to Miriam Makeba, whom he had briefly met several years earlier at a SNCC function. A South African singer who had achieved a measure of international celebrity, in part for performing with Harry Belafonte, Makeba and Carmichael began a whirlwind romance; within a year, they were married and would spend the next decade as husband and wife.[84]

As Carmichael toured Africa, Black Power continued to dominate national headlines. At SCLC's annual convention in 1967, King, surrounded by signs that stressed "Black Is Beautiful and It Is So Beautiful to Be Black," embraced themes of racial pride, calling for a new definition of the word *black* and noting that English-language definitions of the term, in contrast to *white*, were offensive. "They even tell us," he said at one point, "that a white lie is better than a black lie."[85] King's words reflected careful deliberation. His new book, *Where Do We Go from Here: Chaos or Community?*, issued a major statement on Black Power, a portion of which the *New York Times Magazine* excerpted two months before the SCLC convention. The book's subtitle reflected the despair that had infused King's recent organizing and intellectual ruminations, in marked contrast to the earnestly hopeful titles (*Stride Toward Freedom* and *Why We Can't Wait*) of his earlier books. "When a people are mired in oppression," wrote King, "they realize deliverance only when they have accumulated the power to enforce change." These words began King's most detailed analysis of Black Power. Political power, noted King, represented the next logical phase of the civil rights struggle. The key to black political power would be the accumulation of enough leverage to negotiate with government officials from a position of strength, which recent victories, including the passage of the 1964 Civil Rights Act and the 1965 Voting Rights Act, would provide. The exertion of such political pressure, King admitted, represented a new stage in the black freedom movement. "We must frankly acknowledge that in past years our creativity and imagination were not employed in learning how to develop power." King set out to correct this error by analyzing the "ideological, economic, and political forces" at the foundation of society. Civil rights protests, argued King, underscored, rather than ameliorated, African American exclusion from these three areas of social capital, but they also offered the chance for dramatic transformation. Juggling several themes, King's book excerpt stressed the need for protest and politics, self-criticism and self-determination, and economic opportunity and spiritual fulfillment in the pursuit of power that relied more on guile than on guns. "Power is not the white man's birthright; it will not be legislated for us and delivered in neat government packages," he concluded. "It is a social force any group can utilize by accumulating its elements in a planned, deliberate campaign to organize it under its control."[86] Upon its release, observant reviewers of *Where Do We Go from Here?* noted that Carmichael's and King's political views (notwithstanding differences on the question of self-defense) converged more than the two men's public images. King's book would inspire SCLC to adopt new tactics, including a massive civil disobedience campaign, a strategy criticized as anarchistic by mainstream opinion makers but enthusiastically supported by antipoverty and peace activists, just as it was tragically underestimated by Black Power advocates.[87]

In the fall of 1967, shortly after *Where Do We Go from Here?* appeared, Carmichael and Charles Hamilton's *Black Power: The Politics of Liberation in America* was published. Given the enormous levels of expectation among activists, intellectuals, and journalists, *Black Power* promised to be as ambitious as contemporary events seemed to demand. *Black Power* opened with an urgent warning attached, as an epigraph, to the book's dust jacket right before it went to press:

> This book presents a political framework and ideology which represents the last reasonable opportunity for this society to work out its racial problems short of prolonged destructive guerrilla warfare. That such violent warfare may be unavoidable is not herein denied. But if there is the slightest chance to avoid it, the politics of Black Power as described in this book is seen as the only viable hope.[88]

Carmichael and Hamilton's dramatic language underscored the dire racial atmosphere of late-1960s America. "This book is about why, where and in what manner black people must get themselves together," they began. Promising no definitive cure for the nation's tortured racial history, Carmichael and Hamilton instead offered a framework for the concept of Black Power that focused on political and intellectual experimentation, including an emerging "black consciousness" they sought to define. Indeed, Black Power required the ultimate act of self-definition by a people whose long history of bondage forced them to see themselves, at least partially, through the eyes of the very forces that oppressed them.* *Black Power* argued that black people had a responsibility to craft the goals, strategies, and tactics for black liberation.[89] Distinguishing between personal acts of racial animus they characterized as "individual racism," the authors used the term "institutional racism" to define *collective* acts of racial oppression that marginalized millions of African Americans. The distinction was a crucial one. Turning at least a generation of reputable social science scholarship on its head—most notably Gunnar Myrdal's classic *An American Dilemma*—Carmichael and Hamilton described institutional racism as relegating blacks to colonial status within America. This was something of an overstatement even if blacks did constitute a nation within a nation—based on their political powerlessness, white power's indirect rule through corrupt black politicians, and local and national structures that rendered their electoral power virtually irrelevant.

What the authors described as "political colonialism" also shaped the status of black Americans. Businesses, social agencies, and landlords, like colonial missionaries in Africa, practiced exploitation disguised as welfare for poor blacks caged in ghettos. Banished to economically depressed communities that functioned as figurative prisons, blacks experienced vicious cycles of poverty, degradation, and hopelessness whose defeat would require new political strategies.[90] Carmichael and

---

*In his 1903 classic *Souls of Black Folk*, W. E. B. Du Bois had described this struggle as "double consciousness."

Hamilton followed their remarks on white power with an outline of "Black Power: Its Need and Substance." Black Power provoked resistance against "cultural terrorism," especially once African Americans "redefine[d] themselves" by reclaiming their African heritage. It was this reclamation project that would provide blacks with the foundation for an assertive new identity.

Refusing to identify themselves as "Negro," many blacks now called themselves African American, Afro-American, or black people. "When we begin to define our own image," Carmichael and Hamilton wrote, blacks would become immune to the humiliating stereotypes so often deployed externally and parroted within the community. A full appreciation of black history, free from white supremacist distortions of Africa and apologies for slavery, fueled Carmichael and Hamilton's vision for an effective Black Power philosophy. *Black Power* defined the understanding of black history, culture, and American society as a "politics of modernization" that critiqued national values, searched for innovative ways to solve pervasive inequalities, and enlarged the scope of political participation. Carmichael and Hamilton questioned the very meaning of American democracy and confessed that, in the past, "what we have called the movement has not really questioned the middle-class values and institutions in this country."[91]

Readers who feared, or hoped, that *Black Power* would call for the dismantling of liberal democratic capitalism in favor of some revolutionary political order were either greatly relieved or bitterly disappointed. In the *New York Review of Books*, the intellectual historian Christopher Lasch criticized *Black Power* for its failure to offer "concrete proposals" for social change.[92] The *London Observer*, in a sympathetic review of *Black Power* and *Where Do We Go from Here?*, found Carmichael and Hamilton's analysis moderate and at times surprisingly parochial.[93]

Ultimately, *Black Power* retreats from an unsparing examination of American political and economic systems. After vaguely describing "parallel community institutions" that could replace existing ones, the authors abruptly shifted from a call for black political participation to a portrayal of Black Power as simply the latest variant of America's long history of ethnic pluralism.[94] Black Power, in other words, could be considered revolutionary as long as blacks defined the concept for themselves leaving plenty of room for the kind of philosophical and ideological contradictions that so often plagued political organizing efforts. Self-determination would lead to political control, for example, in southern states such as Alabama, where blacks had been excluded. Black Power as "an effective share of power" was contrasted with white power based on "domination or exploitation."[95] Yet Carmichael and Hamilton failed to explain how power sharing could alleviate the poverty and powerlessness they earlier described as endemic to black American life. In its concluding chapters, however, *Black Power* recaptures the earlier, searing eloquence that marked its first pages, with a discussion of new forms of political organizing that would exchange past strategies of racial integration for ones that would promote self-determination in African American communities. According to Carmichael and Hamilton, integration remained political and cultural suicide in a land ruled by white supremacy.[96]

If Carmichael and Hamilton's failure to tout a singular revolutionary strategy disappointed critics, Harold Cruse would earn raves (perhaps not surprisingly) for outlining, with surgical precision, an archaeology of black radical political failure stretching back to the Harlem Renaissance. Published the same fall as *Black Power*, Cruse's *The Crisis of the Negro Intellectual* catalyzed a burgeoning interest in black history and culture while igniting debates among black intellectuals that would linger into the next century. Cruse turned his travails in New York's postwar radical cultural and political circles into a scintillating treatise criticizing prominent black radicals as politically ineffectual, artistically uninspired, and ideologically dogmatic. In Cruse's telling, Julian Mayfield, Lorraine Hansberry, Paul Robeson, and many other luminaries were Communist dupes, the undeserving beneficiaries of political and literary cliques that kept aspiring artists (most notably, though never explicitly mentioned, himself) from achieving their due in the world of arts and letters. Equal parts polemic and political analysis, Cruse's maverick interpretation of postwar black radicalism helped solidify the reputation of *The Crisis of the Negro Intellectual* as perhaps the most boldly imaginative black intellectual history ever conceived.

Cruse's resurgent political activism, between 1960 and 1965 (a period during which he toured Cuba, became involved in the Freedom Now Party, and took an editorial position at *Liberator*, all contacts that led to the book contract for *The Crisis of the Negro Intellectual*), helped him extend his narrative into the civil rights and early Black Power years, providing fodder for his gossipy indictments of former literary colleagues and political allies.[97] The book's critical and commercial success, which was a professional boon for Cruse, contained yet further layers of irony. By enthusiastically, and often uncritically, supporting Cruse's work, both white liberals and black militants embraced a kind of historical amnesia that portrayed America's brutal McCarthy period as a universal embrace of blind-alley politics. *The Crisis of the Negro Intellectual* erased the history of radical black struggle against the Cold War's political and travel restrictions; it smeared black activists such as Robeson and Hansberry as confused opportunists ultimately betrayed by their lack of commitment to racial struggle.

Lasch described Cruse's work as "a monument of historical analysis." Unaware that the book was a polemic in objective history's clothing, Lasch and Cruse's other strident supporters embraced *The Crisis of the Negro Intellectual* as the masterwork of an obscure prophet.[98]

Already fifty-one years old, Cruse had waited a long time to experience critical and commercial success. Speaking engagements from universities, academic conferences, and political workshops poured in. Publishers offered Cruse other book contracts, and he secured a visiting professorship in Afro-American studies at the University of Michigan that would eventually become a tenured position. Engaged in the type of cultural criticism that marked him as incorrigible within black radical circles, he was nonetheless characterized as a breath of fresh air by white critics of Black Power. Whites praised Cruse for condemning Black Power, while black nationalists welcomed the author's warnings against white Communists as proof of the irrelevance of integration. Although certain critics repudiated the book's charges, it would take another generation to vigorously challenge and, at times, methodically refute Cruse's contemporary version of events.[99]

Collectively, the writings of and political analyses by King, Carmichael, Hamilton, and Cruse reflected the complexities of rapidly unfolding international and domestic political events.[100] Toward the end of 1967, Carmichael prepared to return to the United States, armed with invigorating experiences and intellectual ammunition. In December, during the second part of a war crimes tribunal in Denmark, Carmichael spoke with some of America's leading antiwar protesters. In a Copenhagen hotel room, he discussed the meaning of Black Power with Carl Oglesby, former president of Students for a Democratic Society, two American correspondents, and an Italian journalist. In that meeting, Carmichael confronted two of the most explosive issues facing black radicals in the United States: armed rebellion and the role of white radicals. Fresh from his tour of nations liberated by guerrilla warfare, Carmichael proposed a domestic revolution that would progress in stages, first damaging property before growing more sophisticated. Since the United States lacked a "revolutionary white organization," Carmichael argued that progressive whites, including the New Left, should seek to bring about change in their communities. According to Carmichael, white activists, whom the Black Panthers labeled "mother country radicals," compounded racial tensions by resurrecting a paternalistic view of blacks at the same time that they ignored the racism that infected the nation like a cancer.[101] Hardly a blip on the media radar that followed his international tour, Carmichael's off-the-cuff chat in Copenhagen sounded the very themes that would consume him on his return to the United States, a journey he described to a Copenhagen journalist as "going back to hell."[102] Before returning, however, Carmichael stopped in Paris, where he was detained for seventeen hours at the airport as "an undesirable," before French officials granted him a three-month visa (with an option for renewal); the incident fueled rumors that Charles de Gaulle had personally ended Carmichael's detention.[103]

Carmichael arrived in New York's Kennedy Airport on December 11, 1967, to supporters chanting "Ungawa, Black Power!," proving that Carmichael would receive more national attention and political support than Malcolm X on each of the three occasions he returned from African tours. Having crossed international boundaries and enjoyed some of the freedoms associated with his overseas tour, Carmichael came back to a domestic landscape more constricted by race than ever. U.S. marshals confiscated Carmichael's passport, and the Port Authority police escorted him to the Harlem YMCA for his meeting with H. Rap Brown and other SNCC activists.[104]

The White House did not hide its feelings about Carmichael's overseas tour. The same day that he arrived at Kennedy Airport, Undersecretary of State Nicholas Katzenbach petitioned Congress to pass a law making tours like Carmichael's, to banned countries, punishable by criminal penalties that included one year in prison and a stiff fine.[105] According to government officials, Carmichael's travels through Communist countries, liberated African kingdoms, and left-wing European conferences marked him as both dangerous and unpredictable—a civil rights militant turned Black Power revolutionary who trekked through Cuba's mountainous terrain with Fidel Castro, consorted with North Vietnamese leaders, impressed African royalty, and dazzled Western intellectuals, all during the same trip. For Carmichael, the tour served as his formal introduction to Pan-Africanist impulses that would shape the rest of his life. No sooner had he arrived home than he was requested to focus on a retinue of crises that included the recent arrest of the Black Panther Party's minister of defense, Huey P. Newton. The Panthers' significance, if not membership, had grown dramatically during Carmichael's time away.* Traveling to Washington, Carmichael met with Panther leaders Eldridge Cleaver and Bobby Seale, who convinced him to speak in Oakland at a rally on behalf of Newton. This invitation began Carmichael's formal alliance with the Black Panther Party—a relationship born out of mutual admiration and necessity even as it was destined to end in a minefield of recriminations.

---

*At the end of June 1967, Newton issued "Executive Mandate No. 2," which "drafted" Carmichael into the Black Panther Party at the rank of Field Marshal, with power "to establish revolutionary law, order and justice" on the East Coast of the United States.

9

THE TRIAL OF
HUEY PERCY NEWTON

Black Power loomed over the year 1968, which was packed with international crises, political assassinations, racial insurrections, climactic street demonstrations, antiwar protests, and a bitterly contested presidential election.[1] Future histories would look back at 1968 as, effectively, the end of the democratic surges inspired by civil rights struggles, though actual events suggest the exact opposite.[2] Black Power demonstrations would boil over for another seven years, continuing domestic insurgency in the name of revolution as government violence was systematically unleashed in the name of law and order.

Student protests, labor strikes, and democratic movements gripped much of Europe, including Italy, Spain, Germany, and France. For a brief season, Prague exemplified the possibilities of the spread of a global political revolution. That year, May Day celebrations in Czechoslovakia featured the open display of once-forbidden signs (including American flags) attesting to a closed society's desire for freedom. While May brought new hope to Prague, it introduced new anxieties in France, where a general strike that included students and workers paralyzed the country.[3]

For Americans, the January 31 Tet offensive—a series of coordinated attacks by the North Vietnamese against major cities, including Saigon—coincided with the Vietnamese New Year, just nine months after General William Westmoreland's stirring congressional speech. During the month of February, network television, newspapers, and influential periodicals transmitted newsreel images and photographs of American casualties, military executions, and human carnage that were worse than anything the nation had seen. The growing perception that Vietnam had already turned into a quagmire ignored the fact that Tet was a military failure. Walter Cronkite, the distinguished CBS news anchor, covered the Vietnam War amid the Tet crisis. Cronkite concluded his February 27 telecast, *Report from Vietnam,* by characterizing the war as a "stalemate," calling for negotiation as an exit strategy, and defending Americans as an "honorable people" who had done the best they could. While Cronkite's comments reinforced his reputation as the standard bearer of American journalistic forthrightness, Lyndon Johnson—still suffering from the fallout of racial upheavals compounded by increasing calls to end the war—reportedly remarked that, having lost Cronkite's support, American efforts in Vietnam were doomed.[4]

In the eighteen months since the conclusion of the Meredith March, Stokely Carmichael had become an international icon, Black Power's most famous advocate. He was also a national leader in search of an effective vehicle by which he could pursue an urban organizing agenda. Based in Oakland's black community, the Black Panther Party operated with a grassroots sensibility that SNCC lacked. On a more practical level, the Panthers possessed a ruthless desperation that Carmichael might have imagined could be used in fulfilling his agenda.

Huey P. Newton, cofounder of the Panthers and its minister of defense, faced the gas chamber if convicted of first-degree murder charges in the shooting death of Oakland police officer John Frey. Newton's incarceration left the Panthers with a leadership vacuum. Believing that control of the group was up for grabs, Carmichael supported the Free Huey movement in the hopes that he might use the opportunity to influence the philosophy of the Black Panthers, bringing it closer to what SNCC had been unable to do: organize poor blacks in the urban North.[5]

For black Americans, Oakland's postwar history represented dashed hopes and blighted dreams that could be seen in the city's housing patterns, employment structure, and public schools. The city's hopes for utilizing the benefits of postwar prosperity to create an industrial garden during the 1940s receded in subsequent decades, in the face of economic downturns, industrial downsizing, and rancorous debates over property taxes, racial inequality, and urban sprawl. During the 1960s, Oakland, along with its more cosmopolitan and prosperous Bay Area sister city, San Francisco, emerged as a center of Black Power activism and a fertile headquarters for California's left-wing political, social, and cultural radicalism. Both cities represented a microcosm of the state's paradoxical culture, at once politically liberal and racially conservative, increasingly multicultural yet under seemingly permanent white rule. California's edgy frontier highlighted the state's complex, racially divisive, and economically combative histories. In Oakland, Black Power introduced aggressive solutions to historic problems, calling for better housing, jobs, and schools in the inner city and surrounding suburbs, which were marked by segregation, demographic shifts, and a subtly changing economy that ravaged the city's most vulnerable residents.[6]

The Black Panthers were mostly young activists whose personal lives and oftentimes limited professional opportunities were defined by Oakland's increasingly impoverished landscape. The Panthers, after all, owed their name to Carmichael's bold organizing efforts in Lowndes County, Alabama. The South had been the site of the most memorable episodes of direct political action, while inner cities in the North and on the West Coast prided themselves on being the forerunners of a Malcolm X–inspired Black Consciousness movement. Now, unnoticed by many, the Panthers were producing an urban phenomenon with distinctly southern roots.[7]

The Panthers imagined themselves as organizing the contemporary

Field Negroes that Malcolm X had defined. Newton fit Malcolm's description of the black working class: the seventh child of a preacher and a housewife transplanted to Oakland from Louisiana, Newton was a new type of political activist—one as comfortable attending community meetings as consorting with the rough traders and hard cases that populated his West Oakland neighborhood. Newton's adaptability was part of his sometimes jarring personality and perpetually conflicted, at times tortured, soul. The contradictions didn't stop at Newton's political life. Both self-effacing and egotistic, Newton was an enigmatic public speaker and an enthusiastic debater, yet extremely sensitive to criticism. As a respected political leader, he denounced the use of drugs, yet remained in the grip of addiction for much of his life. An admitted criminal who studied the law with the intention of defending his own crimes in court, he became a radical activist who would advocate human rights and social justice for all. Yet, unlike Malcolm X's career, Newton's evolution (which included stints in jail on various charges) did not progress in a linear fashion. His personal transformation would prove to be lurching, unfinished, and often painful.

Huddled in the offices of the North Oakland Service Center in October 1966, Newton dictated the party platform, while Bobby Seale, his slightly older, equally driven but more practical friend and party cofounder, wrote it down. Surrounded by piles of books, articles, and pamphlets, they drew up a ten-point program entitled "What We Want" and "What We Believe." The manifesto called for black self-determination, decent housing, education, and the end to exploitation in the ghetto. Ending police brutality, the inspiration for their initial street patrols, rated number seven on the list—a point, Newton later claimed, that proved that self-defense represented only one of the group's main objectives. The document ended with a rhetorical flourish, with the Panthers demanding "land, bread, housing, education, clothing, justice, and peace."[8] Initially advocating radical reform, by 1968 the group dropped "Self-Defense" from its official name, announcing that the Black Panther Party would be at the forefront of a political revolution.

Their sometimes reckless displays of courage to defend the African American community distinguished the Oakland Panthers from their Black Power–era contemporaries.[9] Panther uniforms also captured attention. Starched powder blue turtlenecks offset their otherwise monochromatic attire of black boots, pants, scarves, berets, and leather jackets. Patrolling the streets of Oakland brandishing shotguns, holstered pistols, and law books, the group quickly solidified its reputation for attracting young black militants with its first member, "Little Bobby" Hutton. A fifteen-year-old part-time antipoverty center worker, Hutton served as the group's treasurer and, two days after the King assassination, its first casualty.

Panther patrols reflected Newton's experience on the street as a convict, hustler, and college student. Black men who engaged in criminal activity, those whom Newton described as "brothers off the block" and the "lumpen," represented an untapped army, potential urban soldiers in search of bold leaders. According to Newton, the time had "come for Black people to arm themselves against . . . terror before it is too late."[10] Through the Black Panthers, Newton set out to organize men and women he considered redeemable but who, in a later era, would become known as the "urban underclass."

Immersing himself in a self-fashioned radical intellectual canon that featured Karl Marx, W. E. B. Du Bois, Malcolm X, Lenin, Mao Tsetung, and Frantz Fanon, Newton tinkered with standard revolutionary concepts, shaping them to local conditions in order to make the politics of revolution comprehensible to average African Americans. The black middle class, he argued, failed to help the poor because they despised their social mores. Black college students did little more than talk about problems—they didn't formulate solutions. In contrast, the patrols would prevent police brutality and inspire the brothers on the block to engage in political struggle. Panthers patrolled Oakland, Richmond, Berkeley, and San Francisco, standing guard when police officers pulled over black motorists. While observing the police from a legally safe distance, Newton and other Panthers would stun cops, bystanders, and suspects alike by reading aloud sections from the penal code in an effort to inform citizens of their rights. Initially, these tactics worked; at the mere sight of Black Panthers, police officers would often halt their arrest and leave the scene.[11]

Successive confrontations between February and October 1967, beginning with the *Ramparts* incident, made Bay Area headlines. The April shooting by police of Denzil Dowell, a black man living in North Richmond, called for a ratcheting up of Panther organizing and community patrols when, at the request of Dowell's family, Newton and the Black Panthers conducted their own investigation, concluding that the young man had been murdered. The Denzil Dowell case prompted the Panthers to produce a mimeographed pamphlet, the *Black Panther,* which would become an invaluable means for distributing information, outlining political ideology, and fund-raising.[12]

In May, Newton sent more than two dozen armed Panthers to Sacramento's capitol building in a dramatic protest against impending gun legislation that would end the group's legal right to openly display arms. The Panther "invasion" of the capitol building made national headlines as images of Bobby Seale surrounded by a phalanx of armed Panthers on the steps of the capitol were seared into the national consciousness, interrupting regularly scheduled news and radio programs. This incident would make the Black Panthers' name, successfully positioning them as new leaders of the nation's burgeoning Black Power movement.

The Sacramento incident would produce two competing mythologies. Left-of-mainstream periodicals, from *Ramparts* to the *National Guardian,* trumpeted the group's Sacramento adventure, comparing the Black Panthers to Cuban revolutionaries.[13] White authorities viewed the Panthers as armed and dangerous, a gang of gun-toting criminals out to murder police officers, while many blacks saw things differently, deluging the party's Oakland storefront headquarters with pleas to join and start their own local chapters.[14] In Oakland, the showdown at the state capitol made the group a target for police surveillance. Police department brass issued beat cops and patrol cars with a list of Panther vehicles and license plates.

By the early morning of October 28, 1967, Newton estimated that the Oakland police had pulled him over upward of fifty times, beginning with the first Panther patrol in 1966. That morning Newton returned from an evening of celebrating the official end of three years' probation for a burglary conviction. Within minutes of being flagged down by a patrol car, Newton lay sprawled on the ground, a bullet lodged in his stomach, as one officer lay mortally wounded, another seriously injured. An all-points bulletin described Newton as the suspected shooter. When he showed up at an emergency room, police handcuffed him before transferring him to another hospital for life-saving surgery.[15]

Mainstream media covered the Black Panthers as the harbingers of an unwanted future populated by misguided, if colorful, urban gangsters whose provocative polemics might very well initiate race war.[16] Coverage in the *Black Panther* would frame these same events as the start of a political revolution. Published weekly beginning in 1968, the *Black Panther* featured essays, editorials, and interviews outlining the group's ten-point program; party rules and regulations; and articles outing suspected informers, agents, and provocateurs. Local reports on police brutality, national stories about the black liberation movement, and international news of guerrilla struggles in Vietnam, Africa, and Latin America illustrated the paper's cosmopolitan and at times controversial editorial direction. Minister of Culture Emory Douglass's popular political cartoons depicted police officers as "pigs," adding yet more controversial flair to the Panthers' image. The paper's combative language—provocatively criticizing rival Black Power organizations, law enforcement officials, politicians, and the black middle class—stripped, at least for its readers, long-standing American institutions of moral and political legitimacy. For Eldridge Cleaver, the point was to examine, through the prism of Marxism-Leninism, the peculiar forces shaping black life. Influenced by what he viewed as the successful application of Marxist theory to indigenous movements in Korea and China, Cleaver proposed adopting a vision of class struggle that intimately considered African American experiences and the long history of racial subordination that confounded conventional Marxist rhetoric and practice.[17]

With Newton incarcerated and awaiting trial and Bobby Seale serving a six-month stretch as a result of the Sacramento confrontation, Eldridge Cleaver took on new responsibilities within, and command of, the Panthers. Recently paroled from prison with the help of the lawyer Beverly Axelrod and progressive activists who spoke up on his behalf, arguing among other defenses that Cleaver's literary skill alone warranted his release, Cleaver enjoyed even greater prominence among Bay Area radicals after his arrest at the capitol. Cleaver's *Ramparts* articles (which included a flattering profile of Stokely Carmichael)—as well as his participation in the Black Panthers, antiwar activities, and friendships with white radicals and hippies—contributed to his reputation as a man of striking literary gifts and speaking talent who attracted a coterie of admirers, including James Baldwin.[18] Fearful of possible parole violations, Cleaver had kept his membership in the Black Panthers a secret. The *Black Panther* followed suit, listing the minister of information as "underground."[19]

A career criminal whose first stretch in prison dated back to 1954, the year of the *Brown v. Board of Education* Supreme Court decision, Cleaver became a black nationalist behind bars and began writing from a combination of boredom, curiosity, and desperation.[20] While Cleaver sought spiritual salvation, his lawyer worked to secure his freedom. Cleaver's love letters to Axelrod from prison, along with political essays, made up *Soul on Ice*, his first book. Published in 1968, it established him as a radical social critic and a premier voice of his generation; it also ended his anonymity.[21] Commercially, *Soul on Ice* proved enormously popular, selling over one million copies within two years.[22]

Initial reviews tended to ignore or gloss over Cleaver's depictions of women, preferring instead to bask in his triumphant machismo: an image of himself that at once defied and embraced American fantasies regarding black men's strength, resilience, and violence. Over time, the book was praised as written by a man who had awakened "from someone else's dream," and also criticized by both black and white feminists as an example of the Black Power era's galloping sexism.[23]

For every truth exposed in Cleaver's controversial analysis of the combustible sexual politics that made up American race relations, he left a trail of stereotypes in their place. Among the idiosyncratic but nonetheless archetypal figures populating Cleaver's work were white men who envied black men's sexual prowess, black women robbed of their sensuality, and black men seeking to conquer white women as proof of their relevance in a racist society. The sexual and racial caricatures in *Soul on Ice* were in the tradition of a long line of antimodernist poseurs and prophets (from white patrons of the Harlem Renaissance to verbal pugilists such as Norman Mailer) who observed poor blacks as premodern beings in possession of a liberating sexual energy. In Cleaver's hands, the caricatures took on new dimensions, actually gaining nuance from the opportunity they represented to recognize and react to black exploitation. Outrageous, confessional, and provocative, *Soul on Ice* held an allure for certain black male activists, reaffirming pulp fiction for an unsettling new age. It also exposed profound dangers. Cleaver's black women, tropes of anger, condescension, and cruelty, were liabilities who viewed black men as worthless. Critics focused on the book's graphic descriptions of Cleaver's activities as a rapist as proof that, in contrast to the postprison Malcolm X, his was a soul still in search of redemption.[24] If Cleaver's analysis of race, sex, and power staked a claim for an oppressive type of black masculinity, it also, perhaps unwittingly, spurred intraparty debates about women's role in the Panthers. More a polemical screed than a conventional intellectual analysis, *Soul on Ice* would haunt the Black Power movement long after Cleaver's public change of heart, as well as the party's, would come to adopt progressive ideas about black women's equality.[25]

Cleaver's transformation from a convicted criminal to a radical Black Power advocate exemplified Newton's thesis regarding the revolutionary potential of gangbangers, hard cases, and criminals consigned to lives of perpetual institutionalization. Newton valorized ex-cons, an admiration that grew out of his time in jail and a high regard for Malcolm X's prison experiences. Hard time in California's toughest prisons made Cleaver a formidable recruit to the Panthers. Cleaver's writing talent, his connections with Bay Area radicals, and rapport with former convicts marked him as an invaluable asset whose influence extended over the entire range of the party's modest infrastructure. As editor of the *Black Panther* newspaper, Cleaver creatively interpreted Newton's revolutionary mandates, publishing political tracts that pushed an ideology of self-defense all the way to the edge of advocating for guerrilla warfare. Cleaver posited the Black Panther Party as the vanguard of an imminent revolution to be waged on American streets and fought by an army of politically conscious former prisoners, reformed street hoodlums, and disgruntled combat veterans. For Cleaver, American life evoked images of Old Testament–style decadence, so much so that he dubbed the United States "Babylon." Armed peasants of Babylon, this army of the forgotten, would, according to Cleaver, liberate African Americans or die trying. Cleaver's seductive rhetoric, partially inspired by the Russian anarchist Mikhail Bakunin, attracted groups of black and white revolutionaries.[26]

Cleaver's involvement with the Panthers eventually placed him on the opposite end of the Bay Area's emergent black cultural nationalism. Initially, Cleaver, along with the writers Marvin X and Ed Bullins, had supported black nationalism through the Black House, a large brownstone located in San Francisco's Fillmore area. Black House, which doubled as Cleaver's primary residence, buzzed with activity, welcoming artists, authors, and political activists. LeRoi Jones, Sonia Sanchez, and Roland Snellings—from Harlem's Black Arts experiment—passed through Black House while helping to launch San Francisco State College's groundbreaking black studies movement. A literary prodigy who had overcome personal obstacles, Sanchez found creative inspiration and professional opportunities in San Francisco. Her poetry, which combined race consciousness with sexually frank imagery, hailed the onset of a literary movement. Snellings, who first encountered Jones at the 1961 United Nations protest, had graduated from street protests to clandestine membership in the Revolutionary Action

Movement, the early Black Power group who dabbled in mainstream civil rights organizing.[27]

The Bay Area's Black Power movement shaped cultural, educational, and community institutions. San Francisco State's Black Student Union was the first campus organization to establish black studies as a legitimate academic enterprise. In the face of charges from administrators and campus conservatives that black studies was an intellectual and political fraud, students marshaled Sanchez, Jones, and Snellings to serve as visiting faculty. San Francisco State would become a launching pad for Black Power on college campuses; ex–SNCC member Jimmy Garrett, who had been a driving force behind Stokely Carmichael's tours of the Bay Area the year before, headed State's militant BSU. It was no ordinary college organization. Skilled planning, tireless organizing, and a charged political climate transformed the former Negro Student Union into a major player in campus, city, and state politics. Many of the Panthers' earliest recruits were students at San Francisco State, including Minister of Education George Murray, whose legal troubles would soon embroil students, Panthers, and college administrators in a political showdown. Within two years, San Francisco State's campus politics would make national headlines, with a combative strike that pitted student radicals and sympathetic professors against a conservative administration willing to deploy military-style tactics.

Organized student takeovers in support of black studies transcended regional, racial, and class differences. Student militants at Ivy League, private, state, and historically black institutions of higher learning outlined proposals demanding black studies majors, faculty, cultural centers, and administrative support based on the program State had established. Although San Francisco State's program evolved peacefully, other universities experienced civil unrest on the road toward black studies. At Cornell University, for instance, black studies came about in part through the threat of force, after armed black students occupied a campus building during the spring of 1969.[28] Concerned over the possibility of disruptions, many universities preemptively started black studies programs, a development that sparked charges of co-optation. Black nationalists responded by forming an independent schools movement promoting autonomously administered, if precariously funded, schools, educational centers, and think tanks whose names (Malcolm X Liberation University, Institute of Positive Education, Center for Black Education, and Institute of the Black World) underscored commitment to a revolutionary ideal.[29]

For a time, black nationalist artists and activists socialized with, and organized on behalf of, the Black Panthers. LeRoi Jones headlined a pro-Panther rally a few days after the Panthers' confrontation in Sacramento. In front of three hundred students and numerous television cameras, Jones argued that the time had come for blacks to arm themselves. A fund-raiser at San Francisco State's commons featuring Newton followed Jones's speech.[30] In the spring of 1967, Panthers, militant poets, and radical students formed tenuous political coalitions. Jones's arrival in the Bay Area with his new wife, Sylvia Robinson (later Amina Baraka), bolstered his political outlook and fueled his personal transformation. Black nationalism, which Jones had flirted with for several years, became the motif for poems, political essays, and plays that horrified literary critics and government officials. Jones's poetry increasingly evoked images of militant art inspiring racial confrontation: "We want 'poems that kill' " read one such declaration of war. In addition to writing about revolution, Jones's meticulous search for political and artistic instruments with which to organize black nationalists would end in the Bay Area.[31]

With Marvin X and Bullins, Jones formed Black Arts West, whose theatrical productions played to packed audiences in Oakland and San Francisco. Black Panthers provided security for arts programs and poets crashing at Black House. In person, Jones and Cleaver proved to be physical and temperamental opposites. Diminutive, energetic, and restless, Jones judged the large, unexpressive, and laid-back Cleaver to be a curiously aloof figure.[32]

Jones would find a better rapport with Ron Karenga, a Los Angeles–based black nationalist. The two had met in Newark several months earlier, with Jones leaving the encounter impressed by the loquacious, fast-talking dynamo flanked by two scowling associates dressed in African garb. Born Ron Everett, Karenga had moved to Los Angeles after high school graduation. In Los Angeles he earned a master's degree in political science from UCLA, achieving fluency in Arabic and Kiswahili. Karenga's historical and anthropological study of Africa made him uniquely suited for the black nationalist explosion of the late 1960s. Even before the Black Power movement made national headlines, Karenga successfully organized a Los Angeles chapter of the Bay Area–based Afro-American Association.[33] Led by Donald Warden, the association inspired Bay Area black nationalists in the early 1960s, attracting precocious young activists, including Newton. Warden's promotion of black history and culture offered no fundamental criticism of America's economic system; instead, he chose to argue for black people's fair share through self-help and the creation of small businesses, a solution that made Newton, for one, suspicious of the revolutionary potential of cultural nationalism. Newton took his own experience with the association to heart; for much of his political career, he would regard cultural nationalism as a fraudulent, rhetorical sleight of hand promoted by fast-talking street speakers more interested in personal profit than political revolution. For Karenga, study of African history supported his theory that black America's biggest burden centered on cultural deficiencies that robbed blacks of political agency. Others, including Marcus Garvey, Elijah Muhammad, Malcolm X, and Stokely Carmichael, had advanced similar claims; the novelty of Karenga's approach lay in its promise of a reclaimable African past through the adoption of creatively interpreted cultural, social, and political practices in an easily digestible and expertly marketed package. Possessing the agile mind of an intellectual and the flair of a natural-born showman, Karenga pushed his philosophy as an inevitable reclamation of an African identity stripped of slavery's brutal legacy of physical displacement, psychological anguish, and social stigma. Organizing a group called US—as opposed to "Them"— Karenga promoted cultural reconstruction through what he called

Kawaida. Roughly translated as a "total way of life," from its Kiswahili roots, *Kawaida* was a multipurpose philosophy, religion, and ideology all in one. US members adopted Swahili names, dressed in traditional West African clothes, and engaged in elaborate rituals. Karenga served as the group's master teacher, or *Maulana*.[34] Karenga's promotion of the *Nguzo Saba* (black value system) included Kwanzaa, an African American holiday, and language classes in Kiswahili. Like Black Muslims, US adopted an authoritarian structure, organized a paramilitary unit called the *Simba Wachanga* (Young Lions), and assigned rigidly subordinate roles to women, ostensibly for their own good. Though Karenga eschewed claims of divinity, a cult of personality mushroomed around him nonetheless, and, in a short time, attached itself to his newest, high-profile, disciple: LeRoi Jones.

Jones flirted with a cultural revolution just as Newton was becoming a legend: an imprisoned guerrilla general whose troops camped outside Oakland's courthouse to demand his release. A poster-size photograph of a pensive-looking Newton, wearing a black beret and holding a spear in his left hand and a rifle in his right while sitting on a wicker chair surrounded by African shields, became one of the iconic portraits of the era.[35] Newton had posed for the photograph at the home of Beverly Axelrod in San Francisco's Haight-Ashbury district months before his arrest. After Newton's incarceration, the BPP printed thousands of posters to raise money for his defense fund as well as for its storefront offices.[36] Newton's value to the Panthers went beyond symbolism; his arrest gave the Panthers their raison d'être.

Inspired by events in Cuba, China, and Vietnam, Newton defined "revolutionary nationalism" as a political philosophy that exposed the inequities blacks lived with under capitalism. The resurgence of black nationalism during the early 1960s introduced Bay Area militants, including Newton, to streams of pamphlets, journals, and political manifestos collectively authored by members of the Revolutionary Action Movement. A pivotal, if also obscure, player in Newton's political awakening, RAM declined at around the same time that the Panthers achieved their iconic status.[37] To be a revolutionary nationalist, Newton informed one journalist, "you would by necessity have to be a socialist." Newton's Socialism came from what he often described as observation, participation, and study—a formula, he suggested, that held the key to understanding most of human behavior. As a black nationalist who claimed that Socialism was intrinsic to political revolution, Newton contrasted the Black Panthers' approach to race and culture with other Black Power groups. Reactionary nationalism, or what the Panthers called "porkchop nationalism," obscured a fundamentally reformist politics hiding behind the strict regimens and rituals invoked by cultural, not political, flourishes (African dress, language, names, diet), propagation of which came at the expense of political transformation. Burdened by the wrong political perspective, groups that Newton, and the rest of the Panthers, defined as "cultural nationalists" were deemed enemies of black people—obstacles to the ascendancy of the "Vanguard Party" that would usher in the political consciousness of the black community. The varying degrees to which Black Panthers and other black nationalists accepted culture as the linchpin of revolution can be traced to the ideological roots of the Panther-US conflict that would explode in Los Angeles by 1969. If the Bay Area belonged to the Black Panthers, Los Angeles was political terrain dominated by Ron Karenga and US. In a California street culture punctuated by rival gangs, a war between Black Power groups (both of which included ex-gang members) over political turf was inevitable.

Part of the Panther-US conflict resulted from the Panthers' faith in white radicals and Marxism, a belief shared by no other major Black Power organization. While certain Black Power groups viewed the black community as a nation within a nation, one that required self-determination (including separate land, an idea propagated by the Nation of Islam and subsequently the Republic of New Afrika), Newton argued that the ghetto was an internal colony. He analyzed the situation of blacks in America from the perspective of dialectical materialism, the Marxist-derived philosophical approach that deals in opposites, or the connection between the positive and the negative. In Newton's eyes, particular contradictions that flourished under capitalism produced both horror and hope: urban poverty elicited its contradictions by forcing bright, articulate young blacks to pursue a life of crime for lack of better options. Newton prescribed for white radicals of the "mother country"—the Panthers' name, alongside "Babylon," for the United States—a historic role in the unfolding revolution. Mother country radicals would jump-start revolution throughout the United States alongside the Panthers' assaults in urban cities. The Panthers would accept aid from, and enter into alliances with, white radicals judged to be genuine revolutionaries. The coexistence of racial oppression and capitalist exploitation necessitated these alliances.

Newton's formulation of political revolution included a separate reclamation of black manhood. Partially influenced by Cleaver's discussion, in *Soul on Ice*, of America's tumultuous history of race and sexuality, Newton defined black men as emasculated, stripped, by slavery, of physical authority and psychological independence, then injured, yet again, by black women who shunned them for these "failures." In an interview, Newton explained that the emasculation of American black men was changing since "the vanguard group, the Black Panther Party along with all revolutionary groups have regained our mind and our manhood."[38] Having been labeled intellectually incompetent as an adolescent, Newton spoke from personal experience. The sum of Newton's thought, what the Black Panthers would famously describe as his "genius," was to highlight, through theoretical improvisations, the consummation of seemingly contradictory sets of ideas: peace and violence, hope and death, manhood and women's equality. In so doing, Newton proved to be an unusual ideologue who stubbornly justified sectarian disputes against cultural nationalists on the grounds that their politics were wrong. Yet Newton was flexible enough to abandon some of his revolutionary principles in the face of evidence suggesting that political events had outpaced his historical analysis.

*   *   *

Newton's brash public image and private displays of intellectual intensity attracted a broad coalition of interests. White radicals of the newly formed Peace and Freedom Party (PFP) openly supported efforts to free Newton and also provided crucial financial and political resources. Berkeley students attached themselves to the Black Power movement at the very moment that interracial political organizing had waned in the wake of an explosion of black consciousness and increasing black separatism. The Free Huey movement gave whites eager for an alliance with black radicals an entrée into Black Power. American Whites for the Defense of Huey P. Newton, self-described "Honkies for Huey," had independently organized support for his case even before the Black Panther Party–Peace and Freedom Party (BPP-PFP) alliance.[39] From Cleaver's perspective, this was good news. White radicals had been instrumental in publicizing Cleaver's metamorphosis from prisoner to social activist. *Ramparts* aided this transition, offering professional respect that lent credibility to Cleaver's political exploits, allowing him to cover the Black Power movement as both a journalist and a participant. Cleaver also understood the psychology of white radicals enthusiastic for the approval and friendship of blacks they regarded as revolutionaries.

Based on a much different set of circumstances, so did Carmichael, who repeatedly cautioned the Panthers against interracial alliances. Carmichael's experiences in SNCC convinced him that blacks and whites needed to organize their respective communities. But Carmichael did not advocate conventional racial separatism; instead, a rough pragmatism influenced his thinking. In SNCC, interracial alliances had been strained by complications, including Black Power's scathing rejection of white liberalism. Now with the stakes higher, Carmichael feared that the Panthers would become "the black shock troops of the white New Left and the 'counterculture.' "[40]

In announcing the BPP-PFP alliance, Cleaver took liberties with Carmichael's stance on interracial coalitions. "The fundamental principle we are working with is Stokely Carmichael's dictum of specific coalitions for specific purposes," he said. "We feel that this fits neatly into that framework."[41] In cautioning the Panthers' new allies, Cleaver observed that "if the PFP tried to hurt us we would have to be in a position to hurt the PFP."[42] Cleaver and the Black Panthers approached Newton's case like a political campaign. Negotiations between the Panthers and the PFP had hinged on several issues, including the group's willingness to nominate Newton for Congress. Eager for a vehicle into Oakland's black community, the PFP agreed.[43]

Sympathetic stories in the radical press of Newton's predicament competed with the local news juggernaut, the *Oakland Tribune*. There was a hint of bathos to *Tribune* publisher William F. Knowland's pugnacious conservatism. One of Oakland's wealthiest patrons, Knowland had unsuccessfully run for California governor in 1958. With his national ambitions dashed, Knowland used the *Tribune* as a bully pulpit for his personal criticism of racial militancy in general and the Black Panthers in particular.[44] While the *Tribune* fired streams of anti-Panther missives, support for Newton's case grew. After seeing a widely distributed photo of Newton handcuffed to his hospital bed while awaiting medical attention, one local physician wrote an eloquent apology to Newton.[45] The Huey P. Newton Defense Fund publicized such expressions of sympathy, announced plans for demonstrations, and touted the appearance of SNCC chairman H. Rap Brown at a press conference in support of Newton.[46] Charles Garry, Newton's lead counsel, followed suit, proclaiming his client's innocence at the same time that he leveled charges of police brutality on Newton's behalf.[47] Newton's arraignment hearing provided a preview of the tactics supporters would deploy during the trial. Leather-jacketed Panthers greeted Newton in court with raised fists and Black Power salutes. As uniformed Panthers demonstrated outside, Peace and Freedom activists distributed pamphlets that described Newton as the latest black victim of a police frameup.[48]

Carmichael gave Newton's case its biggest endorsement. Panther organizers trumpeted Carmichael's keynote speech at a planned February 17, 1968, rally as a virtual guarantee of publicity, while the increased turnout, thanks to his presence, provided much-needed funds for Newton's defense.[49]* National coverage exploded on February 17 and 18, as two rallies took place, the first in Oakland and the other in Los Angeles, in support of Newton. The first fell on Newton's birthday and mixed celebration, fund-raising, and radical speeches. The Black Congress, a coalition of Bay Area Black Power activists, helped to organize the fund-raiser in Los Angeles. Attracting thousands of people and featuring leading Black Power advocates, both rallies gained media attention and supporters nationwide.

Discussions surrounding a proposed alliance between SNCC and the Panthers aroused hopes and anxieties in both camps. In theory the partnership was logical, even serendipitous. SNCC's renowned militancy, organizational energy, and resourcefulness were singled out by civil rights and Black Power activists. Rap Brown's penchant for brash sound bites made him an overnight hero to black militants, a sought-after speaker, and a target of local and federal authorities.

Carmichael, SNCC's biggest asset, was ready for change. His increasingly contentious relationship with the group dated to his tenure as chairman. Fallout from his unauthorized statements and controversial international tour had left him at odds with colleagues. Factionalism in SNCC produced competing camps, one aligned with James Forman's class perspective and the other Carmichael's Pan-Africanism. Carmichael viewed BPP overtures to join its membership as an opportunity, while top Panther leadership jumped at the chance for national influence that his participation promised.[50]

BPP officers introduced Carmichael, Forman, and Brown at the Oakland rally as "honorary" members. Carmichael became prime minister of the Afro-American nation. Forman, bitter at having been

---

*In Los Angeles to work on a screenplay for an eventually aborted Malcolm X film project, James Baldwin described Carmichael as a heroic freedom fighter whose "dreams of love" had been betrayed by a society brimming with hypocrisy. In an essay, "From Dreams of Love to Dreams of Terror," dripping with sarcasm, Baldwin offered trenchant commentary about the recent confiscation of Carmichael's passport. "He is being punished by a righteous government, in the name of justly wrathful people . . . and there appears to be a very strong feeling that this punishment is insufficient. If only, I gather, we had the foresight to declare ourselves at war, we would now be able to shoot Mr. Carmichael for treason."

denied the post of political education director over Carmichael's objection, settled for minister of foreign affairs. Brown would pay dearly for his short-lived stint as the minister of justice. Arrested shortly after completing a swing through California in violation of his parole, Brown faced a lengthy prison term on a federal warrant.[51] Forman spoke in detail of retribution for the assassination of Black Power militants, in the form of targeted assaults on power plants, police stations, and politicians, informing the audience that "the only politics we can be concerned with is the politics of revolution." Guns, claimed Brown, would be the key to liberating Newton. Offering Newton as a prime example of a revolutionary hero, Brown asked, "How many white cops have died since Huey P. Newton has been in jail?" Calling President Johnson a "two-gunned outlaw from Texas," Brown dismissed claims that America's government held moral authority over the use of violence. "We built the country up," he said. "We'll burn it down if it don't hurry up and come around."[52] Brown's speech went on to deploy provocative imagery of organized guerrilla campaigns, government conspiracies to commit genocide, and the specter of a coming race war.

Carmichael took a different approach. The Oakland rally marked Carmichael's first major appearance since returning from his international tour the previous year. An empty wicker chair on the stage symbolized the absent Newton and also marked a change in Carmichael's perspective. Dressed in a colorful dashiki, Carmichael maintained that the struggle for Black Power should be international and complex, and would require black self-determination.[53] As the evening's last speaker, Carmichael delivered the rally's most controversial speech. "Tonight we have to talk about several things. We're here to celebrate Brother Huey P. Newton's birthday. We're not here to celebrate Huey Newton the individual, but Huey Newton as part and parcel of black people wherever we are in the world today." Offering a thinly veiled critique of previous speakers' talk of Socialist revolution, Carmichael continued: "Therefore we are not talking about politics tonight. We are not talking about economics tonight. We are talking about the survival of a race of people." Asserting that the U.S. government was prepared to commit genocide against blacks, Carmichael placed survival at the center of his speech.

Carmichael detailed three measures, or "slogans," as he called them, required for black survival. "We must develop an undying love as is personified in Brother Huey P. Newton. Undying love for our people, undying love . . . Our slogan will become: First, our people, then and only then me and you as individuals. Our people first." The call for love and acceptance for the collective good dovetailed with his second point. "Every Negro is a potential black man," he said. Uncle Toms had been "whitewashed," but it was the job of revolutionaries to show them the error of their ways. White racists and "institutions of racism" were the real enemies. Finally, Carmichael called on blacks to unite in struggle around their racial heritage. "Not the land, but the people," he implored. From this perspective, wherever African descendants lived—Africa, Brazil, Cuba, or Detroit—blacks were at home.

Backpedaling from the Marxist polemics he had articulated in Cuba, Carmichael criticized Communism and Socialism as irrelevant to the needs of blacks. During his international tour, Carmichael had given two major speeches that hinted at his support for Socialist revolution. Press reports from Cuba had highlighted such statements, which outraged American observers—a feeling that Carmichael's time in Africa seemed to have changed. Adopting Kwame Nkrumah's criticism that Black Power in America meant little without a liberated Africa, Carmichael was undergoing a major philosophical and political transformation.[54] At the rally, Carmichael proclaimed that "Communism is not an ideology suited for black people, period. Period. Socialism is not an ideology fitted for black people, period. Period." Carmichael's closing comments cast blacks as refugees in a land of racial oppression. "We are an African people with an African ideology, we are wandering in the United States, we are going to build a concept of peoplehood in this country or there will be no country."[55] Carmichael stopped just short of calling himself a Pan-Africanist, choosing instead to outline a political movement that made Africa central to black liberation in the United States. Although Pan-Africanist impulses had long been a part of black politics, the timing of Carmichael's emphasis was off, coinciding, as it did, with the Panthers' growing acceptance of Socialism.

The rally in Los Angeles the next day featured more participants than the Oakland benefit but less than organizers had anticipated. Los Angeles Panther Alprentice "Bunchy" Carter, an ex-convict, former gang leader, and Cleaver confidant, joined Carmichael, Brown, and Forman onstage.[56] Uniformed Panthers marched with military precision outside the arena as members hawked photos and buttons and waved bright blue flags emblazoned with a black panther. Inside the bustling arena, activists passed around petitions, exchanged information, handed out leaflets, and collected donations.[57]

A series of government reports were released at this time, confirming—if only in the broadest strokes—much of the racial inequality the Panthers alleged. In Washington in early March, the Kerner Commission released its findings that systemic racism, unemployment, and police brutality had fueled the recent riots. Focusing on the political economy of race, the *Report of the National Advisory Commission on Civil Disorders* contained more than six hundred pages of facts, figures, and recommendations in support of public and private employment programs that, along with education, housing, and welfare reform, presented a comprehensive blueprint for the radical reform of the government's antipoverty efforts.[58] "All this serves to underscore our basic conclusion," the report stated, that "the need is not so much for the government to design new programs as it is for the nation to generate new will."[59] Martin Luther King Jr., in the midst of organizing the Poor Peoples Campaign, scheduled to convene in Washington, seized on the finding as a naked confession of racism and economic inequality that would only increase the importance of the summer's planned demonstration.[60] Fueled as it was by a combination of scholarly examination, congressional documents, public testimony, and the moral outrage of political officials and civic leaders, the Kerner Commission's report was the last thing that Lyndon Johnson wanted to hear. The man whose signature domestic policy sought to wage an unconditional war against poverty as a way of building the Great Society refused to meet with the commission he appointed.[61]

The president's unexpected announcement, on March 31, that he would not seek reelection kicked off a spring full of escalating crises. Johnson's move roiled Democratic Party politics, inspiring J. Edgar Hoover to write a moving note thanking the president for his brilliant public service. If Johnson's resignation saddened the FBI director, it left antiwar protesters momentarily bewildered, placing the peace movement's dreams of a showdown at the August Democratic National Convention in jeopardy.

The assassination of Martin Luther King Jr., on Thursday, April 4, 1968, before a Memphis march on behalf of the city's striking black sanitation workers triggered waves of violence in cities across the nation.[62] Chicago officials reported looting and fires, while National Guard units were deployed in Michigan, North Carolina, Tennessee, Illinois, and Massachusetts to keep the peace. Washington, Detroit, Memphis, Toledo, and Nashville imposed curfews, and many other cities canceled police leaves, closed schools and businesses, and placed police officers on round-the-clock shifts. By executive order, President Johnson dispatched four thousand Army and National Guard troops into the District of Columbia; some were deployed to guard the White House and the Capitol.[63] The tally of destruction in the wake of King's death was overwhelming— 125 cities in twenty-nine states experienced racial unrest, and an estimated $45 million in property damage was reported. The human cost included thirty-nine dead and three thousand five hundred injured.[64] Almost seventy thousand troops were required to quell what many black militants characterized as a prelude to the coming revolution.

In Washington, rioting broke out along the Fourteenth Street corridor, in the city's northwest section. Carmichael presided over an emotional press conference that had been originally scheduled to discuss Brown's latest legal crisis. "When white America killed Dr. King last night," he said, the country had declared war on black people. "There will be no crying, and there will be no funeral," he added. Informed by reporters that the majority of Americans joined in mourning King's death, Carmichael reminded them of the waves of hysteria that had engulfed the Poor Peoples Campaign.[65] Afterward, Carmichael led a parade of mourners down Fourteenth Street. Departing from SNCC's storefront offices around eight-thirty in the evening, Carmichael and groups of black supporters demanded that storeowners close their shops in deference to King's death.[66] At Howard University, while some agitated students openly contemplated setting the entire city on fire, other students and faculty members jammed into the university's Crampton auditorium, singing "Precious Lord," the hymn that King had requested in the event of his death. Howard's student association president declared that the assassination had "erased a buffer zone" across America's racial divide. In a brief address, Carmichael warned students "to stay off the streets if you don't have a gun, there's going to be shooting." By Friday evening, the District of Columbia was in the throes of a full-scale rebellion.

While violence engulfed the nation's capital, the Black Panthers prepared for an organized guerrilla assault in Oakland streets. In the weeks leading up to the King assassination, rumors spread that the cops were planning to wipe out the Panthers.[67] An anonymous call to Black Panther headquarters the day after the murder specifically threatened party members, including Cleaver.[68] On April 6, convoys of Panthers engaged in a ninety-minute shootout with the Oakland police that ended with Panthers running for cover, Cleaver and two officers wounded, and seventeen-year-old Bobby Hutton dead. The Black Panthers charged that Hutton had his hands up at the time of his arrest, making his death an assassination. Denying murder allegations, the police countered that they had seized a cache of weapons at the scene as evidence that the Panthers were criminals posing as political revolutionaries.[69] Decades later, Cleaver would describe the evening as a planned "ambush" against police officers that went awry; nonetheless, he remained adamant that Hutton had been deliberately murdered.[70]

Partially to defuse mounting tension, Bobby Seale announced that the party had decided against retribution. During a hastily organized rally in Hutton's memory, Seale stressed the need for black people to arm themselves while cautioning against the kind of reckless bravado that contributed to Hutton's death. The Panthers, he said, refused "to get hundreds of our people shot up, killed and wounded."[71]

As the nation mourned King's death, more than one thousand people attended Bobby Hutton's funeral, including local politicians and Black Power activists. Speaker after speaker eulogized Hutton as a freedom fighter whose death reflected a society at war with itself.[72] Then City Council member Ron Dellums, predicting that the nation was heading toward a rendezvous with "militarism and fascism," compared local outrage over Hutton's death with the King assassination.[73]

Hutton's death was just the beginning of the confrontations between Black Panthers and local police officials that would escalate over the next two years. In September 1968, J. Edgar Hoover's public labeling of the Panthers as an internal security threat led to a series of destructive counterintelligence measures aimed at disrupting the party's effectiveness, partly by fostering dissension with other Black Power organizations. Even as Cleaver gained new levels of fame and notoriety by playing up the party's military image, the Panthers undertook less confrontational initiatives, including the "Free Breakfast Program," which provided hot meals for youngsters in Oakland and other cities across the country. Enormously popular, the Panthers' community service programs represented a softer, more practical side of revolutionary politics, one that contradicted FBI fears and local antagonisms that mistook the Black Panthers for armed terrorists. For Black Power activists, King's death legitimized suspicions of nonviolence and the limits of moral persuasion as a way of effecting lasting social change. As a practical matter, race riots gripped the nation's attention but produced little political power. A new generation of black radicals proposed to do something to break this stalemate.

On Monday, July 15, 1968, more than two thousand protesters surrounded Oakland's ten-story Alameda County Superior Court to reaffirm their support for Newton, who remained there awaiting trial, and to affirm the Panther–Peace and Freedom alliance. Intellectually agile, articulate, and movie star–handsome, Newton was personable, with a somewhat scholarly demeanor that defied media expectations. So did some of his most famous supporters, including James Baldwin, who took time from writing a screenplay for a proposed Malcolm X film to visit Newton. In jail, Baldwin and Newton reminisced over their meeting the previous fall at a Caribbean restaurant in San Francisco.[74] In less than two years, Newton had gone from an obscure, gun-toting local militant to an icon who commanded the respect, attention, and devotion of an impressive group of black leaders.

In early 1968, Carmichael had been called by the Panthers in an effort to lend credibility to the group. By that summer, the Panthers had achieved a measure of fame, taking their place among a pantheon of Black Power groups able to command a national and international stage that would eventually transcend geographical borders and ethnic identity.[75] Newton's trial on first-degree murder charges would emerge as a symbol of protest for a generation, attracting a multiracial cast of supporters who hailed the minister of defense as a political outlaw: a transcendent antihero for a revolutionary age. Politicized Chicanos, radical Puerto Ricans, insurgent Asian and Native Americans, and white New Leftists representing political and cultural rebellions of various stripes invested in Newton and the Black Panthers as a cause, a symbol, and a movement. But there was more. Newton's trial placed legacies of slavery and contemporary racism at the center of modern legal proceedings.

Charles Garry made Black Power a central part of Newton's case. The son of Armenian immigrants who had escaped genocide at the hands of the Turks, Garry had been active in radical politics for three decades. Dr. Carleton Goodlett, a Bay Area physician and publisher of a black newspaper, introduced Garry to the Panthers. "Charles, a brother is shot and in the hospital," Goodlett had informed him. "He's charged with murder. I'd like you to defend him." Fueled by little more than righteous indignation, Garry met Newton at Oakland's Highland Hospital. The attorney's value to Newton would be quickly proven when Garry, responding to complaints that the police were threatening his client, hired private nurses to watch over him. As he prepared Newton's defense, Garry reacquainted himself with the writings of W. E. B. Du Bois, supplementing his reading with works by authors Newton suggested, especially Malcolm X, Richard Wright, and Frantz Fanon.[76] Jury selection took three weeks, as Garry challenged the middle-aged, overwhelmingly white citizens that made up the bulk of Alameda County's jury pool. Exclusion of blacks and poor people, Garry argued, hopelessly prejudiced Newton's case even before testimony began. A barrage of experts, including a psychologist and a sociologist, warned against racism's effects on the judgments and attitudes of white Americans.

Garry was framing Newton's trial in much the same language that protesters outside the courthouse were using to call for Newton to be freed. On July 15, the trial's opening day, an orange Peace and Freedom Party vehicle served as the rally's sound truck. Kathleen Cleaver, outfitted in black knee-high leather boots, skirt, and coat, led supporters in chants demanding Newton's immediate release. Kathleen, the wife of Eldridge, was the Panthers' communications secretary. Her glamorous public image did much to obscure the party's ambiguous treatment of black women. Internally, Panthers debated women's role in a revolution designed to provide black men with the positions of respect and authority that white society had historically denied them. Pivotal players in the development and maintenance of the organization's growing infrastructure, women in the rank and file waged an intense, uphill struggle to be considered full partners in the revolution.[77] The *San Francisco Chronicle*'s description of Kathleen as "strikingly handsome" would be added to other press accounts portraying the Panthers as militants who looked, and at times acted, like movie stars.[78]

Several hundred supporters who had marched three miles from Merritt College met another early-morning contingent at the courthouse just as hundreds more arrived from the Bay Area. Security set new standards for safety and contributed to the assertion—denied by the police and stressed by the Panthers—that Newton's case had become a political trial. Armed and helmeted police officers stalked the corridors as members of the Alameda County's Sheriff's Office and the

Black Panthers engaged in a kind of dueling theater: each side brandishing walkie-talkies, lining up in formation, and maintaining discipline under tense circumstances. Extra security meant limited access for reporters and small humiliations for family members and supporters who braced themselves for the arduous task of gaining entrance to Judge Monroe Friedman's well-protected seventh-floor courtroom.[79] Garry protested the elaborate precautions, charging that they poisoned the atmosphere even before a jury had been chosen. "Every time I enter this court," said Garry, "I feel I am in a police state." Judge Friedman, whose courtroom demeanor and membership in Oakland's exclusive, racially restricted Elks Club rendered him, as far as the defense went, a hostile combatant, dismissed Garry's concerns as "personal" rather than legal.[80]

SNCC, the Panthers, and New Left activists participated in public displays of unity as private tensions began to emerge. A contentious July 17 meeting in Oakland exacerbated feelings of mutual distrust between top leaders in SNCC and the Black Panthers. Willie Ricks, John Wilson, and Ron "Crook" Wilkins represented SNCC, while Eldridge Cleaver, Seale, Field Marshall Donald Cox, and David Hilliard represented the Panthers. James Forman triumphantly distributed a memorandum detailing SNCC's unequivocal support for the Panthers in their ambitious quest to become a national organization. Cleaver reacted to Forman's announcement with a mixture of suspicion and hostility. Questioning SNCC's commitment to the BPP, Cleaver accused SNCC of plotting a takeover.[81]

Newton's comments from jail touched off further confusion. In a wide-ranging interview for the underground press, Newton asserted that SNCC's opposition to white revolutionaries rested on the fact that, in the past, white liberals had dominated civil rights organizations. Stokely Carmichael's militancy, according to Newton, had repudiated white paternalism at the expense of distinguishing between sincere whites and opportunists. "The blacks in SNCC," said Newton, "were completely controlled program-wise; they couldn't do any more than these white liberals wanted them to do, which wasn't much."[82]

Because he chose to ignore SNCC's groundbreaking history, Newton's impressionistic analysis was considered demeaning, naive, and divisive. For SNCC members uneasy about the direction of the proposed alliance, Newton's outburst only amplified underlying anxieties.[83] James Forman's deteriorating health, the Panthers' aggressive political tactics, and the FBI's efforts to stall cooperation between SNCC and the BPP exploded during the second week of Newton's trial, when Forman and a group of Panthers met in New York to plan a press conference and a series of rallies. Subsequent media reports claimed that the Panthers had placed an empty gun in Forman's mouth and squeezed the trigger three times in retaliation for botching a United Nations press conference.[84] While Forman denied rumors of overt threats, he admitted that working with the Black Panthers had made him fear for his personal safety.[85] The ripple effect from the failed SNCC-Panther alliance included Carmichael's public ouster from SNCC and his deepening involvement in the Panthers.[86]

On the day of the contentious SNCC-Panther meeting, Newton gave an interview from a visitor's cell at Alameda County Superior Court, reiterating his belief in the law and informing journalists that he would be given a fair trial if tried by a jury of his peers.[87] On the second day of jury selection, large groups of Panthers and supporters demonstrated outside the courthouse. Under a blazing sun, one hundred Panthers jettisoned their poorly ventilated black leather jackets in favor of sky blue T-shirts. Inside, Garry offered evidence of bias in Oakland's jury pool, based on the lower percentage of blacks registered to vote; he went so far as to bring forward a barrage of experts to document his thesis. University of Chicago law professor Hans Zeisel testified that whites tended to favor capital punishment more than blacks, supporting Garry's motion to let death penalty opponents serve on the jury. Zeisel's empirical data, suggesting that pro–death penalty whites harbored unconscious antiblack sentiment, complemented earlier testimony from a Stanford University psychologist, author of *The Authoritarian Personality*, who asserted that racists lived in denial of the way in which prejudice affected their judgment. Two college professors spoke on behalf of the defense, explaining that poor blacks voted less often and were thus underrepresented as potential jurors.[88] Again rejecting the jury pool as biased, Garry argued that because the government had failed to ensure the participation of Newton's racial and economic peers in his trial, the defendant's constitutional rights had been violated.[89] Assisted by attorney Fay Stender, Garry successfully excised blatant racists, prowar partisans, and antimilitants from the jury. Testimony from expert witnesses on the systemic nature of racism gave Garry latitude in steering the jury pool toward Alameda County residents who acknowledged racism's uncanny ability to touch everyday life. In the process, Newton's defense team was instrumental in introducing a subfield of case law—race and jurisprudence—that shaped, and extended well beyond, Black Power–era criminal law.[90]

While the defense's tactics depended on creatively forged legal breakthroughs, the prosecutor, Lowell Jensen, presented the state's evidence as an open-and-shut case of cold-blooded murder; he promised to prove Newton's guilt through state-of-the-art forensics. For more than two weeks and with the help of over two dozen witnesses, Jensen depicted Newton as a career criminal who had chosen to shoot at police officers rather than return to jail as a parole violator. Charging that Newton had been in possession of both an illegal weapon and marijuana, the prosecution painted the defendant as a desperate fugitive motivated by self-preservation, not politics. Oakland's top criminologist, the ballistics expert John Davis, testified that Officer Frey had been shot at close range, corroborating eyewitness testimony from a bus driver, Henry Grier, on the morning of the shooting; the account was a blow to the defense's theory that Officers Herbert Heanes and John Frey had accidentally shot each other while Newton stood in the middle of the crossfire.[91]

"I hope to put Huey on last," said Garry, "and I hope to present our case in five days."[92] The state's case against Newton, which contained inconsistencies in both the witness statements and the physical evidence, buoyed Garry's confidence. Garry's trump card, to everyone's surprise, was his loquacious defendant. By examining through Newton's eyes the individual events leading up to the shooting, Garry sought to make the overwhelmingly white, middle-class, middle-aged jurors identify with the recently reformed juvenile delinquent turned ghetto revolutionary.

Defense motions, which had become a staple of the trial, delayed the August 19 appearance of Garry's opening witness. Garry called for a direct acquittal almost immediately after the trial began. Judge Friedman, a seventy-two-year-old jurist unimpressed by Garry's courtroom antics and unsympathetic to the case's political implications, denied the motion. Defense witnesses offered dramatic testimony that Officer Frey enjoyed brutalizing West Oakland blacks and consistently referred to them as "niggers."[93]

Tight security accompanied Newton's first day as a witness. Dressed in a gray suit and black turtleneck, he cut an impressive figure. Newton greeted Carmichael with a raised fist and a smile, while noting Eldridge and Kathleen Cleaver in the courtroom.[94] Garry's examination began with two pointed questions: "Did you kill Officer Frey?" "No, I did not," replied Newton. "Did you shoot or wound Officer Herbert Heanes?" Newton repeated his first answer.[95] Only a fraction of Newton's direct testimony focused on the Frey shooting; instead, Garry chose to have Newton spend most of his first day on the witness stand recounting his personal biography and political activism. For instance, Newton detailed how *Plato's Republic* had represented for him a watershed text, both in his pursuit of literacy and in his organizing efforts in Oakland's black community. Garry's line of questioning even allowed his client to explain the Panthers' ten-point program, as part of Newton's wide-ranging lecture on African American history.[96]

Carmichael, just in from Washington to hear Newton testify, held a short press conference after the morning recess. "It is crystal clear," he said, "that this is a political trial of a black man who was trying to liberate his people." Surrounded by Eldridge Cleaver and Panther field marshal Chico Neblett, Carmichael offered gracious words in response to SNCC's public announcement of his departure and the end of the SNCC-Panther alliance. The two groups would exchange recriminations over the next month, with Eldridge Cleaver alleging that Forman's faction had underestimated the group's tenacity and intelligence and Julius Lester countering that the Panthers had all but forced SNCC to the brink of consummating a relationship it had never really wanted.[97]

That evening, Carmichael headlined a Black Panther rally in Marin City. Forecasting a race war waged by guerrilla fighters, he informed the standing-room-only audience that blacks would have to prepare themselves for this new kind of struggle. At the same rally, Cleaver trumpeted his presidential nomination by the Peace and Freedom Party as proof that a growing number of whites had turned a political corner. Cleaver's presidential campaign became the centerpiece of a BPP-PFP alliance in which Newton would run for Congress and Kathleen Cleaver for the state assembly. The nominations represented a personal coup for Cleaver, new allies for the Panthers, and added publicity for Newton's trial.

The prosecution's cross-examination of Newton was noteworthy for what it didn't produce. Despite being baited by the meticulous Jensen, Newton never lost his composure on the stand. Instead, in an elaborate form of testimony that annoyed the prosecution as it also lent his testimony an air of poignant dignity, he calmly recounted previous brushes with the law. Two articles published by Newton in the *Black Panther* newspaper, Jensen argued, bolstered the contention that the organization promoted violence. Excerpts from "The Correct Handling of Revolution" included a bloody scenario describing the execution of a police officer. A poem entitled "Guns Baby Guns!" the prosecution argued, advocated murder. Dr. Herman Blake, a Berkeley professor whose expertise included the exotic field of black urban linguistics, countered Jensen's assertions, offering testimony that explained Newton's polemics (including the Panthers' use of "pig" to describe the police), as signifiers, a type of revolutionary slang that could scarcely be taken literally.[98]

Prosecution and defense closing arguments, respectively, cast Newton as a cop killer and as a humanist. "Who did it?" Jensen asked the jury. "Who is it that was a foot away, eighteen inches away? Who fired a weapon?" Jensen's four-hour closing argument offered a devastating summation of state exhibits, witnesses, and material evidence packaged as an open-and-shut case.[99]

The defense's closing arguments rested on the twin themes of conspiracy and politics.[100] Garry supplemented half a dozen poster-size charts contrasting inconsistencies in Henry Grier's eyewitness testimony with a dramatic demonstration disputing Grier's original statement that Newton had pulled a gun from his jacket pocket. Comparing the Armenian genocide to the historic suffering of black Americans, Garry repudiated the resentment against radical blacks and whites exhibited during the recent Democratic National Convention in Chicago, where ruthless suppression was substituted for open-ended debate. "The black community today, the black ghetto, is fighting for the right of survival," he said. Pointing to the Kerner Commission's findings that traced urban rioting to institutional racism and white hostility, Garry concluded his summation. "I personally know what discrimination is," he said. "This case is a diabolical attempt to put an innocent man in the gas chamber, and my government should not be party to that kind of scheme."[101] Jensen's final rebuttal painted Newton as a changeling, a man who talked "of love in the language of hate" and about "weapons in the language of politics." The case, Jensen went on, necessitated a guilty verdict to ensure that the courts remained safe havens "where we can repair our controversies, where we can declare the truth."[102]

Over four days of jury deliberation, Newton's supporters kept vigil in the empty courtroom, at times venturing into a packed room reserved for the press; Charles Garry huddled with Newton on the tenth floor of the courthouse while the prosecution remained in seclusion.[103] On September 8, 1968, Newton was convicted of voluntary manslaughter in the shooting death of Officer Frey and acquitted on a second count of assaulting Officer Heanes with a deadly weapon. Because the jury also found Newton guilty of an earlier, still-disputed felony offense, he was eligible, under state law, for a sentence of two to fifteen years.[104] By 10:20 P.M., after an exchange of clench-fisted Black Power salutes and shouts of "Power to the People!" between Newton and his supporters, the trial ended.[105]

Over the next two weeks, as newspapers weighed the meaning of the jury verdict, the Black Panthers regrouped. Newton's September 27 sentencing hearing proved anticlimactic. Stunned supporters watched as a court officer whisked Newton away after a five-minute hearing in which his sentence of two to fifteen years was announced.

Newton was not the only Panther in trouble with the law. Eldridge Cleaver's legal problems, stemming from the April shootout with Oakland police in the days following the King assassination, continued. Unexpectedly released back to parole two months after Bobby Hutton's death, Cleaver's fortunes changed that September. On the day of Newton's sentencing, the California District Court of Appeal revoked Cleaver's parole.[106] With Newton incarcerated and his own freedom in doubt, Cleaver went on a public speaking tour. Having recently added best-selling author to his list of credentials, Cleaver became a hot commodity on the lecture circuit. Governor Reagan's objection to Berkeley's offer to Cleaver to deliver a series of lectures set off explosive antagonisms between the two men. In speeches, Cleaver unleashed expletive-laced assaults on Reagan, mocking the governor as "Mickey Mouse," even as he confided to close allies that he would never return to jail.[107]

As the Black Panthers took hold of the political spotlight, Richard Nixon claimed the political prize he had pursued for so long: the White House. In a campaign that mixed racially tinged populism with contempt for a liberal establishment portrayed as having disappointed white middle-class voters, Nixon emerged as front-runner, if also a defiantly uncharismatic one. The strength of Nixon's national support partially stemmed from backroom deals brokered during the summer's

Republican National Convention in Miami. There, Nixon had corralled the party's right wing into submission in exchange for a conservative civil rights policy. George Wallace's surprisingly robust third-party campaign, one that played to southern whites' fears of racial equality, economic irrelevance, and cultural conservatism, aided Nixon's infamous "southern strategy," in the process helping to redefine America's electoral landscape. The strategy was more than just tactical. As vice president, Nixon subordinated his racial prejudice to his presidential aspirations, turning himself into an unlikely civil rights moderate who served as the Eisenhower administration's face in Africa, held cordial meetings with Martin Luther King Jr., and received an honorary NAACP membership. In the current political calculus, blacks formed the kind of target—the Republican Party's literal bête noire—that coalitions of resentment thrived upon. Nixon's victory lay in claiming the portion of disaffected voters unable to support Wallace's openly segregationist candidacy but unwilling to vote for the Democratic Party candidate, Vice President Hubert Humphrey. Publicly, Nixon promoted economic opportunity as the cornerstone of his civil rights platform, defining "black capitalism," the benefits of ownership, and entrepreneurship in the black community as the most constructive definition of Black Power.[108]

While Nixon crafted a coalition of counterrevolutionaries, Humphrey struggled to find his own voice. Shackled to President Johnson's Vietnam policy until the final weeks of the campaign, the vice president presided over a Democratic Party fractured by the war, plagued by racial divisions, and groping for national leadership. Violence in the streets of Chicago during the August national convention routed Humphrey's earlier promise to wage a campaign fueled by the politics of "purpose" and "joy."[109] Convinced that victory lay in exploiting racial divisions, Republican strategists played up the Democratic Party's overwhelming identification with black rights. In the end, Richard Nixon, fighting off an impressive, if late, surge from the Humphrey campaign, became the thirty-seventh president of the United States.

Nixon's spectacular comeback coincided with the self-exile of both

Cleaver and Carmichael. Cleaver did not return to jail. After failing to turn himself over to San Francisco authorities on November 27, he became a fugitive.[110] In the days immediately leading up to that date, a group of colleagues, black and white, had hatched escape plans for Cleaver that ranged from an airplane hijacking to climbing up the Rockies on horseback en route to Canada. The actual getaway was simpler. After arriving at his San Francisco home, Cleaver slipped out the back entrance just as an impersonator, accompanied by Kathleen Cleaver, talked tough to reporters. From San Francisco, he flew to New York in disguise, catching a connecting flight to Montreal before boarding a freighter to Cuba.[111]

During a series of speeches at California colleges in November, Carmichael stepped up his criticism of white liberals; chastising hippies (in a crowd filled with them) as drug-addicted "cowards," while at the same time personally vowing to fight for a global revolution. "We are for revolutionary violence. We are for spitting to killing, whatever is necessary to liberate us," Carmichael informed a crowd of more than one thousand students at San Jose State.[112] However, King's assassination, quiet disagreements with the Black Panthers over political philosophy, and a sense of his own mortality forced Carmichael to take stock of his life. For some time now, he had had his eye on a base from which to mount revolution, thousands of miles away from his adopted homes of the Deep South, Harlem, and the Bay Area. Carmichael's marriage to Miriam Makeba, deepening involvement in African affairs, and Nixon's recent election only accelerated his plans to move to Guinea.

In December, Carmichael and Makeba packed their personal belongings aboard a freighter bound for West Africa. By the next year, Carmichael would officially make Guinea his home.[113] "The revolution," Carmichael had decided, "is not about dying. It's about living."[114]

10

DARK DAYS, BRIGHT NIGHTS

In 1969 the Black Panthers were the major radical organization targeted by a maze of official authority, from local police departments and special services bureaus to the National Guard and federal intelligence agencies. A dense network of informants and agents provocateurs hounded the Panthers, other black nationalist groups, and the New Left, deploying legal and illegal methods. The federal indictment of Bobby Seale on conspiracy charges stemming from protests at the Chicago Democratic National Convention set the stage for the Nixon administration's aggressive prosecution of Black Power radicals. President Nixon took a personal interest in the government's prosecution and surveillance of the party.[1] His administration featured several top-level figures—most notably Vice President Spiro Agnew, Attorney General John Mitchell, and national security advisor Henry Kissinger—whose contempt for civil rights colored domestic policy toward African Americans in general and dissidents in particular. After several years of sparring with Ramsey Clark and Nicholas Katzenbach, J. Edgar Hoover welcomed a group of officials whose political impulses matched his own.[2] Nixon's election in the aftermath of Martin

Luther King Jr.'s murder, the very event that emboldened Black Power activists to argue more vociferously than ever that America was an unrepentantly racist nation, placed civil rights leaders on the defensive. Black Power would fill the vacuum brought by King's death, its focus on politics and culture transforming race relations and black activism in the United States and beyond.

For the Black Panthers, 1969 began just as the previous year did, in a state of crisis. The first blow was the untimely deaths of John Huggins and Alprentice "Bunchy" Carter during a shootout, on the UCLA campus, with members of US, the group founded by Ron Karenga. Although the conflict between US and the Panthers could be traced to a turf war over political influence in southern California, Cointelpro had manipulated partisan antagonisms between the two groups to the edge of violence. In the process, it drove US, which never recovered from the taint associated with its involvement in the Panther shootings, from the national political scene.[3]

The violence in Los Angeles occurred as Oakland headquarters initiated a nationwide purge of the party's ranks. The Black Panther Party's purges were a response to the sudden growth in its membership that had outstripped the party's limited resources. Hundreds of rogue members, suspected agents, common criminals, and loyal advocates were expelled from its ranks, and a three-month moratorium on membership was instituted. "We are going to weed out provocateurs and agents," Seale told reporters at the beginning of the year.[4] The party also reordered its priorities, increasing political education for existing members, instituting tougher requirements for membership, and focusing on community service.[5] Mass arrests of Panthers in New York in April, and in New Haven in May, placed additional pressure on the group. In a case that foreshadowed factional splits, the police charged twenty-one members of the Panthers' iconoclastic New York chapter with plotting a campaign of terror and violence throughout the city. The murder of Panther Alex Rackley the next month linked Seale to a plot of urban destruction that newspapers speculated stretched from Harlem to New England. Cleaver's exile and Seale's legal troubles created a leadership void into which the party's enigmatic chief of staff,

David Hilliard, stepped. A childhood friend of Newton's, Hilliard offended the rank and file as well as white supporters with his tendentious style of leadership. Lacking Cleaver's charisma, Newton's intellectual ambitions, or Seale's earthiness, Hilliard settled on a profane speaking manner that substituted emotion for nuance. The pressure of being the Black Panther Party's national spokesman and most visible leader only magnified Hilliard's shortcomings.[6]

Stokely Carmichael's departure further destabilized the Panthers. Carmichael's resignation, on July 3, 1969, came in the form of a message delivered by his wife, Miriam Makeba. "The Party has become dogmatic in its duly required ideology," Carmichael wrote, with dissidents "lumped into the same category and labeled cultural nationalists, porkchop nationalists, reactionary pigs." Describing BPP attacks against black nationalists as "vicious and dishonest," Carmichael broke with the Panthers from his new home in Conakry, Guinea.[7] The split followed the BPP's dismissal of Chico Neblett, an ex–SNCC activist and Carmichael loyalist. Neblett and sixteen other Boston Panthers were purged for counterrevolutionary activity that included "propagating cultural nationalist madness" rather than embracing "class struggle."[8] Carmichael's role in organizing Panthers on the East Coast contributed to the ideological struggle within the party between black nationalists and Marxists, one that would loom long after Carmichael's association with the group ended.[9]

At the time, Carmichael's exit appeared to be the result of an ideological dispute, but in fact both its cause and effect would symbolize much more. The Panthers' political success exposed the organization's fundamental weaknesses at the same time that it introduced dangers, namely those posed by Cointelpro's surveillance, leaving members on edge. The group's diverse makeup produced internal tensions, with more educated members at odds with some of their working-class counterparts.[10] Cleaver's absence contributed to this state of flux, transforming the party in substantive ways, most specifically by a renewed focus on community organizing. Chapters organized a variety of community programs—what Newton would later characterize as "survival programs"—across the country, which would expand beyond food for the poor to include free health clinics, transportation for the relatives of prisoners, and liberation schools.[11]

The party established a national bureaucracy to coordinate newspaper distribution, consult local leaders, and administer financial management. Ideological development, which had once been broad enough to encompass the divergent philosophies of Newton, Cleaver, and Carmichael, turned rigid, couching a more orthodox Marxist-Leninism as the correct revolutionary line. There was little patience for renegades unable to divest themselves of mere black nationalism. Although the Panthers grew increasingly secure in their approach to racial politics, class and gender matters remained troublesome. Because the organization lacked the infrastructure to rehabilitate hard cases, dysfunctional behavior exhibited by certain recruits wreaked havoc on the Panthers as a whole, especially in terms of discipline and weakened morale, while also exposing the group to even more intense repression.[12]

The Panthers' problems extended to the group's treatment of women. Developed on the cusp of the women's movement, the Panthers' gender politics became more progressive rhetorically yet remained conflicted internally, rife with contradictions that reflected the wider Black Power and New Left's own vertigo. Communal living arrangements among the BPP rank and file inspired hope for harmony between the sexes as it also revealed the frustrations of relationships strained by harassment from local authorities, sexual tension between men and women, and frustration and disappointment with party leaders' autocratic decision making and relatively lavish lifestyles. Efforts to challenge what Seale described as male chauvinism achieved mixed results.[13] Women tended to be assigned cooking, cleaning, and secretarial work while men served as bodyguards, drivers, and public speakers. Combating all kinds of political repression, except their own, nonetheless seemed to inspire women in the BPP to take on leadership roles.

By the early 1970s, at least outwardly, the party had turned several important corners. The BPP's increasing focus on welfare rights and women's issues corresponded with Newton's support for women's equality. While Newton's public pronouncements clashed with his private reputation as a womanizer, BPP internal policy still produced tangible results, culminating in Elaine Brown's meteoric rise to the position of party chair.[14]

Carmichael had attempted to address some of the Panthers' other internal problems, yet his lack of personal chemistry with the members undermined those efforts. Second-tier Panther leaders regarded Carmichael as personally distant and intellectually arrogant, while the rank and file's admiration for Carmichael coexisted uneasily with envy of his iconic stature.[15] Carmichael's maverick political behavior, which had been accepted in SNCC, strained his already fraught, as well as new, ties with the Panthers. Over time, Eldridge Cleaver's poker-faced regard for Carmichael turned to simmering frustration when Carmichael's political independence and candor, including remarks that suggested pessimism regarding the outcome of Newton's trial and Cleaver's legal troubles, became apparent. Cleaver's soaring political profile and penchant for overstatement made him confident enough to characterize SNCC as a group of "black hippies" who had become radicalized through their association with the Panthers.[16] For Cleaver, Panther efforts to form a coalition between Black Power, the New Left, and assorted radicals represented a shift in the BPP's philosophy, one that paralleled his change of heart during Newton's trial. "Before last fall we agreed with Stokely's position" that blacks and whites needed to organize separately, admitted Cleaver. But Newton's arrest raised the stakes, forcing a search for other options. "We tried it. We decided to join with them. We are glad we did that."[17]

Carmichael viewed the Panthers as a group of politically naive amateurs who bluffed their way through a historical tide that he had initiated. He chafed when ordered by neophytes to wear the Panther uniform, staging small protests by wearing a dashiki underneath his leather jacket. During several meetings with the incarcerated Newton, Carmichael reiterated his position that nothing short of guerrilla warfare would free the minister of defense, a point of view that alienated key Panthers. In turn, the party's lack of organizational discipline and increasing ties with whites alienated Carmichael. In an "Open Letter to Stokely Carmichael," published in *Ramparts* and reprinted in the *Black Panther*, Cleaver charged Carmichael with a fear of interracial alliances based on Carmichael's experiences in SNCC. Newton had leveled similar allegations in the wake of the failed SNCC-Panther alliance. The Panthers attacked Carmichael's advocacy of Pan-Africanism as simply another version of cultural nationalism that ignored class conflict at the root of black oppression. Carmichael countered that the BPP had formed premature coalitions with white radicals eager to use armed blacks as fodder for political bloodshed unleashed in purely fictional, if no less violent, revolutionary fantasies.[18]

At the end of July 1969, Carmichael and Cleaver met in Africa, during Algeria's twelve-day Pan-African Cultural Festival, to discuss their differences. Even before Carmichael's resignation, Cleaver had expressed continued admiration for Carmichael while at the same time venting his disappointment over Carmichael's failure to play a more active role in the Panthers. The festival marked Cleaver's first appearance since his flight from the United States, quashing rumors that he had been assassinated. Cleaver had arrived in Algeria after almost six disappointing months in a Cuban apartment that locals called "Casa de las Panteras," or House of the Panthers, upset over the Cuban government's unfulfilled promises to furnish him with support that included guerrilla training.[19] Cleaver and Carmichael's private meetings exposed an ideological gulf that no amount of negotiations could repair. Carmichael publicly admitted as much, telling reporters that he had no plans to rejoin the group. Cleaver responded with a series of coordinated attacks that ensured that Carmichael's resignation would be shaped by the Black Panther Party. For example, Cleaver's "Open Letter to Stokely Carmichael" painted Carmichael as a narrow black nationalist whose antiwhite prejudice rendered him immune to the party's developing cosmopolitanism. Cleaver's letter also included his classic rhetorical flourishes, elegant feints away from legitimate criticisms, instead, choosing to gently question Carmichael's courage, while also hinting at his possible collaboration with government officials.[20] Ultimately, the Panthers' perspective would prevail, influencing the way history understands Carmichael's association with the group. Subsequent Panther writings would describe Carmichael as an "opportunist" frightened by the group's daring alliances with whites.[21]

Bobby Seale's attachment to the Chicago Eight conspiracy trial seemed to confirm Carmichael's warnings against interracial alliances. While major Black Power groups had stayed away from the August 1968 Democratic Convention protest, Seale's fringe role in the week's tumultuous events placed him at the center of one of the year's oddest legal trials. Seale's codefendants (Tom Hayden, Jerry Rubin, Rennie Davis, Abbie Hoffman, Dave Dellinger, Lee Weiner, and John Froines) had been key figures in the Chicago demonstrations. For Seale, the conspiracy trial would be just a prelude to murder charges stemming from the New Haven case. The gallbladder surgery that Charles Garry, Seale's defense lawyer, had recently undergone only added to Seale's woes after Judge Julius Hoffman refused a six-week stay and appointed noted civil liberties attorney William Kunstler (who almost a decade before represented William Worthy) as Seale's counsel. Seale's reaction sparked a showdown with Judge Hoffman on the trial's opening day, when Seale read a statement declaring the judge to be a racist. Denied the right to represent himself, Seale displayed behavior that turned the courtroom into a spectacle. The trial would feature allegations of jury tampering, suggestions of a government conspiracy to destroy the Black Panthers, and Judge Hoffman's escalating hostility toward Seale. Hoffman, after engaging in harsh banter with Seale over the matter of legal representation (Hoffman insisted that the court appoint Kunstler while Seale was equally insistent that he be fired), the judge ordered the defendant to be bound, shackled, and gagged for future courtroom proceedings. Seale's supporters charged Eighth Amendment violations, as did his codefendants, civil libertarians, and observers. On November 5, 1969, the acrimonious courtroom relationship between

Hoffman and Seale reached its climax when Hoffman ordered Seale's case severed from his codefendants' and, citing sixteen instances of Seale's refusal to remain silent in court, sentenced him to four years for contempt.[22]

In December, confrontations between Black Panthers and law enforcement reached new levels of intensity. The December 4 murders of Chicago Panthers Fred Hampton and Mark Clark, in a coordinated police raid, renewed questions about police tactics, earning the Panthers public sympathy. Four days later in Los Angeles, a special tactical squad unleashed a predawn raid of the party's fortified headquarters. Charles Garry, responding to the waves of raids, shootings, and harassment, released a list of nineteen Panthers he claimed had been killed by the police since March 1968.[23]

The BPP's high-profile legal battles drew support from a multiracial coalition of liberals, radicals, and civil liberties activists. "The test of a civil libertarian today," wrote Michael Harrington during the final weeks of 1969, "is whether one is willing to defend the rights of the Black Panthers."[24] The hounding of the Black Panthers by local and federal law enforcement brought with it the generosity of white liberals and civil rights moderates who mounted a kind of civic defense of the Panthers through high-profile commissions, books, editorials, even cocktail parties.[25] Perhaps no writer more eloquently expressed support for the Black Panthers than James Baldwin, who compared domestic assaults against the party with America's destruction in Vietnam:

> Now, in the interest of the public peace, it is the Black Panthers who are being murdered in their beds, by the dutiful and zealous police. But, for a policeman, all black men, especially young black men, are probably Black Panthers and all black women and children are probably allied with them: just as, in a Vietnam village, the entire population, men, women, children, are considered as probable Vietcong.[26]

While the Panthers tried to regroup, black and white radicals bombarded the nation with waves of protests, civil disobedience, student strikes, and bombings. This last measure marked a split within the Left over the use of violence, one that would destroy the Students for a Democratic Society and reverberate within the BPP.

Disillusioned by the Nixon administration's escalation of bombing in Vietnam and burdened by revelations of secret military campaigns against Cambodia the previous year, the Weatherman faction of the Students for a Democratic Society committed reckless, improvised acts of violence that first captured national headlines on March 6, 1970, after the group's bomb-making "factory" in New York's West Village exploded, killing three members and sending the rest of the group into exile and hiding. The explosion marked the beginning of a year that would include fifty thousand bomb threats and three thousand domestic bombings.[27]

At the same time, rumors that Cleaver planned to return from exile magnified perceptions of a leadership gap within the Panthers. Nationwide assaults on the Panthers and mounting evidence that Fred Hampton had been executed spurred liberal outrage. A citizens' committee cochaired by Roy Wilkins investigated whether the Panthers' constitutional rights had been violated during the late 1960s. Composed of many of the party's biggest critics, the Commission of Inquiry into the Black Panthers and Law Enforcement Officials—which included Whitney Young, former attorney general Ramsey Clark, and American Jewish Committee president Phillip Hoffman—found that the Panthers' civil liberties had indeed been violated.

Meanwhile, the harsh treatment meted out to Seale—the lone black defendant in the Chicago Eight conspiracy case, now standing trial alone—strained the party's relationship with the New Left. David Hilliard accused white radicals of betraying the Panthers, leading to Hilliard's near-physical assault of Tom Hayden. From prison, Newton responded to the BPP's legal troubles with taped directives, never publicly broadcast, which placed a moratorium on members' cursing in public and warned that the *Black Panther*'s penchant for splashy covers featuring international icons of Communism risked alienating moderate sectors of the black community. Newton's political reevaluation took place against the backdrop of New Left factionalism, including splits between advocates of radical reform and supporters of revolutionary action. Proponents of radical reform promoted community organizing, antipoverty programs, and strategic voter participation while advocates of revolution favored riskier tactics, including guerrilla warfare. The Panthers' bold words touting self-defense and political revolution had radicalized segments of the New Left. Having helped unleash the anger and ideological consciousness of a generation of black and white radicals, Newton now moved to mediate these passions.[28]

On May 29, 1970, the California Court of Appeals overturned Newton's voluntary manslaughter conviction.[29] While Newton's release from prison, on August 5, was historic, it was provisional, pending the outcome of a new trial. Feelings of anger, paranoia, and bewilderment soon replaced the initial euphoria that Newton felt on his return. Privately, Newton bristled against his revolutionary poster boy image. The Panthers had changed dramatically during his incarceration adding thousands of new warriors to the cause. White radicals, who had been tangential in the group's early days, now comprised a core of supporters eager to embrace Newton as their leader. Most important, while Newton languished in prison, the Panthers' rhetoric of self-defense had, through the political activism of Cleaver and others, been ratcheted up toward advocacy of revolutionary violence. The party's broader ideology mirrored this progression as it evolved from revolutionary nationalism to advocacy of a worldwide Socialist revolution. There were reformist elements within the Panthers that tempered these revolutionary yearnings, arguing that gun-centered rhetoric obscured popular programs, like breakfast for schoolchildren, that, in fact, exemplified the Panthers' search for "land, peace, and justice."

Newton's release from jail coincided with a failed prison break that drew the Panthers into the kind of deeper sectarian conflicts that threatened to break the party apart. On August 7, 1970, seventeen-year-old Jonathan Jackson entered the Marin County Courthouse and pulled out a gun. After handing three other defendants firearms, Jackson kidnapped Judge Harold Halsey, the prosecutor, and three jurors. Courthouse photographers snapped pictures in the middle of the kidnapping, as the fugitives marched toward a waiting van with a sawed-off shotgun crudely taped to Judge Halsey's neck. Jail officials attempted to thwart the planned escape; in the ensuing shootout, prison guards killed Jackson, along with convicts James McClain and William Christmas, while one of the escaping inmates fatally shot Judge Halsey and wounded the prosecutor, who was left a paraplegic.

The failed prison break was part of an ill-conceived plan to free George Jackson, who was not in court that day. Jonathan's older brother, George, a legend in the California State Prison system, had requested and been granted Black Panther Party membership by an imprisoned Newton. Jackson's acceptance of a plea bargain for robbery at the age of seventeen had turned his long record of juvenile delinquency into an indefinite sentence under state law. In Soledad prison, Jackson's thoughtful articulateness and ruthlessly imposing physical presence made him a natural leader and jailhouse authority, a status that would thrust him into the center of a war of attrition between inmates and correction officials at Soledad that would result in the killing of one guard in retaliation for the death of a black inmate. In the aftermath, prison officials charged George Jackson and two other prisoners with murder. While Malcolm X, Cleaver, and Newton had used prison as a springboard for political activism, Jackson's indefinite sentence afforded him no such luxury.

Supporters characterized the three as the Soledad Brothers, political prisoners whose revolutionary beliefs and activism had made them targets of jailhouse officials. Publicity surrounding the case introduced the Panthers to a wide circle of radicals organizing around prisoner rights issues. *Soledad Brother,* a collection of Jackson's prison letters published in 1970, turned him into a new kind of Black Power icon. Jackson's published writings resonated among Black Power activists, particularly black and white proponents of immediate armed revolution. The Marin County shooting raised the Soledad Brothers above the thicket of California's Black Power politics—and triggered a nationwide hunt for Angela Davis, the Communist philosophy professor and registered owner of one of the guns used that day.

Meanwhile, by 1970, the Black Panthers had split into two factions. Top leaders in Oakland, while acknowledging that blacks had to protect themselves against racist assaults, identified arms as only one part of radical politics, shifting more weight onto the BPP's popular neighborhood service programs as the key to building a base in the black community. In contrast, advocates of immediate revolution regarded Panther headquarters as an overly bureaucratic, politically reformist clique that subverted Newton's original vision. Newton's writings, which included tracts on the necessity of armed struggle as well as eloquent narratives defining revolution as a painstaking process that required patience and close ties to the black community, lent credibility to both sides.

Despite the Panthers' attempts at reform, the incarceration, exile, or assassination of national leaders such as Chicago Panther Fred Hampton in 1969 meant that individual chapters operated with a great deal of autonomy. Members of the New York chapter asserted this independence as a badge of honor, adopting African names such as Shakur and Cetewayo to set them even further apart as dissidents.[30]

The *Black Panther* chronicled the group's split between hardcore revolutionaries and sensitive community caretakers. Photographs of Jonathan Jackson in the midst of his doomed courthouse assault formed half of the August 15, 1970, front page, while two pictures of Newton (one with David Hilliard; the other with the recently released Newton gently hugging a little black girl) dominated the rest. Jackson's assault placed new pressures on Newton to choose which image properly represented the party. Through emissaries, Cleaver complained that the Panthers no longer set a revolutionary example, having been surpassed by radicals such as the Weather Underground, who continued their bombing campaign against American institutions. Advocates of instant revolution argued that the party's logical evolution lay in guerrilla warfare, reasoning that government repression justified political violence.

Newton attempted to negotiate a balance between the Panthers' political and military wings. His offer of an "indeterminate" number of Panthers to be sent to North Vietnam to aid national liberation fighters followed the party's well-publicized support of Jonathan Jackson's attempted prison break. Newton's alliance with George Jackson won him protection against military-minded Panthers who looked upon Jonathan as a martyr and George as a living revolutionary.

Politics continued to fuel Newton's public bravado. Privately, he expressed anger and disbelief over the BPP's image as gun-toting desperados, laying out plans for extensive political education to reform the group's rank and file. While his critics chafed, Newton set out to reinvent the BPP in accordance with his original vision. A leader whose identity as part street preacher and part ghetto enforcer was reinforced in jail, Newton would retain this duality as head of the Panthers, disappointing some and renewing the hopes of others.[31]

Publicly, Newton described Jonathan as a hero and authorized the Panthers to organize a "revolutionary funeral" for him and others killed in the Marin County shootout. On August 11, 1970, four days after Jonathan's death, Newton characterized the attempted jailbreak as a "colossal event" more significant than 1965's Watts rebellion and the Detroit uprising two years later, because it signaled an attempt at organized revolutionary violence. Newton singled out the teenaged Jonathan as an exemplar of his often-repeated axiom that "the corrupt racist lords can make no law that the oppressed people are bound to respect."[32] Behind the scenes, Newton rejected Jonathan's methods as a reckless stunt that illustrated the breadth of Cleaver's influence, alienated the Panthers from the community, and justified official repression. Cleaver disagreed, dispatching statements from Algeria that supported guerrilla campaigns. Cleaver's views found support among the party's fiercely independent New York chapter, which stood accused by local authorities of plotting revolutionary violence in the tristate area. While both factions expressed doubts about Newton's commitment to guerrilla tactics, George Jackson's partisan support for Newton served as a trump card. Jackson's loyalty was strategic, for, in his mind, the BPP represented the most likely vehicle to liberate blacks. From this perspective, Newton provided vital cover for organizing a "people's army" that would unleash revolution against an unsuspecting public.[33]

In September 1970, amid a climactic two-year state of siege between the Black Panthers and law enforcement officials, the Revolutionary People's Constitutional Convention took place in Philadelphia. The convention drew more than ten thousand participants, including sizable numbers of white radicals. Plans called for drafting a "people's constitution" that would be ratified at a second convention, in Washington, two months later. Newton had been uncomfortable with the convention from the start, since it had been Cleaver's idea, the kind of event that attracted thousands of New Leftists who respected the minister of information as a revolutionary hero. While incarcerated, Newton was perhaps the one man who held greater appeal than Cleaver. In person, however, Newton proved to be a major disappointment. Expecting the kind of rhetorical flourishes that had marked Cleaver's public speaking, the crowd instead listened to abstract, philosophical discussions—another Newton trademark.[34]

The Panthers dominated media coverage and discussion of the Black Power movement as a second wave of Black Power political and cultural organizations gained momentum.[35] On Labor Day weekend, as Newton led the Panthers in Philadelphia, *Imamu* Amiri Baraka (formerly LeRoi Jones) presided over a meeting of four thousand black nationalists in Atlanta. The Congress of African People's (CAP) Conference attempted to draw Black Power groups from the United States and abroad into a coalition. In the three years since being beaten in Newark during the riots, Baraka had emerged as a political activist and black nationalist theoretician, eclipsing his mentor Ron Karenga. Baraka's group, Committee for a Unified Newark (CFUN), retained *Kawaida* as its philosophy. Patterned after Karenga's US group, in Los Angeles, CFUN was a disciplined social organization that reflected sectarian beliefs derived from African culture, including rigid roles for men and women, a precise chain of command, and specific cultural and spiritual rituals. Baraka's newfound asceticism meant that he no longer drank or smoked, was referred to as *Imamu*—a title that made him *Kawaida*'s second-ranking member, nominally subordinate only to Karenga, the *Maulana*—and presided over organizational practices that included written directives requiring members to bow when leaving his presence.

CFUN retained the gender blinders of the US organization. Experiments with polygamy, theories of women's "natural submissiveness," and blatant examples of sexual exploitation marred its vision of black nationalism. Women in the movement fought back; Baraka's wife, Amina, led political struggles challenging CFUN and the larger black nationalist movement on charges of sexism. Global considerations also fueled reassessments of gender politics. Over time, the role of women in the movement would undergo extensive debate, dialogue, and transformation.[36]

In 1969, *Ebony* treated readers to an in-depth look at Baraka's metamorphosis. Splashy color photos of Baraka, resplendent in dashiki and African medallions, surrounded by CFUN members, accompanied an interview that described the writer as a new kind of icon who blended art and politics, spirituality and intellect, confident enough in his staggering literary abilities to move back and forth between the worlds of art and politics. Citing the recent publication of Baraka's groundbreaking anthology *Black Fire* (coedited with the Black Arts pioneer Larry Neal), writer David Llorens declared the poet the avatar of a historic literary movement. While Baraka's position as a literary advocate was not new, his political leadership was. As a minister in the *Kawaida* faith, Baraka was at the center of rituals that included naming ceremonies, overseeing religious schools, and cultural and paramilitary components all administered under his direction. From his multipurpose headquarters, Spirit House, Baraka organized Newark's postriot black community into a disciplined cadre of cultural and political workers whose success at grabbing local political office pointedly dispelled myths that Black Power was romantic and apolitical.

Part of *Ebony*'s special issue on the "Black Revolution," the magazine's profile of Baraka heralded the arrival of a new kind of political activist, reflecting Black Power's growing reach.[37] *Ebony*'s publisher, John H. Johnson, editorialized that "a nation more divided black against white than at any time in history" required a forum for leading figures in art and politics to explain the black revolution to the magazine's middle-class readers. Critics, activists, and authors debated the merits of the Black Consciousness movement, catalogued the history of African American political rebellions, and focused on the activism of local and national Black Power groups. The results were startling in their confirmation that Black Power nationalism had succeeded in touching black America's jagged edges—for instance, black prisoners in Colorado who were taking classes in Swahili.

Baraka's political ambitions paralleled the increasing cultural significance of the Black arts. "The Black Arts movement," wrote Larry Neal in the same *Ebony* issue, "seeks to link, in a highly conscious manner, art and politics in order to assist in the liberation of black people." Such an effort would require nothing less than the search for an epistemology to analyze, criticize, and ruminate about a misunderstood blues people held hostage—literally and figuratively—by an oppressive society. Black Arts activists set out to exorcise the demons behind what Baraka called "a John Coltrane people being ruled by Lawrence Welk."[38] Critics and theorists trumpeted the emergence of a Black Aesthetic in a burst of (largely self-published) anthologies, journals, and books. While a mainstream trade publisher released the landmark *Black Fire,* scores of poets and writers of fiction and nonfiction developed independent ventures to circulate art crafted to promote political liberation. Detroit's Broadside Press, founded by the poet Dudley Randall, anticipated the new wave of publishing, introducing poets such as Sonia Sanchez to national audiences. The Third World Press, established by the Chicago poet Haki Madhubuti (formerly Don L. Lee), organized a publishing outlet for Black Power activists that would last long after the movement's decline.[39]

Baraka's 1966 call for politically conscious lyrics based on black protest proved to be the tip of a sizable iceberg. Fueled by the duel impulses of profit and politics, black recording artists helped propel

Black Power into American popular culture.[40] Spoken-word artists Watts Prophets, Last Poets, and Gil Scot-Heron (whose "The Revolution Will Not Be Televised" became an instant classic of the period) used jazz-inflected vocals, live bands, and African drums to innovate a sound that presaged aspects of rap music and hip-hop culture. Jazz artists and contemporary rhythm and blues acts creatively responded to the push for a new Black Aesthetic, which was also developed in a mural movement that painted iconic images of Black Power activists on ghetto walls across America and in theatrical productions that pointedly reflected rage and desire for a new black nation. Mainstream expressions of Black Power–era radicalism would eventually include soul singer James Brown's "Say It Loud—I'm Black and I'm Proud," a hopeful anthem of resistance, and Marvin Gaye's contemplative masterpiece, "What's Going On."

If the Black Arts exploded nationally through Baraka's high profile, literary black nationalism thrived regionally as well. Activists in urban centers such as Detroit and Chicago succeeded where Baraka had failed in Harlem, building cultural institutions to showcase the "new black poetry," thereby galvanizing the relationship between established African American writers such as Gwendolyn Brooks and young upstarts like Haki Madhubuti. Southern manifestations of Black Arts activism penetrated cities, including Atlanta, New Orleans, and Miami, providing a counterpoint to better-known activists on both coasts, in the Midwest, and in northeastern cities such as Philadelphia and Boston.[41]

Perhaps the most notable Pan-Africanist missing from the CAP conference was Carmichael, who sent a message of endorsement from Guinea, calling Pan-Africanism "the highest political expression of Black Power." Carmichael's message renewed a plea for black unity that he had conveyed in person earlier that year. On March 18, 1970, Carmichael returned to the United States after a fourteen-month absence. Immediately jumping back into Black Power politics, he led a rally at the United Nations in support of independence movements in Rhodesia, Angola, and South Africa.[42] Having "flirted with but never accepted the dream" that revolution could be achieved without bloodshed, Carmichael privately reminisced about his evolution from a precocious West Indian teenager who dallied with members of the Young Communist League into a world-weary activist. "I have had lunch with Ho Chi Minh, I spent a week-end with Fidel Castro," Carmichael wrote to Lorna D. Smith, an elderly white civil rights activist he remained in close touch with. "I have met most of the guerilla [sic] fighters in the liberation movements in the world, I have met the white left, I have been to China, and I have met most of the African leaders. I now work and study under Dr. Nkrumah, the most brilliant man this century has produced. I knew Martin Luther King and I knew Malcolm X. I observe President Ahmed Sékou Touré as he governs a state against insurmountable odds. I am twenty-eight but I feel older."[43]

Within a week of his return to the United States, a federal subpoena would accelerate Carmichael's political maturity. A two-hour appearance before the Senate subcommittee on internal security elicited no major revelations. Pleading the Fifth Amendment to most questions, he agreed to participate in the secret hearings only after learning that the legal consequences of refusal included time in jail.[44] After Carmichael offered no information to the subcommittee on links between domestic radicals and international Communists, committee members resumed their grilling of a more cooperative Robert F. Williams, just back from China.[45] During this trip, Carmichael laid the groundwork for organizing a domestic and international pan-African movement. In speeches at Federal City College in Washington and at Morehouse College in Atlanta, Carmichael defended himself from charges that he had abandoned the movement, as well as from rumors that he was a CIA agent.[46] According to Carmichael, the Black Panther Party's recent misfortunes exposed the group as unschooled Marxists whose premature alliances with white radicals caused their own unnecessary imprisonment and even death. Carmichael's discussion of the Black Panthers revealed a renewed willingness to discuss issues of class. "I want to say that I am not a

Marxist-Leninist myself but I understand Karl Marx better than many people who call themselves Marxist-Leninists," he declared at one point.[47] If Pan-Africanism provided a continental land base to aid political struggles in the United States and around the world, Carmichael declared, Black Power would be its highest form. Dismissing physical migration to Africa as impractical, Carmichael advocated supporting African independence struggles while gaining control of black communities in the United States through the consolidation of political power at all levels, the creation of independent institutions, and the development of a unity of purpose. On the subject of unity, Carmichael's words implicitly rebuked the Panthers, warning activists against "attacking each other, calling names like 'porkchop nationalists' and 'cultural nationalists' or 'CIA agents' and playing into the hands of our enemies."[48] Published in 1971, *Stokely Speaks: Black Power Back to Pan-Africanism* documented Carmichael's evolution from a brand of black nationalism that skirted the edges of retaliatory violence to advocacy of an international revolution spearheaded by Africa's restoration as a global superpower. During a speech at the University of Texas in March 1971, Carmichael cautioned those who had initially come in for his patented brand of militancy to be aware that his ideas had dramatically changed. "The period of entertainment is over," he told students, before discussing "concepts basic to the problems" that plagued the African American community. Reminding students that "we are Africans, we are Africans," he singled out a lack of ideological clarity as crippling the black world's potential for a successful revolution.[49] Despite a political landscape marked by a proliferation of views within black organizations, Carmichael's revised political orientation resonated with black nationalists.[50]

Carmichael toured the United States with news of the global revolution that he would lead from Africa, even as Baraka jump-started the process that would give Black Power mainstream cachet and newfound political leverage. Kenneth Gibson's 1970 mayoral election in Newark established him as the first black leader of a major northeastern city, a victory that black nationalists perceived as offering them a wider mandate for gaining elected political power. Baraka emerged as a major proponent of coalitions between nationalists and politicians, dismissing his critics by noting that dreams of worldwide revolution started at the local level. In other words, activists would deploy strategic resources in local, state, and national elections. Having achieved preliminary victory in Newark, Baraka set his sights on the rest of the nation.

Black Power activists heeded this call. Chief among them was Owusu Sadaukai, a North Carolina militant who read Carmichael's message at the CAP convention. For a time, Sadaukai and Carmichael shared broad political objectives, establishing ties between Guinea and North Carolina. By 1970, many former SNCC workers, including Cleveland Sellers, Courtland Cox, Charlie Cobb, and Jimmy Garrett, had become committed Pan-Africanists. Both the southern-based Student Organization of Black Unity (SOBU) and Malcolm X Liberation University (MXLU) were products of what might be called a SNCC diaspora, reflecting a new organizing direction, which included the Washington-based Center for Black Education. Coordinated efforts to build black cultural and political institutions meant expanding identification with Africa from the merely ideological to the practical. Promoting knowledge of the continent, fund-raising for independence movements, and instituting cultural exchange programs made up their day-to-day activities. Members of SOBU attempted to apply tactics learned from SNCC to a global liberation project that would take them from colleges to union halls. Discerning that American universities were losing the political relevance they had enjoyed in the late 1960s, SOBU saw itself as the student arm of Black Power, a group of committed activists whose goal was to organize young people around a revolutionary Pan-Africanist ideology.[51]

For Baraka, "Nation Time" was more than just a poetic phrase: it encapsulated the evolution of Black Power from spontaneous urban rebellions to the creation of political institutions that promoted vibrant black communities. Grand plans hatched in Atlanta required small, incremental steps. Blacks who talked about nation building but could not win a local election were not up to the task.[52] Major metropolitan centers, like Newark, would be the political bases for the black nation. From slavery's legacy of urban decay and poverty, Baraka set out to create pan-African paradises of intellectual rigor, cultural celebration, and political power. Ballots—not bullets—would fuel this transformation.

The unity of black nationalists during the early 1970s paralleled the beginning of the Panthers' decline. Once free, Newton managed to squander much of the political capital he had earned during his almost three years of incarceration, largely due to a wider crisis of relevancy that engulfed him and the Black Panthers. Most of the Panthers that he had known were now in jail or in exile, and Newton felt uncomfortable around many of the new leaders, including Deputy Minister of Defense Elmer "Geronimo" Pratt. A poor public speaker, Newton endured the quiet disdain of rank-and-file Panthers, who walked out of his political education classes, leading Newton to confide to David Hilliard that "they think the Chairman is more important than me." The suggestion that he change his title to "supreme commander" to avoid confusion only added to growing skepticism about Newton's decision to live in a penthouse apartment, his refusal to curtail the power of Hilliard and his brother, Assistant Chief of Staff June Hilliard, not to mention the increasingly large coterie of Hollywood insiders and hangers-on who exacerbated the tensions.[53] Rumors of Newton's descent into a world of drugs, exotic alcohols, and wealthy, fashionable, and star-struck supporters just ratcheted up the concerns.[54] Expectations that Newton would end internal corruption and financial mismanagement were dashed by reports that he willingly participated in administrative graft. Out of jail, Newton's recreational drug use drifted into a serious addiction that party members suspected yet still ignored.

A series of debates at Yale University in February 1971 foreshadowed Newton and the party's fall. New Haven was the home of one of the party's strongest chapters, and was also where Seale and other Panthers faced criminal charges for the torture and murder of suspected informer Alex Rackley. Newton attended the trial while at the same time delivering a series of lectures as part of his debates with the human-development scholar Erik Erikson that would be published two years later as *In Search of Common Ground*. When not debating, Newton conducted high-level negotiations with Richard "Dhoruba" Moore, Connie Matthews, and Michael "Cetewayo" Tabor over their dissatisfaction with the party and his leadership. Prominent members of the New York Panthers, Tabor and Moore were defendants in the Panther 21 case while Matthews was part of the party's International Section in Algeria and married to Tabor. The trio charged Newton with betraying his responsibility to the party by refusing to support underground military campaigns like those led by Los Angeles Panther Geronimo Pratt.[55] A Vietnam veteran who had served in the Special Forces in Southeast Asia, Pratt possessed the military training to plan the kind of revolutionary activities that Cleaver loved; in fact, Pratt had protected Los Angeles Panthers during a violent police raid in 1969. By 1970, Pratt had risen to deputy minister of defense, important enough to accompany Hilliard to Newton's prison release; as Pratt ascended through the Panther ranks, coordinated efforts by the FBI to fuel Newton's suspicions of him were successful. After Pratt's arrest in Texas while organizing a safe house for Panther underground operations, Newton expelled him as an agent provocateur and "enemy of the people." Forged letters authored by the FBI and routed between Algeria and Oakland described a web of intrigue that placed Pratt at the center of a Panther "coup" that would include Newton's assassination. An open letter from Panther 21 defendants that appeared in an underground newspaper at the beginning of the year, criticizing Newton and the party, seemed to confirm Newton's worst fears that his life was in danger, moving him to act against both Pratt and the New York chapter. Suspicion grew that renegade Panthers were in contact with Cleaver, the most outspoken and well-known advocate of armed struggle. Recognition from the Algerian government, the distribution of his writings overseas, and a recent tour of North Korea made Cleaver a formidable, if somewhat distant, political adversary.[56]

Trust would be the first casualty of successful counterintelligence measures. Distance between Cleaver and Newton, the result of a stream of imaginative FBI measures, conspired to poison a relationship forged in mutual admiration. Less than six months after Newton's release from jail, an FBI memo emphasized his deteriorating psychological state, taking pains to note that he appeared "on the brink of mental collapse" before suggesting a stepped-up disinformation campaign against the Panthers.[57]

At Yale, Newton proved himself to be an impressive if sometimes erratic, theorist. Beginning with an opening monologue defining dialectical materialism, Newton resisted polemical flourishes, offering instead a detailed description of "Intercommunalism," the Panthers' new philosophy. Outlining the party's evolution from black nationalism to Third World "internationalism," he announced that "the world today is a dispersed collection of communities." Accordingly, American technological superiority, military and economic might, combined with an increasingly diversified global population, had rendered conventional notions of class struggle, imperialism, and revolution outdated. Therefore, the road to international revolution lay not in geographic territory but in building a culture within contemporary global communities oppressed by "a small ruling circle" headquartered in the United States.[58]

As a political analysis, Newton's theory of "Intercommunalism" anticipated later discussions of globalization and multiculturalism, but at Yale it produced only puzzlement and confusion. Newton's penchant for answering straightforward questions with long, rambling analogies didn't help matters; he acknowledged his weakness when questioned about his efforts to simplify the BPP's ideology for a general audience. "Yes, that's our big burden," he said. "So far I haven't been able to do it well enough to keep from being booed off stage, but we are learning."[59] If Newton faltered in front of large audiences, he was an affable raconteur in smaller academic settings. Wearing wire-rim glasses that highlighted his professorial demeanor, Newton discussed the paradox of opposing identity politics within an organization that restricted membership to blacks. He also described the party's recently founded Ideological Institute, developed for the purpose of instilling revolutionary theory in rank-and-file Panthers, and his support for the women's movement and gay rights.

Erik Erikson began the second day of his debate with Newton the way Newton had begun the first, with a long statement that expressed admiration for his fellow speaker, before confessing confusion about the previous day's lecture on dialectics. The scholar offered, as a point of unity, his personal biography as a psychoanalyst who dabbled in history. Newton's answers to anxious questions from students regarding the Panthers' strategy and future tactics provided a glimpse into what would soon become a major turning point in the group's history. Quoting Chairman Mao's famous slogan that "power grows out of the barrel of a gun," Newton suggested that the statement related to self-determination rather than to a call to arms. Mao, he claimed, was "not interested in spreading the Communists' influence" through guerrilla tactics but instead focused on amassing genuine political power.[60] The BPP's future, as envisioned by Newton, ultimately lay in politics rather than in violent revolution.

The third and final day of Newton's Yale lecture featured moments of frustration on the part of both the speakers and the students, all of whom found the theoretical exchanges too abstract and Newton's particular unwillingness to engage in a nuts-and-bolts revolutionary polemic disappointing. Annoyed as he was with the Yale students, Newton enjoyed conversing with Erikson, an eminent intellectual who lavished him with the praise and the respect of a colleague. Just as the conference concluded, a crisis erupted. The three Black Panthers (Matthews, Tabor, and Moore) who accompanied Newton to Yale disappeared, throwing into stark relief the growing bicoastal feud that Newton had been unable to resolve. Secret negotiations between the three Panthers and Newton had produced only temporary agreements that were quickly shattered by their disappearance. Matthews, who doubled as Newton's personal secretary and Cleaver's handpicked emissary from Algeria, functioned as the conduit between disgruntled Panthers on the East Coast and members of the newly formed International Section. By February 6, Tabor and Matthews had seen enough. After a series of contentious meetings regarding the treatment of the Panther 21, Newton's behavior, and the direction of the BPP, they abruptly left (along with Richard Moore), taking some of Newton's personal papers and Panther funds. That same day, they announced their decision and the differences that inspired it on a local radio station. A few days later, Tabor and Matthews turned up in Algeria.

Stunned, Newton responded by expelling the missing trio as well as nine of the thirteen New York defendants.[61]

Cleaver lashed out at Newton during a televised international conference call on February 26, which had been originally designed as a show of unity between Oakland and Algeria. As the interview ended, Cleaver surprised Newton by discussing internal problems over the air, calling for the reinstatement of Pratt and the Panther 21, as well as the expulsion of David Hilliard. Ambushed, Newton immediately called Cleaver in Algeria to find out why he had discussed party business in public. From Algeria, Cleaver taped the telephone conversation that would start a war. "Eldridge, you dropped a bombshell this morning," Newton began. "It was very embarrassing for me," he continued. "It had to be dealt with," Cleaver replied. Over the phone, each steadfastly maintained that the other was in error, until Newton dropped his own bombshell. "The International Section is expelled," said Newton. Vowing to write to the North Korean, Algerian, and Chinese embassies, which had formally recognized the Panthers, to inform them that Cleaver was no longer a part of the group, Newton also promised to end Cleaver's political sanctuary by publicizing news of the expulsion. "I like a battle, brother. We'll battle it out," he said. Protesting "that's not the best way to deal with that," Cleaver warned Newton of his willingness to fight. Cleaver, responded Newton, was a "coward and a punk" who leveled charges against Hilliard in lieu of an attack against the party's cofounder. Astonished at the rage he had unleashed, Cleaver backpedaled by saying, "I'm not going to call you that, you see," just in time to have a furious Newton abruptly hang up the telephone.[62]

Newton's expulsion of Cleaver and the entire International Section broke through a festering organizational impasse that had been brewing since Cleaver's exile. Renegade Panthers in New York and New Jersey looked to Cleaver as a revolutionary leader who could end the financial mismanagement and creeping conservatism that, they felt, plagued the Panthers. Newton, on the defensive, countered

Cleaver's charges by accusing Cleaver's cadre of betraying the black community through an ill-fated partnership with white radicals mesmerized by revolutionary fantasies. Carmichael's warning against an alliance with white radicals, Newton would later admit, had come true.[63]

The specter of civil war within the Panthers gave both Newton and Cleaver renewed purpose. Cleaver's life in exile had been marked by long days in the company of fugitive Panthers, tours of North Korea and Hanoi, and unexpected visits from hijackers, political refugees, and other questionable characters. Newton, whose métier since his youth was overcoming rough obstacles, relished confrontation. The Black Panthers were *his* organization, and, over the next several months, Newton set out to ensure that both his supporters and his enemies understood this.

Over the next year, the Black Panthers continued to engage in bitter sectarian struggles, replete with accusations of "revisionism" and "infantile leftism" that grafted Old Left language onto their own contemporary conflicts. Cleaver's faction charged that the party had been split into a right wing and a left wing, with Newton's leadership reflecting "bureaucracy and fear" over proactive revolutionary politics. During the first week of March 1971, a taped denunciation of the Panthers' Oakland leadership from Central Committee members Eldridge and Kathleen Cleaver, Donald Cox, and rank-and-file Panthers, exiled in Algeria, offered detailed accusations against Hilliard and more measured criticism directed at Newton. Cleaver's taped charges argued that the party's right wing devoted itself to mass mobilization and the creation of an infrastructure capable of organizing rallies, publishing a newspaper, and raising political consciousness. In contrast, left-wing forces favored the type of urban guerrilla tactics that had turned Jonathan Jackson into a martyr. The party, Cleaver continued, was a "vanguard organization," not a "mass membership" group. From this perspective, Newton's emphasis on community programs was also the promotion of counterrevolution, by preventing a disciplined group of revolutionaries from taking action while large numbers within the community underwent a prolonged period of political education. In prison, Newton had come to symbolize the symmetry between the party's political and military identities; freed from prison, Newton now stood charged with abandoning armed struggle for political reform. For partisans who, in Cleaver's words, had "transformed politics into war," the shift was unacceptable.[64]

Journalists eagerly followed the "Newton-Cleaver" clash while quoting anonymous party sources who expressed doubts about the group's future.[65] The March 8, 1971, shooting death of Cleaver loyalist Robert Webb in Harlem turned rumors of war into reality. Panther insiders interpreted Webb's murder as the work of Newton supporters, and a response to the death talk emanating from Algeria.

Against a torrent of threats circulating between Algeria and Oakland, Sam Napier, the well-liked head of the party's newspaper distribution, was tortured and killed at the *Black Panther*'s New York headquarters on April 17. Unaware of who was culpable, the press treated the story as a battle of wills between Cleaver and Newton, each of whom threatened to do what the police had, so far, been unable to accomplish: destroy the party. While Webb's murder remained unsolved, the successful apprehension of Napier's killers sparked rumors that Newton and Oakland's top Panthers had received special treatment from law enforcement officials through back-channel cooperation.[66]

The deaths of Webb and Napier signaled the beginning of the end of the Black Panther Party as a national organization. What newspapers described as a "transoceanic" battle between leading organizational officials quickly turned into a rout. In the following months, Newton consolidated his power over the Black Panthers through tight control of its newspaper, party funds, and the loyalty of liberal allies. Elaine Brown, who had joined the Black Panthers shortly after Newton's imprisonment and would become a close political and personal confidant after his release, proved pivotal in this regard. Tough, outspoken, and temperamental, Brown accused Eldridge Cleaver of holding Kathleen hostage in Algeria and of being a philandering husband who committed numerous acts of mental and physical abuse against his wife. Kathleen

Cleaver forcefully denied these charges—going so far as to make a tour of the United States in 1972 to raise support for Panthers loyal to Eldridge—yet it was Newton's faction, in the form of Brown's accusations, that shaped public perception of the Panthers' dispute.

Nationally, hundreds of Panthers quit or resigned, confused and disgusted by the constant stream of recriminations and acts of random violence that punctuated the party's split. Exiled members compared the Panthers to the NAACP, castigating Newton and Hilliard in particular as con men who had betrayed the revolution.[67] At the same time, the party outlined its new agenda, one point of which was a rapprochement with the black church. During a May 19, 1971, speech, Newton surprised observers by describing the black church as a vital part of the community. The Panthers, he confessed, had been guilty of "revolutionary cultism" over the past two years. As an example, Newton pointed to his impulsive offer to send a group of Black Panthers to serve as soldiers on the side of the North Vietnamese. Newton's discussion drew a clear distinction between the party's current leadership and those recently expelled. "The revolutionary cultist uses the words of social change," but lacked patience for the arduous process of political revolution. Indeed, "revolutionary cultists" committed behavior "so far divorced from the process of revolution" that they ended up "living in a fantasy world" of partisans who called themselves the "vanguard." Since they did not have the support of the black community, Newton reasoned, "revolutionary cultists" were not the vanguard. After the speech, Newton recounted his recent visit to a church, for the first time in a decade, to exemplify the Panthers' need to reconnect with the grassroots as part of a larger reevaluation.[68]

Part of this reevaluation included Newton's first stab at international diplomacy. After his second manslaughter trial ended in a mistrial in August 1971, Newton, accompanied by Elaine Brown, embarked on a two-week visit to the People's Republic of China. He returned just in time for the third manslaughter trial (after failing to convict for a third time, the DA dropped the charges) while still basking in the glow of meetings with Chinese premier Chou En-lai and African guerrilla leader Samora Machel.[69] By the next year, Newton would order all BPP chapters closed as part of his ambitious plan to concentrate on developing local political power in Oakland.

Portions of the "left wing" of the party, after an aborted attempt to operate an independent BPP—including the publication of a competing newspaper called *Right On!*—elaborated on Cleaver's definition of "politics as war" through the formation of the Black Liberation Army (BLA). Loosely organized and united principally by the belief that the time for guerrilla warfare had come, ex-Panthers who joined the BLA engaged in clandestine warfare against the police—convinced, even after the incarceration and the death of many colleagues, that they could start the revolution themselves.[70] In the short term, Newton would have the last word. His *Revolutionary Suicide* philosophically narrated the sordid episode of the Panthers' unraveling as a product of Eldridge Cleaver's misguided "defection" from both the Black Panther Party and the African American community. The concept of "revolutionary suicide" represented Newton's rejection of "reactionary suicide"—the political status quo that led blacks to self-murder. "Revolutionary suicide does not mean that I and my comrades have a death wish," wrote Newton. "It means just the opposite." Blacks "had such a desire to live with hope and human dignity" that they were willing to face death to achieve this dream. Newton's theory of "revolutionary suicide" argued that the hallmark of a better life—one that comprised struggles against war, racism, and poverty—was a good death. If death was the inevitable consequence of a revolutionary life, then hope, which sprang from a "resolute determination to bring about change," would be its ultimate corollary and contradiction.[71]

George Jackson exemplified Newton's assertion that "revolutionary suicide" comprised an intrinsic part of a well-lived life. Jackson was one of Newton's greatest assets during the BPP's internal turmoil; his death, on August 21, 1971, in what authorities described as a jailbreak and supporters labeled an assassination, marked the highpoint of the prisoner rights movement that united liberals and revolutionaries in a wide-scale reform effort. Jackson's book, *Soledad Brother,* recounted his years in prison in a series of carefully edited letters; the book was published less than a year before his death. Although initially pleased at his newfound fame, Jackson soon tired of the public persona that had spun largely beyond his control.

Gregory Armstrong, Jackson's white, middle-aged editor, shaped *Soledad Brother*'s portrait of Jackson's life, soft-pedaling the author's more incendiary Marxist rhetoric in favor of a softer narrative of moral redemption in the face of inhumane treatment. Flush with book royalties to pay his defense committees and interview requests from major media outlets, Jackson, in spite of remaining imprisoned, took control of his destiny. During Jackson's last year alive, the Black Panther Party oversaw his defense committee, published his articles in the party's newspaper, and safeguarded his image. Weeks before his death, Jackson admitted to one reporter that he hoped to escape from prison—the public confession of a doomed man, fueled by the wish to avenge his brother's death and energized by the belief that a domestic street war was on the brink of exploding if only ignited by the proper spark.[72] Newton eulogized "Comrade George" as a revolutionary hero even as he refrained from supporting the kind of armed insurrection that Jackson's most radical writings advocated.

Black prisoners in Attica took a different course. Partially inspired by Jackson's death, inmates at the upstate New York correctional facility staged a rebellion in September 1971 that sent shock waves throughout the nation. At Attica, what Huey Newton described as "revolutionary cultism" would combine with genuine inmate grievances and outrage over the death of George Jackson to inspire a prison takeover that made headlines around the world. Five days of tense negotiations produced near-breakthroughs that, tragically, still ended in bloodshed. In the end, gunfire during the takeover of the prison by state authorities killed thirty-nine men—twenty-nine prisoners and ten guards taken as hostages. Medical examinations showing that the guards died of bullet wounds contradicted initial media reports that the hostages "died when convicts slashed their throats with knives."[73]

Angela Davis's criminal trial for aiding Jonathan Jackson's prison break began on February 28, 1972, and would, by its end, complete the circle of major Black Power–era legal battles.[74] Because Davis was a political prisoner, a Communist, and a black activist, her trial was closely watched by a spectrum of the Left. Among the more obscure organizations interested in her fate was the Third World Women's Alliance (TWWA), a small group of black women who, like many of the key activists within the women's movement, traced their feminist consciousness to having come of age politically in SNCC. Shrouded in legend, Mary King and Casey Hayden's landmark position paper at SNCC's 1964 Waveland, Mississippi, conference described a battle of the sexes featuring protagonists with ties to civil rights, Black Power, and the New Left. Perhaps Waveland would be best known as the site of Stokely Carmichael's humorous—and profoundly sexist—remark that the position of women in the organization was "prone."[75] For white SNCC activists, the organization's adoption of Black Power left many searching for their own political identities, which considerable numbers found respectively within the antiwar and women's movements.

Black women in SNCC traveled a different road. Founded by Frances Beal, SNCC's Black Women's Liberation Committee (BWLC) represented one of the few bright spots in the organization's final days. Progressive SNCC activists (some of whom attended classes on Marxism taught by James Forman), who found Black Power nationalism overly macho and yet who judged the women's movement as reeking of class bias and racism, organized the BWLC in December 1968. By 1970, the BWLC had changed its name to the Third World Women's Alliance to reflect a diverse constituency that included Puerto Rican women. Through agitprop, consciousness-raising sessions, and guerrilla theater, TWWA introduced what might be called Black Power feminism into the larger debate over women's roles in liberation struggles.[76] The prominent role of women defendants in Panther trials in New York and New Haven reflected TWWA's fight against what it termed the "triple oppression" of race, class, and gender bias, while the organization's immediate energies were focused on combating the mythology of the black family that had sprung from the publication of the controversial findings released by Daniel Patrick Moynihan. The report mourned the black community's loss of male figures, a phenomenon that could be traced to slavery. Convicted, as it were, without trial for collaborating with the enemy, black women in nationalist circles subscribed to concepts of family that deemed male-centered households as the key to restoring African cultural practices. Yet black feminists drew strength from the growing number of published writings, including *The Black Woman,* a collection of essays and poetry edited by Toni Cade Bambara, that featured Beal's groundbreaking "Double Jeopardy" essay, heralded by future scholars as a manifesto ahead of its time.[77] Beal's radical feminism partially informed the Free Angela Davis movement, while her political organizing grew out of the larger movement's mistreatment of black women. Based in New York City, TWWA marched in defense of Davis (in the face of white feminists, who angrily told them that Davis's case was unrelated to the women's movement), attended national conferences, and forged alliances with trade unionists in the tristate area.[78] Juggling identities as a black feminist, nationalist, and Socialist, Beal carved out space for female Black Power heretics in a political landscape dominated by black men. Compared to more visible organizations, the efforts of these bold women stood on the fringes of Black Power activism. Channeled through Angela Davis's international profile, they took on new meaning.

A native of Birmingham, Alabama, Angela Davis grew up in an area nicknamed Dynamite Hill due to the frequency of Klan-related violence there. Davis was the daughter of middle-class parents, whose ties to radical politics were part of Birmingham's historic, though ultimately unsuccessful, efforts to forge a new civic order, based on racial equality, that included New Deal liberals and black Communists.[79] A French literature major at Brandeis University, Davis spent her junior year at the Sorbonne, in Paris, where she witnessed Algerian students being harassed by police as suspected agitators. Courses with the scholar Herbert Marcuse at Brandeis sparked her life-long interest in philosophy. After a period of study at Goethe University, in Frankfurt, West Germany, she returned to the States to pursue a doctoral degree under Marcuse's direction at the University of California, San Diego. A committed leftist, Davis would find herself impressed with aspects of the burgeoning Black Power movement. In southern California, she became involved with three groups, the Black Panther Political Party (which had no relation to the Oakland BPP and would change its name to Los Angeles SNCC), the Los Angeles branch of the Black Panthers, and the Che-Lumumba Club, a Communist Party club. Davis arrived into an atmosphere where the majority of Black Power activists defined revolution as a man's job. As she remembered, "The constant harangue by US men was that I needed to redirect my energies and use them to give my man strength and inspiration so that he might more effectively contribute his talents to the struggle for Black liberation."[80] Having judged the almost feudal sexual politics of certain groups absurd, Davis developed a working relationship with the Los Angeles Panthers but reserved her complete political commitment for the Communist Party.

Davis's burgeoning radicalism would gain her notoriety after her appointment to UCLA's faculty in the fall of 1969. Under pressure from Governor Ronald Reagan, the California Regents almost immediately began proceedings to dismiss Davis from her teaching post. As America's most famous female Communist, Davis required constant protection, and not only because of her involvement in the Soledad Brothers case but also because the case placed her in the middle of the political intrigue attached to George Jackson. Over the course of the winter, spring, and summer of 1970, Davis's involvement in the Bay Area Soledad Defense Committee evolved from a purely political commitment into a close relationship with George Jackson, his family, and supporters, making Davis an immediate suspect in Jonathan Jackson's ill-fated courthouse assault. Placed on the FBI's Most Wanted list, Davis evaded capture for two months before her arrest by agents in New York, on October 13, 1970, after the discovery that she had purchased one of the guns used in the assault. Posters of Davis sporting a huge Afro hairstyle became the female equivalent of Newton's famous Panther portrait, making it virtually impossible for her to stay underground. Four days after her arrest, four hundred supporters gathered in Los Angeles to form the National United Committee to Free Angela Davis and All Political Prisoners (NUC-FAD). While the Communist Party spearheaded these efforts, NUC-FAD received broad support from black activists, most notably James Baldwin, whose open letter to Angela Davis appeared in both London's *New Statesman* and the *New York Review of Books*.

Some of the correspondence between Jackson and Davis published in *Soledad Brother* revealed their intense love affair blooming against a backdrop of urban guerrilla warfare, in which neither party was afraid to make mutual promises of lifetime commitment. Support for Davis's legal case would continue throughout 1971, with two hundred local defense committees in the United States and sixty-seven international sections. Taking place on the heels of George Jackson's death in San Quentin and the Attica prison rebellion, Davis's trial in the winter and spring of 1972 in Santa Clara County found her spending time in jail working on her case, writing political essays, and receiving letters from thousands of supporters. The prosecution presented their case as a crime of passion motivated by Davis's desire to be with George; several letters to Jackson as well as edited portions of Davis's diary were admitted into evidence to buttress this theory. Revelations about Davis's love for Jackson, which had already been publicized in two books, cast a strobe light on the weakness of the prosecution's case. Lacking incriminating physical evidence, the prosecution resorted to passages written after the August 7, 1970, shootout, to establish Davis's involvement in a premeditated conspiracy.

The defense presented its case in two and a half days, arguing that the charges against Davis were based on flimsy evidence and innuendo that amounted to a legal obscenity. After deliberating for just two days, the jury acquitted Davis of all charges, on June 4, 1972. As Davis hugged her mother, Sallye, the courtroom exploded in cheers while the presiding judge futilely sought to restore order.[81]

Davis's trial represented the denouement of a series of climactic political struggles that briefly united Black Panthers, hard-core prisoners, liberal intellectuals, and left-wing radicals into a coalition that dreamed of justice for political prisoners but would, eventually, settle for exposing rough truths about the prison system. In the process, Davis became the most popular female icon of the Black Power era and one of the few black women to emerge as a national symbol of political revolution. Davis's trial also marked a subtle shift away from the politics of insurrection and revolutionary violence that had reached a peak during the early 1970s. While proponents of armed struggle still had supporters, most Black Power activists focused on political transformation through imaginative acts of creation, political and otherwise, rather than on urban guerrilla warfare.

11

DASHIKIS AND DEMOCRACY

Shortly after the start of the Angela Davis trial, more than eight thousand people gathered in Gary, Indiana, for the 1972 National Black Political Convention. It was perhaps the most important political, cultural, and intellectual gathering of the Black Power era, chiefly because of its scope and the diversity of its attendees. The convention's motto of "Unity Without Uniformity" brought together students, labor activists, elected officials, welfare rights organizers, and feminists in the hopes of building a permanent National Black Political Assembly. Thomas Fortune, a Brooklyn assemblyman, summed up the feelings of many participants after the convention's conclusion: "We Met—Therefore We Won!"[1]

Black Power came of age at Gary, temporarily displacing civil rights as the representative movement for social and political progress. The presence of major civil rights organizations at a convention organized by black nationalists attested to this changing of the guard. Ralph Abernathy, Martin Luther King's successor as head of the Southern Christian Leadership Conference, possessed neither the personal chemistry nor the intellectual heft to lead a national organization and yet, lead one he did. Within SCLC, a power struggle between Abernathy and Jesse Jackson, the dynamic young Chicago activist, further diffused the civil rights landscape. After leaving SCLC, Jackson formed his own group, People United to Save Humanity (PUSH). As head of PUSH, Jackson blended the pragmatic and the militant in rhetorical flourishes that borrowed from the Black Power movement. The Congress of Racial Equality, now headed by the charismatic Roy Innis, was also in attendance in Gary, increasingly drawn by the early 1970s to a rhetoric of black self-reliance that included support for Richard Nixon and opposition to busing. With the exception of the NAACP, which chafed at the convention's all-black makeup, every major civil rights and Black Power organization participated.

Gary's diverse attendance reflected the maturity of Black Power radicalism after its eclipse of the civil rights old guard and its newfound domination of community activism and politics. Rather then being at the mercy of outside forces, many of the delegates made history.[2]

Delegates walked through sunny downtown streets decorated, courtesy of Gary mayor and convention speaker Richard Hatcher, in the black nationalist colors of red, black, and green.[3] The city's welcoming atmosphere shocked Ben Chavis, a delegate from North Carolina who had once engaged in ugly confrontations with Wilmington police.[4] Official courtesies inspired Bobby Seale to applaud the city's police force. "I won't call my brothers 'pigs'—not in Gary, Indiana," Seale informed the conventioneers, who cheered his statement.[5] Seale's presence hinted at the Black Panther Party's transformation. Over the next year, the Panthers would embrace electoral politics, running Seale and Elaine Brown as high-profile candidates for Oakland mayor and city council, while Huey P. Newton masterminded the campaign strategy from behind the scenes.

Part of the united front that emerged out of Gary, the Black Panther Party had, by the early 1970s, closed most of its chapters in order to shore up its organizational base where it all began, in Oakland. While still calling themselves revolutionaries, the group had turned several corners, going from open confrontation with authorities to a strategy of community empowerment, by consolidating local strength as power brokers within Oakland's municipal politics.

More than three hundred journalists and reporters from various organizations, including the *Black Scholar*, *Newsweek*, the *Washington Post*, the *New York Times*, and *Black World*, covered the event.[6] In most published accounts, Amiri Baraka emerged as Gary's premier backroom negotiator. Baraka, Hatcher, and Michigan congressman Charles Diggs presided over a meeting that, as one reporter put it, was "supported by every major Black organization, group, cult, church, profession, and elected official."[7] These groups also brought considerable resources, raising upward of $200,000 to finance the event, increasing the stakes of what many participants considered to be a defining historical moment. Even before the banging of the gavel formally opened the convention, excitement, tension, and anxiety approached a fever pitch.[8] Thousands of delegates and observers descended on West Side High School as delegates and journalists secured their credentials. A sign, "Welcome to Gary: BLACK NATIONAL POLITICAL CONVENTION," greeted participants.[9]

Inside the convention, politics played out along predictable ideological lines. Black nationalists wanted to prevent the meeting from being hijacked by politicians, while elected officials tried to steer the proceedings into the mainstream or, at the very least, away from the kind of radical pronouncements, so common to Black Power events, that made them cringe. Welfare rights activists promoted an increase in benefits to keep pace with inflation, and trade unionists dreamed of a strong prolabor platform while trying not to alienate the Democratic Party machine that provided them with vital support. Certain groups, such as the Republic of New Afrika, caucused for their own political dreams (in this case, the idea that the five Black Belt states in the South constituted a separate nation) in hopes that they might be validated by the larger body; representatives of the Nation of Islam, the Panthers, and others walked around debating various issues, and activists recently back from Mozambique gave interviews about African independence movements.[10]

The convention's draft preamble catalogued these political rhythms. "We come to Gary in an hour of great crisis and tremendous promise for Black America," it declared. The United States was a nation on "the brink of chaos" and controlled by politicians who "offer no hope of real change." African Americans were "standing on the edge of history"; they could either join a "decadent" society spiraling out of control or create a more humane political culture. "The choice was large," the agenda dramatically intoned, "but the time is very short."[11]

Longtime marchers in the freedom movement reminded attendees of their almost religious devotion to certain causes, including some recently embraced by a younger generation. Reparations advocate "Queen Mother" Audley Moore handed out petitions to all who would listen, as she lamented that slavery had robbed her "of her pretty black color," while black feminists such as Frances Beal attempted to gain their share of influence through creative lobbying.[12] At least two FBI informants, authorized by the bureau to ferret out illegitimate political activities, attended the convention.[13] Reporters milled around the meeting rooms, gymnasium, and backroom caucuses to get a feel for the ongoing story as documentarian William Greaves filmed the event.

The convention's more colorful side revealed itself in spectacles reminiscent of Harlem's 125th Street corridor of speakers. Outside, one man handed out leaflets, with a huge sign draped over his body that read: "JESUS WAS BLACK."[14] Journalists took note of it all, describing the "denim-clad band" playing "gutsy" music that possessed the "force and undercurrent of driving drums."[15]

On March 11, the convention's second day, Richard Hatcher delivered a rousing opening keynote. "As we look out over this vast and expectant assemblage, we can imagine how Moses and the People of Israel thrilled when they witnessed the parting of the Red Sea," he began.[16] Hatcher's peroration referenced black America's most revered civil rights leader and intellectual pioneer. "We know the spirit of triumph and determination that infused Dr. Du Bois and his fellow warriors at the first gathering of the Niagara Movement."[17]

Bolting from his seat on the platform directly behind Hatcher, Jesse Jackson rushed to extend his congratulations.[18] The self-described "country preacher" from Chicago, who had been at King's side that fateful day in Memphis, Jackson represented a bridge between two generations of civil rights activists. A liberal integrationist, Jackson took the unusual measure of aligning himself with the convention's black nationalists, repeatedly asking delegates "What time is it?" "Nation Time!" they responded, supporting the widespread notion that they were in the process of building a "black nation" in America. Inspired by a Baraka poem, the idea of building a black nation reached its zenith at Gary, coursing through many delegates and momentarily seizing even integrationists. Jackson stepped into territory that Hatcher refused to enter, publicly calling for an independent political party, even suggesting a name: the Black Liberation Party.[19] His memorable address compared the flowering of a new black movement to a mother giving birth. "When the baby is gonna be born, everybody gets scared," he said. "The water has broke. The blood is spilled. A new black baby is going to be born." He concluded his rousing speech with one final question, "When we form our own political party what time is it?" "Nation Time!" the entire convention hall enthusiastically declared.[20]

Jackson's speech inspired hope and frustration, while his flamboyant appearance (sporting a gigantic afro and a large medallion of King's likeness) struck an image of a civil rights activist adorned in the robes of Black Power militancy.[21] For many, however, Jackson's speech inspired deep, revelatory chords. Among young people and black nationalists, Jackson ratcheted up the wish to stage a formal, public break from major party politics. If Gary would be the birth of a black political movement, it seemed only natural that an actual political party be formed.

For professional political activists, the proceedings elicited caution. Even those sympathetic to the feelings of black nationalists had pragmatic reasons for sticking with major party politics: the money. Afro-America, whatever its form, possessed no parallel structures to replace the financing it received from Democratic Party machine politics, labor unions, and other traditionally liberal constituencies. Many black politicians had come to Gary to leverage their local standing into a possible shot at national recognition; depending on the convention's tone, it could help or hurt their careers.

State delegations and caucuses stayed up throughout the night hammering out the details of a national agenda. The most pressing matter was how much power black nationalists and elected officials, the convention's two main political constituencies, would wield in the National Black Political Assembly. Elected officials tried to blunt the influence of local organizers, who were culled almost exclusively from the ranks of black nationalists. Despite harboring resentment over their treatment by the Democrats, most elected officials refused to abandon the party. Nationalists pushed their agenda, which reflected the hard-earned fruits of years of organizing. Black nationalism, as evidenced by the sheer numbers of people, including politicians, at the convention, would achieve a kind of dominance unmatched before or since.

The conference's final day, March 12, began with early morning sessions to smooth out the national agenda. Volunteers distributed thousands of copies of the draft agenda, which resembled a typical newspaper.[22] Led by Howard University political scientist Ron Walters, organizers had finished the document at two in the morning, when a relieved Hatcher sent it to a local printer. Young people walked around impassively, disappointed at the convention's failure to call for an independent black party, disgusted by some of the wheeling and dealing they had witnessed, and angry that the $25 registration fee had, as one young woman put it, virtually "excluded from the meeting" sectors of the working class.[23] For twenty-one-year-old Georgia delegate L. P. Banks, there was "no need to deal with Democrats or Republicans anymore," and eighteen-year-old delegate Ray Standard, from Washington, wanted to "be about the business" of forming a third party.[24]

Baraka chaired the last general session, his role as a conciliator surprising many. *Newsweek*'s comment (under the title "Black and Angry") that "only a few years ago it might have seemed improbable for one of America's angriest black writers to emerge as a respected chairman of a national black convention" echoed the sentiment of national commentators, including a sizable number of black observers.[25]

Two resolutions passed that Sunday, one calling for an end to busing and the other supporting a Palestinian homeland. Both resolutions
sparked a minor controversy, and were reported by the national press
as reflections of the tone of the meeting as a whole.[26] Nonetheless, the
convention closed in a remarkable gesture of unity as the Black National Anthem played; Baraka, Jesse Jackson, Coretta Scott King, and
others raised clenched fists as thousands shouted that, for black America, it was, at long last, "Nation Time!"[27]

As exhausted delegates made their way home, journalists and political prognosticators analyzed the weekend's historic significance and
future implications. Black periodicals gave detailed accounts of the deliberations, generally praising the convention as a resounding success.
Jet provided lavish coverage, complete with pictures and captions that
read, " 'Right on' Mayor Shows Militants How Black Power Works."[28]
The *African World* described the meeting as a "black beginning in
Gary," criticizing the white media for playing up divisions.[29] There was
some truth to this criticism. *Newsweek* claimed that the convention displayed "more energy than unity."[30] Similarly, the *New York Times* intoned that the assembly was "divided" regarding its role in politics.[31]
The aftermath of Gary would prove that the true measure of the convention lay somewhere in between these contrasting viewpoints.

Removed from the tumult and optimism of both the convention and
the Black Power era, the agenda proposed in Gary reads like an out-
sized dream. In the bright sunshine that beamed down on that mid-
western city, however, the plans seemed difficult but not impossible.
Calls for political revolution hatched in grimy basements, deserted
coffeehouses, dingy diners, and late-night bars had given way to grand
political meetings in cities governed by black leaders. To this day, the
convention's significance remains partially obscured by its association
with an era characterized as violent, antiwhite, and politically unso-
phisticated; yet policy recommendations that emerged from Gary challenge that view. As a template for organizing diverse communities
fragmented by political and ideological struggles, the National Black
Political Assembly promoted an agenda of radical political reform that

focused on urban renewal, quality education, welfare rights, and economic opportunity fueled by the redistribution of wealth. If Black Power could be described as a loosely defined slogan before Gary, it became something more after; national opinion makers took note of the shift, with the *Washington Post* editorializing its support for the convention's goals of political participation as proof that "black power comes of age."[32] Embracing protest *and* politics, Gary illustrated the new political understanding that revolution, far from being the hundred-yard dash that many had predicted during the late 1960s, was in fact a marathon that required a community of long-distance runners.[33]

Baraka's political evolution after Gary showcased both Black Power's practical success at organizing as well as its internal ideological fractures. Characterizing a nation as "a large institution" and "world African unity" as an even larger one, Baraka defined "expressions of concrete Pan-Africanism" as growing out of alliances between local and national activists working together for specific objectives.[34] Nationally, Pan-Africanism was found among black studies programs and departments, black student unions, cultural organizations, think tanks, and elected officials. Internationally, Pan-Africanism provided visible support for, and established links with, existing progressive governments and guerrilla fighters in Africa, the Caribbean, and the larger Third World. African Liberation Day (ALD) exemplified Baraka's idea of institution building as part of the larger process of nation building. Held on May 27, 1972, eight days after the release of the Gary agenda, ALD coincided with the Organization of African Unity's celebration of continental independence.

Owusu Sadaukai, a leading Black Power advocate in North Carolina, organized ALD. A trip to Tanzania in the fall of 1971, under the auspices of the Interreligious Foundation for Community Organization (IFCO), internationalized Sadaukai's thinking. Created in 1967, IFCO was an ecumenical agency that aided a wide variety of social justice groups. Funded by churches and public donations, IFCO provided assistance to leading Black Power groups and institutions, including Sadaukai's independent school, Malcolm X Liberation University, which was located in North Carolina. In the Tanzanian capital of Dar es Salaam, Sadaukai encountered African revolutionaries and black American exiles drawn to President Julius Nyerere's Ujamaa Movement.[35] After being introduced to Mozambican guerrillas waging a successful campaign against the Portuguese, Sadaukai accepted an invitation to visit war-torn southern Africa. Sadaukai's month in the heart of Portuguese Africa included marching alongside guerrilla fighters, eating indigenous foods, and the acquisition of a new perspective on his pan-African activities.[36] By journey's end, he wondered, "What can we do to help?"[37]

The African Liberation Day coordinating committee answered this question. The national movement, spearheaded by Sadaukai, created bridges between dreams of African restoration and the political realities facing black Americans. Introduced to the wonders of the African continent via Black Power, black nationalists in America reacted by organizing locally. Grassroots activists in North Carolina, New York, Chicago, Atlanta, and dozens of other cities started schools, consortiums, and exchange programs that focused on ways to aid the African revolution. Fund-raisers, boycotts, and agitprop fostered pragmatic international links that punctured romantic notions of Africa among certain groups of nationalists.[38]

The ALD coordinating committee drew strength from a broad range of Black Power activists and politicians, including Baraka, Cleveland Sellers, Angela Davis, and Charles Diggs. ALD succeeded in uniting politicians and Black Power activists around African independence struggles as a complement to the strategy outlined in Gary.

On May 27, 1972, African Liberation Day demonstrations took place in Washington, San Francisco, Montreal, and the Caribbean islands of Antigua, Grenada, and Dominica.[39] Organizers dedicated the rallies to the memory of Kwame Nkrumah, whose recent death produced an outpouring of global support highlighted by Fidel Castro's attendance at Nkrumah's state funeral.[40] Among the notable attendees at the ALD event was Black Panther Elaine Brown, her presence a symbolic exorcism of the group's criticism of black nationalists; she described the proceedings as "the most beautiful thing I've ever seen in my life."[41] Within the Black Panther Party, Newton's criticism of Pan-Africanism as the "highest stage of cultural nationalism" had been replaced by the party's willingness to cooperate with a pan-African movement whose national composition, international contacts, and local connections surpassed its own.[42]

If Gary represented a move toward a national black political agenda, African Liberation Day reflected the movement's evolving global awareness. It also illustrated the continuation of an alliance between Black Power activists and African American politicians that had been brokered through several years of public and private negotiations before its consummation in Gary. The presence of Charles Diggs, chair of the House Subcommittee on Africa, underscored this point. Addressing the Washington demonstration in a colorful dashiki, Diggs provided Black Power activists with congressional support. "We are sounding a warning," he announced, "that no longer will the movement stop at the water's edge."[43]

Local nationalists promoted Black Power's pan-African impulses and looked to the continent as a practical if also ideological symbol that held the key to black liberation in the United States. The push to build nationalist institutions reflected the general adoption of aspects of Stokely Carmichael's advocacy of Pan-Africanism. However, ideological differences threatened the stability of this united front. Baraka, a protean figure whose political leadership and poetry accelerated the spread of black consciousness from American ghettos to college campuses, stood at the center of increasingly rancorous debates between Black Power activists committed to black nationalism and those committed to Marxism. National and regional meetings of the African Liberation Support Committee became the site for major discussions about Black Power's future. Pan-Africanism, lauded for its ability to appeal simultaneously to moderates, militants, and revolutionaries, now proved incapable of overcoming the very philosophical and personal rifts it inspired. Certain black nationalists advocated an exclusively racial politics that—in its basest form—rationalized the defense of African dictators under a misguided notion of racial solidarity.[44] Revolutionary Pan-Africanists, while allowing aspects of Marxism to influence their beliefs, agreed that a united continent would play a pivotal role in shaping domestic and international struggles against racism and colonialism. The final group, black Marxists, saw class struggle as the key to liberation and were suspicious of all forms of racial solidarity, a position that offended many black nationalists.[45]

The Black Panthers' political organizing in Oakland complemented the ALD's pursuit of a global agenda with its focus on local politics. Intercommunalism, the party's controversial philosophy, defined local and international politics as the flip sides of the same coin. Newton's decision to close Panther chapters outside of Oakland, cooperate with grassroots institutions such as the black church, and promote "survival programs," all in the name of radical reform, augmented the party's local strength even as it diminished the Panthers' national profile. Seale's mayoral campaign was meant to remedy the lack of black political power in Oakland. With Seale's announcement, the *Black Panther* sprang into action, documenting a litany of abuses by local authorities. Seale summed up the party's efforts to build an urban political base as consistent with its past revolutionary posture. "To use Oakland's institutions as a means to run the survival program is to organize and unify the people, and make those institutions serve the people," he remarked. "But the main thing to do, of course, is get the racist flunkies and lackeys of the capitalist ruling class out of the system."[46] Newton directed the party's remaining members and resources to Seale's and Minister of Information Elaine Brown's (who was running for city council) respective campaigns, both of which touted a platform that called for new corporate taxes, revenue sharing, and a residency requirement for Oakland police officers. Hampered by scandals and only recently resolved legal trials, Seale's and Brown's campaigns nevertheless presented a challenge to the city's Democratic establishment and turned the Panthers into major players in Oakland politics—despite their defeat in the elections.

If Seale and Brown represented the new public face of the Black Panther Party of the early 1970s, Newton remained in limbo, intent on making Oakland a base of operations for radical politics yet still drawn to the city's street culture. An acrimonious boycott launched by the Panthers during the summer of 1971 against black businesses that refused Newton's demand to contribute to survival programs drew expected criticism from long-standing enemies, such as the *Oakland Tribune,* as well as anxiety from various sectors of Oakland's black community. The Panthers' protests represented the stark transformation of the easy solidarity of the Black Power era of the late 1960s to the methodical, sober approaches that would characterize the early 1970s.

At times, Newton's reevaluation of black capitalism crossed the line separating legal protests and extortion. By the time the Panthers reached a settlement with Cal-Pak (a coalition of black-owned liquor and package stores) in 1972, Newton had shifted his energies to consolidating power over a more lucrative arena: Oakland's black underworld. The FBI documented allegations that ranged from the sordid (Newton's alleged efforts to shake down black social clubs) to the outrageous (the Panthers' demand for money from the producers of the "blaxploitation" film *The Mack*). In these instances, Newton the revolutionary had been replaced by Newton the racketeer.[47]

Rumors of Newton's drug dependency, fistfights, and bizarre behavior (including Seale's arbitrary dismissal from the Panthers) made his arrest in 1974 on charges of beating his tailor and shooting a prostitute unsurprising. Prior to his arrest, Newton, surrounded by a hand-picked security detail, would spend late nights at the Lamp Post, a nightclub owned by the party, in pursuit of a substitute for the clarifying danger he felt on early Panther patrols. Although Newton clearly retained traces of his earlier rakish bravado, his personal impulses leaned squarely toward the predatory. Haunted by substance abuse, Newton's revolutionary politics atrophied into a quest for material wealth and personal pleasure, punctuated by intermittent moments of sobriety. Under the influence of drugs and alcohol more often than not, Newton's star was on the descent at the exact time that the Black Panthers came closest to approximating his early vision of a radical community organization able to meet the needs of the people rather than the whims of political leaders. Faced with a string of criminal charges, Newton jumped bail and, after a treacherous journey, arrived in Cuba around Thanksgiving 1974.[48]

As the Black Panthers turned to local activism and Newton's personal life spiraled out of control, the united front established at Gary revealed itself to be broader than it was deep. Tensions between Baraka and politicians who had participated in the Gary convention presaged conflicts that would cripple Black Power radicalism and lead to the almost simultaneous dissolution of the Congress of African People and the National Black Political Assembly. For Black Power activists, the pressing order of business throughout 1973 was the organization of the Sixth Pan-African Congress, to be held the following year. The "6-PAC," as it came to be known, was a reprisal of five meetings that had been organized by W. E. B. Du Bois during the first half of the twentieth century. Pan-Africanists took great pride in the fact that the upcoming conference would be the first of its kind to be convened in Africa. The success of the second annual African Liberation Day, in May 1973, prompted organizers to establish a permanent body—the African Liberation Support Committee—that would serve as both a pro-Africa lobby and a national educational and community organizing tool. Baraka played a major role in facilitating these efforts, which included publicizing resistance against Portuguese colonialism in Mozambique and Angola. Anticolonial struggles in tiny Guinea-Bissau and the islands of Cape Verde also loomed large. Amilcar Cabral (from whom Stokely Carmichael had requested assistance in 1967), the leader of the resistance, was a respected revolutionary and pragmatic Marxist whose beliefs remained compatible with Black Power and the promotion of African culture.

In Tanzania, President Nyerere's definition of Socialism as "Ujamaa," or cooperative economics, struck a chord with stateside Pan-Africanists seeking an alternative to free-market capitalism and dogmatic Marxism. By the early 1970s, Baraka's essays on building black nationalist institutions revolved around "Nationalism, Pan-Africanism, and Ujamaa," which he characterized as "African Scientific Socialism," a blend of cultural nationalism, internationalism, and Socialism.[49]

Two years after the Gary convention, Black Power's national decline would begin in earnest. At the National Black Political Convention, in Little Rock, Arkansas, in April 1974, Baraka's call for Socialist revolution stunned delegates and observers, many of whom had been unaware of his deep disgust with the very style of progressive black nationalism and Pan-Africanism that he had helped to initiate. Little Rock was notable, as well, for the scarcity of black elected officials; presumably they were put off by a direction that left the National Black Political Assembly open to charges of red-baiting and worse. Internal debates over Black Power's future would evolve into bitter struggles, highlighted by the Little Rock convention's refusal to support the creation of an independent political party—a stance that Harold Cruse characterized as "a betrayal of the Black militant potential built up during the struggles of the Sixties."[50]

One month after Little Rock, in May 1974, black nationalists convened a conference at Howard University to discuss the future of the Black Power movement. Held amid a flurry of May activities dubbed "African Liberation Month," the conference's theme of "Which Road Toward Black Liberation?" sparked quarrels between factions committed to Pan-Africanism and those advocating Marxism. Boldfaced names, including Baraka, Sadaukai, and Carmichael, presented major theoretical statements at the convention.

At Howard, redefining the role of class struggle in domestic and international politics dominated the agenda. One group attempted to reconcile its Pan-Africanist consciousness with the brutal realities of American racism. Black Marxists, countering with a historical materialist view, argued that blacks constituted an exploited working class whose liberation lay in a global movement for a Socialist revolution.

Wearing the green military fatigues of the Guinean Army and representing the All African People's Revolutionary Party, Carmichael, after
acknowledging the importance of class struggle, drifted back to a focus on race that had been the hallmark of his original call for Black
Power. "The only question before the black community," said
Carmichael, "is the question of nationalism!" The primary objective
for black activists, according to Carmichael, was the restoration of
Africa. For Carmichael, Pan-Africanism represented "the total liberation and unification of Africa under scientific socialism." Carmichael's
advocacy of Socialist revolution reflected the ideological evolution that
had taken place during his five years in Africa spent in personal study
and meetings with Nkrumah and Sékou Touré.

Carmichael's attempts to reassert his leadership over Black Power
politics through annual speaking tours of American universities and
community groups produced mixed results. While he made significant
inroads promoting the All African People's Revolutionary Party, establishing a base for it at Howard University and garnering national press
attention through interviews and television appearances, he proved less
successful convincing black leaders of his contemporary political relevance, in part because his efforts at building a broad coalition among
blacks of all ideological stripes met with a lukewarm response.[51]

If Carmichael's plans to lead a "National Black United Front" remained scattershot, his role as a global organizer of Pan-Africanist ideology proved more successful. By 1974, Pan-Africanism, which
Carmichael had described to skeptical audiences six years earlier in
Oakland, became the dominant mode of radical black activism around
the country. Indeed, a cross-section of Afro-America, from Black Panthers to the Congressional Black Caucus, paid homage to the continent's ascension in domestic affairs by participating in coalitions led by
pan-African activists. This political synergy made Carmichael's appearance at Howard even more bittersweet. Having coaxed race consciousness and a pan-African identity out of a generation of radicals, at
Howard Carmichael confronted former protégés and others who
doubted that his dazzling oratory still held the key to an international
political revolution.[52]

Both Baraka's and Sadaukai's statements at Howard evinced the shifting perspectives of nationalist partisans. Sadaukai confessed the error of his earlier understanding of black liberation at the beginning of a speech in which he stressed the need to study both classical Marxist theorists and contemporary African innovators—a remarkable position considering that Sadaukai had, at one time, counseled against reading Marx and Lenin because they were white. The audience responded to the confessional tone and naked candor of Sadaukai's speech with a standing ovation. Baraka then began his speech with Lenin's definition of imperialism as a unique and volatile stage within capitalism. The quotation kicked off a tortured address that took theoretical leaps and historical somersaults in its quest to reconcile class struggle with black nationalism. After quoting Cabral, Baraka argued that black nationalism remained essential to the development of the liberation movement. Lenin's notion of a "vanguard party"—a group of highly trained activists and agitators who would channel mass alienation toward a political revolution—also shaped Baraka's speech. Privately, Baraka doubted his own words. "The people on the left who had defeated nationalism," recalled Baraka, "did not have all of their theoretical arguments together, but they at least did provide a point of departure, a jumping-off place, and I was ready to jump off."[53]

Political struggles unleashed during the Howard conference set the stage for the Sixth Pan-African Congress, convened in Dar es Salaam, Tanzania, in June 1974. While past congresses had mapped out strategies for African liberation from Europe, the current meeting confronted growing debates about neocolonialism. The idea for the "6-PAC" grew out of the efforts of an international body of organizers spearheaded by Black Power activists. Three SNCC veterans—Jimmy Garrett, Courtland Cox, and Charlie Cobb—coordinated a series of planning meetings, fund-raising ventures, and political negotiations that took place in the United States, Europe, Africa, and the Caribbean. C. L. R. James, whose return to the United States in the late 1960s had introduced his radical writings to a new generation of activists, advised them on the complex internal divisions among pan-African constituents within Africa and the Caribbean.[54]

In Africa, Black Power activists split into two opposing camps over support for class struggle or black nationalism. Baraka's ideological transformation alienated him from the large delegation of African American nationalists yet drew him closer to the conference host, Julius Nyerere, who, Baraka noted, proudly displayed Lenin's entire works in his bookcase. From June 19 to 27, upward of two hundred American delegates attended the meeting at Tanzania's University of Dar es Salaam. Nyerere provided inspiration for advocates of class struggle. "Let us make it quite clear," he remarked in his opening speech, "we oppose racial thinking." Pan-Africanism was part of a larger struggle for human rights that, although born out of racial oppression, was color-blind in its quest for social, political, and economic justice. Admitting that black skin too often correlated with poverty, Nyerere argued that color alone could not explain this phenomenon. "We are neither poor, nor are we kept poor, because we are black," he told the assembly. "We remain poor because of the world trading and monetary systems—and these, whatever their other disadvantages, are color-blind."[55]

For Baraka, the congress forced him to confront painful truths regarding Africa, Black Power, and global revolution. Baraka now judged his past political activism as at best naive and at worst foolish. The congress's final declaration called for a global pan-African movement to restore the continent, offering an assortment of plans that touched on free trade and democratization, the promotion of Socialism, and the curtailing of the influence of Western superpowers in African affairs.[56] Ultimately, the success of the congress's radicals in defining Pan-Africanism through the prism of class instead of race undermined the unity that "6-PAC" had hoped to broker.[57] The lack of a permanent structure to implement the final declaration issued from the congress led some critics to label the entire event a spectacular failure, while others claimed as a victory (just like at Gary) the fact that the meeting took place at all.[58]

Baraka's full-scale adoption of Marxism by the end of the year upset the fragile unity among Black Power activists. Critics chalked up his conversion to a Communist conspiracy by white radicals intent on disrupting African American political independence.[59] Back in the States, a "two line struggle," between black nationalists and Marxists, continued, with predictable results.

Baraka formally announced his advocacy of "Marxism-Leninism-Maoism" on October 7, 1974, his fortieth birthday. Defending his change of heart as the result of a discovery that "merely putting Black faces in higher places" would not lead to fundamental social change, Baraka's shift to Marxism would complete an ideological journey that had begun at Howard University and continued in the Air Force, Cuba, Greenwich Village, Harlem, Newark, and San Francisco before this, his final epiphany, off of Tanzania's Indian Ocean.[60]

Political turmoil among Black Power activists mirrored larger crises within American politics. Watergate, which in the span of two years had moved from whispered allegations to a full-blown crisis, would soon become the shorthand for unfettered government corruption. Revelations of government secrets that had trickled in through the Pentagon Papers and stolen FBI documents during the early 1970s, mushroomed into a national scandal in the wake of Watergate and the systemic abuses of federal power uncovered by the Senate committee chaired by Frank Church, Democrat of Idaho. The committee's exposé of the FBI's and Cointelpro's clandestine role in the dismantling of the Black Power, New Left, and antiwar movements would spur reform of the domestic intelligence infrastructure and, in the process, provide further evidence of the pitfalls of unchecked government power.

There was little unity in Black Power activists' interpretation of these events. For some, the exposure of widespread political corruption represented an opportunity for dramatic and long-hoped-for social and economic reforms; others derided this view as hopelessly optimistic. Black nationalists continued community organizing that focused on cultural renewal, institution building, and, at times, strategic alliances with elected officials. At the opposite end of the spectrum, newly converted black Marxists vowed to start the revolution by themselves, armed with ideological blueprints that (proponents claimed) made success a virtual scientific certainty.[61]

For Black Power activists, the second half of the 1970s would prove far less romantic and politically cohesive than the first. But even if the political heat surrounding Black Power organizations and leaders had cooled, protest would still continue. Black Power contributed to the multiplicity of social justice movements that, on the surface, seemed more splintered than in the decade before. Struggles for black feminism, a cleaner environment, affirmative action, and gay and lesbian rights became synonymous with identity politics and political correctness, twin shibboleths deployed by both conservatives and disillusioned former radicals who decried America's social and cultural fragmentation. The 1970s would prove to be more democratic and diverse than the mythic 1960s and therefore harder to categorize.

Yet by their overlapping, contentious, and messy efforts to extract, maintain, and extend hard-won victories, radical social movements of the 1970s did transform the United States, forcing hallowed institutions in both the public and the private spheres to come to grips with school desegregation, voting rights, affirmative action, environmental protection, and other issues. Accomplished against a backdrop of political scandal, economic misery, and racial tensions that became known as a "crisis of confidence," the end of the Vietnam War, the rise of the women's movement, and the gains of black elected officials appeared in a national landscape that also featured a jumble of opinion makers and ordinary people questioning the country's moral compass.[62]

In 1975 in Oakland, the Black Panther Party, with a significantly scaled back membership led by Elaine Brown, settled into its new, still controversial identity as a local political organization. That same year, organized opposition to Amiri Baraka's Marxist politics resulted in his removal as secretary general of the National Black Political Assembly. Stokely Carmichael, still an energetic speaker and enthusiastic organizer, receded further into the national background while remaining an important international figure. As Black Power's glow faded, Malcolm X would in death age best, frozen in memory as the era's progenitor, a martyred people's champion whose confident exterior, fiery speeches, and perpetual youth would symbolize the historic progress and unfulfilled promise of Afro-America.

EPILOGUE

LEGACIES, 1975–2005

The influence of the Black Power movement's most revered icon, Malcolm X, extended beyond the era. During the late 1980s and early 1990s, a new generation of rap musicians and hip-hop artists deployed Malcolm X (and to a lesser extent other Black Power icons) as symbols of racially conscious and historically resonant political defiance. The rap group Public Enemy, in particular, helped to introduce the movement's legacy to a post–Black Power generation with anthems such as "Fight the Power," an objective further aided by the 1992 release of Spike Lee's film *Malcolm X*. Renewed attention to *The Autobiography of Malcolm X* helped make Malcolm mainstream enough to be memorialized on a U.S. Postal Service stamp. Through Malcolm, contemporary black urban youth embraced other symbols of Black Power. Some of hip-hop's angry young men and women were themselves echoes of the Black Power activists of four decades earlier. While hip-hop reported reality from the street (from Los Angeles to New Orleans to Brooklyn)—in the form of urban violence, drug abuse, and ennui not covered by the mainstream media—it also reveled in aspects of the sexism, commercialism, and exploitation that characterized the worst aspects of the Black Power era.[1]

In some spectacular instances, both movements shared bloodlines. Panther 21 defendant Afeni Shakur's son, Tupac, became a groundbreaking hip-hop artist and an icon after his 1996 death. Tupac Shakur came of age in an era seemingly bereft of the type of political movements that had inspired his mother. For Tupac, the connection between urban poverty, racism, and economic inequality fueled some of his most poignant, controversial, and successful music.

If Black Power influenced urban youth, the Black Arts enjoyed their own renaissance through the popularity of hip-hop–inflected poetry slams and organized tributes to cultural icons including Sonia Sanchez, Nikki Giovanni, Askia Touré (Rolland Snellings), and Amiri Baraka.[2]

Black Power's demise as a national movement coincided with the deepening, from coast to coast, of America's urban crisis that would continue to unfold over the next decades. In the post–Black Power era African Americans took political control over metropolitan centers at the very moment that cities were, due to federal neglect, shrinking tax bases, and loss of industries, made most vulnerable to crime, poverty, and failing public schools. Ironically, a range of activists—from Malcolm X and the Black Panthers to Stokely Carmichael and SNCC— had anticipated these very ills. While we will never know how a thriving Black Power movement might have confronted soaring gang violence, the crack epidemic, and poverty that gripped much of the African American community during the late 1970s and 1980s, we can guess how Black Power activists might have helped ease the heartbreaking transition from the hopeful Great Society rhetoric of the 1960s to the conservatism that characterized the Reagan revolution of the 1980s.

In November 1975, Eldridge Cleaver surrendered to American authorities in Paris after seven years of exile had exacted steep personal and political costs. A *Newsweek* interview published in advance of his return described Cleaver as a sort of international tramp, isolated in France, adrift from the radical political currents that had once sustained him, homesick, his relationship with former allies marred by mutual hostilities. The Black Panthers denounced him as a federal agent even as Kathleen Cleaver toured the country raising support for his case. American journalists covered Eldridge Cleaver's bizarre political transformation with a mixture of sympathy and condescension; Cleaver's own attempts at explanation did nothing to clear the air. In one breath he described Watergate as "America's greatest contribution" to political change and, in the next, settled old scores by denouncing Fidel Castro.

In 1978, Cleaver published *Soul on Fire,* a somewhat scattershot autobiography and sequel to *Soul on Ice,* which described his religious conversion and proud association with conservative evangelists such as Billy Graham. By the 1980s, the uproar over Cleaver's defection from Black Power and New Left radicalism dissipated, allowing him to settle into a life of quiet obscurity. Cleaver periodically resurfaced in Berkeley during the 1990s as a public speaker and sidewalk raconteur, sometimes sporting a dashiki as he fashioned an office from a public pay phone and an outdoor bench. Somehow, Cleaver retained a rakish twinkle in his eye that even the ravages of time did little to diminish. Part madcap showman, part street philosopher until the end, Cleaver was wistful in his final days, before his 1998 death in California; bereft of the revolutionary panegyrics of the 1960s, Cleaver nonetheless retained the era's resilience, if little else.[3]

Eldridge Cleaver's diminished influence paralleled the professional ascent of his ex-wife Kathleen. Rebounding from their tumultuous relationship to raise two children, Kathleen Cleaver graduated from Yale Law School in 1989 and continues to work as a professor, human rights activist, and occasional chronicler of the era her activism helped shape. In the midst of writing a memoir of her movement days, Kathleen Cleaver represents one of the era's ultimate survivors.

Angela Davis, Black Power's most famous female political prisoner, has also flourished. An internationally recognized prisoner rights and anti–death penalty advocate, today Davis is a professor, author, and public intellectual. While many of their fellow activists faced profound difficulties adjusting to the new political realities of postradical America,

both Cleaver and Davis successfully reinvented themselves by returning to the respective intellectual activist roots that had nurtured them.

The Black Panther Party's transition from national political mobilization to grassroots organizing continued into the late 1970s, with
the group serving as advisors to Oakland's first black mayor, Lionel
Wilson. The Panthers' transformation from revolutionary outsiders
to urban powerbrokers would be remarkable, unexpected, and short-
lived.[4]

Huey P. Newton returned from Cuba on July 3, 1977, hastening
the party's demise. Arriving at San Francisco's airport, Newton called
for the newly elected Mayor Wilson to help the Panthers eliminate
drug abuse and "to work for progressive change in our society." It was
vintage Newton, displaying the bravado and charisma that had made
him an icon. Only the times had changed. Journalists still noted his
physical beauty, quick smile, and contemplative answers, but now
Newton was asked questions that the press wouldn't have dreamed of
asking a few years before: "The Movement is over, and the rallies and
the crowds have disappeared. Does anyone really care any more what
Huey Newton thinks about America, its injustices or system?" Newton responded with humor. "Believe it or not, I'm rather shy. I've never
liked large crowds." Chain-smoking his way through interviews in
which he announced plans to write a book about his time as an exile,
Newton would refuse, in one breath, to criticize the Cuban government and, in another, would deny allegations of drug abuse.[5] Acquitted of criminal charges, Newton began a fresh start, completing a
doctorate (a study of repression against the Black Panther Party) at the
University of California at Santa Cruz.

The party officially ended in 1982, a relic of its former strength,
though still staffed by devoted members who persevered in the face of
devastating journalistic exposés and uninspired and, even at times, corrupt leadership. Newton, who outlived the party by seven years, would
suffer his own personal decline. On August 22, 1989, he was shot three
times in the early hours of the morning near a crack house in Oakland.

Newton's unseemly death fueled a chorus of conservatives and former radicals, who portrayed the party's entire operation as a front for criminal activity obscured by a political posture that carried a whiff of fraudulence from the start. Former Panthers and sympathizers countered that the party's legacy was infinitely more complex, and also positive.[6]

Amiri Baraka found intermittent peace as a Marxist.[7] For a time, he became a leading spokesman for efforts to build a "new" Communist movement during the 1970s before being hired as a professor at Stony Brook University, in Long Island. Baraka's literary production as a writer and poet, which had profoundly shaped African American consciousness during the 1960s and 1970s, now featured more universal themes of class struggle and anti-imperialism. Publishers once eager to showcase Baraka's work found his new political perspective untenable, relegating him, as well as much of his work, to the literary margins. Despite personal and professional setbacks, he has endured, remaining among the last of the controversial breed of activists who, for a brief moment, promised, in Eldridge Cleaver's inimitable phrase, a "new day in Babylon."[8]

Stokely Carmichael never abandoned his dreams to liberate Africa as part of a larger quest for global revolution. Having reached the peak of his international notoriety in his twenties, Carmichael would spread his wings by regrouping in Guinea, where he became a leading Pan-Africanist organizer and proponent of Third World revolution. Carmichael's exile denied him the grand stage and media attention that had characterized his time as a Black Power activist in the States, yet he was able to settle comfortably into the role of a professional revolutionary, satisfied that the passage of time had done nothing to dampen his restless energy, intellectual curiosity, or maverick politics. In contrast to the ideological shifts and declining personal fortunes of some of his famous contemporaries, Carmichael, who by the late 1970s had changed his name to Kwame Ture (in honor of his mentors

Kwame Nkrumah and Sékou Touré), maintained a rigorous globe-hopping schedule that included frequent speaking tours of American colleges.[9]

In Africa, Ture engaged in new conflicts at once larger and more obscure than those of his early civil rights activism, focusing on promoting African progress by extolling the continent's potential as a base for international social and economic revolution. Ture's adopted home of Conakry, Guinea, became a kind of center for the international intrigues and clandestine activities that made the young Stokely Carmichael's dreams of global transformation seem tantalizingly real.[10] But Ture's unwavering insistence on the viability of a pan-African revolution appeared anachronistic in an era during which Ronald Reagan and Margaret Thatcher dominated Western politics and the world witnessed the brutal effects of the continuing crises of African nation building (which would eventually touch Guinea, leading to Ture's brief incarceration in the 1980s). Meanwhile, the official legacy of the civil rights movement seemed to have written Ture out of the story.[11]

During the 1990s, however, Africa made a comeback of sorts, galvanized by a global anti-apartheid movement led, at least in part, by forces that first emerged during the Black Power era. Randall Robinson founded TransAfrica, which picked up where the African Liberation Support Committee left off to become the most important group lobbying for U.S. foreign policy in Africa during the post–Black Power period.[12]

Twenty-five years after *Black Power*'s initial publication, Ture continued his advocacy of the revolutionary Pan-Africanism that he first adopted one fateful summer on the continent.[13] Diagnosed with prostate cancer in 1996, Ture spent the next two years, in between medical treatments and various political commitments, completing his autobiography, *Ready for Revolution*. After two years combating a diagnosis of terminal cancer, Kwame Ture died in Guinea on November 15, 1998.[14]

* * *

Portions of the coalition that gathered in Gary, Indiana, in 1972 would thrive long after the movement seemed to be over. Harold Washington's successful run, in spite of long odds, for mayor of Chicago in 1983 rallied a black radical movement adrift just a decade after declaring victory to be within reach, only to witness the onset of a mean season of racial setbacks. It was Washington's surprising win at the polls that helped propel Jesse Jackson's historic 1984 presidential candidacy. In both campaigns, veterans of the movement served as key grassroots organizers, mature activists who helped shape Washington's and Jackson's optimistic rhetoric in the face of soaring unemployment, urban blight, and poverty—the legacy of a movement left for dead.[15] For other Black Power figures, particular instances of unfinished business have produced poignant reversals of fortune, most notably Panther Geronimo Pratt's 1997 release from prison after more than a quarter of a century of unjust incarceration.[16]

The final word on the Black Power era has yet to be written. In the nation's historical memory, the movement pales in comparison with the celebrations, political legislation, and landmark court cases associated with the civil rights movement. Black Power most often serves as a twisted folklore, a cautionary tale featuring gun-toting militants who practiced politics without portfolio, vowed to die in the name of revolution, and who dragged down more promising movements for social justice.[17] Yet such a perspective ignores Black Power's complex relationship to the civil rights era. Inspired in part by the same legacy that buoyed civil rights activists, Black Power advocates took the notion of righting historical wrongs to a whole new, if also more combative, level.

Black Power's impact remains powerfully resonant—if also fraught and contentious—in American social and political institutions. Indeed, a generation of politicians, artists, and intellectuals have channeled black identity as first articulated by Black Power in ways that found a creative outlet in domestic and international affairs, education, and political and cultural activism. Black Power emerged alongside civil rights activism during a moment of national racial crisis pregnant with world historic possibilities. Postwar American prosperity, with its expansive promise of middle-class contentment, home ownership, and educational opportunity, largely excluded the very generation of blacks who helped to enable the nation's social, political, and economic progress.

African Americans responded in different ways to America's postwar landscape. Southern civil rights activists during the 1950s advocated a brand of social justice that, although dramatically scaled back from the radical politics of the 1930s and 1940s, retained elements of World War II–era racial militancy. Black Power activists embraced a different political radicalism altogether, one that promoted self-reliance, self-defense, Pan-Africanism, internationalism, and cooperation among blacks—and, at times, violence and misogyny. While some were more effective as political activists and others better at grabbing headlines, Black Power radicals ultimately discovered, just as their civil rights counterparts did, that there were no easy solutions to America's racial crisis. In the new millennium, more than thirty years after the Gary convention, its agenda for urban reform, political accountability, and the promotion of strong local communities through the strategic deployment of black political power remains remarkably relevant, if historically uncommemorated. The convention's major themes periodically pop up in coalitions, marches, and meetings seeking solutions for an African American community still in peril.

Civil rights struggles are rightfully acknowledged as having earned black Americans a historic level of dignity. Black Power accomplished a no-less-remarkable task, fueling the casually assertive identity and cultural pride that marks African American life today. In this way, there remains between the movements a poetic symmetry that briefly transcended political differences while ultimately transforming the very landscape of race relations. Future expressions of racial pride, from the late 1960s to the present, would achieve enough mainstream legitimacy to be co-opted by corporate entities and liberal politicians. Yet Black Power's legacy remains relevant to contemporary political organizing taking shape on street corners, in labor unions, on college campuses, and at ballot boxes. For both the generation who found its political bearings during some of America's most dangerously hopeful years and for those who have come after, the work to bring racial justice to the United States and to the world continues. For the men and women who found inspiration and courage through their acceptance of the ideal of racial equality, the movement never ended. They continue the fight to build a more hopeful and humane world that, like some ancient buried treasure, might be rediscovered any day now.

NOTES

INTRODUCTION: TO SHAPE A NEW WORLD

1. Martha Biondi, *To Stand and Fight: The Struggle for Civil Rights in Postwar New York City* (Cambridge: Harvard University Press, 2003); Thomas J. Sugrue, *The Origins of the Urban Crisis: Race and Inequality in Postwar Detroit* (Princeton: Princeton University Press, 1996); Diane McWhorter, *Carry Me Home: Birmingham, Alabama: The Climactic Battle of the Civil Rights Revolution* (New York: Touchstone, 2002); Robert O. Self, *American Babylon: Race and the Struggle for Postwar Oakland* (Princeton: Princeton University Press, 2003).

2. Elinor Des Verney Sinnette, *Arturo Alfonso Schomburg: Black Bibliophile and Collector* (Detroit: New York Public Library and Wayne State University Press, 1989), p. 182.

3. Winston James, *Holding Aloft the Banner of Ethiopia: Caribbean Radicalism in Early Twentieth-Century America* (London: Verso, 1998), pp. 187–88; David Levering Lewis, *When Harlem Was in Vogue* (New York: Penguin Books, 1997) and *W.E.B. Du Bois: The Fight for Equality and the American Century, 1919–1963* (New York: Henry Holt, 2000); Wilson J. Moses, *The Golden Age of Black Nationalism, 1850–1925* (New York: Oxford University Press, 1988).

4. "Van Gosse Interview with Harold Cruse," in William Jelani Cobb, ed., *The Essential Harold Cruse: A Reader* (New York: Palgrave Macmillan, 2002), p. 285.

5. "Van Gosse Interview with Harold Cruse," p. 284; Lewis, *When Harlem Was in Vogue*.

6. "Van Gosse Interview with Harold Cruse."

7. See Biondi, *To Stand and Fight*.

8. Carol Anderson, *Eyes Off the Prize: The United Nations and the African Amer-

ican Struggle for Human Rights, 1944–1955 (Cambridge, U.K.: Cambridge University Press, 2003), pp. 8–57.

9. Anderson, *Eyes Off the Prize*; Gerald Horne, *Communist Front?: The Civil Rights Congress, 1946–1956* (Rutherford: Fairleigh Dickinson University Press, 1988).

10. See Martin Duberman, *Paul Robeson* (New York: New Press, 2005).

11. William H. Chafe, *Civilities and Civil Rights: Greensboro, North Carolina, and the Black Struggle for Freedom* (New York: Oxford University Press, 1981); Robert Rodgers Korstad, *Civil Rights Unionism: Tobacco Workers and the Struggle for Democracy in the Mid-Twentieth Century South* (Chapel Hill: University of North Carolina Press, 2003); Biondi, *To Stand and Fight*; John Dittmer, *Local People: The Struggle for Civil Rights in Mississippi* (Urbana: University of Illinois Press, 1995); and Charles Payne, *I've Got the Light of Freedom: The Organizing Tradition and the Mississippi Freedom Struggle* (Berkeley: University of California Press, 1995). See also Jeanne F. Theoharis and Komozi Woodard, eds., *Freedom North: Black Freedom Struggles Outside the South, 1940–1980* (New York: Palgrave Macmillan, 2003).

12. Barbara Ransby, *Ella Baker and the Black Freedom Movement: A Radical Democratic Vision* (Chapel Hill: University of North Carolina Press, 2003), pp. 132–34.

13. Paul Robeson, *Here I Stand* (Boston: Beacon Press, 1988); Penny Von Eschen, *Race Against Empire: Black Americans and Anticolonialism, 1937–1957* (Ithaca: Cornell University Press, 1997); Brenda Gayle Plummer, *Rising Wind: Black Americans and U.S. Foreign Affairs, 1935–1960* (Chapel Hill: University of North Carolina Press, 1996); Anderson, *Eyes Off the Prize*; Biondi, *To Stand and Fight*; Korstad, *Civil Rights Unionism*.

14. Duberman, *Paul Robeson*; Robeson, *Here I Stand*; Von Eschen, *Race Against Empire*; Plummer, *Rising Wind*; Anderson, *Eyes Off the Prize*. Truman's relatively progressive initiatives on race reflected, rather than contradicted, the international arena's growing influence on America's color line. For a fascinating discussion, see Azza Salama Layton, *International Politics and Civil Rights Policies in the United States, 1941–1960* (Cambridge, U.K.: Cambridge University Press, 2000). Jacqueline Dowd Hall examines the civil rights movement from the New Deal to the 1970s' "movement of movements," arguing that only by acknowledging the era's diversity can civil rights be rescued from clichés that water down the black freedom struggle's challenge to white supremacy and the New Right's appropriation of colorblind politics. See "The Long Civil Rights Movement and the Political Uses of the Past," *Journal of American History* 91, no. 4 (2005), pp. 1233–63.

15. Nikhil Pal Singh, *Black Is a Country: Race and the Unfinished Struggle for Democracy* (Cambridge: Harvard University Press, 2004), pp. 109–18. See also Robin D. G. Kelley, *Hammer and Hoe: Alabama Communists During the Great Depression* (Chapel Hill: University of North Carolina Press, 1990), and Mark Naison, *Communists in Harlem During the Depression* (Urbana: University of Illinois Press, 1983).

16. Duberman, *Paul Robeson*, p. 431.

17. Richard Wright fell in love with the idea of Bandung. For Wright the conference elicited nostalgia for his youthful dreams of political revolution, flights of fancy that had ended in mutual recriminations after his public break with the Communist Party during the 1940s. Reading about the upcoming conference from his home in France, Wright was impressed by the breadth of the proceedings—a bright spot in a career marred by disappointment. Celebrated as a literary genius after the publication of *Native Son* in 1941, his early success had given way to political disillusionment, literary failures, and finally, personal exile. Well into what should have been his professional prime, Wright sought work as a roving journalist, traveling across continents writing eyewitness accounts of political revolutions raging across the Third World. See

Richard Wright, *The Color Curtain: A Report on the Bandung Conference* (Cleveland: World Publishing Company, 1956), p. 11. For an examination of the Bandung Conference, see Plummer, *Rising Wind*, pp. 247–56, and Cary Fraser, "An American Dilemma: Race and Realpolitik in the American Response to the Bandung Conference, 1955," in Brenda Gayle Plummer, ed., *Window on Freedom: Race, Civil Rights, and Foreign Affairs, 1945–1988* (Chapel Hill: University of North Carolina Press, 2003), pp. 115–40.

18. See Hall, "The Long Civil Rights Movement and the Political Uses of the Past"; Kelley, *Hammer and Hoe*; Korstad, *Civil Rights Unionism*. Certainly Nikita Khrushchev's 1956 revelations, at the Twentieth Party Congress, of the carnage inflicted by Stalinism marked the end of a kind of left-wing activism. Many CP members left the party, disillusioned and embittered. For some radical activists, the news allowed them to chart an independent course. See, for example, Duberman, *Paul Robeson*, p. 437. See also James Edward Smethurst, *The Black Arts Movement: Literary Nationalism in the 1960s and 1970s* (Chapel Hill: University of North Carolina Press, 2005).

19. While scholars such as Clayborne Carson, William Chafe, John Dittmer, and Charles Payne have stressed the profound significance of local movements, the conventional narrative places King as the primary representative of a complex array of forces, squared off against the federal government in the face of, first, John F. Kennedy and Robert F. Kennedy and, later, Lyndon B. Johnson. See, for example, Nick Kotz, *Judgment Days: Lyndon Baines Johnson, Martin Luther King Jr., and the Laws That Changed America* (New York: Houghton Mifflin, 2005). See also Taylor Branch, *Parting the Waters: America in the King Years, 1954–1963* (New York: Touchstone Books, 1989); Adam Fairclough, *To Redeem the Soul of America: The Southern Christian Leadership Conference and Martin Luther King, Jr.* (Athens: University of Georgia Press, 2001); David Garrow, *Bearing the Cross: Martin Luther King Jr. and the Southern Christian Leadership Conference* (New York: Harper Perennial, 1999); Chafe, *Civilities and Civil Rights*; Clayborne Carson, *In Struggle: SNCC and the Black Awakening of the 1960s* (Cambridge: Harvard University Press, 1981); Dittmer, *Local People*; and Payne, *I've Got the Light of Freedom*.

20. Ferruccio Gambino, "The Transgression of a Laborer: Malcolm X in the Wilderness of America," *Radical History Review* 55, no. 1 (1993), pp. 7–31; Clayborne Carson, *Malcolm X: The FBI File* (New York: Carroll & Graf, 1991). See also Robert Korstad and Nelson Lichtenstein, "Opportunities Found and Lost: Labor, Radicals, and the Early Civil Rights Movement," *Journal of American History* 75, no. 3 (1988), pp. 786–811; Theoharis and Woodard, *Freedom North*; Biondi, *To Stand and Fight*; Clarence Taylor, *Knocking at Our Own Door: Milton A. Galamison and the Struggle to Integrate New York City Schools* (New York: Columbia University Press, 1997); Plummer, *Rising Wind*; Anderson, *Eyes Off the Prize*; Ransby, *Ella Baker and the Black Freedom Movement*; Von Eschen, *Race Against Empire*; James H. Meriwether, *Proudly We Can Be Called Africans: Black Americans and Africa, 1935–1961* (Chapel Hill: University of North Carolina Press, 2002); Robin D. G. Kelley, *Race Rebels: Culture, Politics, and the Black Working Class* (New York: Free Press, 1994); Payne, *I've Got the Light of Freedom*; Dittmer, *Local People*; Plummer, *Window on Freedom*; Thomas Borstelmann, *The Cold War and the Color Line: American Race Relations in the Global Arena* (Cambridge: Harvard University Press, 2001); Sugrue, *The Origins of the Urban Crisis*; Singh, *Black Is a Country*; Jeanne Theoharis and Komozi Woodard, eds., *Groundwork: Local Black Freedom Movements in America* (New York: New York University Press, 2005). See also Gerald Horne, *Black and Red: W.E.B. Du Bois and the African-American Response to the*

Cold War, 1944–1963 (Albany: State University of New York Press, 1986); *Communist Front?*; *Black Liberation and Red Scare: Ben Davis and the Communist Party* (Newark: University of Delaware Press, 1994); and *Race Woman: The Lives of Shirley Graham Du Bois* (New York: New York University Press, 2000).

1. FORERUNNERS

1. The name of the black Muslim, Johnson Hinton, has been identified as Hinton Johnson in certain sources. Benjamin Karim goes as far as to say that Malcolm X mistakenly refers to him as Johnson Hinton in his autobiography. Bruce Perry, citing court papers, asserts that his name was Johnson Hinton. FBI documents refer to the member as Johnson X. See Peter Goldman, *The Death and Life of Malcolm X* (New York: Harper & Row, 1973), pp. 55–65; Benjamin Karim, with Peter Skutches and David Gallen, *Remembering Malcolm*, (New York: One World, 1992), pp. 45–46; and Karim, ed., *The End of World White Supremacy: Four Speeches by Malcolm X* (New York: Arcade Publishing, 1971), pp. 2–6, in which he claims Malcolm conflated Johnson's name. In his autobiography, Malcolm refers to him as "Brother Johnson Hinton." See Alex Haley, *The Autobiography of Malcolm X* (New York: Ballantine Books, 1998), p. 257; Bruce Perry, *Malcolm X: The Life of a Man Who Changed Black America* (Barrytown: Station Hill Press, 1992), pp. 164–66, 437. FBIMX 100-399321 (Part 3), "Malcolm Little," April 30, 1958, p. 29.

2. *New York Amsterdam News*, May 18, 1957, pp. 1, 38.

3. Goldman, *The Death and Life of Malcolm X*, pp. 55–59; Karim, *Remembering Malcolm*, pp. 45–47.

4. Perry, *Malcolm X*, pp. 165–66.

5. Goldman, *The Death and Life of Malcolm X*, p. 59.

6. *New York Amsterdam News*, May 1957, p. 1.

7. FBIMX 100-399321-21 (Part 3), p. 79, quoting Malcolm X from *Pittsburgh Courier*, November 9, 1957; Johnson was awarded $70,000. Perry, *Malcolm X*, p. 166.

8. Haley, *The Autobiography of Malcolm X*, p. 256.

9. Goldman, *The Death and Life of Malcolm X*, pp. 52–53.

10. William Sales Jr., *From Civil Rights to Black Liberation: Malcolm X and the Organization of Afro-American Unity* (Boston: South End Press, 1994), pp. 59–60.

11. See Timothy B. Tyson, *Radio Free Dixie: Robert F. Williams and the Roots of Black Power* (Chapel Hill: University of North Carolina Press, 1999); Lance Hill, *The Deacons for Defense: Armed Resistance and the Civil Rights Movement* (Chapel Hill: University of North Carolina Press, 2004); Christopher B. Strain, *Pure Fire: Self-Defense as Activism in the Civil Rights Era* (Athens: University of Georgia Press, 2005); Simon Wendt, "The Roots of Black Power?: Armed Resistance and the Radicalization of the Civil Rights Movement," in Peniel E. Joseph, ed., *The Black Power Movement: Rethinking the Civil Rights–Black Power Era* (New York: Routledge, 2006).

12. Claude Andrew Clegg III, *An Original Man: The Life and Times of Elijah Muhammad* (New York: St. Martin's Press, 1997), pp. 109–45.

13. Robert Caro, *The Power Broker: Robert Moses and the Fall of New York* (New York: Vintage Books, 1975), p. 5.

14. Sales, *From Civil Rights to Black Liberation*, pp. 59–60.

15. Haley, *The Autobiography of Malcolm X*, pp. 238–39.

16. Plummer, *Rising Wind*, pp. 247–56; Fraser, "An American Dilemma," pp. 115–40.

17. FBIMX 100-399321 (Part 5), Malcolm Little, November 17, 1959, p. 45; Invitation to Abyssinian Baptist Church, FBIMX 100-399321-21 (Part 3), pp. 74–75, citing *Los Angeles Herald* dispatch, August 8, 1957; Karim, *End of World White Supremacy*, pp. 14–15; Goldman, *The Death and Life of Malcolm X*, p. 68. For competition between Malcolm and Powell, see Goldman, *The Death and Life of Malcolm X*, pp. 134–35; Perry, *Malcolm X*, pp. 302–4; and Taylor Branch, *Pillar of Fire: America in the King Years, 1963–1965* (New York: Simon and Schuster, 1998), p. 96.

18. FBIMX 100-399321 (Part 21), Sub A, *Pittsburgh Courier*, January 25, 1958, and *Los Angeles Herald Dispatch*, February 13, 1958; FBIMX 100-399321-33 (Part 4), Airtel, July 17, 1959.

19. FBIMX 100-39321-29 (Part 4), Malcolm Little, October 17, 1958, pp. 1–4; FBIMX 100-39321-27 (Part 4), November 19, 1958, pp. 9–10; Hakim Jamal, *From the Dead Level: Malcolm X and Me* (New York: Warner Books, 1973), pp. 94–122.

20. Goldman, *The Death and Life of Malcolm X*, p. 88.

21. Rebeccah Welch, "Black Art and Activism in Postwar New York, 1950–1965," Ph.D. diss., New York University, 2002, p. 2.

22. Branch, *Parting the Waters*, pp. 592–93.

23. Clegg, *An Original Man*, pp. 159–60; Haley, *The Autobiography of Malcolm X*, pp. 259, 287–88; Perry, *Malcolm X*, pp. 213–14; Louis Lomax, *When the Word Is Given: A Report on Elijah Muhammad, Malcolm X, and the Black Muslim World* (Winnipeg: Signet Books, 1964), pp. 73, 147–49.

24. Haley, *The Autobiography of Malcolm X*, pp. 230–89; Goldman, *The Death and Life of Malcolm X*, pp. 49–91; Perry, *Malcolm X*, pp. 160–66, 174–86.

25. Haley, *The Autobiography of Malcolm X*, pp. 3–256; Perry, *Malcolm X*, pp. 2–186; Goldman, *The Death and Life of Malcolm X*, pp. 3–106.

26. Lomax, *When the Word Is Given*, p. 18.

27. Ibid., p. 19.

28. Branch, *Pillar of Fire*, p. 3.

29. Ibid., pp. 25–26.

30. Goldman, *The Death and Life of Malcolm X*. See Farah Jasmine Griffin, "'Ironies of the Saint': Malcolm X, Black Women, and the Price of Protection," in Bettye Collier-Thomas and V. P. Franklin, eds., *Sisters in the Struggle: African American Women in the Civil Rights–Black Power Movement* (New York: New York University Press, 2001), pp. 214–29.

31. Lomax, *When the Word Is Given*, p. 24.

32. Plummer, *Rising Wind*; Von Eschen, *Race Against Empire* and *Satchmo Blows Up the World: Jazz Ambassadors Play the Cold War* (Cambridge: Harvard University Press, 2005); Dudziak, *Cold War Civil Rights*; Borstelmann, *The Cold War and the Color Line*; Meriwether, *Proudly We Can Be Called Africans*.

33. *Baltimore-Washington Afro-American*, Mar. 9, 1957. Ghana's recruitment efforts rescued one high-profile leader from political oblivion. W. E. B. Du Bois, two years before his death, expatriated to Ghana to start his proposed *Encyclopedia Africana* at Nkrumah's personal request. The long-delayed project—it had been conceived of as the "Encyclopedia of the Negro"—was planned as a multivolume history that would trace the black presence on several continents and the Caribbean. Perpetually denied funding for this ambitious venture, Du Bois, at ninety-three, became a citizen of Ghana and embarked on his lifelong dream of completing the encyclopedia. See Lewis, *W.E.B. Du Bois: The Fight for Racial Equality*, pp. 389, 442–49.

34. Kevin Gaines, "African-American Expatriates in Ghana and the Black Radical Tradition," *Souls* 1, no. 4 (Fall 1999), pp. 64–71 and "Revisiting Richard Wright in

Ghana: Black Radicalism and the Dialectics of Diaspora," *Social Text* 67 (Summer 2001), pp. 75–101.

35. *New York Amsterdam News*, December 28, 1957, pp. 1, 3.

36. *Baltimore-Washington Afro-American*, August 2, 1958.

37. *New York Amsterdam News*, August 2, 1958, p. 1.

38. Robeson, *Here I Stand*, pp. 33–36, 104–8.

39. Tyson, *Radio Free Dixie*, p. 191.

40. Ibid., pp. 146–48.

41. Julian Mayfield, "Tales from the Lido," pp. 25–27, in Julian Mayfield Papers. Hereafter cited as JMP.

42. FBIMX 100-399321 (Part 4), Memo, July 16, 1959, p. 1.

43. Ibid., July 21, 1959, pp. 1–20.

44. Louis Lomax, *To Kill a Black Man* (Los Angeles: Holloway House, 1968), pp. 65–76.

45. *New York Amsterdam News*, August 1, 1959, pp. 1, 31.

46. Clegg, *An Original Man*, pp. 129–30.

47. FBIMX 100-399321-36 (Part 5), Airtel, July 27, 1959, p. 1.

48. FBIMX 100-399321 (Part 21), Sub A, *Pittsburgh Courier*, August 15, 1959.

49. FBIMX 100-399321-39 (Part 5), November 17, 1959, pp. 31–36; FBIMX 100-399321-40, May 17, 1960, pp. 21–22. Clegg, *An Original Man*, p. 139.

50. Clegg, *An Original Man*, pp. 138–45.

51. *New York Amsterdam News*, January 16, 1960, p. 1.

52. Haley, *The Autobiography of Malcolm X*, p. 325.

53. Goldman, *The Death and Life of Malcolm X*, p. 112; Perry, *Malcolm X*, p. 214; Clegg, *An Original Man*, p. 181.

54. See *Muhammad Speaks* newspapers circa 1962 and 1963.

55. *Muhammad Speaks* also generated significant amounts of income. Members hawked copies on street corners in an effort to meet sales quotas. High sales figures were rewarded with fleeting fame in the pages of *Muhammad Speaks* while slackers were verbally chided and at times beaten by Muslim enforcers. For hundreds of thousands of readers who were not aware of the pressures to meet sales quotas or the punishments doled out to those who didn't, *Muhammad Speaks* offered detailed coverage of the era's unfolding events by employing a group of skillful journalists, including many unaffiliated with the Nation. The paper's coverage of Africa was particularly informative, offering details about revolutionary movements breaking out all over the continent. See Perry, *Malcolm X*, pp. 220–21; Branch, *Pillar of Fire*, p. 260; Karim, *Remembering Malcolm*, pp. 153–54. See also Von Eschen, *Race Against Empire*, pp. 173–74, and Smethurst, *The Black Arts Movement*, pp. 181–83.

56. See Mary Helen Washington, "Alice Childress, Lorraine Hansberry, and Claudia Jones: Black Women Write the Popular Front," in Bill V. Mullen and James Smethurst, eds., *Left of the Color Line: Race, Radicalism, and Twentieth Century Literature of the United States* (Chapel Hill: University of North Carolina Press, 2003), pp. 183–204. See also Ruth Feldstein, " 'I Don't Trust You Anymore': Nina Simone, Culture, and Black Activism in the 1960s," *Journal of American History*, March 2005, <http://www.historycooperative.org/jah/91.4/feldstein.htm> (6 Apr. 2005); and Kevin K. Gaines, "From Center to Margin: Internationalism and the Origins of Black Feminism," in Russ Castronovo and Dana D. Nelson, eds., *Materializing Democracy: Toward a Revitalized Cultural Politics* (Durham: Duke University Press, 2002), pp. 294–313. The black lesbian feminist Audre Lorde received intellectual mentoring from the Harlem Writers Guild in the early 1950s; see Alexis De

Veaux, *Warrior Poet: A Biography of Audre Lord* (New York: Norton, 2004), pp. 38–39.

57. John Oliver Killens, "Lorraine Hansberry: On Time!" *Freedomways* 19, no. 4 (1979), pp. 273–76.

58. Purportedly, Cruse's criticisms of Hansberry were personal. According to legend, Hansberry had turned down his request to read one of his proposed musical plays. In his analysis of postwar black intellectual activists, Cruse devoted more time to Hansberry than Paul Robeson (whom he equally detested). See Harold Cruse, *The Crisis of the Negro Intellectual* (New York: Quill, 1984), pp. 267–84. Rebeccah Welch historically contextualizes Hansberry's literary work and political activism within the radical milieu of 1950s Harlem, with its many-layered cultural and political networks. See Welch, "Black Art and Activism," pp. 200–260.

59. Mary Helen Washington persuasively argues that the untold story of radical black women political activists and literary figures during the 1950s represents a political tradition and literary canon that complicates Cold War historiography. See Washington, "Alice Childress, Lorraine Hansberry, and Claudia Jones." Ben Keppel's analysis of Hansberry's impact on the politics of race traces some of the play's most poignant criticisms of American democracy to Hansberry's childhood. Hansberry's father, Chicago real estate entrepreneur Carl Hansberry, successfully challenged segregated housing in the 1943 Supreme Court decision *Hansberry v. Lee*, only to find the decision unenforceable after which time he made plans to move his family to Mexico before his premature death in 1945. See Ben Keppel, *The Work of Democracy: Ralph Bunche, Kenneth B. Clark, Lorraine Hansberry, and the Cultural Politics of Race* (Cambridge: Harvard University Press, 1995), pp. 21–26.

60. Komozi Woodard argues that Robeson's elaboration on W. E. B. Du Bois's notion of black culture inspired Black Arts and Black Power activists, most notably the young LeRoi Jones; see Woodard, "Amiri Baraka, the Congress of African People and Black Power Politics: From the 1961 United Nations Protest to the 1972 Gary Convention," in Joseph, *The Black Power Movement*.

61. Of course, Black Power nationalists were among Hansberry's most vociferous critics. Cruse's dismissive analysis of Hansberry in his 1967 classic, *The Crisis of the Negro Intellectual*, capped a discourse imposed by Cold War liberals who defined the play and Hansberry's politics on their own terms, setting the stage for a distorted debate. See Keppel, *The Work of Democracy*, pp. 177–214, 227–29. More than twenty-five years later, former critics of Hansberry, including Amiri Baraka, would issue re-evaluations, declaring the play to be on "the cutting edge" of the black movement's "class and ideological struggles." See also Robert Nemiroff, "Introduction," to Hansberry, *A Raisin in the Sun* (New York: Modern Library Edition, 1995), p. xx.

62. Tyson, *Radio Free Dixie*, pp. 203–5.

63. FBIRW 100-387728 (Section 1), Memo, July 14, 15, 18, 1959, from Director to Charlotte SAC.

64. *New York Amsterdam News*, February 7, 1959, p. 1.

65. Van Gosse, *Where the Boys Are: Cuba, Cold War America, and the Making of a New Left* (London: Verso, 1993), pp. 147–48.

66. Tyson, *Radio Free Dixie*, pp. 223–24.

67. Ibid., p. 225.

68. LeRoi Jones, "Cuba Libre," in *Home: Social Essays* (New York: Norton, 1998), p. 16.

69. Ibid., p. 17.

70. Cruse, *The Crisis of the Negro Intellectual*, p. 356.

71. Harold Cruse, "A Negro Looks at Cuba," in Cobb, *The Essential Harold Cruse*, p. 11.

72. Robin D. G. Kelley and Betsey Esch, "Black Like Mao: Red China and Black Revolution," *Souls* 1 (Fall 1999), pp. 6–41; Robin D. G. Kelley, *Freedom Dreams: The Black Radical Imagination* (Boston: Beacon Press, 2002), pp. 72–73.

73. Cruse, "A Negro Looks at Cuba," p. 12.

74. Ibid., p. 13.

75. Cruse, *The Crisis of the Negro Intellectual*, p. 357.

76. Cruse, "A Negro Looks at Cuba," p. 16.

77. Jones, "Cuba Libre," p. 52.

78. Amiri Baraka, *The Autobiography of LeRoi Jones* (Chicago: Lawrence Hill Books, 1997), p. 125.

79. FBILJ 100-425307, Security Memo, November 16, 1957, Amiri Baraka Papers, Box 9, Moorland-Spingarn, Howard University. For Jones's experiences in the Air Force, see Baraka, *The Autobiography of LeRoi Jones*, pp. 137–78. In a bit of historical sleuthing, Komozi Woodard has discovered that among the magazines Jones was cited for reading was Paul Robeson's radical periodical *Freedom*. See Woodard, "Amiri Baraka, the Congress of African People and Black Power Politics."

80. Baraka, *The Autobiography of LeRoi Jones*, p. 181.

81. *New York Amsterdam News*, June 25, 1960, pp. 1, 18.

82. Williams's subsequent flight to Cuba galvanized radicals around the country. Jones, Calvin Hicks, Mayfield, Richard Gibson, and Dan Watts were part of the Monroe Defense Committee (MDC), organized to raise money and publicity for the defendants held as accomplices in Williams's trumped-up kidnapping charges. Activists connected with the Socialist Workers Party started the rival Committee to Aid the Monroe Defendants (CAMD), which the MDC criticized as an attempt by the white Left to take over the radical black movement. While the CAMD was composed of an interracial group of activists, MDC exemplified a largely black nationalist effort, although one that was cosmopolitan enough to attract Bayard Rustin as a sponsor. MDC members and sponsors reflected the overlapping circles of black activism during the early 1960s. Participants from the United Nations 1961 demonstrations, the Fair Play for Cuba Committee, Watts's Liberation Committee for Africa and *Liberator* writers, and Hicks and LeRoi Jones's *On Guard* all were connected with the MDC, which would later affiliate themselves with the Freedom Now Party. See FBIMDC 100-146353, "Monroe Defense Committee: Internal Security—Miscellaneous," November 16, 1961, pp. 1–36.

2. AT HOME IN THE WORLD

1. *New York Times*, September 20, 1960, p. 1.

2. Goldman, *The Death and Life of Malcolm X*, p. 56; Rosemari Mealy, *Fidel and Malcolm X: Memories of a Meeting* (Melbourne, Australia: Ocean Press, 1993), p. 42.

3. *Pittsburgh Courier*, August 15, 1959, in FBIMX 100-399321 (Part 21), Sub A.

4. Ibid.

5. *New York Amsterdam News*, September 24, 1960, p. 1.

6. Mealy, *Fidel and Malcolm X*, p. 42.

7. Ibid., pp. 43–44.

8. Personal recollection by Cuban reporter Reinaldo Penalver in Mealy, *Fidel and Malcolm X*, p. 58; *Baltimore-Washington Afro-American*, October 8, 1960, p. 1.

9. FBIMX 100-399321 (Part 6), "Malcolm K. Little," November 17, 1960, p. 20.

10. Gosse, *Where the Boys Are*, p. 151.

11. *New York Times*, September 20, 1960, p. 16.

12. Ibid., p. 17.

13. Photograph in *New York Citizen-Call*, September 24, 1960, in Mealy, *Fidel and Malcolm X.*

14. *New York Amsterdam News*, September 24, 1960, p. 1.

15. Maya Angelou, *The Heart of a Woman* (New York: Bantam Books, 1997), p. 111.

16. *Baltimore-Washington Afro-American*, October 1, 1960, p. 1.

17. *New York Amsterdam News*, September 26, 1959, p. 1.

18. *Baltimore-Washington Afro-American*, October 1, 1960, p. 9.

19. *New York Amsterdam News*, October 1, 1960, p. 35.

20. William Worthy, "Writer Sees No Need to Stay Out of Cuba," *Baltimore-Washington Afro-American*, October 8, 1960, p. 1.

21. *New York Amsterdam News*, October 1, 1960, pp. 1, 35.

22. *New York Times*, September 27, 1960, p. 1.

23. *New York Amsterdam News*, August 6, 1960, p. 4; September 17, 1960, pp. 1, 11; October 22, 1960, pp. 1, 35.

24. Ludo De Witte traces Lumumba's assassination to Belgian officials; he argues that, although Western forces (including the United States) wanted to oust Lumumba, the CIA had abandoned covert operations against the prime minister by December 1960. See De Witte, *The Assassination of Lumumba* (London: Verso, 2001).

25. Welch, "Black Art and Activism," p. 308; Angelou, *The Heart of a Woman*, p. 173.

26. Farah Jasmine Griffin, *If You Can't Be Free, Be a Mystery: In Search of Billie Holiday* (New York: Free Press, 2001), pp. 163–82.

27. Ibid., pp. 170–72.

28. Baraka, *Autobiography of LeRoi Jones*, p. 259; see Craig Werner, *A Change Is Gonna Come: Music, Race and the Soul of America* (Edinburgh: Payback Press, 1998), pp. 124–36.

29. Eric Porter provides an excellent analysis of Abbey Lincoln's artistic development during the 1950s and 1960s, especially the way in which her embrace of a politicized jazz aesthetic and activist black nationalist identity converged with the country's emerging dialogue about race, culture, gender, and civil rights. See Eric Porter, *What Is This Thing Called Jazz?: African American Musicians as Artists, Critics, and Activists* (Berkeley: University of California Press, 2002), pp. 149–90. See also Griffin, *If You Can't Be Free, Be a Mystery.*

30. Angelou, *The Heart of a Woman*, pp. 169–80.

31. *New York Times*, February 16, 1961, p. 1.

32. Angelou, *The Heart of a Woman*, pp. 186–87.

33. Baraka, *Autobiography of LeRoi Jones*, p. 267. Carlos Moore, the young black Cuban who would become one of revolutionary Cuba's biggest critics, was in the thick of the action. So was Harlem's senior Carlos, Carlos Cooks, who had kept the fires of Garvey-styled Pan-Africanism burning well past their heyday, a distinction exemplified by the fact that Ghanaian Prime Minister Kwame Nkrumah personally escorted him to a scheduled rally after careless organizers had snubbed the distinguished nationalist. See Plummer, *Rising Wind*, p. 282.

34. *New York Times*, February 16, 1961, p. 10.

35. Ibid.

36. Ibid., February 17, 1961, p. 1.

37. Calvin Hicks, "African-American Literary and Political Movements, 1960's, on New York's Lower East Side" (New York: Cultural Dimensions, 1994), pp. 1–2 (pamphlet in author's personal possession). Some of the Lower East Side's artists and activists, including Tom Dent, Roland Snellings, and Nora Hicks (Calvin Hicks's wife), would go on to form Umbra an avant garde writing collective whose workshops drank in the era's eclectic radicalism while resisting sectarianism. For oral histories of Umbra, see Umbra Oral History Collection. See also Eben Y. Wood, "Black Abstraction: The Umbra Workshop and an African American Avant-garde," Ph.D. diss., University of Michigan, 2004; Smethurst, *The Black Arts Movement*.

38. *New York Amsterdam News*, February 18, 1961, p. 8.

39. *New York Times*, February 16, 1961, p. 1.

40. Meriwether, *Proudly We Can Be Called Africans*, pp. 233–38; Woodard, *A Nation Within a Nation*, pp. 57–59.

41. *New York Amsterdam News*, February 25, 1961, pp. 1, 9.

42. Welch, "Black Art and Activism," p. 321.

43. James Baldwin, "A Negro Assays the Negro Mood," *New York Times Magazine*, March 12, 1961, p. 25.

44. Baldwin, "A Negro Assays the Negro Mood." Hansberry, in a letter to the *New York Times* commenting on Baldwin's essay, took offense at rumors connecting the United Nations demonstrations with Communist subversion. Hansberry railed against "the continuation of intrigues against African and American Negro freedom" before apologizing to Mme. Pauline Lumumba (Patrice Lumumba's widow) for Dr. Ralph Bunche (who had publicly apologized for the behavior of black protesters outside the United Nations). See Lorraine Hansberry, "Congolese Patriot," *New York Times Magazine*, March 26, 1961, p. 4.

45. David Gallen, *Malcolm X As They Knew Him* (New York: Carroll & Graf, 1992), pp. 31–32.

3. WAGING WAR AMID SHADOWS

1. William Worthy, "A Close Look at the Black Muslims," *National Guardian*, September 19, 1964, p. 6; "Malcolm X Says a Group Will Stress Politics," *National Guardian*, March 21, 1964, p. 4.

2. John D'Emilio, *Lost Prophet: The Life and Times of Bayard Rustin* (Chicago: University of Chicago Press, 2004), p. 230.

3. *Baltimore-Washington Afro-American*, October 8, 1960, pp. 1–2.

4. Ibid., September 15, 1956, p. 2.

5. *New York Times*, June 23, 1955, p. 14.

6. William Worthy interview.

7. Worthy's relationship with Rustin during the 1940s and 1950s illustrates the fluidity of a black freedom movement in which radical pacifists, antiracists, black nationalists, liberals, and activists overlapped. See D'Emilio, *Lost Prophet*, pp. 133, 135, 145–48.

8. Worthy interview.

9. *Baltimore-Washington Afro-American*, February 16, 1957, p. 1.

10. Ibid., January 4, 1958. Worthy's refusal to accept this deal lost him the chance to become CBS News' first black correspondent, a job that went to Richard Gibson. See Besenia Rodriguez, " 'De la esclavitud yanqui a la libertad cubana': U.S. Black Radicals, the Cuban Revolution, and the Formation of a Tricontinental Ideology," *Radical History Review* 9 (2005), pp. 1–2, 67.

11. *Baltimore-Washington Afro-American*, May 5, 1962, pp. 1–2.

12. *Muhammad Speaks*, January 15, 1963, p. 14.

13. Worthy interview.

14. *Baltimore-Washington Afro-American*, February 11, 1961, p. 6.

15. Ibid., August 5, 1961, p. 1; Worthy interview.

16. *Baltimore-Washington Afro-American*, July 29, 1961, pp. 1, 5.

17. Ibid., October 7, 1961, p. 2.

18. Ibid., October 21, 1961, p. 6.

19. Ibid., p. 6.

20. Ibid., June 30, 1962, pp. 1–2.

21. Worthy interview.

22. Phil Ochs, *All the News That's Fit to Print* (1964) http://walterlippman.com/worthy.html. See also Worthy interview and Gosse, *Where the Boys Are*, p. 152.

23. *Baltimore-Washington Afro-American*, June 30, 1962, pp. 1–2.

24. Ibid., August 18, 1962, p. 2.

25. *Illustrated News*, January 29, 1962, p. 6.

26. See Branch, *Parting the Waters*, and McWhorter, *Carry Me Home*.

27. The social, political, economic, and cultural impact of black migration to urban centers in the North, Midwest, and the West Coast after World Wars I and II has been well documented. See James Weldon Johnson, *Black Manhattan* (New York: Da Capo Press, 1991); St. Clair Drake and Horace Cayton, *Black Metropolis: Negro Life in a Northern Community* (Chicago: University of Chicago Press, 1993); Gilbert Osofsky, *Harlem: The Making of a Ghetto* (Chicago: Dee, 1996); Kenneth Kusmer, *A Ghetto Takes Shape: Black Cleveland, 1870–1930* (Urbana: University of Illinois Press, 1976); Arnold Hirsch, *Making the Second Ghetto: Race and Housing in Chicago 1940–1960* (Chicago: University of Chicago Press, 1998); Joe William Trotter, *Black Milwaukee: The Making of an Industrial Proletariat, 1915–1945* (Urbana: University of Illinois Press, 1985); Lewis, *When Harlem Was in Vogue*; Albert Broussard, *Black San Francisco: The Struggle for Racial Equality in the West, 1900–1954* (Lawrence: University Press of Kansas, 1994); Sugrue, *The Origins of the Urban Crisis*; Douglas Flamming, *Bound for Freedom: Black Los Angeles in Jim Crow America* (Berkeley: University of California Press, 2005). The classic work remains W. E. B. Du Bois's pioneering study *The Philadelphia Negro: A Social Study* (Philadelphia: University of Pennsylvania Press, 1998). See also Michael B. Katz, ed., *The Underclass Debate: Views from History* (Princeton: Princeton University Press, 1993). What remains less well documented is how black activists in the North started local initiatives that were part of the broad sweep of civil rights activism in the post–World War II era. See Taylor, *Knocking at Our Own Door*; Biondi, *To Stand and Fight*; Self, *American Babylon*; Rhonda Y. Williams, *The Politics of Public Housing: Black Women's Struggles Against Urban Inequality* (New York: Oxford University Press, 2004); Theoharis and Woodard, *Freedom North* and *Groundwork*. Specific instances of black radical activism in Harlem, Detroit, Oakland, and other urban areas outside of the South during the late 1950s and early 1960s were not simply a prelude to Black Power activism; it was Black Power, at least in a local sense, complete with urban militants who used the language, style, and tactics that would become a nationwide movement. See also Matthew Countryman, *Up South: Civil Rights and Black Power in Philadelphia* (Philadelphia: University of Pennsylvania Press, 2006).

28. Sugrue, *The Origins of the Urban Crisis*; Sydney Fine, *Violence in the Model City: The Cavanaugh Administration, Race Relations, and the Detroit Riot of 1967* (Ann Arbor: University of Michigan Press, 1989).

29. See Sugrue, *The Origins of the Urban Crisis*.

30. William Van Deburg, *New Day in Babylon: The Black Power Movement and American Culture* (Chicago: University of Chicago Press, 1992), p. 237.

31. Grace Lee Boggs interview.

32. Grace Lee Boggs, *Living for Change: An Autobiography* (Minneapolis: University of Minnesota Press, 1998), p. 122.

33. Albert Cleage Jr., *Black Christian Nationalism: New Directions for the Black Church* (New York: William Morrow, 1972), pp. 32–34.

34. *Illustrated News*, November 13, 1961, p. 3.

35. Fine, *Violence in the Model City*, p. 24.

36. FBIMX 100-399321-21 (Part 3), April 30, 1958, pp. 22–35.

37. FBIGOAL 100-442379-3, Memorandum, August 10, 1964, p. 1.

38. Boggs, *Living for Change*, p. 119.

39. FBIGOAL 100-442379-2X2, August 6, 1964, p. 4.

40. Boggs, *Living for Change*, p. 118.

41. While the couple had no children of their own, James Boggs had children from a previous relationship.

42. Breitman went so far as to secure issues of *Liberator* to be distributed at the Friday night forums. See Breitman, Correspondence, January 28, 1963, Socialist Workers Party Papers, Wisconsin State Historical Society; Angela D. Dillard, "Religion and Radicalism: The Reverend Albert B. Cleage, Jr., and the Rise of Black Nationalism in Detroit," in Theoharis and Woodard, *Freedom North*, p. 165.

43. *Michigan Chronicle*, October 19, 1963, pp. 1, 4.

44. Boggs, *Living for Change*, p. 118.

45. Phillip Abbott Luce, *The New Left*, p. 183, in Revolutionary Action Movement Papers, Reel 9.

46. RAM's anonymity did not last long. See Kelley and Esch, "Black Like Mao," pp. 6–41.

47. *Illustrated News*, May 28, 1962, p. 3.

48. Ibid., June 11, 1962, p. 1

49. Ibid., January 8, 1962, p. 2.

50. Fine, *Violence in the Model City*, pp. 17–37.

51. *Detroit News*, June 24, 1963, p. 1.

52. Fine, *Violence in the Model City*, p. 36.

53. *Illustrated News*, July 9, 1962, p. 4.

54. Ibid., July 2, 1962, p. 2.

55. For a detailed account, see Branch, *Pillar of Fire*, pp. 4–15. See also *Muhammad Speaks*, June 1962, pp. 1–3, 5, 10.

56. Jamal, *From the Dead Level*, p. 194; Goldman, *The Death and Life of Malcolm X*, p. 98; Karim, *Remembering Malcolm*, p. 138; Perry, *Malcolm X*, p. 192; Branch, *Pillar of Fire*, p. 13.

57. Branch, *Pillar of Fire*, p. 13.

58. Jamal, *From the Dead Level*, pp. 196–98.

59. FBIMX 100-399321-48 (Part 7), Internal Security, NOI, November 17, 1961, p. 9; Jamal, *From the Dead Level*, pp. 95, 196–200.

60. The term used by NOI members to describe blacks.

61. Karim, *Remembering Malcolm*, p. 140.

62. Goldman, *The Death and Life of Malcolm X*, pp. 98–99; Jamal, *The Dead Level*, pp. 200–201; Branch, *Pillar of Fire*, p. 14.

63. *Los Angeles Sentinel*, May 3, 1962, p. 4A.

64. *Los Angeles Times*, August 29, 1962, p. 1.

65. *California Eagle*, May 3, 1962, p. 4.

66. Malcolm X 1962. PRA BB0541.

67. Branch, *Pillar of Fire*, pp. 14–15; Goldman, *The Death and Life of Malcolm X*, pp. 97–106.

68. "The Challenge of Racism," flyer, Freedom Now Party Organizational Files, Tamiment Institute, New York University.

69. "The Crisis of Racism," Palm Gardens, New York, May 1, 1962. Sound Recording, Schomburg Center.

70. Ibid.

71. Ibid.

72. Ibid.

73. Ibid.

4. LIBERATORS

1. Scholar James Edward Smethurst suggests that even though Watts's relationship to Old Left Communists was marked by ambivalence, he had close associations with radicals in the past and during the 1960s, and allowed members of Left-nationalist groups such as the Revolutionary Action Movement to publish frequently in the *Liberator*. *Freedomways*, whose title suggests Robeson's *Freedom* magazine, served as an important publishing outlet for activists associated with the Black Arts and Black Power. See Smethurst, "Poetry and Sympathy: New York, the Left, and the Rise of Black Arts," in Mullen and Smethurst, *Left of the Color Line*, pp. 259–78; and Smethurst, *The Black Arts Movement*.

2. Daniel Watts transcript. Moorland-Spingarn Collection, Howard University.

3. Cruse, who later broke with Watts, wrote a series of provocative and highly influential articles for *Liberator* between 1963 and 1964. It was largely through these articles—and his 1962 essay in *Studies on the Left*—that he was known to a generation of black radicals before the publication of *The Crisis of the Negro Intellectual*. See Van Gosse, "More Than Just a Politician: Notes on the Life and Times of Harold Cruse," in Jerry Watts, ed., *Harold Cruse's The Crisis of the Negro Intellectual Reconsidered* (New York: Routledge, 2004), pp. 32–35.

4. Carol Polsgrove, *Divided Minds: Intellectuals and the Civil Rights Movement* (New York: Norton, 2001), pp. 155–72.

5. Sylvester Leaks, "James Baldwin—I Know His Name," *Freedomways* 3, no. 1 (1963), pp. 102–8.

6. John Henrik Clarke to Julian Mayfield, June 18, 1963, p. 2. John Henrik Clarke Papers, Box 6, f-r.

7. Julian Mayfield, "And Then Came Baldwin," *Freedomways* 3, no. 2 (1963), pp. 143–55.

8. John Henrik Clarke, "James Baldwin Talks of Fire," *National Guardian*, March 21, 1963, p. 10.

9. James Baldwin, "Not 100 Years of Freedom," *Liberator*, January 1963, p. 7.

10. James Baldwin, *The Fire Next Time* (New York: Dell Books, 1964), p. 100.

11. Ibid., p. 72.

12. James Baldwin, *No Name in the Street* (New York: Dell Books, 1972), p. 95.

13. Ibid., p. 122.

14. Branch, *Pillar of Fire*, p. 89. In Baldwin's recollection, Hansberry ended the meeting with a comment to Kennedy, "But I am worried about the state of the civilization

which produced that photograph of the white cop standing on the Negro woman's neck in Birmingham." See Baldwin, "Lorraine Hansberry at the Summit," *Freedomways* 19, no. 4 (1979), pp. 269–72.

15. Joanne Grant, "The Little Man Who Wasn't There," *National Guardian*, June 13, 1963, p. 5.

16. FBIRFK 77-51387, vol. 5, Teletype, May 29, 1963.

17. George Breitman, ed., *Malcolm X Speaks* (New York: Pathfinder Press, 1989), p. 16. If James Baldwin's *The Fire Next Time* represented black radicalism's literary manifesto, Nina Simone's "Mississippi Goddamn" became its musical equivalent, a scalding protest anthem that repudiated America's vigorous self-congratulation after the March on Washington. A classically trained pianist born in the rural South, Simone took the jazz world by storm in the early 1960s through a deft combination of blues, jazz, classical, and soul music. With political mentors that included Lorraine Hansberry, James Baldwin, and Langston Hughes and friendships with SNCC activist Stokely Carmichael, Simone's growing identification with the black freedom struggle's most radical elements placed her in the company of the same activists who participated in the 1961 United Nations demonstrations. Written in a flush of anger and creativity following news of Birmingham's Sixteenth Street church bombing in September 1963, "Mississippi Goddamn" expressed stark political anger and with it a heightened critical consciousness poised on civil rights' outer edges. Judging America a "country full of lies," Simone issued a grim prediction of death and violence ("You're all gonna die like flies"), more popularly associated with Malcolm X and the Nation of Islam. Simone's criticism of civil rights liberals who preached patience was less a turning point in the civil rights era than a window into a world of radical black art and activism that would galvanize the Black Arts movement and Black Power. Headlining the Student Non-Violent Coordinating Committee (SNCC) benefit concerts in the South as well as successful European tours, Nina Simone proudly wore African dress, unabashedly proclaimed loyalty to the black movement's most militant sectors, and in the process emerged as a powerful voice among Afro-American radicals. See Feldstein, " 'I Don't Trust You Anymore.' "

18. *Illustrated News*, March 4, 1963, p. 3.

19. *Correspondence*, January 1963, p. 2 (of supplement).

20. *Muhammad Speaks*, February 4, 1963; Elombe Brath interview.

21. Branch, *Pillar of Fire*, pp. 75–154; Kelley, *Race Rebels*, pp. 77–100.

22. *Baltimore-Washington Afro-American*, April 20, 1963, p. 1.

23. *Muhammad Speaks*, May 13, 1963, p. 8.

24. Robert F. Williams, "Radio Free Dixie," broadcast, May 1963. I am grateful to Ernie Allen for making this material available to me.

25. "Radio Free Dixie," May 1963. In Philadelphia, African Americans, led by militant NAACP and CORE activists, organized contentious protests against the city's restricted trade unions. Marked by violent skirmishes between police, protesters, and construction workers, Philadelphia's protests revealed the intersection of southern civil rights, northern protest, and federal policy. On June 22, 1963, influenced by racial turmoil in Birmingham, which seemed to be spreading to trouble spots including Philadelphia, President Kennedy signed an executive order banning discrimination in federally sponsored construction. See Thomas J. Sugrue, "Affirmative Action from Below: Civil Rights, the Building Trades, and the Politics of Racial Equality in the Urban North, 1945–1969," *Journal of American History* 91, no. 1 (June 2004), pp. 145–73.

26. See *Muhammad Speaks*, May 24, 1963, p. 2, and June 21, 1963 (cover). For an analysis of this photo, see McWhorter, *Carry Me Home*, pp. 374–75.

27. *Illustrated News*, May 27, 1963, p. 1.

28. *Michigan Chronicle*, June 1, 1963, p. 4.

29. Boggs, *Living for Change*, p. 124.

30. Suzanne Smith, *Dancing in the Street: Motown and the Cultural Politics of Detroit* (Cambridge: Harvard University Press, 1999), pp. 41–42.

31. Nick Salvatore challenges the assumption that Albert Cleage was the primary source behind the Great March. See *Singers in a Strange Land: C. L. Franklin, the Black Church, and the Transformation of America* (New York: Little, Brown, 2005), pp. 244–51.

32. *New York Herald Tribune*, May 5, 1963, p. 16, in NYFBIMX 105-8999-3617 (Section 50); Perry, *Malcolm X*, pp. 234–36.

33. *Newark Star-Ledger*, May 10, 1963, in NYFBIMX 105-8999-3622 (Section 50).

34. *Chicago Defender*, May 6, 1963, in NYFBIMX 105-8999-3618 (Section 50).

35. *Chicago Defender*, May 25–31, 1963, in NYFBIMX 100-8999-3608 (Section 50).

36. Branch, *Pillar of Fire*, p. 100.

37. *New York Times*, May 17, 1963, p. 17, in NYFBIMX 105-8999-3628 (Section 50).

38. *New York Times*, June 30, 1963, p. 45, in NYFBIMX 105-8999-3709 (Section 51).

39. Ibid.

40. FBIMX 100-399321-59 (Part 8), Memo, May 13, 1963, pp. 1–2.

41. FBIMX 100-399321 (Part 9), Airtel, May 15, 1963, p. 1; Perry, *Malcolm X*, p. 210.

42. Perry, *Malcolm X*, p. 210.

43. Lomax, *When the Word Is Given*, p. 74.

44. Malcolm equated news that Jackie Robinson and Floyd Patterson were planning trips to Birmingham with a futile attempt by white liberals to stave off a growing black tide of anger; *New York Times*, May 11, 1963, p. 9, in NYFBIMX 105-8999-3623 (Section 50), and *New York Amsterdam News*, May 25, 1963, p. 2, in NYFBIMX 105-8999-3623 (Section 50).

45. Branch, *Parting the Waters*, p. 343.

46. Plummer, *Rising Wind*, p. 290.

47. *New York Amsterdam News*, November 2, 1963, p. 46.

48. Ibid., November 16, p. 49.

49. Ibid., November 30, 1963, p.1, in NYFBIMX 105-8999-3966 (Section 55).

50. Gallen, *Malcolm X*, pp. 139–40.

51. For Malcolm's discussion of Birmingham, see Lomax, *When the Word Is Given*, pp. 178–79. See also McWhorter, *Carry Me Home*, p. 437.

52. *New York Times*, April 23, 1963, p. 20.

53. Ibid.

54. Ibid.

55. Branch, *Pillar of Fire*, p. 97.

56. For a time, Malcolm conducted separate interviews at the same hotel with Lomax and Haley. See Perry, *Malcolm X*, p. 214.

57. Goldman, *The Death and Life of Malcolm X*, p. 111; Perry, *Malcolm X*, p. 214.

58. *Illustrated News*, June 10, 1963, p. 4.

59. *Michigan Chronicle*, June 15, 1963, pp. 1, 4.

60. Smith, *Dancing in the Street*, p. 26.

61. Dillard, "Religion and Radicalism," p. 167.

62. Payne, *I've Got the Light of Freedom*, pp. 285–86.
63. *Detroit News*, June 24, 1963, p. 2A.
64. Branch, *Parting the Waters*, p. 843.
65. *Detroit News*, June 24, 1963, p. 1.
66. Ibid., p. 4A.
67. Ibid.
68. Ibid.
69. Ibid.
70. Ibid.
71. *Correspondence*, June 1963, p. 1.
72. *Michigan Chronicle*, June 29, 1963, p. 4.
73. Ibid.
74. Ibid.
75. *Illustrated News*, June 24, 1963, p. 3. Motown Records recorded and distributed King's speech in August, calling it "The Great March to Freedom." The sound engineer was GOAL activist Richard Henry. See Smith, *Dancing in the Street*, pp. 21–53.
76. *Detroit News*, June 24, 1963, p. 16.
77. Worthy interview.
78. "The Declaration of Washington," August 28, 1963, Freedom Now Party Organizational File, Tamiment Institute, New York University.
79. The day after the meeting between Hoover and Freedom Now Party representatives, letters of commendation were requested for special agents and two supervisors who provided intelligence about the FNP sit-in plot. FBIFNP 105-123706-13, Memo, August 30, 1963, pp. 1–2.
80. FBIFNP 105-123706-12, "Freedom Now Movement's Visit to Director's Office," Memo, August 29, 1963, pp. 1–8.
81. FBIFNP 105-123706, Memo, August 30, 1963, pp. 1–9, 15; SAC Letter, September 4, 1963, pp. 1–2.
82. Dillard, "Religion and Radicalism," p. 168.
83. *Illustrated News*, October 28, 1963, pp. 3, 6.
84. Ibid.
85. See Peter B. Levy, *Civil War on Race Street: The Civil Rights Movement in Cambridge, Maryland* (Gainesville: University Press of Florida, 2003), and "Gloria Richardson and the Civil Rights Movement in Cambridge, Maryland," in Theoharis and Woodard, *Groundwork*, pp. 97–115; Sharon Harley, " 'Chronicle of a Death Foretold': Gloria Richardson, the Cambridge Movement, and the Radical Black Activist Tradition," in Bettye Collier-Thomas and V. P. Franklin, eds., *Sisters in the Struggle: African American Women in the Civil Rights–Black Power Movement* (New York: New York University Press, 2001), pp. 174–96; Goldman, *The Death and Life of Malcolm X*, p. 116.
86. Malcolm X, "Message to the Grassroots," in Breitman, *Malcolm X Speaks*, pp. 4–17.
87. Ibid., p. 5.
88. Haley, *The Autobiography of Malcolm X*, p. 415.
89. Breitman, *Malcolm X Speaks*, p. 9.
90. Haley, *The Autobiography of Malcolm X*, pp. 306–7. Such accusations were not far off the mark. Behind the scenes, events leading up to the March on Washington featured false starts, political blackmail, illegal surveillance, backroom deals, and tense discussions. President Kennedy's attempts to stall the march failed. After standing their ground with Kennedy, civil rights leaders convened privately. Roy Wilkins handpicked the "Big Six"—A. Philip Randolph; John Lewis of SNCC; Whitney Young of the Urban

League; James Farmer of CORE; King of SCLC; and himself—as the main recipients of foundation money. The financial support, while eagerly pursued by the NAACP and the Urban League, threatened less established groups such as SCLC and the young mavericks of SNCC (who received the smallest amount of money) with burdensome restrictions. See Garrow, *Bearing the Cross*; Branch, *Parting the Waters*, pp. 276–78, 846–48.

91. *Michigan Chronicle*, November 16, 1963, pp. 1, 4.

92. Goldman, *The Death and Life of Malcolm X*, pp. 118–19; Branch, *Pillar of Fire*, pp. 184–86.

93. FBIMX 100-399321 (Part 9), "Internal Security—Nation of Islam," November 15, 1963, p. 1.

94. *New York Amsterdam News*, December 7, 1963, p. 1.

95. NYFBIMX 105-8999-3959 (Section 55), pp. 1–3.

96. *Illustrated News*, November 25, 1963, pp. 3, 6–7.

97. Ibid., December 9, 1963, p. 3.

98. Sterling Gray, "Architect of a Revolution," *Liberator*, December 1963, pp. 8–9.

99. Lomax, *When the Word Is Given*, p. 179.

5. POLITICAL KINGDOMS

1. Branch, *Pillar of Fire*, p. 201; NYFBIMX 105-8999-4073, Wiretap transcript of December 31, 1963, telephone conversation, pp. 1–3. Memorandum, January 27, 1964.

2. *New York Amsterdam News*, February 1, 1964, p. 1.

3. Ibid., February 15, 1964, p. 1.

4. Ibid., February 22, 1964, p. 1.

5. *Baltimore-Washington Afro-American*, February 22, 1964, p. 1, in NYFBIMX 105-8999-4103 (Section 57).

6. *New York Times*, February 27, 1964, p. 23, in NYFBIMX 105-8999-4229 (Section 58); *New York Times*, February 26, 1964, p. 39, in NYFBIMX 105-8999-4229; *Newark Star Ledger*, February 22, 1964, in NYFBIMX 105-8999-4224; *New York Amsterdam News*, February 22, 1964, p. 1, in NYFBIMX 105-8999-4223.

7. Lomax, *When the Word Is Given*, p. 177; Branch, *Pillar of Fire*, p. 255.

8. *New York Courier*, February 29, 1964, and *Chicago Defender*, March 2, 1964, in FBIMX 100-399321-A (Part 21), Sub A.

9. *Chicago Defender*, March 2, 1964, p. 10, in NYFBIMX 105-8999-4133 (Section 57).

10. Branch, *Pillar of Fire*, pp. 251–53.

11. *New York Amsterdam News*, March 7, 1964, p. 1.

12. Branch, *Pillar of Fire*, pp. 251–62.

13. Ibid., p. 256.

14. FBIMX 100-399321-125 (Part 10), Memo, March 26, 1964, pp. 2–4.

15. FBIMX 100-399321 (Part 11), June 18, 1964, p. 27; Goldman, *The Death and Life of Malcolm X*, p. 133.

16. Breitman, *Malcolm X Speaks*, p. 22.

17. Malcolm responded affirmatively to one reporter's question about whether he would keep "X" as his name. See Goldman, *The Death and Life of Malcolm X*, p. 135.

18. William Worthy, "Malcolm X Plan for Rifle Clubs," *Baltimore-Washington Afro-American*, March 21, 1964.

19. *Baltimore-Washington Afro-American*, March 21, 1964, pp. 1–2; and Sales, *From Civil Rights to Black Liberation*, p. 126.

20. *Philadelphia Inquirer*, March 15, 1964. *Philadelphia Evening Bulletin*, Newspaper Clipping Collection. Temple University Library, Urban Archives. Hereafter cited as PEBUA.

21. FBIMX 100-399321-55 (Part 8), Memo, March 28, 1963, p. 1.

22. *National Guardian*, March 21, 1964, p. 9; Goldman, *The Death and Life of Malcolm X*, pp. 144–45; Taylor, *Knocking at Our Own Door*, pp. 158–60.

23. William Worthy, "Muhammad's Empire Is Heading for Oblivion," *National Guardian*, September 26, 1964, p. 4.

24. *New York Post*, March 10, 1964, p. 5, in NYFBIMX 105-8999-4153 (Section 57); FBIMX 100-399321 (Part 10), Airtel, March 26, 1964, pp. 1–7.

25. FBIMX 100-399321 (Part 21), Sub A; "Muslim Leader Rules Out Violence in Aide Split," *Arizona Republic*, March 10, 1964, p. 39.

26. FBIMX 100-399321 (Part 10), Airtel, March 12, 1964, pp. 1–3; Branch, *Pillar of Fire*, pp. 255–60.

27. *New Crusader*, April 4, 1964, p. 5, in NYFBIMX 105-8999-4330 (Section 59).

28. *New York Times*, March 23, 1964, p. 18, in NYFBIMX 105-8999-4203 (Section 58).

29. Gertrude Samuels, "Feud Within the Black Muslims," *New York Times Magazine*, March 22, 1964, p. 105.

30. A. B. Spelman, "Interview with Malcolm X," *Monthly Review*, May 1964, pp. 14–24.

31. *Washington Evening Star*, March 26, 1964, p. A5, in NYFBIMX 105-8999-4257 (Section 58); Branch, *Pillar of Fire*, pp. 267–68; Perry, *Malcolm X*, p. 255.

32. *Washington Evening Star*, March 26, 1964, p. A5, in NYFBIMX 105-8999-4257 (Section 58).

33. Branch, *Pillar of Fire*, p. 268.

34. FBIMX 100-399321 (Part 10), Airtel, March 26, 1964, pp. 1–7; Branch, *Pillar of Fire*, p. 261.

35. Honed at Harlem's Rockland Palace and Cleveland's Cory Methodist Church, Malcolm delivered the definitive version in Detroit the day before leaving for Africa. See Goldman, *The Death and Life of Malcolm X*, p. 150; Breitman, *Malcolm X Speaks*, p. 23.

36. Breitman, *Malcolm X Speaks*, pp. 23–44.

37. FBIMX 100-399321-97 (Part 10), Airtel, April 14, 1964, pp. 1–3.

38. Sales, *From Civil Rights to Black Liberation*, pp. 99–100; Branch, *Pillar of Fire*, p. 269.

39. Malcolm's trip to Ghana is drawn from the following sources. Malcolm X, "We Are All Blood Brothers," *Liberator*, July 1964, pp. 4–6; Haley, *The Autobiography of Malcolm X*; Leslie Alexander Lacy, *The Rise and Fall of a Proper Negro: An Autobiography* (New York: McMillan, 1970), pp. 207–27; Goldman, *The Death and Life of Malcolm X*, pp. 172–82; Angelou, *All God's Children Need Traveling Shoes*.

40. Malcolm X, "We Are All Blood Brothers," p. 4.

41. Angelou, *All God's Children Need Traveling Shoes*, p. 23; Gaines, "African-American Expatriates in Ghana and the Black Radical Tradition," p. 68.

42. Lewis, *W.E.B. Du Bois*, p. 568.

43. Gallen, *Malcolm X*, p. 75.

44. Lacy, *The Rise and Fall of a Proper Negro*, pp. 148–91; JMP.

45. FBIMX 100-399321 (Part 14), January 20, 1965, p. 94.

46. Haley, *The Autobiography of Malcolm X*, pp. 384–86.

47. Ibid., p. 385.

48. *Ghanaian Times*, May 18, 1964, in NYFBIMX 105-8999-5279 and May 19, 1964, 105-8999-5278 (Section 72); Branch, *Pillar of Fire*, p. 314.

49. Horne, *Race Woman*, pp. 188–90.

50. Haley, *The Autobiography of Malcolm X*, 389.

51. Goldman, *The Death and Life of Malcolm X*, p. 179.

52. Malcolm X, "We Are All Blood Brothers," p. 5.

53. Sales, *From Civil Rights to Black Liberation*, pp. 131–32.

54. Haley, *The Autobiography of Malcolm X*, pp. 303–4.

55. *New York Amsterdam News*, May 23, 1964, p. 14, in NYFBIMX 105-8999-4512 (Section 61).

56. Haley, *The Autobiography of Malcolm X*, pp. 450–51.

57. FBIGOAL 100-HQ-442379-1, Memorandum, July 15, 1964, p. 4.

58. Ibid., p. 3.

59. Ibid.

60. Maxwell C. Stanford, "Revolutionary Action Movement (RAM): A Case Study of an Urban Revolutionary Movement in Western Capitalism," M.A. thesis, Atlanta University, 1986; Askia Muhammad Touré interview; Kelley and Esch, "Black Like Mao," pp. 6–41; Hill, *The Deacons for Defense*, pp. 222–23.

61. *New York World Telegram*, June 18, 1964, in NYFBIMX 105-8999-4589 (Section 63).

62. Sales, *From Civil Rights to Black Liberation*, pp. 104–13.

63. Breitman, *By Any Means Necessary*, p. 38.

64. Ibid., pp. 59–64.

65. Branch, *Pillar of Fire*, pp. 380–81.

66. Ibid., pp. 384–86.

67. Ibid., p. 386.

68. Memo, July 10, 1964, pp. 11–16, in NYFBIMX 105-8999-4710 (Section 65); Clegg, *An Original Man*, pp. 223–24.

69. *New Crusader*, July 11, 1964, p. 5, in NYFBIMX 105-8999-4792 (Section 66); Clegg, *An Original Man*, pp. 223–24.

70. *Baltimore-Washington Afro-American*, August 1, 1964, p. 1.

71. *New York Times*, July 20, 1964, p. 16.

72. Ibid.; Branch, *Pillar of Fire*, p. 418.

73. *National Guardian*, August 1, 1964, p. 5.

74. *Muhammad Speaks*, August 14, 1964, p. 1.

75. OAAU Press Release, July 17, 1964; Vertical Files, OAAU, Bentley Library Special Collections, University of Michigan.

76. Breitman, *Malcolm X Speaks*, pp. 72–77.

77. *New York Post*, July 17, 1964, p. 32, in NYFBIMX 105-8999-4742 (Section 65).

78. Breitman, *By Any Means Necessary*, p. 137.

79. FBIMX 100-399321 (Part 14), Jan. 20, 1965, pp. 106-8; Horne, *Race Woman*, p. 187.

80. *New York Journal-American*, July 25, 1964, p. 20, in NYFBIMX 105-8999-4790 (Section 66).

81. FBIMX 100-399321 (Part 14), Jan. 20, 1965, p. 142.

82. *New York Times*, August 17, 1964, p. 22, in NYFBIMX 105-8999-4783 (Section 67).

83. John Lewis and Michael D'Orso, *Walking with the Wind: A Memoir of the Movement* (New York: Simon and Schuster, 1998), pp. 294–98.

84. Goldman, *The Death and Life of Malcolm X*, pp. 219–20; Lacy, *The Rise and Fall of a Proper Negro*, pp. 221–27.

85. *New York Courier*, December 5, 1964, pp. 1, 9, in NYFBIMX 105-8999-5221 (Section 72).

86. *New York Times*, November 11, 1964, p. 48, in NYFBIMX 105-8999-5143 (Section 71).

87. *New York Amsterdam News*, December 5, 1964, in NYFBIMX 105-8999-5222 (Section 72).

88. Branch, *Pillar of Fire*, pp. 547–48; Breitman, *Malcolm X Speaks*, pp. 105–14.

89. Branch, *Pillar of Fire*, pp. 550–51.

90. *New York Times*, January 2, 1965, p. 6, in NYFBIMX 105-8999-5334 (Section 73).

91. *Philadelphia Independent*, December 5, 1964, p. 20, in NYFBIMX 105-8999-5183 (Section 72).

92. Branch, *Pillar of Fire*, pp. 578–79; Goldman, *The Death and Life of Malcolm X*, pp. 230–32; Perry, *Malcolm X*, pp. 348–49.

93. Branch, *Pillar of Fire*, pp. 573–75. Malcolm wrote Julian Mayfield in Ghana, asking his old friend for help in the event of his death. See Goldman, *The Death and Life of Malcolm X*, p. 256; Russell J. Rickford, *Betty Shabazz: A Remarkable Story of Survival and Faith Before and After Malcolm X* (Naperville: Sourcebooks, 2003), p. 215.

94. *The Record*, February 15, 1965, p. 2, in NYFBIMX 105-8999-5581 (Section 75).

95. *New York Daily News*, February 16, 1965, in NYFBIMX 105-8999-5829 (Section 78); *New York Journal American*, February 16, p. 3, in NYFBIMX 105-8999-5827 (Section 78).

96. Branch, *Pillar of Fire*, p. 596; Goldman, *The Death and Life of Malcolm X*, pp. 267–74.

97. Clegg, *An Original Man*, p. 229; Branch, *Pillar of Fire*, pp. 596–97, 601–3.

98. *New York Herald Tribune*, February 24, 1965, p. 1, in NYFBIMX 105-8999-5903 (Section 79).

99. *New York Post*, February 24, 1965, p. 3, in NYFBIMX 105-8999-5904 (Section 79).

100. *New York Herald Tribune*, February 23, 1965, p. 14, in NYFBIMX 105-8999-5885 (Section 79); *New York Post*, February 26, 1965, p. 3, in NYFBIMX 105-8999-5719 (Section 77).

101. *New York Times*, February 23, 1965, p. 1, in NYFBIMX 105-8999-5886 (Section 79).

102. *New York Times*, February 24, 1964, p. 1, in NYFBIMX 105-8999-5895 (Section 79).

103. *New York Daily News*, February 22, 1965, p. 3, in NYFBIMX 105-8999-5889 (Section 79).

104. *New York World Telegram and Sun*, February 22, 1965, p. 1, in NYFBIMX 105-8999-5860 (Section 79); *New York Herald Tribune*, February 24, 1965, pp. 1, 10, in NYFBIMX 105-8999-5906 (Section 79); *New York Times*, February 24, 1965, p. 1, in NYFBIMX 105-8999-5895 (Section 79).

105. *Chicago Daily News*, February 23, 1965, p. 4, in NYFBIMX 105-8999-5882 (Section 79).

106. *New York Times*, February 22, 1965, p. 20, in NYFBIMX 105-8999-5855 (Section 79); *New York Times*, February 27, 1965, p. 74, in NYFBIMX 105-8999-5944 (Section 80).

107. *New York Times*, February 26, 1965, in NYFBIMX 105-8999-5923 (Section 80); *New York Daily News*, February 26, 1965, p. 3, in NYFBIMX 105-8999-5929 (Section 80).

108. *New York Amsterdam News*, March 20, 1965, p. 39, in NYFBIMX 105-8999-6168 (Section 82).

6. "BLACK" IS A COUNTRY

1. Baraka, *The Autobiography of LeRoi Jones*, pp. 273–77; Woodard, *A Nation Within a Nation*, pp. 64–68.

2. LeRoi Jones, *Home: Social Essays* (New Jersey: Ecco Press, 1998), pp. 10, 82–86.

3. Gosse, "More Than Just a Politician," in Watts, *Harold Cruse's The Crisis of the Negro Intellectual Reconsidered*, pp. 35–36. See also Diane C. Fujino, *Heartbeat of Struggle: The Revolutionary Life of Yuri Kochiyama* (Minneapolis: University of Minnesota Press, 2005).

4. Woodard, *A Nation Within a Nation*, pp. 66–67. James Smethurst's history of the Black Arts movement illustrates the way in which BARTS benefited from a preexisting landscape of radical cultural and political activism. See also Smethurst, *The Black Arts Movement*.

5. *Time*, August 20, 1965, p. 13.

6. For Parker's statement, see *Los Angeles Times*, August 16, 1965, p. 4; for Yorty's, see *Los Angeles Times*, August 18, 1965, pp. 3, 16.

7. Garrow, *Bearing the Cross*, p. 439. Jeanne Theoharis argues that King had visited Watts twice before the uprising and had placed struggles in Los Angeles in the context of the liberation movement sweeping America. See Theoharis, " 'Alabama on Avalon': Rethinking the Watts Uprising and the Character of Black Protest in Los Angeles," in Joseph, *The Black Power Movement*.

8. *Los Angeles Herald-Examiner*, August 16, 1965.

9. *Philadelphia Evening Bulletin*, June 5, 1965. PEBUA.

10. LBJ Oral History Archives, tape no. 8578, April 20, 1965.

11. Branch, *Pillar of Fire*, p. 601.

12. *New York Times*, October 29, 1965, p. 41, and November 5, 1965, in NYFBIMX 105-8999-A,B,C.

13. Carmichael quote from *Eyes on the Prize II*, Episode 2, "The Time Has Come, 1964–1966."

14. "SNCC Charts a Course," June 4, 1966, p. 9, *National Guardian* pamphlet.

15. Stokely Carmichael with Ekwueme Michael Thelwell, *Ready for Revolution: The Life and Struggles of Stokely Carmichael (Kwame Ture)* (New York: Scribner, 2003), pp. 22–43.

16. Ibid., pp. 55–59.

17. Ibid., pp. 83–109.

18. Ibid., pp. 92–93.

19. Ibid., pp. 100–101.

20. Ibid., p. 113.

21. Ibid., pp. 137–38.

22. Ibid., pp. 118–19, 136–54.

23. Gordon Parks, "Whip of Black Power," *Life*, May 19, 1967, p. 79.

24. Carmichael, *Ready for Revolution*, p. 194.

25. Ibid., p. 148.

26. Ibid., p. 435. See also Payne, *I've Got the Light of Freedom*, p. 240.

27. Cleveland Sellers interview; Judy Richardson interview. At the Waveland Conference, two white women members of SNCC had produced well-thought-out position papers on the organization's treatment of women. This approach, if not the substance of their complaint, turned some members off. See Carmichael, *Ready for Revolution*, pp. 430–35, and Carson, *In Struggle*, pp. 147–48.

28. Carmichael, *Ready for Revolution*.

29. Henry Hampton and Stephen Fayer, eds., *Voices of Freedom: An Oral History of the Civil Rights Movement from the 1960s to the 1980s* (New York: Bantam Books, 1990), p. 268; Carmichael, *Ready for Revolution*, p. 460. For a look at Lowndes County that emphasizes the indigenous nature of the movement, see Hasan Jeffries, "Organizing for More Than the Vote: The Political Radicalization of Local People in Lowndes County, Alabama, 1965–1966," in Theoharis and Woodard, *Groundwork*, pp. 140–63.

30. *Look*, November 16, 1965.

31. Carson, *In Struggle*, pp. 161, 165; Carmichael, *Ready for Revolution*, pp. 466–71.

32. Bernard Weinraub, "The Brilliancy of Black," *Esquire*, January 1967, pp. 133–34; Parks, "Whip of Black Power," p. 80.

33. Parks, "Whip of Black Power," p. 80.

34. Carson, *In Struggle*, p. 163.

35. *The Movement*, May 1966, p. 107, Carson Bound Personal Archives King Center. Hereafter cited as CAKC.

36. *The Movement*, June 1966, p. 127. CAKC.

37. Historian Charles Payne provides the most detailed account of the organizing tradition of careful, painstaking, and deliberative community activism that crossed generational lines between the Depression-era South and the civil rights era. See Payne, *I've Got the Light of Freedom*. See also Kelley, *Hammer and Hoe*, and Dittmer, *Local People*.

38. *The Movement*, June 1966, p. 124. CAKC.

39. Carson, *In Struggle*, p. 164; Carmichael, *Ready for Revolution*, p. 474.

40. *The Movement*, June 1966, p. 124. CAKC.

41. Carson, *In Struggle*, p. 203.

42. *The Movement*, July 1966, p. 5. CAKC.

43. *New York Times*, May 28, 1966, pp. 1, 9.

44. Carmichael, *Ready for Revolution*, p. 484.

7. "WHAT WE GONNA START SAYIN' NOW IS BLACK POWER!"

1. Branch, *Parting the Waters*, pp. 647–53.

2. *New York Times*, June 7, 1966, pp. 1, 27.

3. Ibid., June 8, 1966, p. 1.

4. Garrow, *Bearing the Cross*, p. 475.

5. *Newsweek*, June 20, 1966, p. 30; *New York Times*, June 8, 1966, p. A1.

6. *Newsweek*, June 20, 1966, p. 27.

7. *New York Times*, June 7, 1966, p. 29.

8. Ibid., June 8, 1966, p. 26.
9. "The New Racism," *Time*, July 1, 1966, p. 11; *Memphis Commercial Appeal*, June 10, 1966, p. 3. See also Dittmer, *Local People*, pp. 389-407.
10. *Newsweek*, June 20, 1966, p. 29.
11. *New York Times*, June 8, 1966, p. 1.
12. Cleveland Sellers interview.
13. *New York Times*, June 8, 1966, p. 32.
14. *Newsweek*, June 20, 1966, p. 29.
15. Carmichael, *Ready for Revolution*, p. 494.
16. Ibid., p. 494.
17. Ibid., p. 490.
18. *Newsweek*, June 20, 1966, p. 30.
19. Ibid., p. 30.
20. Sellers interview; Fairclough, *To Redeem the Soul of America*, pp. 314–15.
21. Hampton and Fayer, *Voices of Freedom*, p. 289.
22. *Chicago Daily News*, June 8, 1966, p. 6.
23. *Newsweek*, July 4, 1966, p. 14.
24. Carmichael, *Ready for Revolution*, p. 510.
25. *Chicago Daily News*, June 8, 1966, p. 6.
26. *Eyes on the Prize II*, "The Time Has Come, 1964–1966."
27. Cleveland Sellers, *The River of No Return: The Autobiography of a Black Militant and the Life and Death of SNCC* (New York: William Morrow, 1973), p. 162.
28. Branch, *Parting the Waters*, p. 180.
29. Historian Lance Hill has written the first in-depth account of the Deacons. See Hill, *The Deacons for Defense*, pp. 1–51, 245–73.
30. Sellers interview.
31. Carmichael, *Ready for Revolution*, p. 504.
32. *New York Times*, June 9, 1966, p. 1.
33. Ibid., p. 33.
34. Ibid., June 11, 1966, pp. 1, 19.
35. Ibid., June 12, 1966, p. 82.
36. Ibid., June 14, 1966, p. 19.
37. Ibid., June 15, 1966, p. 26.
38. Ibid., June 26, 1966, p. 40; Paul Good, "A White Look at Black Power," *The Nation*, Nov. 21, 1966, pp. 534–38; *Chicago Daily News*, June 14, 1966, p. 42.
39. *New York Times*, June 15, 1966, p. 26.
40. Ibid.
41. Ibid., p. 1.
42. *Time*, June 24, 1966, p. 31.
43. *New York Times*, June 26, 1966, p. 40; Good, "A White Look at Black Power," p. 113.
44. Sellers interview.
45. Ibid.
46. *New York Times*, June 16, 1966, p. 35.
47. Garrow, *Bearing the Cross*, p. 481; *New York Times*, June 16, 1966, p. 35.
48. Garrow, *Bearing the Cross*, p. 481; *New York Times*, June 17, 1966, p. 1.
49. Hampton and Fayer, *Voices of Freedom*, p. 289.
50. *Los Angeles Times*, June 17, 1966, p. 1.
51. *New York Times*, June 17, 1966, p. 1.

52. Ibid., September 25, 1966.
53. Sellers, *The River of No Return*, p. 168.
54. *New York Times*, June 19, p. 28; Garrow, *Bearing the Cross*, p. 482.
55. Garrow, *Bearing the Cross*, p. 482.
56. *Chicago Daily News*, June 20, 1966, p. 1.
57. Ibid.
58. *New York Times*, June 19, 1966, p. 60.
59. *Face the Nation*, CBS Television, June 19, 1966. *SNCC Papers* (Microfilm), Reel 2, 58. See also FBIKT 100-446080-2, pp. 1–2.
60. *Face the Nation*, June 19, 1966, p. 6.
61. Ibid., pp. 16–17.
62. Ibid., p. 4.
63. Garrow, *Bearing the Cross*, p. 486; *New York Times*, January 25, 1966, p. 1.
64. Meredith had, at various points during his convalescence, expressed displeasure over the march's lack of organization and the perceived opportunism of those who assumed its leadership. There were other statements as well. Most were various timetables announcing when he would rejoin the march. Others were delivered in television or radio interviews. On NBC's *Meet the Press*, Meredith claimed that the FBI had stood by during his ambush. In a radio interview, he declined to say whether or not, on his return to the Magnolia State, he would carry a gun. "There are an awful lot of people who plan to go back with me and I don't know what they are going to do." *New York Times*, June 16, p. 35; June 20, p. 21; June 22, p. 24; and June 26, 1966, p. 1.
65. *New York Times*, June 26, 1966, p. 1.
66. Garrow, *Bearing the Cross*, p. 487.
67. *New York Times*, June 26, 1966, p. 40.
68. Ibid.; *New York Times*, June 27, 1966, p. 1.
69. *New York Times*, June 27, 1966, p. 1.
70. Ibid.
71. Ibid., p. 29.
72. Ibid.
73. Carson, *In Struggle*, p. 211; *Eyes on the Prize II*, "The Time Has Come, 1964–1966."
74. *New York Times*, June 27, p. 9; June 28, 1966, p. 23.
75. "The Nation," *Time*, July 1, 1966, p. 11; "Distorted Cry?" *Newsweek*, August 8, 1966, p. 54; "A New White Backlash?" *Saturday Evening Post*, September 10, 1966, p. 88; *U.S. News and World Report*, July 11, 1966, p. 52.
76. *New York Times*, July 1, 1966, p. 1.
77. Ibid., April 21, 1966, p. 38.
78. Ibid.
79. Sellers, *The River of No Return*, p. 132.
80. Ibid., p. 130.
81. Stokely Carmichael, "What We Want," *New York Review of Books*, September 22, 1966, p. 5.
82. *New York Times*, July 2, 1966, p. 2.
83. Ibid., June 30, 1966, p. 1.
84. Ibid., July 2, 1966, p. 24.
85. Ibid.
86. Ibid., July 4, 1966, p. 16.
87. Ibid., July 5, 1966, pp. 1, 22.
88. Ibid., July 7, 1966, p. 1.

89. Ibid., July 10, 1966, p. 53.

90. Parks, "Whip of Black Power," p. 78.

91. Comparisons to Belafonte were appropriate. Approaching forty, Belafonte was a legendary singer and actor. Over the preceding decade, he had added human rights activist to an already impressive résumé. A close friend and advisor of King's, he served as the movement's unofficial confidant, moneyman, and negotiator. His devotion to struggle and acceptance of its cost to his personal wealth garnered him the respect of student activists. See Lerone Bennett, "Stokely Carmichael: Architect of Black Power," *Ebony*, June 1966; see also Stokely Carmichael–Lorna D. Smith Collection, M0170, Dept. of Special Collections, Stanford University Libraries, Stanford, Calif. Hereafter cited as SCLDSC.

92. FBIKT 100-446080-2, June 20, 1966, p. 1–2.

93. Ibid.

94. FBIKT 100-446080-2X, July 13, 1966, p. 9.

95. Carmichael, *Ready for Revolution*, pp. 542–43; Carson, *In Struggle*, p. 273.

96. Parks, "Whip of Black Power," p. 78.

97. See Steve Estes, *I Am a Man!: Race, Manhood, and the Civil Rights Movement* (Chapel Hill: University of North Carolina Press, 2005). See also Hill, *Deacons for Defense*; Tyson, *Radio Free Dixie*.

98. For examples of the press's treatment of Carmichael, see "Stoke Here to Back Huey," *Berkeley Barb*, February 16–22, 1968; "Stokely Carmichael Still Kingpin of Militant Urban Negro Leaders," *Daily Enterprise*, February 27, 1968; "King and Carmichael Map Summer Strategy," *Human Events*, March 2, 1968; " 'Poor March' on April 22," *San Francisco Mercury*, March 5, 1968. SCLDSC. For anti-Carmichael letters sent to the FBI, see FBIKT 100-446080-6, Correspondence to Director Hoover, August 2, 1966, and FBIKT 100-446080-7, August 21, 1966.

99. "A 'Black Power' Speech That Has Congress Aroused," *U.S. News and World Report*, August 22, 1966, p. 6.

100. Carmichael, "What We Want," pp. 4, 8.

101. Stokely Carmichael, "We Are Going to Use the Term 'Black Power' and We Are Going to Define It Because Black Power Speaks to Us," in John Bracey, August Meier, and Elliot Rudwick, eds., *Black Nationalism in America* (Indianapolis: Bobbs-Merrill, 1970), p. 470.

102. Bracey, Meier, and Rudwick, *Black Nationalism in America*, pp. 471–72; Estes, *I Am a Man!*, pp. 107–29.

103. Bracey, Meier, and Rudwick, *Black Nationalism in America*, p. 472.

104. Ibid., p. 474.

105. Ibid., p. 475.

106. Ibid., p. 476.

107. *New York Times*, July 14–17, 1966. See also Adam Cohen and Elizabeth Taylor, *American Pharaoh: Mayor Richard J. Daley, His Battle for Chicago and the Nation* (Boston: Back Bay Press, 2001), pp. 387–92.

108. *Chicago Sun Times*, July 29, 1966, p. 4, quoted in FBIKT 100-446080-6X, p. 6. For King's Chicago campaign, see Garrow, *Bearing the Cross*, pp. 431–525, and Fairclough, *To Redeem the Soul of America*, pp. 279–307. See also James R. Ralph, *Northern Protest: Martin Luther King, Jr., Chicago, and the Civil Rights Movement* (Cambridge: Harvard University Press, 1993).

109. *New York Times*, August 1, 1966, p. 13; Branch, *Parting the Waters*, pp. 661–63, 796–97.

110. *New York Times*, August 1, 1966, p. 14.

111. Ibid., August 2, 1966, p. 2.

112. Ibid., August 3, 1966, p. 19.

113. Ibid., August 4, 1966, p. 32.

114. FBIKT 100-446080-3X, July 29, 1966, pp. 1–11.

115. Despite the taint of Malcolm X's assassination, Elijah Muhammad and the Nation of Islam achieved a kind of reverence in the eyes of certain Black Power activists, as forerunners to the era's race consciousness and black nationalism. See Clegg, *An Original Man*, pp. 239–41.

116. FBIKT 100-446080, Memorandum, August 9, 1966, p. 1.

117. *Philadelphia Inquirer*, August 13 and 14, 1966. PEBUA.

118. Forman, *The Making of Black Revolutionaries*; Goode, "Out to Get SNCC: A Tale of Two Cities," *The Nation*, November 21, 1966, pp. 534–38.

119. *Philadelphia Evening Bulletin*, September 3, 1966. PEBUA.

120. Carson, *In Struggle*, p. 225.

121. *Philadelphia Inquirer*, April 22, 1967. PEBUA.

122. *New York Times*, August 18, 1966, pp. 1, 31.

123. FBIKT 100-446080. See letters dated August 10, 17, 18, 22, and 25, 1966, p. 1.

124. FBIKT 100-446080-33, October 6, 1966; *Meet the Press* transcript, August 21, 1966.

125. FBIKT 100-446080-33, October 6, 1966, p. 3.

126. FBIKT 100-446080, Memorandum, August 23, 1966, and Memorandum, F. J. Baumgardner to W. C. Sullivan, August 26, 1966.

127. FBIKT 100-446080, Airtel from Director Hoover, August 18, 1966, p. 1; Airtel, SAC, August 26, 1966.

128. FBIKT 100-446080, Memorandum, August 10, 1966, p. 1.

129. FBIKT 100-446080, Airtel, August 18, 1966, p. 1.

130. The Vine City dispute between militant project staffers and national SNCC officers has been told largely from the viewpoint of partisans critical of local staffers' at times disruptive tactics. See, for example, Carson, *In Struggle*; Carmichael, *Ready for Revolution*. Askia Muhammad Touré, a coauthor of SNCC's Black Position Paper, offers an alternative view, asserting that project members were labeled disruptive as a way to prevent debate on issues raised in the position paper. In fact, SNCC would adopt much of the paper's themes of self-determination and race consciousness over the next two years. Askia Muhammad Touré interview. See also Winston A. Grady-Willis, "A Changing Tide: Black Politics and Activism in Atlanta, Georgia, 1960–1977," Ph.D. diss., Emory University, 1998.

131. *Washington Post*, September 7, 1966, pp. 1, 3.

132. Ibid., p. 3.

133. Ibid., p. 1.

134. *Washington Post*, September 8, 1966, p. 21.

135. *U.S. News and World Report*, September 19, 1966, p. 36.

136. *Atlanta Constitution*, September 9, 1966, p. 1.

137. *New York Times*, September 10, 1966, pp. 1, 14.

138. Ibid., September 11, 1966, pp. 1, 50.

139. Ibid., September 12, 1966, p. 50.

140. Garrow, *Bearing the Cross*, p. 527.

141. FBIKT 100-446080, Summary of Carmichael Activity, September 21, 1966, pp. 1–2.

142. Garrow, *Bearing the Cross*, p. 531; *New York Times*, September 12, 1966, p. 49.

143. Fairclough, *To Redeem the Soul of America*, pp. 322–23.

144. *New York Times*, September 21, 1966, p. 33.

145. Ibid., September 25, 1966.

146. Bayard Rustin, "'Black Power' and Coalition Politics," *Commentary*, September 1966, pp. 35–40.

147. Ibid., pp. 35–36.

148. David Danzig, "In Defense of 'Black Power,'" *Commentary*, September 1966, pp. 41–46.

149. Rustin, "'Black Power' and Coalition Politics," p. 35.

150. Bayard Rustin, "From Protest to Politics: The Future of the Civil Rights Movement," *Commentary*, February 1965, pp. 25–31.

151. See D'Emilio, *Lost Prophet*, pp. 393–416.

152. Rustin, "'Black Power' and Coalition Politics," p. 40.

153. Carmichael, "What We Want."

154. Ibid., p. 8.

155. *New York Times*, September 22, 1966, p. 1.

156. FBIKT 100-446080, Memorandum, Deke DeLoach to Clyde Tolson, October 27, 1966, pp. 1–5.

157. Richard Powers, *Secrecy and Power: The Life of J. Edgar Hoover* (New York: Free Press, 1987), pp. 400–401.

158. Roger Wilkins, *A Man's Life: An Autobiography* (New York: Touchstone, 1984), pp. 171–75, 204–7; Powers, *Secrecy and Power*, pp. 400–402; *New York Times*, March 1, 1967, pp. 1, 24.

159. *Philadelphia Evening Bulletin*, August 25, 1966, (SC, 1966). PEBUA.

160. *New York Times*, October 29, 1966, p. 1.

161. *Philadelphia Evening Bulletin*, October 1, 1966. PEBUA.

162. Lyndon Johnson and Abe Fortas, October 3, 1966. Side A, tape K66.03. LBJ Library.

163. *New York Times*, October 27, 1966, pp. 1, 14.

164. Ibid., pp. 1, 20.

165. FBIKT 100-446080-78, Memorandum, November 18, 1966, pp. 1–9.

166. *New York Times*, October 29, 1966, pp. 1, 9.

167. Ibid., October 30, 1966, p. 62.

168. Ibid.

169. Ibid., p. 63.

170. Pacifica Radio Archives (hereafter cited as PRA) BB1709 and *New York Times*, October 30, 1966, p. 63.

171. Catherine Ellis and Stephen Drury Smith, eds., *Say It Plain: A Century of Great African American Speeches* (New York: New Press, 2005), p. 58.

172. Ellis and Smith, *Say It Plain*, p. 61; PRA BB1709.

173. Ellis and Smith, *Say It Plain*, pp. 61–73; PRA BB1709.

174. FBIKT 100-446080-41, Memorandum, October 31, 1966, p. 1.

175. Ibid., pp. 1–3.

176. Carson, *In Struggle*, p. 230.

177. Ibid.

178. *The Movement*, December 1966, p. 183. CAKC.

179. Sellers, *The River of No Return*, p. 154.

180. *The Movement*, p. 176. CAKC.

181. *New York Times*, November 9, 1966, p. 1.

182. Ibid., p. 25.

183. Ibid., December 13, 1966, pp. 1, 30.

184. FBIKT 100-446080-92, "Stokely Carmichael," November 28, 1966, p. 3.

185. FBIKT 100-446080-98, Teletype, November 25, 1966, pp. 1–2.

186. D'Emilio, *Lost Prophet*, pp. 427–29.

187. FBIKT 100-446080-100, "Re: Stokely Carmichael," December 19, 1966, pp. 1–4.

8. STORM WARNINGS

1. FBIKT 100-446080, January 13, 1967, "Stokely Carmichael, Racial Matter," p. 1. Stokely Carmichael and SNCC rank and file, after expressing initial support, had decided against participating in Powell's Black Power Conference during the fall of 1966. See Charles Hamilton, *Adam Clayton Powell, Jr.: The Political Biography of an American Dilemma* (New York: Collier Books, 1992), p. 28.

2. *New York Times*, January 11, 1967, pp. 1, 20.

3. Hamilton, *Adam Clayton Powell, Jr.*, pp. 445–78.

4. Less than two weeks after announcing that he would not seek a second term as SNCC chairman, Carmichael visited Puerto Rico, where he was enthusiastically received. He marched into San Juan with groups of students waving Puerto Rican flags and a banner that read *"Apoyamos Black Power en los Estados Unidos* (We support Black Power in the U.S.)." Carmichael condemned American involvement in Vietnam and stressed political ties between black Americans and Puerto Ricans; black people were "a colony" of the U.S. just as Puerto Rico was. Speaking in Spanish at the university, he emphasized the importance of Puerto Ricans' "cultural identity," stripped away by years of oppression. See *Muhammad Speaks*, March 10, 1967.

5. Reginald Major, *A Panther Is a Black Cat* (New York: William Morrow, 1971), pp. 70–71; *Berkeley Barb*, February 10, 1967, p. 3.

6. Eldridge Cleaver, "Courage to Kill: Meeting the Panthers," in *Post-Prison Writings and Speeches* (New York: Random House, 1970), pp. 23–29.

7. Carson, *In Struggle*, pp. 245–49.

8. *New York Times*, April 11, 1967, p. 16.

9. Ibid., p. 46.

10. Carson, *In Struggle*, pp. 222–51.

11. Garrow, *Bearing the Cross*, pp. 545–56. Simon Hall's case study documents the tension between white peace activists and an increasingly radicalized black movement. See Simon Hall, *Peace and Freedom: The Civil Rights and Antiwar Movements in the 1960s* (Philadelphia: University of Pennsylvania Press, 2005).

12. *New York Times*, April 16, 1967, p. 3; Gilbert Moore, *A Special Rage* (New York: Harper & Row, 1971), pp. 71–72; Earl Anthony, *Picking Up the Gun: A Report on the Black Panthers* (New York: Pyramid, 1971), p. 60.

13. *New York Times*, April 16, 1967, p. 3.

14. Garrow, *Bearing the Cross*, pp. 556–57.

15. *Muhammad Speaks*, April 28, 1967, p. 4.

16. Garrow, *Bearing the Cross*, pp. 556–57.

17. *New York Times*, April 29, 1967, pp. 1, 10, 12.

18. Carson, *In Struggle*, pp. 251–57.

19. Ibid., pp. 254–55; *New York Times*, June 14, p. 31, and June 15, 1967, p. 33.

20. *New York Times*, June 12, pp. 1, 88; June 14, p. 1; June 15, 1967, pp. 1, 31, 34.

21. *Wall Street Journal*, June 23, 1967, p. 1.

22. FBIKT 100-446080, Memo, May 18, 1967, pp. 1–5; Airtel (Director to SAC, WFO), May 18, 1967, pp. 1–2 ; Airtel (SAC, WFO to Director), May 19, 1967, pp. 1–2; Correspondence to White House, May 24, 1967, pp. 1–2; Memo, May 17, 1967, pp. 1–2. FBI surveillance included probes into Carmichael's sexual life and his financial information. See Airtel, May 25, 1967, pp. 1–2.

23. *Wall Street Journal*, June 23, 1967, p. 1.

24. By January 1968, a cross-section of politicians, militants, civil rights moderates, and journalists predicted that urban violence would soon evolve into protracted guerrilla warfare. See *U.S. News and World Report*, January 8, 1968, p. 62.

25. *New York Times*, July 13, 1967, p. 1.

26. Ibid., July 15, 1967, p. 10.

27. Ibid., p. 11.

28. Tom Hayden, *Reunion: A Memoir* (New York: Random House, 1988), pp. 154–55.

29. Tom Hayden, *Rebellion in Newark: Official Violence and Ghetto Response* (New York: Vintage Books, 1967), pp. 45–72.

30. Jones's demands during the press conference included a request for U.N. intervention, prosecution of police officers who had shot blacks during the rebellion, and the release of blacks arrested during the violence. He also called for new elections to replace the existing city bureaucracy. LeRoi Jones Press Conference, July, 1967. PRA No. BB5262.

31. Woodard, *A Nation Within a Nation*, pp. 78–172; *New York Times*, July 15, 1967, p. 11.

32. *New York Times*, July 16, pp. 1, 55; July 17, 1967, p. 28.

33. FBIAC 100-448517-1 Airtel, December 15, 1967, pp. 1–14. For an inside account of Black Power labor radicalism in the riot's aftermath, see Dan Georgakas and Marvin Surkin, *Detroit: I Do Mind Dying* (Boston: South End Press, 1998), and Ernest Allen Jr., "Dying from the Inside: The Decline of the League of Revolutionary Black Workers," in Dick Cluster, ed., *They Should Have Served That Cup of Coffee: Seven Radicals Remember the Sixties* (Boston: South End Press, 1979), pp. 71–109.

34. *New York Times*, July 24, 1967, p. 15.

35. Ibid., p. 1.

36. Ibid., July 25, 1967, p. 1.

37. Wilkins, *A Man's Life*, pp. 194–99.

38. Powers, *Secrecy and Power*, pp. 339–43, 404–27.

39. Ibid.

40. Carson, *In Struggle*, p. 255; *New York Times*, July 25, 1967, pp. 1, 20.

41. Peter B. Levy questions historical accounts regarding Brown's Cambridge appearance as well as characterizations of the subsequent violence as a riot. See *Civil War on Race Street*, pp. 133–59.

42. *New York Times*, July 27, 1967, pp. 1, 18.

43. Ibid., pp. 1, 19.

44. Ibid.

45. Ibid., July 27, 1967, p. 34.

46. Ibid., July 26, 1967, p. 1; July 29, 1967, p. 1.

47. Ibid., July 29, 1967, p. 1.

48. Ibid., p. 9.

49. Ibid., July 31, 1967, pp. 1, 19.

50. Ibid., July 29, p. 9; July 28, 1967, p. 14.

51. Ibid., July 28, 1967, p. 14.

52. Carson, *In Struggle*, p. 273.

53. *New York Times,* July 28, 1967, p. 10.

54. Ibid., August 2, 1967, p. 36; Julius Lester, *All Is Well* (New York: William Morrow, 1976), p. 140.

55. *Washington Post,* August 18, 1967, p. B11.

56. Ibid., July 26, 1967, p. 8.

57. Carson, *In Struggle,* p. 274.

58. *National Guardian,* August 5, 1967, p. 1.

59. *Newsweek,* August 21, 1967, p. 18.

60. Ibid., pp. 20–25.

61. *The Movement,* September 1967, p. 1. CAKC.

62. *Washington Post,* August 2, 1967, p. 1.

63. Ibid., p. 14.

64. Carson, *In Struggle,* p. 274; *Muhammad Speaks,* August 25, 1967, p. 7; *National Guardian,* July 29, 1967, p. 6. By the time a version of this bill became law in 1968, tacked onto the Federal Housing Act, it was known as an anti–H. Rap Brown bill.

65. *New York Times,* July 13, 1967, p. 11.

66. *Washington Post,* July 28, 1967, p. 9.

67. Carmichael, *Ready for Revolution,* p. 583.

68. *The Movement,* September 1967, p. 4. CAKC.

69. *National Guardian,* August 1967, p. 1.

70. Stokely Carmichael, "Black Power and the Third World," August 1967, p. 1. SNCC Papers (Microfilm).

71. Ibid., p. 3.

72. Ibid.

73. Carmichael, *Ready for Revolution,* pp. 594–601.

74. The French occupation of Algiers and the subsequent war for liberation was immortalized in the film *The Battle for Algiers;* see *National Guardian,* September 16, 1967, p. 8.

75. Carmichael, *Ready for Revolution,* p. 584.

76. For analysis of the controversy, see Carson, *In Struggle,* pp. 267–69, and Carmichael, *Ready for Revolution,* pp. 559–63, 605. Carmichael's vociferous support for Palestinian liberation led to charges of anti-Semitism. Many black radicals identified Palestine as a colony and its people as a community of color under siege. The formulation produced an uncomfortable stalemate in which representatives of two long-standing minority groups attacked each other as racist and anti-Semitic. In his posthumously published autobiography, Carmichael denies charges of anti-Semitism, invoking his early Bronx youth surrounded by Jewish liberals and leftists who taught him to sing "Hava Nagila." See *Ready for Revolution,* p. 557. However, at least two of Carmichael's letters from the early 1970s contain passages that come closer to criticizing Jews in general than Israel in particular. See Correspondence from Stokely Carmichael to Lorna D. Smith, July 23 and August 9, 1972. SCLDSC.

77. Carmichael, *Ready for Revolution,* pp. 626–28; Carson, *In Struggle,* p. 276.

78. Piero Gleijeses, *Conflicting Missions: Havana, Washington, and Africa, 1959–1976* (Chapel Hill: University of North Carolina Press, 2002), pp. 185–213.

79. Jules Milne, ed., *Kwame Nkrumah: The Conakry Years: His Life and Letters* (London: Panaf Books, 1990), p. 186.

80. Carmichael, *Ready for Revolution,* p. 617.

81. Ibid., p. 622.

82. Milne, *Kwame Nkrumah,* pp. 183–85.

83. Ibid., pp. 186–87.

84. Miriam Makeba, with James Hall, *Makeba: My Story* (New York: New American Library, 1987), pp. 147–57. In Cairo, Carmichael scribbled Nkrumah a letter explaining his decision to return to the States earlier than planned. Grim news from America included reports of SNCC's organizational crises as well as Rap Brown's latest legal troubles. Nkrumah, who privately feared for Carmichael's safety after an episode in Guinea where American State Department officials attempted to confiscate his passport, conceded that, considering the circumstances, he understood the urgency of Carmichael's return. See Nkrumah to Shirley Graham Du Bois, November 12, 1967, p. 2. Kwame Nkrumah Papers, Box 154, folder 3, Moorland-Spingarn Collection, Howard University.

85. *New York Times*, August 19, 1967, p. 12.

86. *New York Times Magazine*, June 11, 1967, pp. 26–27, 93–97, 100–103.

87. Peace activists were among King's most enthusiastic supporters. In October, antiwar protesters unleashed a massive demonstration at the Pentagon, reflecting "existential unity between words and deeds." Six months after the "Spring MOBE," the National Mobilization Against the War organized a demonstration whose militancy overwhelmed the movement's moderate elements. Divisions among militants focused on political disruption versus cultural symbolism. At the Pentagon, the two coexisted uneasily, with observances of Che Guevara's death competing with efforts by a group of hippies to rid the Department of Defense of evil spirits. Scattered protesters placed flowers in the helmets of soldiers. Others broke through barricades and camped in a parking lot adjacent to the Pentagon. After club-wielding federal marshals removed the squatters during the night, reinforcements arrived the next day, and the ensuing confrontation resulted in hundreds of arrests for trespassing and a feeling among protesters that a new chapter of protest had been written at the Pentagon. See David Farber, *Chicago '68* (Chicago: University of Chicago Press, 1988), pp. 56–59. For King's announcement that he would step up his nonviolent tactics to promote civil disobedience, see Garrow, *Bearing the Cross*, pp. 567–74. See also Hall, *Peace and Freedom*.

88. Stokely Carmichael and Charles Hamilton, *Black Power: The Politics of Liberation in America* (New York: Random House, 1967).

89. Ibid., pp. vii–x.

90. Ibid., pp. 2–32.

91. Ibid., p. 41.

92. Christopher Lasch, "The Trouble with Black Power," *New York Review of Books*, February 29, 1968, p. 6.

93. Mark Bonham Carter, "Prophet of Violence," *London Observer*, March 24, 1968. SCLDSC.

94. Carmichael and Hamilton, *Black Power*, p. 44.

95. Ibid., p. 47.

96. Ibid., p. 155–77.

97. Cruse, *The Crisis of the Negro Intellectual*.

98. Lasch, "The Trouble with Black Power," p. 10.

99. *New York Times*, November 21, 1967, p. 21. The most complete criticism of Cruse to date is found in Watts, *Harold Cruse's The Crisis of the Negro Intellectual Reconsidered*. See also James, *Holding Aloft the Banner of Ethiopia*, pp. 262–91. For a comprehensive critique of Cruse's take on postwar Harlem, see Welch, "Black Art and Activism in Postwar New York." For a sampling of Cruse's essays, see Cruse, *Rebellion or Revolution?* (New York: William Morrow, 1968), and Cobb, *The Essential Harold Cruse*. See also Robert Allen, *Black Awakening in Capitalist America: An Analytic History* (Trenton: Africa World Press, 1990).

100. Stephen Steinberg has described 1960s analyses (by both black and white authors) challenging racial conventions as the "scholarship of confrontation." See *Turning Back: The Liberal Retreat from Racial Justice in American Thought and Policy* (Boston: Beacon Press, 1995).

101. *National Guardian*, December 16, 1967, pp. 1, 14.

102. *Muhammad Speaks*, December 15, 1967, p. 2.

103. Carmichael told reporters that De Gaulle himself had initiated his release. See *San Francisco Sunday Examiner*, December 10, 1967, and *Greensboro Daily News*, December 7, 1967. SCLDSC.

104. *New York Times*, December 12, 1967, p. 14.

105. Ibid., December 17, 1967, p. 188.

9. THE TRIAL OF HUEY PERCY NEWTON

1. Olympic sprinters John Carlos and Tommie Smith stirred international controversy (and were subsequently stripped of their medals) by wearing black socks and gloves on the podium during the medals ceremony. Pictures of Smith and Carlos giving a clench-fisted Black Power salute remain among the era's iconic photographs. For the Olympic protest, see Amy Bass, *Not the Triumph but the Struggle: The 1968 Olympics and the Making of the Black Athlete* (Minneapolis: University of Minnesota Press, 2002). For the Columbia strike, see Hayden, *Reunion*, pp. 272–84, and Stefan Bradley, " 'Gym Crow Must Go!': Black Student Activism at Columbia University, 1967–1968," *Journal of African American History* 88, no. 2 (2003), pp. 163–81. For a perceptive analysis of the Ocean Hill–Brownsville controversy, see Jane Ana Gordon, *Why They Couldn't Wait: A Critique of the Black-Jewish Conflict over Community Control in Ocean Hill–Brownsville, 1967–1971* (New York: Routledge-Falmer, 2001).

2. A body of scholarship, memoirs, and histories explicitly and implicitly posits 1968, which included the assassinations of King and Robert Kennedy, the passage of the last major civil rights legislation, the decline of SNCC and SDS, and the election of Richard M. Nixon as president as the end of the most promising political and social activism first ignited by the black freedom movement. See, for example, Todd Gitlin, *The Sixties: Years of Hope, Days of Rage* (New York: Bantam Books, 1989); Garrow, *Bearing the Cross*; Mark Kurlansky, *1968: The Year That Rocked the World* (New York: Ballantine Books, 2004); Carson, *In Struggle*; Levy, *Civil War on Race Street*. See also Taylor Branch, *At Canaan's Edge: America in the King Years, 1965–68* (New York: Simon and Schuster, 2006).

3. George Katsiaficas, *The Imagination of the New Left: A Global Analysis of 1968* (Boston: South End Press, 1987), pp. 3–116; Kurlansky, *1968*, pp. 92–93, 238–50, 287–305; Cleaver, *Post-Prison Writings*, p. 77. See also Jeremi Suri, *Power and Protest: Global Revolution and the Rise of Détente* (Cambridge: Harvard University Press, 2003).

4. Kurlansky, *1968*, pp. 50–63.

5. Transcript of Stokely Carmichael interview with Clayborne Carson, October 18, 1977, p. 10. CAKC.

6. Self, *American Babylon*, pp. 1–60, 217–55, 291–316.

7. Both Newton and Bobby Seale were originally from the South.

8. Bobby Seale, *Seize the Time: The Story of the Black Panther Party and Huey P. Newton* (New York: Random House, 1970).

9. There were other groups, inspired by the Lowndes County Freedom Organization, that called themselves the Black Panthers, including one group in New York and two in California. Oakland's Black Panther Party for Self-Defense would claim the use of the name through a combination of intimidation and publicity.

10. Huey P. Newton, *To Die for the People* (New York: Writers and Readers, 1995), p. 10.

11. Huey P. Newton, *Revolutionary Suicide* (New York: Ballantine Books, 1974), pp. 127–42.

12. Ibid., pp. 155–61.

13. *National Guardian*, May 27, 1967, p. 8.

14. Newton, *Revolutionary Suicide*, pp. 190–208.

15. Ibid.

16. For an example of mainstream media coverage of the Black Panthers, see *Newsweek*, April 22, 1968; *Time*, October 4, 1968; and *Wall Street Journal*, August 29, 1969. Earl Caldwell, a crusading black journalist and former *New York Times* reporter, made the Panthers his personal beat during much of this era, providing some of the most balanced coverage of the group. See Caldwell, "Huey Newton's Conviction Reversed by Coast Court," May 30, 1970, p. 1, and "Internal Dispute Rends Panthers," May 7, 1972, p. 26, both in the *New York Times*. For an example of Panther coverage by the radical press, see *Berkeley Barb*, February 17, 1967, p. 1, and October 4–10, 1967, pp. 8–9. For coverage of the Panthers in the black press, see *Ebony*, August 1969, pp. 107–8, 110–12.

17. Christian Davenport, "Reading the 'Voice of the Vanguard': A Content Analysis of the Black Panther Intercommunal News Service, 1969–1973," in Charles Jones, ed., *The Black Panther Party Reconsidered* (Baltimore: Black Classic Press, 1998), pp. 193–209; Kelley and Esch, "Black Like Mao," pp. 22–23.

18. Huey P. Newton, "Eldridge Cleaver: He Is No James Baldwin, 1973," in David Hilliard and Donald Weise, eds., *The Huey P. Newton Reader* (New York: Seven Stories Press, 2002), pp. 285–89; Baldwin, *No Name in the Street*.

19. Moore, *A Special Rage*, pp. 72–73; Seale, *Seize the Time*, pp. 132–34; Newton, *Revolutionary Suicide*, pp. 148–52.

20. Eldridge Cleaver, *Soul on Ice* (New York: Dell, 1968), pp. 26–27.

21. Melanie Margaret Kask's compelling study of Eldridge Cleaver and Beverly Axelrod's letters sheds light on the creation of *Soul on Ice*. Kask argues that Axelrod was instrumental in establishing Cleaver as a formidable presence among the Left even before his prison release. See "Soul Mates: The Prison Letters of Eldridge Cleaver and Beverly Axelrod," Ph.D. diss., University of California, Berkeley, 2003.

22. Ibid., pp. 115–18.

23. Ibid., p. 121.

24. Cleaver, *Soul on Ice*, pp. 145–75. Cleaver's allegorical essay classified black men as "Supermasculine Menials," black women as "Subfeminine," white men as "Omnipotent Administrators," and white women as "Ultrafeminine."

25. Tracye Matthews, " 'No One Ever Asks What a Man's Place in the Revolution Is': Gender and the Politics of the Black Panther Party, 1966–1971," in Jones, *The Black Panther Party Reconsidered*, pp. 267–304; Jeffrey O. G. Ogbar, *Black Power: Radical Politics and African American Identity* (Baltimore: Johns Hopkins University Press, 2004), pp. 100–106.

26. David Hilliard and Lewis Cole, *This Side of Glory: The Autobiography of David Hilliard and the Story of the Black Panther Party* (New York: Little, Brown, 1993), p. 181.

27. Askia Muhummad Touré interviews.

28. Donald Alexander Downs, *Cornell 69: Liberalism and the Crisis of the American University* (Ithaca: Cornell University Press, 1999).

29. *New York Times*, April 6, 1969, pp. 25–26, 60, 65, 68–70, 75; Harry Edwards, *Black Students* (New York: Free Press, 1970); Van Deburg, *New Day in Babylon*, pp. 64–82; Joy Ann Williamson, *Black Power on Campus: The University of Illinois, 1965–1975* (Urbana: University of Illinois Press, 2003).

30. *Daily Gator*, May 5, 1967, p. 1; Amiri Baraka Papers, Box 18, Moorland-Spingarn, Howard University.

31. Amiri Baraka, "Black Art," *Liberator*, January 1966, p. 18.

32. Baraka, *The Autobiography of LeRoi Jones*, p. 355.

33. Scot Brown, *Fighting for US: Maulana Karenga, the US Organization, and Black Cultural Nationalism* (New York: New York University Press, 2003), pp. 10–11.

34. Ibid., p. 43.

35. Seale, *Seize the Time*, p. 182.

36. Hilliard and Cole, *This Side of Glory*, p. 140.

37. The Black Panther Party for Self-Defense's debt to the Revolutionary Action Movement has been obscured, partly because of Newton's (and to a lesser extent Seale's) fear of having their own contributions to the Black Power movement and the black freedom struggle upstaged by RAM. However, RAM's influence on Newton and Seale cannot be discounted. The young radicals who were members of, or associated with, RAM received a political education that provided them with theoretical tools as well as a framework to conceptualize liberation struggles at the local, national, and international level. For the way Newton and Seale regarded RAM, see Newton, *Revolutionary Suicide*, pp. 77–78; Seale, *Seize the Time*, pp. 24–34. For discussion of RAM, see Stanford, "Revolutionary Action Movement (RAM)"; Kelley and Esch, "Black Like Mao," pp. 6–41; Kelley, *Freedom Dreams*, pp. 72–93; Ogbar, *Black Power*, pp. 78–81; Hill, *The Deacons for Defense*, pp. 221–23, 255–56; Tyson, *Radio Free Dixie*, pp. 297–98; Smethurst, *The Black Arts Movement*, pp. 166–71.

38. Philip S. Foner, ed., *The Black Panthers Speak* (New York: Da Capo Press, 2002), p. 61.

39. *Berkeley Barb*, December 8–14, 1967. The following discussion of Newton's trial is drawn from clippings files and trial transcripts in the Dr. Huey P. Newton Foundation Papers at Stanford University, especially Boxes 19–23, and 26. Hereafter cited as NFP.

40. Carmichael, *Ready for Revolution*, p. 663.

41. *Berkeley Barb*, December 28, 1967. NFP.

42. *Berkeley Gazette*, February 12, 1968. NFP.

43. *New York Times*, February 5, 1968. NFP.

44. See *Berkeley Barb*, December 28, 1967, and *People's World*, November 25, 1967, in NFP. On William F. Knowland, see Kay Boyle, *The Long Walk at San Francisco State* (New York: Grove Press, 1970), pp. 102–3; Self, *American Babylon*, pp. 183–85, 248; Hugh Pearson, *The Shadow of the Panther: Huey Newton and the Price of Black Power in America* (Reading: Addison Wesley, 1994), pp. 243, 246.

45. *San Francisco Sun-Reporter*, November 11, 1967. NFP.

46. *Berkeley Barb*, November 17–23, 1967.

47. *People's World*, November 25 and December 2, 1967; *Berkeley Barb*, January 26, 1968. NFP.

48. *Oakland Tribune*, January 11, 1968. NFP.

49. *Oakland Tribune*, February 17, 1968; *Berkeley Gazette*, February 17, 1968. NFP.

50. Newton, *To Die for the People*, pp. 9–10; Seale, *Seize the Time*, pp. 215–22.

51. *Santa Rosa Press Democrat*, February 20, 1968. NFP.

52. Rap Brown, February 17, 1968. PRA BB4525b.

53. Hilliard and Cole, *This Side of Glory*, p. 173; Seale, *Seize the Time*, p. 222.

54. Carmichael's speeches at the Dialectics of Liberation Conference in London and at the Organization of Latin American Solidarity Conference in Cuba articulated sympathy with Socialist-inspired revolution that his Oakland keynote lacked. See *Stokely Speaks: Black Power Back to Pan-Africanism* (New York: Vintage Books, 1971), pp. 77–110. For reactions from two Black Power activists to Carmichael's keynote, see Hilliard and Cole, *This Side of Glory*, pp. 173–74; Angela Davis, *An Autobiography* (New York: International Publishers, 1988), p. 168.

55. "Stokely Speaks," *Aframerican News Service*, March 11, 1968, pp. 1–11.

56. *Oakland Tribune*, February 19, 1968. NFP.

57. Elaine Brown, *A Taste of Power: A Black Woman's Story* (New York: Pantheon Books, 1992), p. 126; Carson, *In Struggle*, pp. 282–83.

58. U.S. Riot Commission Report, *Report of the National Advisory Commission on Civil Disorders* (New York: Bantam Books, 1968), pp. 410–83.

59. Ibid., p. 412.

60. Garrow, *Bearing the Cross*, p. 600.

61. Wilkins, *A Man's Life*, p. 209; Transcript, Ramsey Clark Oral History Interview IV, April 16, 1969, by Thomas Harrison Baker, pp. 8–11, LBJ Library. http://lbjlib.utexas.edu/johnson/archives.hom/oralhistory.hom/ClarkR/clark-r4.pdf (August 13, 2005).

62. Garrow, *Bearing the Cross*, pp. 575–624.

63. *New York Times*, April 6, 1968, p. 1.

64. *U.S. News and World Report*, April 22, 1968, p. 27.

65. Stokely Carmichael Press Conference, Transcript, April 4, 1968, p. 8. CAKC.

66. *Washington Post*, April 5, 1968, p. 3.

67. Seale, *Seize the Time*, pp. 228–30.

68. FBIEC 100-447251-844, *People of the State of California vs. Eldridge Cleaver*, December 29, 1977, pp. 3–4.

69. *Berkeley Gazette*, April 8, 1968. NFP. In his autobiography, David Hilliard claims that Eldridge Cleaver orchestrated an ambush of the police that went awry. See Hilliard and Cole, *This Side of Glory*, pp. 185–87.

70. Hampton and Fayer, *Voices of Freedom*, pp. 515–17.

71. Seale, *Seize the Time*, p. 236.

72. *Berkeley Gazette*, April 18, 1968. NFP.

73. Ibid.

74. *San Francisco Sun-Reporter*, May 11, 1968, NFP; Baldwin, *No Name in the Street*, pp. 169–78.

75. The Black Panthers' influence on the multicultural New Left extended to Asian American and Chicano radicals on the West Coast and Puerto Rican and white radicals on the East Coast. See Ogbar, *Black Power*, pp. 159–89.

76. Charles Garry and Art Goldberg, *Streetfighter in the Courtroom: The People's Advocate* (New York: Dutton, 1977), pp. 7–9, 97–99; Seale, *Seize the Time*, p. 274. In many instances, this was based on a misread of Frantz Fanon's *The Wretched of the Earth*, bypassing his radical humanism and zeroing in on sections that touted revolutionary upheavals as part of the process of creating a more humane civilization. Lewis R. Gordon offers the best contemporary analysis of Fanon. See Lewis Gordon, *Fanon and the Crisis of European Man: An Essay on Philosophy and the Human Sciences* (New York: Routledge, 1995).

77. Brown, *A Taste of Power*; Matthews, "'No One Ever Asks What a Man's Place in the Revolution Is'," pp. 267–304; Seale, *Seize the Time*, pp. 393–403.

78. *San Francisco Chronicle*, July 16, 1968. NFP.

79. *Palo Alto Times*, July 15, 1968; *San Francisco Chronicle*, July 16, 1968; *San Francisco Sun-Reporter*, July 27, 1968. NFP.

80. Boyle, *The Long Walk at San Francisco State*, p. 104.

81. James Forman, *The Making of Black Revolutionaries* (Washington: Open Hand, 1985), p. 534.

82. *The Movement*, August 1968, pp. 419–20. CAKC.

83. Julius Lester, *Revolutionary Notes* (New York: Grove Press, 1969), pp. 144–49.

84. *New York Times*, October 7, 1968.

85. Carson, *In Struggle*, p. 285; Sellers, *River of No Return*, pp. 248–49; Forman, *The Making of Black Revolutionaries*, pp. 537–38.

86. Key SNCC activists followed Carmichael into the Panthers, including Chico Neblett and Bob Brown, who emerged as important organizers. See Carson, *In Struggle*, p. 283.

87. Boyle, *The Long Walk at San Francisco State*, p. 118.

88. *Oakland Tribune*, July 17, 1968. NFP.

89. *San Francisco Sun-Reporter*, July 27, 1968. NFP.

90. *San Francisco Examiner*, July 17, 1968; *Oakland Tribune*, July 19, 1968; *San Francisco Chronicle*, July 19, 1968; Boyle, *The Long Walk at San Francisco State*, pp. 110–12; Mark S. Weiner, *Black Trials: Citizenship from the Beginnings of Slavery to the End of Caste* (New York: Knopf, 2004), pp. 302–21. Fay Stender's political activism would end in tragedy. One of the most outspoken activist lawyers representing black prisoners (most notably George Jackson) during the early 1970s, Stender was shot and paralyzed in 1979 by an ex-con who accused her of betraying Jackson. She ultimately committed suicide. See Lori Andrews, *Black Power, White Blood: The Life and Times of Johnny Spain* (Philadelphia: Temple University Press, 1999).

91. *San Francisco Chronicle* and *San Jose Mercury News*, Aug. 15, 1968. NFP.

92. *San Francisco Examiner*, August 16, 1968. NFP.

93. *San Francisco Chronicle*, August 20, 1968. NFP.

94. Ibid., August 23, 1968. NFP.

95. *San Francisco Examiner*, August 22, 1968. NFP.

96. Ibid., August 22, 1968; *San Francisco Chronicle*, August 23, 1968; Newton, *Revolutionary Suicide*, pp. 258–59.

97. *Los Angeles Free Press*, September 6, 1968, pp. 5–6.

98. Garry and Goldberg, *Streetfighter in the Courtroom*, pp. 138–42.

99. Edward M. Keating, *Free Huey!* (Berkeley: Ramparts, 1971), pp. 193–96.

100. *Oakland Tribune*, September 5, 1968. NFP.

101. Garry and Goldberg, *Streetfighter in the Courtroom*, pp. 143–45.

102. Keating, *Free Huey!*, pp. 215–21.

103. Garry and Goldberg, *Streetfighter in the Courtroom*, pp. 146–47.

104. *Oakland Tribune*, September 9, 1968; *San Francisco Examiner*, September 9, 1968; *San Francisco Chronicle*, September 9, 1968. NFP.

105. Keating, *Free Huey!*, p. 251; Garry and Goldberg, *Streetfighter in the Courtroom*, p. 151.

106. *San Francisco Chronicle*, September 11, 1968; *San Jose Mercury*, September 21, 1968; *San Francisco Chronicle*, September 28, 1968; *Redwood Tribune*, September 28, 1968. NFP.

107. Hilliard and Cole, *This Side of Glory*, pp. 210–11.
108. Van Deburg, *New Day in Babylon*, pp. 118–19.
109. Gitlin, *The Sixties*, p. 287.
110. FBIEC 100-447251-886, Airtel, November 5, 1970, p. 2.
111. Eldridge Cleaver, *Soul on Fire* (Waco: Word Books, 1978), pp. 142–43. See also Lowell Bergman and David Weir, "Revolution on Ice: How the Black Panthers Lost the FBI's War of Dirty Tricks," *Rolling Stone*, September 9, 1976.
112. *Spartan Daily*, November 13, 1968; *The Mercury*, November 13, 1968; *San Jose News*, November 13, 1968; *La Voz*, November 15, 1968. SCLDSC.
113. *News Press* (Glendale, Calif.), December 16, 1968; *The Oregonian*, August 7, 1968; *Washington Post*, July 8, 1968. Carmichael's passport was reinstated shortly after his marriage to Miriam Makeba, ostensibly after he requested it for their honeymoon. See *San Francisco Chronicle*, July 26, 1968. SCLDSC.
114. *London Times*, November 3, 1969. SCLDSC.

10. DARK DAYS, BRIGHT NIGHTS

1. Richard Nixon, *The Memoirs of Richard Nixon* (New York: Grosset & Dunlap, 1978), pp. 469–75.
2. Kenneth O'Reilly, *Nixon's Piano: Presidents and Racial Politics, from Washington to Clinton* (New York: Free Press, 1995), pp. 287–313; Powers, *Secrecy and Power*, pp. 439–40.
3. Brown, *Fighting for US*, pp. 107–30.
4. *San Francisco Chronicle*, January 14, 1969. NFP; *The Movement*, March 1968, p. 11. CAKC.
5. In July 1969, a National Committee to Combat Fascism conference was held in Oakland. Black Panther chapters were transformed into local NCCF chapters. See Floyd W. Hayes III and Francis A. Kiene III, " 'All Power to the People': The Political Thought of Huey P. Newton and the Black Panther Party," in Jones, *The Black Panther Party Reconsidered*, p. 167; Errol Anthony Henderson, "Shadow of a Clue," in Kathleen Cleaver and George Katsiaficas, eds., *Liberation, Imagination, and the Black Panther Party* (New York: Routledge, 2001), p. 200.
6. Major, *A Panther Is a Black Cat*, pp. 111–17; Hilliard and Cole, *This Side of Glory*.
7. *Washington Post*, July 4, 1969, pp. 1, 10.
8. *The Black Panther*, July 19, 1969, p. 15.
9. Carmichael, *Ready for Revolution*, pp. 666–67; Carmichael interview with Carson, October 18, 1977, pp. 11–12. CAKC.
10. *San Francisco Chronicle*, January 14, 1969. NFP.
11. JoNina Abron, " 'Serving the People': The Survival Programs of the Black Panther Party," in Jones, *The Black Panther Party Reconsidered*, pp. 177–92.
12. William Lee Brent, *Long Time Gone: A Black Panther's True-Life Story of His Hijacking and Twenty-Five Years in Cuba* (Lincoln: Excel Books, 2000), pp. 119–24.
13. Seale, *Seize the Time*, pp. 393–403.
14. Matthews, " 'No One Ever Asks What a Man's Place in the Revolution Is'," and Angela D. LeBlanc-Ernest, " 'The Most Qualified Person to Handle the Job': Black Panther Party Women, 1966–1982," in Jones, *The Black Panther Party Reconsidered*, pp. 267–304, 305–34; Brown, *A Taste of Power*; Seale, *Seize the Time*; Hilliard and Cole, *This Side of Glory*; Pearson, *The Shadow of the Panther*.

15. Hilliard and Cole, *This Side of Glory*, pp. 171–74.

16. Carson, *In Struggle*, p. 281.

17. *Berkeley Barb*, August 8, 1968. NFP.

18. Carmichael interview with Carson. CAKC.

19. Lee Lockwood, *Conversation with Eldridge Cleaver: Algiers* (New York: McGraw-Hill, 1970), pp. 18–32.

20. *New York Times*, July 25, 1969, p. 16; July 26, 1969, p. 9; *Black Panther*, August 16, 1969, p. 5.

21. Seale, *Seize the Time*, pp. 211–22, 254–56; Newton, *Revolutionary Suicide*, pp. 172–75, 218–19; Hilliard and Cole, *This Side of Glory*, pp. 171–74.

22. Seale, *Seize the Time*, pp. 323–49; *Contempt: Transcript of the Contempt Citations, Sentences, and Responses of the Chicago Conspiracy 10* (Chicago: Swallow Press, 1970), pp. 1–37. See also William Kunstler, with Sheila Isenberg, *My Life as a Radical Lawyer* (New York: Birch Lane Press, 1994), pp. 29–32.

23. *Philadelphia Evening Bulletin*, December 12, 15, 16, 21, and 27, 1969; *New York Times*, December 16, 1969. (Black Panther-Misc., 1969). PEBUA.

24. *Philadelphia Evening Bulletin*, December 21, 1969. PEBUA.

25. *Philadelphia Evening Bulletin*, December 15, 16, 27, 1969. PEBUA.

26. Baldwin, *No Name in the Street*, p. 131.

27. Powers, *Secrecy and Power*, p. 448; Gitlin, *The Sixties*, pp. 400–401. For a history of violence and the New Left, see Jeremy Varon, *Bringing the War Home: The Weather Underground, the Red Army Faction, and Revolutionary Violence in the Sixties and Seventies* (Berkeley: University of California Press, 2004).

28. *Newsweek*, February 23, 1970, pp. 26–30; Hilliard and Cole, *This Side of Glory*, pp. 224, 259–60; Major, *A Panther Is a Black Cat*, pp. 113–17. For the BPP's relationship with the New Left and historical memory, see Gitlin, *The Sixties*; Jones, *The Black Panther Party Reconsidered*; Cleaver and Katsiaficas, *Liberation, Imagination, and the Black Panther Party*; Brown, *A Taste of Power*.

29. *New York Times*, May 30, 1970, pp. 1, 49.

30. Hilliard and Cole, *This Side of Glory*, p. 168; see also Murray Kempton, *The Briar Patch: The People of the State of New York v. Lumumba Shakur et Al.* (New York: Dutton, 1973); Peter L. Zimroth, *Perversions of Justice: The Prosecution and Acquittal of the Panther 21* (New York: Viking Press, 1974).

31. See Newton Press Conference, August 11, 1970. PRA BB2531; August 26, 1970. PRA BC1460.

32. Newton Press Conference, August 11, 1970. PRA BB2531.

33. For the relationship between Jackson and the Black Panthers, see Jo Durden-Smith, *Who Killed George Jackson?* (New York: Knopf, 1976); Gregory Armstrong, *The Dragon Has Come* (New York: Harper & Row, 1974); Eric Cummins, *The Rise and Fall of California's Radical Prison Movement* (Stanford: Stanford University Press, 1994); Andrews, *Black Power, White Blood*; Winston Grady-Willis, "The Black Panther Party: State Repression and Political Prisoners," in Jones, *The Black Panther Party Reconsidered*, pp. 363–89.

34. George Katsiaficas, "Organization and Movement: The Case of the Black Panther Party and the Revolutionary People's Constitutional Convention of 1970," in Cleaver and Katsiaficas, *Liberation, Imagination, and the Black Panther Party*, pp. 141–55.

35. I use the term "second-wave" Black Power organizing to describe the proliferation of meetings and cultural groups that took place after 1970. This includes the founding of the Congress of African Peoples, African Liberation Support Committee, and the Gary convention, as well as the Student Organization for Black Unity, and Mal-

colm X Liberation University. Some of the main currents of the second wave-
organizations are discussed in this chapter and the next.

36. Woodard, *A Nation Within a Nation*, pp. 180–84; Brown, *Fighting for US*, pp.
56–58, 62–65.

37. David Llorens, "Ameer (LeRoi Jones) Baraka," *Ebony*, August 1969, pp.
75–78, 80.

38. Peter Bailey, "The Black Theater," *Ebony*, August 1969, p. 134.

39. Through the Chicago-based Third World Press and the Institute of Positive Education, Haki Madhubuti emerged as one of the most significant black nationalists advocating
institution building as a vehicle for liberation. See Brown, *Fighting for US*, pp. 151–54.

40. Brian Ward, *Just My Soul Responding: Rhythm and Blues, Black Consciousness, and Race Relations* (Berkeley: University of California Press, 1998), pp. 360–61.

41. Smethurst describes the historical tendencies that led to the eruption of Black
Arts activism nationally. His study sheds light on the movement's regional diversity and
impact. See Smethurst, *The Black Arts Movement*.

42. *Greensboro Daily News*, March 25, 1970. SCLDSC. Carmichael led the
protest with Howard Fuller (Owusu Sadaukai) of North Carolina's Malcolm X Liberation University. Carmichael mentored young Pan-Africanists who organized the Student
Organization for Black Unity, which evolved into the Youth Organization for Black
Unity and the February First Movement. Fuller (who was known as Owusu Sadaukai
but never legally changed his name) became an organizer for African liberation, joined
by former SNCC activists including Jimmy Garrett and Charlie Cobb.

43. Correspondence from Stokely Carmichael to Lorna D. Smith, February 23,
1970. SCLDSC.

44. *San Francisco Examiner*, March 25, 26, 1970; *Washington Post*, March 26,
1970. SCLDSC.

45. Ibid.; Tyson, *Radio Free Dixie*, pp. 302–3.

46. Three weeks after his release, Newton, reacting to reports that Carmichael was
leading a delegation of rogue Panthers in the Middle East, denounced Carmichael as a
CIA agent. Newton Press Conference, August 26, 1971. PRA BC146.

47. Carmichael, *Stokely Speaks*, p. 192.

48. Ibid., pp. 206–7.

49. Carmichael speech at the University of Texas, March 1971. Tape 1 of 2, side a.
CAKC.

50. *Muhammad Speaks*, April 17, 1970; *Greensboro Daily News*, April 27, 1970;
San Francisco Chronicle, August 17, 1970; *Los Angeles Herald-Examiner*, August 17,
1970. SCLDSC.

51. SOBU suggests that the African American "organizing tradition" that scholars
such as Clayborne Carson, Charles Payne, and John Dittmer have documented did not disappear after SNCC's demise in the late 1960s. Many former organizers applied techniques
learned during their tenure in SNCC in a variety of Black Power–inspired groups such as
SOBU, Malcolm X Liberation University, and the Center for Black Education. See, for example, Fanon C. Wilkins, "'In the Belly of the Beast': Black Power, Anti-Imperialism, and
the African Liberation Solidarity Movement, 1968–1975," Ph.D. diss., New York University, 2001; Garrett and Sellers interviews; and especially Countryman, *Up South*.

52. Poinsett, "It's Nation Time."

53. Hilliard and Cole, *This Side of Glory*, p. 318.

54. For reports of Newton's drug abuse, see Hilliard and Cole, *This Side of Glory*,
pp. 340, 353; Brown, *A Taste of Power*, p. 271; Pearson, *The Shadow of the Panther*,
pp. 248–50.

55. Yohuru Williams, *Black Politics/White Power: Civil Rights, Black Power, and the Black Panthers in New Haven* (New York: Brandywine Press, 2000), p. 160; Jack Olsen, *Last Man Standing: The Tragedy and Triumph of Geronimo Pratt* (New York: Doubleday, 2000).

56. *Washington Evening Star*, July 15, 1970, in FBIEC 100-447251.

57. Ward Churchill, " 'To Disrupt, Discredit and Destroy': The FBI's Secret War Against the Black Panther Party," in Cleaver and Katsiaficas, *Liberation, Imagination, and the Black Panther Party*, pp. 110–11.

58. Erik H. Erikson and Huey P. Newton, *In Search of Common Ground* (New York: Dell Books, 1974), pp. 21–30.

59. Ibid., pp. 36–37.

60. Ibid., p. 64.

61. For details surrounding the trial, see Kempton, *The Briar Patch*; Zimroth, *Perversions of Justice*. For discussions of the Panthers' split, see Kathleen Cleaver, "Back to Africa: The Evolution of the Black Panther Party (1969–1972)," pp. 211–54; Grady-Willis, "The Black Panther Party," pp. 363–89; and Ollie A. Johnson, "Explaining the Demise of the Black Panther Party: The Role of Internal Factors," pp. 391–414, in Jones, *The Black Panther Party Reconsidered*.

62. Eldridge Cleaver taped this telephone call with Newton, a portion of which was later aired on public radio as part of a broadcast that showcased the International Section's perspective on the split within the group. See "Contradictions Within the Black Panther Party: Reactions from Algiers." PRA BB4265a/b.

63. Newton, *Revolutionary Suicide*, p. 219.

64. Cleaver shifted much of the blame for the confusion to Charles Garry and David Hilliard, calling them ambitious intermediaries who had stifled Newton's ability to comprehend the liberation struggle after his release from prison. Cleaver described Newton as unable or unwilling to acknowledge Hilliard's alienation from left-wing forces within the party. Donald Cox asserted that Oakland's leadership had abandoned principles of democratic centralism (in which a committee formed policy for the organization through deliberative, theoretically democratic debates among themselves), opting instead for authoritarianism. Testimonials from various Panthers, who described a dysfunctional headquarters characterized by sexism, favoritism, and petty personal disputes, followed Cox's demands for the reinstatement of expelled Panthers. See "Contradictions Within the Black Panther Party," March 5, 1970, PRA BB4265a and b.

65. *New York Times*, March 7, 1971, p. 26.

66. Johnson, "Explaining the Demise of the Black Panther Party," pp. 401–3.

67. *New York Times*, May 12, 1971, p. 43.

68. Newton, *To Die for the People*, pp. 61–75.

69. *San Francisco Chronicle*, October 9, 1971, p. 1; Brown, *A Taste of Power*, pp. 295–304.

70. Newton, *Revolutionary Suicide*, pp. 366–70. For examination of the left wing of the Black Panther Party and the Black Liberation Army, see Jones, *The Black Panther Party Reconsidered*; Cleaver and Katsiaficas, *Liberation, Imagination, and the Black Panther Party*; Assata Shakur, *Assata: An Autobiography* (Chicago: Lawrence Hill, 1987); Olsen, *Last Man Standing*. For revolutionary violence and the New Left, see Varon, *Bringing the War Home*; Susan Braudy, *Family Circle: The Boudins and the Aristocracy of the Left* (New York: Anchor Books, 2003). See also "Black Liberation Army" newspaper clippings in PEBUA.

71. Newton, *Revolutionary Suicide*, pp. 1–6. See also William T. Vollman, *Rising Up and Rising Down: Some Thoughts on Violence, Freedom and Urgent Means* (New York: Ecco Press, 2004).

72. Armstrong, *The Dragon Has Come*; Jo Durden-Smith, *Who Killed George Jackson?* See also George Jackson, *Soledad Brother: The Prison Letters of George Jackson* (Chicago: Lawrence Hill Books, 1994) and the posthumously published *Blood in My Eye* (Baltimore: Black Classic Press, 1990).

73. *New York Times*, September 14, 1971, p. 1.

74. The Black Power era witnessed dozens of legal trials including defendants from the Black Panthers, SNCC, US, and the Republic of New Africa. Cases involving Newton, Cleaver, Jackson, and Davis captured the movement's imagination in ways that other cases failed to do.

75. For a recollection that emphasizes the playfulness behind Carmichael's words, see *Ready for Revolution*, pp. 431–35; Carson, *In Struggle*, pp. 147–48.

76. See, for example, Beverly Guy-Sheftall, ed., *Words of Fire: An Anthology of African-American Feminist Thought* (New York: New Press, 1995); Feldstein, " 'I Don't Trust You Anymore' "; Gaines, "From Center to Margin"; Washington, "Alice Childress, Lorraine Hansberry, and Claudia Jones," pp. 183–204; Matthews, "No One Ever Asks What a Man's Place in the Revolution Is"; LeBlanc-Ernest, "The Most Qualified Person to Handle the Job"; Woodard, *A Nation Within a Nation*; Brown, *Fighting for US*; Ogbar, *Black Power*; E. Francis White, *Dark Continent of Our Bodies: Black Feminism and the Politics of Respectability* (Philadelphia: Temple University Press, 2001); Collier-Thomas and Franklin, *Sisters in the Struggle*; Kimberly Springer, ed., *Still Lifting, Still Climbing: African American Women's Contemporary Activism* (New York: New York University Press, 1999).

77. TWWA Pamphlet, August 1970. NCNW; Farah Jasmine Griffin, "Conflict and Chorus: Reconsidering Toni Cade's *The Black Woman: An Anthology,*" in Eddie S. Glaude Jr., ed., *Is It Nation Time?: Contemporary Essays on Black Power and Black Nationalism* (Chicago: University of Chicago Press, 2002), pp. 113–29.

78. Frances Beal interview; *New York Times*, November 17, 1970, pp. 47, 60.

79. See McWhorter, *Carry Me Home*; Kelley, *Hammer and Hoe*.

80. Davis, *An Autobiography*, p. 161.

81. Bettina Aptheker, *The Morning Breaks: The Trial of Angela Davis* (Ithaca: Cornell University Press, 1997).

11. DASHIKIS AND DEMOCRACY

1. Thomas A. Johnson, "Black Politics," March 12, 1972, Amiri Baraka Papers (microfilm).

2. Ronald Walters interview. Walters, a key convention organizer, described the meeting as having "a distinctly historical flavor in marking an epoch in black political history."

3. Ben Chavis, quoted in Hampton and Fayer, *Voices of Freedom*, p. 572.

4. Ibid., p. 573.

5. Warren Brown, "Black Convention Solves Problems Without Clubs, Bullets, or Blood," *Jet*, March 30, 1972, p. 24.

6. *New York Times*, March 12, 1972, p. 38.

7. Simeon Booker, "Black Convention Is Successful Despite Splits and Tactical Differences," *Jet*, March 30, 1972, p. 12.

8. William Greaves's documentary "Nationtime: Gary" is the best illustration of these feelings. Narrated by Sydney Poitier, with poetry (by Amiri Baraka) read by Harry Belafonte, the work showcases the grandeur of the convention as well as the hope, controversy, and excitement generated at Gary. See "Nationtime: Gary," William Greaves Productions, 1972.

9. Ibid.

10. Ibid.

11. Hampton and Fayer, *Voices of Freedom*, pp. 565–66.

12. *Eyes on the Prize II*, Part 5, "A Nation of Law? 1968–1971"; Beal interview, April 22, 2003.

13. "FBI Teletype," FBI Director to Boston SAC, March 9, 1972, and FBI Director to Washington Field Office SAC, March 9, 1972. FBIBNPC 157-5215-72 and 73.

14. *Jet*, March 30, 1972, p. 28.

15. *The Times* (Indiana), March 12, 1972, in FBIBNPC 157-5215-91.

16. Richard Hatcher, Keynote Address, March 11, 1972, p. 1. Institute of Black World Papers, Schomburg Library. Hereafter cited as IBWSL.

17. Ibid.

18. Greaves, "Nationtime."

19. *New York Times*, March 12, 1972, p. 38.

20. Greaves, "Nationtime."

21. By this time, Jackson's high profile as a militant country preacher was taking shape in major print media. See, for example, *Wall Street Journal*, March 16, 1972, p. 1; *New York Times*, July 6, 1972, p. 21.

22. *Chicago Tribune*, March 13, 1972, p. 2.

23. Ibid.

24. Ibid.

25. *Newsweek*, March 27, 1972, p. 30.

26. *New York Times*, March 16, 1972.

27. Ibid., March 14, 1972, p. 42.

28. *Jet*, March 30, 1972, pp. 12–36.

29. *African World*, April 1, 1972, pp. 1, 8–9.

30. *Newsweek*, March 27, 1972, p. 30.

31. *New York Times*, March 12, 1972, p. 1.

32. *Washington Post*, June 22, 1972. SCLDSC.

33. Formally released on May 19, 1972, Malcolm X's birthday, the fifty-five-page "Gary Agenda" supported a renewed war on poverty, the redistribution of wealth, political representation for the District of Columbia, aid for welfare mothers, and adequate legal representation for prisoners. See, for example, *New York Times*, May 20, 1972, p. 14; see also Woodard, *A Nation Within a Nation*.

34. Imamu Amiri Baraka, "Black Nationalism: 1972," *Black Scholar*, September 1972, p. 25.

35. "National Black Political Agenda," pp. 53–59. IBWSL.

36. Owusu Sadaukai, "Inside Liberated Mozambique," *African World*, January 8, 1972, pp. 8–9.

37. *African World*, May 27, 1972, p. 8.

38. Ronald W. Walters, *Pan-Africanism in the African Diaspora: An Analysis of Modern Afrocentric Political Movements* (Detroit: Wayne State University Press, 1977), pp. 68–69.

39. Wilkins, "In the Belly of the Beast," p. 147.

40. *African World*, May 27, 1972, p. 12.
41. *Jet*, April 27, 1972. SCLDSC.
42. Newton Press Conference, August 26, 1970. PRA BC1460; "The Black Scholar Interviews Bobby Seale," *Black Scholar*, September 1972, pp. 15–16.
43. Woodard, *A Nation Within a Nation*, pp. 175–76. Diggs's commitment was practical as well as rhetorical. Shortly before the march, he was a key plaintiff in a suit against federal officials and corporate leaders that sought to prevent chrome from being imported from southern Rhodesia. See *African World*, May 27, 1972, p. 11.
44. Carmichael's support for Ugandan dictator Idi Amin's ruthless regime, which ousted non-Africans, placed him in the uncomfortable, and reprehensible position of siding with conservative black nationalists who lacked his cosmopolitan intellect, political experiences, or commitment to human rights. See *The Star* (Jamaica), March 19, 1973, and *Voice of Uganda*, June 7 and 18, 1973. SCLDSC.
45. A preliminary showdown between these forces came at a regional ALSC meeting in Frogmore, South Carolina, June 28 to July 1, 1973. Attended by eighty delegates and observers from local ALSC committees, the meeting featured ideological disputes between black nationalists and groups drifting toward a Marxist-tinged anti-imperialism. Delegates agreed to table certain issues until the next meeting, scheduled for Greensboro, North Carolina. See *African World*, July 14, 1973, p. 2; Baraka, *The Autobiography of LeRoi Jones*, pp. 433–34.
46. "The Black Scholar Interviews Bobby Seale," p. 7. The Panthers indicated their interest in electoral politics through their endorsement of Shirley Chisholm's 1972 presidential candidacy. See, for example, documentarian Shola Lynch's "Chisholm '72—Unbought and Unbossed," Realside Productions, 2004.
47. For Panthers' boycott against Cal-Pak, see FBIHPN 92-1271-X-20, San Francisco Bureau, September 21, 1971 (Covering July 30–September 21, 1971), pp. 1–141. For Newton's alleged attempts to shake down the producers of *The Mack*, see FBIHPN 92-13682, "Black Panther Party Demonstration at 'Showcase Bar,'" October 4, 1972, pp. 1–5. For Newton's alleged attempts to organize Oakland's criminal underground, see FBIHPN 92-14778-4, "Huey P. Newton, Anti-Racketeering," July 18, 1974, pp. 1–16. See also Pearson, *The Shadow of the Panther*, pp. 240–47, 251–68.
48. For Newton's decline, see Brown, *A Taste of Power*; Hilliard and Cole, *This Side of Glory*; Pearson, *The Shadow of the Panther*; Johnson, "Explaining the Demise of the Black Panther Party," pp. 391–414. See also Olsen, *Last Man Standing*.
49. Amiri Baraka, "The Beginning of National Movement," August 1972. ABP, Box 12.
50. Harold Cruse, "The Little Rock National Black Political Convention," in Cobb, *The Essential Harold Cruse*, p. 127.
51. For Carmichael's speaking tours, see *Spartan Daily*, March 16, 1971; *San Francisco Chronicle*, March 18, 1971 and January 27, 1973; *San Jose Mercury*, March 19, 1971 and February 14, 22, 1973; *Jet*, April 8, 1971; *Washington Post*, October 18, 1972; *Howard Hilltop*, October 20, 1972; *The Oregonian*, January 26, 1973; *Seattle Post-Intelligencer*, October 4, 1973; *University of Washington Daily*, October 5, 1973. For reaction to Carmichael's plans for a Black United Front, see *Washington Evening Star*, October 31, 1972; *Memphis Commercial Appeal*, November 16, 1972; *Los Angeles Times*, November 24, 1972; *San Jose Mercury News*, December 3, 1972. SCLDSC.
52. Sellers interview; Garrett interview; Wilkins, "In the Belly of the Beast," pp. 204–7.

53. Baraka, *The Autobiography of LeRoi Jones*, p. 440.
54. James Garrett, "A Historical Sketch: The Sixth Pan-African Congress," *Black World*, March 1975, pp. 4–21.
55. "Julius K. Nyerere's Speech to the Congress," *Black Scholar*, July–August, 1974, pp. 20–21. Nyerere's words carried unusual weight. Tanzania's seminal 1967 "Arusha Declaration" represented an important manifesto toward the development of African Socialism, an idea that many Black Power activists in the United States eagerly attempted to incorporate. African American identification with Ujamaa, or the collective approach to building a nation, was both philosophical and practical. Black nationalists developed courses in Swahili (Tanzania's official language), and civil rights burnouts (most notably SNCC's Robert Moses) and political fugitives sought exile under the country's progressive leadership. By 1974, Nyerere's Socialism, once rooted in a vision that focused less on the technical aspect of class struggle and more on the promotion of humanism and political equality, was moving toward a more orthodox Marxism. See Walters, *Pan-Africanism in the African Diaspora*, pp. 64–67; Anthony Bogues, *Black Heretics, Black Prophets: Radical Political Intellectuals* (New York: Routledge, 2003), pp. 102–10.
56. FBISPAC 157-24813-51, Memo, August 29, 1974, pp. 34–36.
57. Walters, *Pan-Africanism in the African Diaspora*, pp. 79–81.
58. David Lawrence Horne, "The Pan-African Congress: A Positive Assessment," and Earl Ofari, "A Critical Review of the Pan-African Congress," in *Black Scholar* (July–August 1974), pp. 2–15; "African Americans Differ at African Congress," *Race Relations Reporter*, July 15, 1974, pp. 1, 3–6.
59. See Jerry Gafio Watts, *Amiri Baraka: The Politics and Art of a Black Intellectual* (New York: New York University Press, 2001), pp. 420–32. Haki Madhubuti, the poet, Black Arts activist, and a former Baraka ally, provided some of the most stinging rebukes. See Madhubuti, *Enemies: The Clash of Races* (Chicago: Third World Press, 1978); Robert C. Smith, *We Have No Leaders: African-Americans in the Post–Civil Rights Era* (New York: SUNY Press, 1996).
60. Amiri Baraka, "Why I Changed My Ideology: Black Nationalism and Socialist Revolution," *Black World* 24, no. 9 (July 1975), pp. 30–42; Baraka, *The Autobiography of LeRoi Jones*, p. 443. Covered by *Black Scholar* and *Black World*, debates between black nationalists and Marxists and the rise and decline of alliances brokered at the Gary convention were overshadowed by the shifting national political climate. See also *New York Times*, April 28, 1975, pp. 1, 61, in which John Oliver Killens, activist, novelist, and Malcolm X ally, describes Baraka as an "instant Marxist."
61. The story of black nationalists and Pan-Africanists-turned-Marxists and their efforts to build a Communist movement remains largely untold. See Baraka, *The Autobiography of LeRoi Jones*; Rod Bush, *We Are Not What We Seem: Black Nationalism and Class Struggle in the American Century* (New York: New York University Press, 1999), pp. 193–213; Watts, *Amiri Baraka*. After a bitter, brief effort to build a multiracial Communist Party, Owusu Sadaukai returned to Milwaukee (as Howard Fuller) and became an educator and community organizer. Fuller interview. See also Max Elbaum, *Revolution in the Air: Sixties Radicals Turn to Lenin, Mao, and Che* (London: Verso, 2002).
62. In an age without heroes, collective social movements went on the offensive, dismissing politics as corrupt, and once-respected elected leaders as fakes, yet continuing to fight for a range of social, political, and economic reforms. See Van Gosse, "A Movement of Movements: The Definition and Periodization of the New Left," in Jean-Christophe Agnew and Roy Rosenzweig, eds., *A Companion to Post-1945 America* (Malden: Blackwell, 2002), pp. 277–302. See also Peter N. Carroll, *It Seemed Like*

Nothing Happened: America in the 1970s (New Brunswick: Rutgers University Press, 2000); Bruce J. Schulman, *The Seventies: The Great Shift in American Culture, Society, and Politics* (New York: Da Capo Press, 2001); Beth Bailey and David Farber, eds., *America in the '70s* (Lawrence: University Press of Kansas, 2004). For a view that the 1970s promoted political fragmentation whose unintended consequences bolstered conservatives, see Todd Gitlin, *The Twilight of Common Dreams: Why America Is Wracked by Culture Wars* (New York: Metropolitan Books, 1995). Robin D. G. Kelley offers a reinterpretation of the legacy of Black Power–era racial identities. See *Yo' Mama's Dysfunktional!: Fighting the Culture Wars in Urban America* (Boston: Beacon Press, 1997) and "Into the Fire: 1970 to the Present," in Robin D. G. Kelley and Earl Lewis, eds., *To Make Our World Anew: A History of African Americans* (New York: Oxford University Press, 2000), pp. 543–95.

EPILOGUE: LEGACIES, 1975–2005

1. The literature on hip-hop is dense. See Tricia Rose, *Black Noise: Rap Music and Black Culture in Contemporary America* (Middletown: Wesleyan University Press, 1994); Mark Anthony Neal, *What the Music Said: Black Popular Music and Black Public Culture* (New York: Routledge, 1998); Michael Eric Dyson, *Holler If You Hear Me: Searching for Tupac Shakur* (New York: Basic Books, 2001); Raquel Rivera, *New York Ricans from the Hip-Hop Zone* (New York: Palgrave Macmillan, 2003); Bakari Kitwana, *The Hip-Hop Generation: Young Blacks and the Crisis in African American Culture* (New York: Basic Civitas Books, 2003); S. Craig Watkins, *Hip-Hop Matters: Politics, Popular Culture, and the Struggle for the Soul of a Movement* (Boston: Beacon Press, 2005); and Jeff Chang, *Can't Stop, Won't Stop: A History of the Hip-Hop Generation* (New York: St. Martin's Press, 2005).

2. Smethurst, *The Black Arts Movement*.

3. *Newsweek*, March 17, 1975, p. 40; *East Bay Voice* 1, no. 3 (1976), pp. 1, 16. NFP; Cleaver, *Soul on Fire*; Kask, "Soul Mates," pp. vii–xiv.

4. In 1976, BPP chair Elaine Brown served as a delegate at the Democratic National Convention in support of California governor and Panther ally Jerry Brown's unsuccessful presidential candidacy.

5. *Los Angeles Times*, August 27, 1977, pp. 1, 12–15. NFP.

6. Brown, *A Taste of Power*, pp. 336–76; Pearson, *The Shadow of the Panther*, pp. 1–9, 269–310; Hilliard and Cole, *This Side of Glory*; Johnson, "Explaining the Demise of the Black Panther Party," pp. 391–414; Cleaver and Katsiaficas, *Liberation, Imagination, and the Black Panther Party*; Ogbar, *Black Power*; Jon Rice, "The World of the Illinois Panthers," in Theoharis and Woodard, *Freedom North*, pp. 41–64; Reynaldo Anderson, "Practical Internationalists: The Story of the Des Moines, Iowa, Black Panther Party," and Robyn Ceanne Spencer, "Inside the Panther Revolution: The Black Freedom Movement and the Black Panther Party in Oakland, California" in Theoharis and Woodard, *Groundwork*, pp. 282–99, 300–317. Perhaps the most provocative analysis of Newton is artist Roger Gueneveur Smith's award-winning one-man show, "A Huey P. Newton Story," directed for cable television by Spike Lee in 2001.

7. Named New Jersey's poet laureate, Baraka was asked to step down from the honorary position because of an incendiary poem he wrote following the September 11, 2001, World Trade Center attacks. Critics charged that the poem was anti-Semitic, while supporters countered that Baraka's words were taken out of context. Throughout the fray, Baraka refused even to consider resigning.

8. Eldridge Cleaver, quoted in Van Deburg, *New Day in Babylon*.

9. By the mid-1970s, Owusu Sadaukai's commitment to Marxist politics had buckled under the strain of sectarian battles. Following a series of debilitating personal and professional setbacks, Sadaukai resumed his identity as Howard Fuller, earned a doctoral degree in education, and became a leading activist in his hometown of Milwaukee. While Fuller's zeal for organizing remained strong, his provocative views on education reform in inner cities thrust him into a bitter national debate and local controversy over school choice. Former Black Power activists viewed Fuller's ascendancy to Milwaukee's superintendent of public schools and close ties to Republican politics as a betrayal. For Fuller, school choice offered black youth a way out of poverty that ex–Black Power activists and civil rights leaders failed to acknowledge. See Fuller interview; see also Jack Dougherty, *More Than One Struggle: The Evolution of Black School Reform in Milwaukee* (Chapel Hill: University of North Carolina Press, 2004), pp. 173–93.

10. Carmichael, *Ready for Revolution*, pp. 680–727.

11. See Hall, "The Long Civil Rights Movement and the Political Uses of the Past," pp. 1233–63.

12. Fuller interview.

13. Kwame Ture, "Afterword," in Kwame Ture and Charles V. Hamilton, *Black Power: The Politics of Liberation* (Vintage, 1992), pp. 187–99.

14. Ture completed this autobiography with the assistance of Ekwueme Michael Thelwell, a SNCC colleague-turned-university-professor from Howard's NAG group. See *Ready for Revolution*.

15. Manning Marable has provided an important analysis of black radicalism during the 1980s in a series of historical accounts. See *Black American Politics: From the Washington Marches to Jesse Jackson* (London: Verso, 1985); *Race, Reform, and Rebellion: The Second Reconstruction in Black America, 1945–1990* (Jackson: University Press of Mississippi, 1990); *How Capitalism Underdeveloped Black America* (Boston: South End Press, 1983). See also Harold Washington, "It's Our Turn," and Jesse Jackson, "Keep Hope Alive," in Manning Marable and Leith Mullings, eds., *Let Nobody Turn Us Around: Voices of Resistance, Reform, and Renewal: An African American Anthology* (Lanham: Rowman & Littlefield, 2003), pp. 535–37 and 567–77. For a critique of Jackson's presidential campaign, see Adolph L. Reed Jr., *The Jesse Jackson Phenomenon: The Crisis of Purpose in Afro-American Politics* (New Haven: Yale University Press, 1986).

16. Olsen, *Last Man Standing*.

17. See, for example, Gitlin, *The Sixties*; Pearson, *The Shadow of the Panther*; David Burner, *Making Peace with the '60s* (Princeton: Princeton University Press, 1996).

BIBLIOGRAPHY

MANUSCRIPT SOURCES

Atlanta, Georgia
Auburn Avenue Research Library on African-American Culture and History, Atlanta-Fulton Public Library

Atlanta University Research Center
Hoyt Fuller Papers

Robert W. Woodruff Library Special Collections
Vincent Harding Papers
Matt Crawford Collection
Constance Curry Collection
Thulani Davis Periodicals

Detroit, Michigan
Wayne State University Labor Archives
James and Grace Lee Boggs Collection

University of Michigan
Labadie Collection

Los Angeles, California
Los Angeles Public Library
California Eagle (Microfilm)
Los Angeles Times (Microfilm)

Southern California Library for Social Science and Research
Angela Davis Los Angeles Defense Committee Papers
Black Panther Party Collection

KPFA, Pacifica Radio Archives

Special Collections, Charles E. Young Library, UCLA
Peace and Freedom Party Collection

New York, New York
Tamiment Institute, Bobst Library, New York University
Harold Cruse Papers
George Breitman Papers
Socialist Workers Party Papers
African Liberation Support Committee Organizational Files
Freedom Now Party Organizational Files

Schomburg Center for Research in Black Culture, New York Public Library
Robert S. Browne Papers
Julian Mayfield Papers
Larry Neal Papers
Institute for the Black World Papers
Umbra Oral History Collection
Catherine Clarke Papers
IFCO Papers
William Strickland Papers
Vicki Garvin Papers
James Baldwin Papers
St. Claire Drake Papers
American Society of African Culture Papers
John Henrik Clarke Papers
National Alliance Against Racist and Political Repression Papers

Palo Alto, California
Stokely Carmichael–Lorna D. Smith Collection, Green Library, Stanford University
Newton Foundation Papers, Green Library, Stanford University
New Left Collection, Hoover Institute, Stanford University
Clayborne Carson Collection, Martin Luther King Jr. Center, Stanford University

Providence, Rhode Island
Brown University
The John Hay Library
Hall-Hoag Collection

Madison, Wisconsin
State Historical Society of Wisconsin
Robert Carl Cohen Papers
Social Action Files
Socialist Workers Party Papers (Microfilm)

Washington, D.C.
Ralph J. Bunche Oral History Collection, Moorland-Spingarn Research Center, Howard University
Amiri Baraka Papers, Moorland-Spingarn Research Center, Howard University
Kwame Nkrumah Papers, Howard University

Mary McLeod Bethune Council House, National Historic Site
Frances Beal Collection, National Council of Negro Women Papers

MANUSCRIPTS ON MICROFILMS

Revolutionary Action Movement Papers, 1962–1996
Robert F. Williams Papers
Student Non-Violent Coordinating Committee Papers
Amiri Baraka Papers

FBI FILES

FBIOAAU	File No. 100-442235 (Organization of Afro American Unity)
FBIMX	File No. 100-399321 (Malcolm X)
NYFBIMX	File No. 105-8999 (Malcolm X New York)
FBIMMI	File No. 100-441765 (Muslim Mosque Incorporated)
FBIMDC	File No. 100-HQ-436190 (Monroe Defense Committee)
FBIBN	File No. 100-448006 (Black Nationalist-Hate Groups)
FBIKT	File No. 100-446080 (Kwame Ture/Stokely Carmichael)
FBIEC	File No. 100-HQ-447251 (Eldridge Cleaver)
FBIRW	File No. 100-HQ-387728 (Robert F. Williams)
FBIHPN	File No. 92-HQ-13682/14778 (Huey Percy Newton)
FBISPAC	File No. 157-HQ-24813 (Sixth Pan-African Congress, Tanzania, 1974)
FBIOG	File No. 100-HQ-435011 (On Guard Committee for Freedom)
FBISS	File No. 157-11096 (Sonia Sanchez)
FBILN	File No. 100-443802 (Larry Neal)
FBIAC	File No. 100-448517 (Albert Cleage Jr.)
FBISNCC	File No. 100-147963 (Student Non-Violent Coordinating Committee)
FBIJM	File No. 100-412872 (Julian Mayfield)
FBIJHC	File No. 97-4575 (John Henrik Clarke)
FBIRAM	File No. 100-442684 (Revolutionary Action Movement)
FBIFNP	File No. 105-123706 (Freedom Now Party)
FBIGOAL	File No. 100-442684 (Group On Advance Leadership)
FBIUH	File No. 157-1022 (UHURU)
FBIRFK	File No. 77-51387 (Robert F. Kennedy)
FBIBNPC	File No. 157-5215 (Black National Political Convention, 1972)
FBIALSC	File No. 157-25073 (African Liberation Support Committee)

PRIVATE COLLECTIONS

Howard Fuller Papers
John Bracey Papers
Ernest Allen Jr. Papers
James Garrett Papers
Gwen Patton Papers

ORAL HISTORIES AND INTERVIEWS

Ahmed, Muhammad (Max Stanford). Telephone interview, Dec. 18, 1999. Audiotape.
Allen, Ernie. Telephone interview, Jan. 5, 2000. Audiotape. Telephone interview, Apr. 24, 2003. Audiotape.
Al Mansour, Khalid. Telephone interview, Apr. 5, 2002. Audiotape.
Anderson, Sam. Telephone interview, Jan. 21, 2000. Audiotape.
Baraka, Amiri. Telephone interview, Feb. 3, 2000. Audiotape. Newark, N.J. July 7, 2004. Audiotape.
Beal, Frances M. Telephone interview, Feb. 16, 2000. Audiotape. Telephone interview, Apr. 22, 2003. Audiotape.
Boggs, Grace Lee. Telephone interview, Jan. 11, 2000. Audiotape. Telephone interview, Dec. 17, 2002. Audiotape.
Bracey, John. Telephone interview, Oct. 30, 2002. Audiotape. Telephone interview, Oct. 23, 2002. Audiotape. Telephone interview, Nov. 6, 2002. Audiotape.
Brath, Elombe. Telephone interview, Nov. 15, 2002. Audiotape.
Bush, Rod. Telephone interview, Jan. 20, 2000. Audiotape.
Chrisman, Robert. Telephone interview, Mar. 1, 2000. Audiotape.
Cleaver, Kathleen. New Haven, Conn., Dec. 18, 2003. Audiotape.
Cobb, Charlie. Washington, Dec. 17, 2003. Audiotape. Telephone interview, Dec. 20, 2003. Audiotape.
Davis, Celeste Lacy. Telephone interview, Jan. 26, 2000. Audiotape.
Fuller, Howard. Telephone interview, Nov. 19, 2002. Audiotape. Telephone interview, July 1, 2003. Audiotape.
Garrett, James. Telephone interview, Mar. 19, 2003. Audiotape. Telephone interview, Apr. 2–3, 2003. Audiotape. Telephone interview, Apr. 27, 2003. Audiotape. Telephone interview, May 14, 2003. Audiotape. Telephone interview, Aug. 4, 2003. Audiotape. Oakland, Calif., June 6 and 10, 2004. Audiotape.
Harding, Vincent. Telephone interview, Jan. 6, 2000. Audiotape.
Hicks, Calvin. Telephone interview, Sept. 29, 2002. Audiotape.
Hiebert, Diedra. Telephone interview, June 8, 2003. Audiotape.
Lynch, Acklyn, Washington, D.C., Apr. 3, 2003. Audiotape.
Miller, Ethelbert. Telephone interview, Apr. 28, 2003. Audiotape.
Muhammad, Saladeen. Telephone interview, Feb. 20, 2002. Audiotape.
Patton, Gwen. Telephone interview, Feb. 8, 2000. Audiotape. Telephone interview, Apr. 15, 2003. Audiotape.
Richardson, Judy. Telephone interview, Apr. 19, 2003. Audiotape.
Rivera, Louis Reyes. Telephone interview, Aug. 9, 2002. Audiotape.
Sales, William. Telephone interview, Jan. 19, 2000. Audiotape.
Sanchez, Sonia. Telephone interview, Dec. 12, 14, and 18, 2002. Audiotape. Telephone

interview. Jan. 28, 2003. Audiotape. Provincetown, Mass., June 28, 2003.
Audiotape. Telephone interview, Aug. 25, 2003. Audiotape.
Sellers, Cleveland. Telephone interview, Mar. 27, 2003. Audiotape.
Simanga, Michael. Telephone interview, Jan. 22, 2000. Audiotape.
Stokely, Brenda. Telephone interview, Jan. 24, 2000. Audiotape.
Strickland, William. Telephone interview, Jan. 6, 2000. Audiotape.
Thelwell, Michael. Telephone interview, Nov. 16, 2002. Audiotape. Amherst, Mass.,
Dec. 16, 1999. Audiotape.
Touré, Askia Muhammad. Telephone interview, Feb. 1 and 17, 2001. Audiotape.
Telephone interview, Nov. 5, 2002. Audiotape.
Tripp, Luke S. Telephone interview, Aug. 9, 2002. Audiotape.
Wagner, Patricia. Telephone interview, Feb. 3, 2000. Audiotape.
Walters, Ronald W. Telephone interview, Apr. 25, 2003. Audiotape.
Woodard, Komozi. Telephone interview, Jan. 12, 2000. Audiotape.
Woods, Diane. Telephone interview, Jan. 24, 2000. Audiotape.
Worthy, William, Washington, D.C., Oct. 20 and Nov. 10, 2002. Audiotape.

RALPH J. BUNCHE ORAL HISTORY COLLECTION,
MOORLAND-SPINGARN RESEARCH CENTER,
HOWARD UNIVERSITY, WASHINGTON, D.C.

Allen, Ernie
Boutelle, Paul
Clarke, John Henrik
DeBerry, Clifton
Harding, Vincent
Mayfield, Julian
Richardson, Gloria
Watts, Dan
Williams, Robert F.
Worthy, William

LBJ LIBRARY

Transcript. Whitney M. Young Jr. Oral History Interview I, June 18, 1969, by Thomas
Harrison Baker. http://www.lbjlib.utexas.edu/johnson/archives.hom/oralhistory.hom/
YoungW/YoungW.asp. (Feb. 1, 2005)
Transcript. Ramsey Clark Oral History Interview IV, April 16, 1969, by Thomas
Harrison Baker. http://www.lbjlib.utexas.edu/johnson/archives.hom/oralhistory.
hom/clarkR/clark-r4.pdf (Aug. 13, 2005)
Transcript. Roy Wilkins Oral History Interview I, Apr. 1, 1969, by Thomas Harrison
Baker. http://www.lbjlib.utexas.edu/johnson/archives.hom/oralhistory.hom/Wilkins/
wilkins.pdf (Aug. 13, 2005)

Tape WH6508.05 (Conversation with Abe Fortas, Aug. 16, 1965)
Tape WH6508.07 (Conversation with Martin Luther King, Aug. 20, 1965)
Tape K66.03 (Conversation with Abe Fortas, Oct. 3, 1966)

AUDIO ARCHIVES

Howard Fuller Collection (Private)
Speeches from Howard University Conference "Which Road Toward Black Liberation?"
  May 1974
King Center, Stanford University
Stokely Carmichael, March 1971, Whittier College

PACIFICA RADIO ARCHIVE, KPFA, LOS ANGELES

PRA No. BB3014	Malcolm X and Bayard Rustin, 1960
PRA No. BB5322	Malcolm X: Black Muslims vs. the Sit-Ins, 1962
PRA No. BB0541	Dick Elman Interviews Malcolm X, 1962
PRA No. BB3049a/b	Malcolm X and William Worthy, 1962
PRA No. BB3528	Speech by Malcolm X on December 20, 1964
PRA No. BB3101	Malcolm X: The Ballot or the Bullet, 1964
PRA No. BB3785.01	The Black Revolution and the White Backlash, 1964
PRA No. BB3103a/b	Malcolm X: The Prospects for Freedom, Jan. 7, 1965
PRA No. BB1709	Stokely Carmichael Berkeley Black Power Speech, 1966
PRA No. BB5262	LeRoi Jones Press Conference, 1967
PRA No. BB5463	Huey P. Newton Interview from Prison, 1968
PRA No. BB1708	Huey P. Newton Rally, 1968
PRA No. BB425a/b/c	Huey P. Newton Rally, 1968
PRA No. BB4532	Huey P. Newton Rally, 1968
PRA No. BB4315	Kathleen Cleaver Interview, 1969
PRA No. BB5137	Challenge '70/LeRoi Jones, 1970
PRA No. BB2531	Huey P. Newton Press Conference, Aug. 11, 1970
PRA No. BC1460	Huey P. Newton Press Conference, Aug. 26, 1970
PRA No. BB4265a/b	Contradictions Within the Black Panther Party: Reactions from Algiers, 1971
PRA No. BC0153	Stokely Carmichael at Whittier College, 1971
PRA No. BB3993	Black Academy of Arts and Letters, Moderated by Harry Belafonte, 1971
PRA No. PZ0468a/b/c	Defining Black Power, 2001

PAMPHLETS

Black Liberation Now! (1966). Radical Pamphlet Collection, Tamiment Institute, New York University.

Black Women's United Front, *Congress of Afrikan People on the Woman Question* (1975). Radical Pamphlet Collection, Tamiment Institute, New York University.

An End to the Neglect of the Problems of the Negro Woman! (1950). Radical Pamphlet Collection, Tamiment Institute, New York University.

IBW and Education for Liberation (1973). Robert Woodruff Special Collections, Emory University.

National Welfare Rights Organization, *Do You Really Want to Know About Welfare in the U.S.?* (1972). Radical Pamphlet Collection, Tamiment Institute, New York University.

National Women's Commission, *Women in the Struggle for Peace and Security* (1950). Radical Pamphlet Collection, Tamiment Institute, New York University.

Perspective on the Atlanta Rebellion (1967). Robert Woodruff Special Collections, Emory University.

The Plot Against Black America (1966). Radical Pamphlet Collection, Tamiment Institute, New York University.

Progressive Labor Party, *We Accuse* (1966). Radical Pamphlet Collection, Tamiment Institute, New York University.

A Report of IFCO Concerns (1973). Robert Woodruff Special Collections, Emory University.

Third World Women's Alliance, *Our History, Our Ideology, Our Goals* (1970). Bethune-Cookman Historical Society, Washington, D.C.

NEWSPAPERS AND PERIODICALS

African Review
African World (SOBU Newsletter)
Baltimore Washington Afro-American
Berkeley Barb
Black America
Blacklash
Black Panther Intercommunal News Service
Black Scholar
Black World (Negro Digest)
Black World View
Correspondence
Crusader
Ebony
Esquire
Fair Play
Freedomways
IBW Monthly Report
Illustrated News
Jet
Liberator
Los Angeles Free Press

Los Angeles Times
Movement
Muhammad Speaks
Nation
National Guardian
Newsweek
New York Amsterdam News
New York Times
Now!
Oakland Tribune
On Guard
Philadelphia Inquirer
Présence Africaine
Ramparts
Realist
San Francisco Chronicle
Soulbook
Triple Jeopardy
Unity and Struggle
U.S. News and World Report
Washington Post

UNPUBLISHED DISSERTATIONS AND PAPERS

Alkebulan, Paul. "The Role of Ideology in the Growth, Establishment, and Decline of the Black Panther Party: 1966 to 1982." Ph.D. diss., University of California, Berkeley, 2003.

Bracey, John Jr. "Marxism and Black Nationalism in the 1960s: The Origins of Revolutionary Black Nationalism." Paper presented at the Organization of American Historians, New Orleans, Apr. 14, 1979.

Countryman, Matthew J. "Civil Rights and Black Power in Philadelphia, 1940–1971." Ph.D. diss., Duke University, 1998.

Grady-Willis, Winston A. "A Changing Tide: Black Politics and Activism in Atlanta, Georgia, 1960–1977." Ph.D. diss., Emory University, 1998.

Jackson, Thomas F. "Recasting the Dream: Martin Luther King, Jr., African-American Political Thought and the Third Reconstruction, 1955–1968." Ph.D. diss., Stanford University, 1994.

Stanford, Maxwell C. "Revolutionary Action Movement (RAM): A Case Study of an Urban Revolutionary Movement in Western Capitalism." M.A. thesis, Atlanta University, 1986.

Ward, Stephen Michael. " 'Ours Too Was a Struggle for a Better World': Activist Intellectuals and the Radical Promise of the Black Power Movement, 1962–1972." Ph.D. diss., University of Texas, Austin, 2002.

Welch, Rebeccah. "Black Art and Activism in Postwar New York, 1950–1965." Ph.D. diss., New York University, 2002.

Wilkins, Fanon Che. " 'In the Belly of the Beast': Black Power, Anti-Imperialism, and the African Liberation Solidarity Movement, 1968–1975." Ph.D. diss., New York University, 2001.

GOVERNMENT DOCUMENTS

Riots, Civil and Criminal Disorders. Hearings before the Permanent Subcommittee on Investigation of the Committee on Government Operations, Part 6. U.S. Senate, Mar. 1967.

Testimony of Stokely Carmichael. Hearing before the Subcommittee to Investigate the Administration of the Internal Security Laws of the Committee on the Judiciary. U. S. Senate, Mar. 1970.

ARTICLES AND BOOK CHAPTERS

Baldwin, James. "From Dreams of Love to Dreams of Terror." *Los Angeles Free Press*, Feb. 23–29, 1968, pp. 1, 3.

Baraka, Amiri. "A Black Value System." *Black Scholar* 1, no. 1 (1969), pp. 54–60.

———. "Toward the Creation of Political Institutions for All African Peoples: From Gary and Miami Before and After." *Black World* 21, no. 12 (1972), pp. 54–78.

———. "Why I Changed My Ideology: Black Nationalism and Socialist Revolution." *Black World* 24, no. 9 (1975), pp. 30–43.

Bates, Beth Tompkins. "A New Crowd Challenges the Agenda of the Old Guard in the NAACP, 1933–1941." *American Historical Review* 102, no. 2 (1997), pp. 340–77.

Beckles, Colin. "Black Bookstores, Black Power, and the FBI: The Case of Drum and Spear." *Western Journal of Black Studies* 20 (1996), pp. 63–70.

Brown, Scot. "The US Organization, Black Power Vanguard Politics, and the United Front Ideal: Los Angeles and Beyond." *Black Scholar* 31, nos. 3–4 (2001), pp. 21–30.

Campbell, Jennifer. " 'It's a Time in the Land': Gendering Black Power and Sarah E. Wright's Place in the Tradition of Black Women's Writing." *African American Review* 31, no. 2 (1997), pp. 211–22.

Carmichael, Stokely. "Pan-Africanism—Land and Power." *Black Scholar* 1, no. 1 (1969), pp. 36–43.

Chrisman, Robert. "The Crisis of Harold Cruse." *Black Scholar* 1, no. 1 (1969), pp. 77–84.

Clemons, Michael L., and Charles E. Jones. "Global Solidarity: The Black Panther Party in the International Arena." *New Political Science* 21, no. 2 (1999), pp. 177–203.

Cruse, Harold. "Revolutionary Nationalism and the Afro-American." *Studies on the Left* 2, no. 3 (1962), pp. 12–25.

Danielson, Leilah. "The 'Two-Ness' of the Movement: James Farmer, Nonviolence, and Black Nationalism." *Peace & Change* 29, nos. 3–4 (2004), pp. 431–52.

Drake, St. Clair. "Black Studies and Global Perspectives: An Essay." *Journal of Negro Education* 53 (1984), pp. 226–42.

Du Cille, Ann. "The Occult of True Black Womanhood: Critical Demeanor and Black Feminist Studies." *Signs* 19, no. 3 (1994), pp. 591–629.

Essien-Udom, E. U. "The Nationalist Movements of Harlem." *Freedomways* 3 (Summer 1963), pp. 335–42.

Gaines, Kevin K. "African-American Expatriates in Ghana and the Black Radical Tradition." *Souls* 1, no. 3 (1999), pp. 64–71.

———. "From Center to Margin: Internationalism and the Origins of Black Feminism." In Russ Castronovo and Dana D. Nelson, eds., *Materializing Democracy: Toward a Revitalized Cultural Politics* (Durham: Duke University Press, 2002), pp. 294–313.

———. "Revisiting Richard Wright in Ghana: Black Radicalism and the Dialectics of Diaspora." *Social Text* 67 (2001), pp. 75–101.

Gambino, Ferrucio. "The Transgression of a Laborer: Malcolm X in the Wilderness of America." *Radical History Review* 55, no. 1 (1993), pp. 7–31.

Gosse, Van. "A Movement of Movements: The Definition and Periodization of the New Left." In Jean-Christophe Agnew and Roy Rosenzweig, eds., *A Companion to Post-1945 America* (Malden: Blackwell, 2002), pp. 277–302.

Hall, Simon. "On the Tail of the Panther: Black Power and the 1967 Convention of the National Conference for New Politics." *Journal of American Studies* 37 (2003), pp. 59–78.

Harding, Vincent. "Wrestling Toward the Dawn: The Afro-American Freedom Movement and the Changing Constitution." *Journal of American History* 74, no. 3 (1987), pp. 718–39.

Hare, Nathan. "An Open Letter to Black Students in the North: New Creation or Familiar Death." *Negro Digest* 18 (1969), pp. 5–14.

———. "Report on the Pan-African Cultural Festival." *Black Scholar* 1 (1969), pp. 2–10.

Higginbotham, Evelyn Brooks. "African-American Women's History and the Metalanguage of Race." *Signs* 17, no. 1 (1992), pp. 251–74.

Holt, Thomas C. "Marking: Race, Race-Making, and the Writing of History." *American Historical Review* 100, no. 1 (1995), pp. 1–20.

Hopkins, Chuck, "Malcolm X Liberation University." *Negro Digest* 19 (March 1970), pp. 39–43.

James, Joy. "Radicalizing Feminism." *Race and Class* 40, no. 4 (1999), pp. 15–31.

Jeffries, Hasan Kwame. "Searching for a New Freedom." In Alton Hornsby Jr., ed., *A Companion to African American History* (Malden: Blackwell, 2005), pp. 499–511.

Jeffries, Judson L. "Black Radicalism and the Political Repression in Baltimore: The Case of the Black Panther Party." *Ethnic and Racial Studies* 25, no. 1 (2002), pp. 64–98.

Johnson, Cedric. "From Popular Anti-Imperialism to Sectarianism: The African Liberation Support Committee and Black Power Radicals." *New Political Science* 25, no. 4 (2003), pp. 477–507.

Jones, LeRoi. "Cuba Libre." In *Home: Social Essays* (New York: Norton, 1998).

Joseph, Peniel. "At the Crossroads: Black Radicalism's Global Vision During the Age of Civil Rights." In Niyi Afolabi, ed., *Marvels of the African World: African Cultural Patrimony, New World Connections, and Identities* (Trenton: Africa World Press, 2003), pp. 425–50.

———. "Black Liberation Without Apology: Rethinking the Black Power Movement." *Black Scholar* 31, nos. 3–4 (2001), pp. 2–17.

———. "Dashikis and Democracy: Black Studies, Student Activism, and the Black Power Movement." *Journal of African American History* 88, no. 2 (2003), pp. 182–203.

———. "Introduction: Toward a Historiography of the Black Power Movement." In Joseph, ed. *The Black Power Movement: Rethinking the Civil Rights–Black Power Era* (New York: Routledge, 2006).

———. "Where Blackness Is Bright? Cuba, Africa, and Black Liberation During the Age of Civil Rights." *New Formations*, no. 45 (2001–2), pp. 111–24.

Kaiser, Ernest. "The Crisis of the Negro Intellectual." *Freedomways* (1969), pp. 24–41.

———. "Recent Literature on Black Liberation Struggles and the Ghetto Crisis." *Science and Society* (1969), pp. 168–96.

Kelley, Robin D. G. " 'But a Local Phase of a World Problem': Black History's Global Vision, 1883–1950." *Journal of American History* 86, no. 3 (1999), pp. 1045–77.

———. "Notes on Deconstructing 'The Folk.' " *American Historical Review* 97, no. 5 (1992), pp. 1400–1408.

Kelley, Robin D. G., and Betsey Esch. "Black Like Mao: Red China and Black Revolution." *Souls* 1, no. 4 (1999), pp. 6–41.

Kelley, Robin D. G. and Tiffany Patterson. "Unfinished Migrations: Reflections on the African Diaspora and the Making of the Modern World." *African Studies Review* 43, no. 1 (2000), pp. 11–45.

Korstad, Robert, and Nelson Lichtenstein. "Opportunities Found and Lost: Labor, Radicals, and the Early Civil Rights Movement." *Journal of American History* 75, no. 3 (1988), pp. 786–811.

Kusmer, Kenneth L. "African Americans in the City Since World War II: From the Industrial to the Post-Industrial Era." *Journal of Urban History* 21 no. 4 (1995), pp. 458–504.

Lang, Clarence. "Between Civil Rights and Black Power in the Gateway City: The Action Committee to Improve Opportunities for Negroes (ACTION), 1964–1975." *Journal of Social History* 37, no. 3 (2004), pp. 725–54.

Lipsitz, George. "The Possessive Investment in Whiteness: Racialized Social Democracy and the 'White' Problem in American Studies." *American Quarterly* 47 no. 3 (1995), pp. 369–87.

Marable, Manning. "Rediscovering Malcolm's Life: A Historian's Adventures in Living History." *Souls* 7, no. 1 (2005), pp. 20–35.

O'Reilly, Kenneth. "The FBI and the Politics of the Riots, 1964–1968." *Journal of American History* 75, no. 1 (1988), pp. 91–114.

Painter, Nell Irvin. "Malcolm X Across the Genres." *American Historical Review* 97, no. 2 (1993), pp. 432–39.

Rodriguez, Besenia. " 'De la esclavitud yanqui a la libertad cubana': U.S. Black Radicals, the Cuban Revolution, and the Formation of a Tricontinental Ideology." *Radical History Review* 92 (Spring 2005), pp. 62–87.

Singh, Nikhil Pal. "Culture/Wars: Recoding Empire in an Age of Democracy." *American Quarterly* 50, no. 3 (1998), pp. 471–522.

Strickland, Bill. "The Gary Convention and the Crisis of American Politics." *Black World* 21, no. 12 (1972), pp. 18–26.

Sugrue, Thomas J. "Affirmative Action from Below: Civil Rights, the Building Trades, and the Politics of Racial Equality in the Urban North, 1945–1969." *Journal of American History* 91, no. 1 (2004), pp. 144–73.

Thelwell, Michael. "1968: A Score-Settling, Ass-Kicking, Head-Whipping, Dues-Taking, Hypocrisy-Exposing, Innocence-Destroying, Delusion-Ending Year." *Village Voice*, Mar. 8, 1988, pp. 29–30, 32–34.

Tyson, Timothy B. "Robert F. Williams, 'Black Power,' and the Roots of the African American Freedom Struggle." *Journal of American History* 85, no. 2 (1998), pp. 540–70.

Umoja, Akinyele Omawale. "Repression Breeds Resistance: The Black Liberation Army and the Radical Legacy of the Black Panther Party." *New Political Science* 21, no. 2 (1999), pp. 131–55.

———. "Searching for Place: Nationalism, Separatism, and Pan-Africanism." In Alton Hornsby Jr., ed., *A Companion to African American History* (Malden: Blackwell, 2005), pp. 529–44.

Walters, Ronald. "The New Black Political Culture." *Black World* 21, no. 12 (1972), pp. 4–17.

Ward, Stephen. " 'Scholarship in the Context of Struggle': Activist Intellectuals, the Institute of the Black World (IBW), and the Contours of Black Radicalism, 1967–1970." *Black Scholar* 31, nos. 3–4 (2001), pp. 42–53.

Wendt, Simon, "God, Gandhi, and Guns: The African American Freedom Struggle in Tuscaloosa, Alabama, 1964–1965." *Journal of African American History* 89, no. 1 (2004), pp. 36–56.

Williams, Rhonda Y. " 'We're Tired of Being Treated like Dogs': Poor Women and Power Politics in Black Baltimore." *Black Scholar* 31, nos. 3–4 (2001), pp. 31–41.

Williams, Yohuru. "No Haven: From Civil Rights to Black Power in New Haven, Connecticut." *Black Scholar* 31, nos. 3–4 (2001), pp. 54–66.

Young, Cynthia. "Havana Up in Harlem: LeRoi Jones, Harold Cruse, and the Making of a Cultural Revolution." *Science and Society* 65 (2001), pp. 12–38.

BOOKS

Afolabi, Niyi, ed. *Marvels of the African World: African Cultural Patrimony, New World Connections, and Identities*. Trenton: Africa World Press, 2003.

Allen, Robert. *Black Awakening in Capitalist America: An Analytic History*. Trenton: Africa World Press, 1990.

———. *Reluctant Reformers: Racism and Social Reform in the United States*. Washington: Howard University Press, 1983.

Al Mansour, Khalid. *Black Americans at the Crossroads: Where Do We Go from Here?* New York: First African Arabian Press, 1990.

Anderson, Carol. *Eyes Off the Prize: The United Nations and the African American Struggle for Human Rights, 1944–1955*. Cambridge: Cambridge University Press, 2003.

Angelou, Maya. *All God's Children Need Traveling Shoes*. New York: Random House, 1986.

———. *Gather Together in My Name*. New York: Bantam Books, 1993.

———. *The Heart of a Woman*. New York: Bantam Books, 1997.

Anthony, Earl. *Picking Up the Gun: A Report on the Black Panthers*. New York: Pyramid, 1971.

Aptheker, Bettina. *The Morning Breaks: The Trial of Angela Davis*. Ithaca: Cornell University Press, 1997.

Armstrong, Gregory. *The Dragon Has Come*. New York: Harper & Row, 1974.

Aronowitz, Stanley. *The Death and Rebirth of American Radicalism*. New York: Routledge, 1996.

Baldwin, James. *The Fire Next Time*. New York: Dell Books, 1964.

———. *No Name in the Street*. New York: Dell Books, 1972.

———. *Notes of a Native Son*. New York: Bantam Books, 1968.

———. *One Day When I Was Lost*. New York: Dial Books, 1973.

Baraka, Amiri. *African Congress: A Documentary of the First Modern Pan-African Congress*. New York: William Morrow, 1972.

———. *The Autobiography of LeRoi Jones*. New York: Lawrence Hill Books, 1997.

———. *Home: Social Essays*. Hopewell, NJ: Ecco Press, 1998.

———. *Raise, Race, Rays, Raze: Essays Since 1965*. New York: Random House, 1971.

Barlow, William, and Peter Shapiro. *An End to Silence: The San Francisco State Student Movement in the 60s*. New York: Bobbs-Merrill, 1971.

Bell, Derrick. *Faces at the Bottom of the Well: The Permanence of Racism*. New York: Basic Books, 1992.

Biondi, Martha. *To Stand and Fight: The Struggle for Civil Rights in Postwar New York City*. Cambridge: Harvard University Press, 2003.

Black Public Sphere Collective, ed. *The Black Public Sphere*. Chicago: University of Chicago Press, 1995.

Blake, John. *Children of the Movement*. Chicago: Lawrence Hill Books, 2004.

Boggs, Grace Lee. *Living for Change: An Autobiography*. Minneapolis: University of Minnesota Press, 1998.

Bogues, Anthony. *Black Heretics, Black Prophets: Radical Political Intellectuals*. New York: Routledge, 2003.

Borstelmann, Thomas. *The Cold War and the Color Line: American Race Relations in the Global Arena*. Cambridge: Harvard University Press, 2001.

Boyle, Kay. *The Long Walk at San Francisco State*. New York: Grove Press, 1970.

Boyle, Kevin. *Arc of Justice: A Saga of Race, Civil Rights, and Murder in the Jazz Age*. New York: Henry Holt, 2004.

Bracey, John, August Meier, and Elliot Rudwick, eds. *Black Nationalism in America*. Indianapolis: Bobbs-Merrill, 1970.

Branch, Taylor. *Parting the Waters: America in the King Years, 1954–1963*. New York: Touchstone Books, 1989.

———. *Pillar of Fire: America in the King Years, 1963–1965*. New York: Simon and Schuster, 1998.

———. *At Canaan's Edge: America in the King Years, 1965–68*. New York: Simon and Schuster, 2006.

Braudy, Susan. *Family Circle: The Boudins and the Aristocracy of the Left*. New York: Anchor Books, 2003.

Breitman, George. *The Assassination of Malcolm X*. New York: Pathfinder Press, 1988.

———. *By Any Means Necessary: Speeches, Interviews, and a Letter by Malcolm X*. New York: Pathfinder Press, 1970.

———. *The Last Year of Malcolm X: The Evolution of a Revolutionary*. New York: Merit Publishers, 1967.

———, ed. *Malcolm X Speaks*. New York: Pathfinder Press, 1989.

Brown, Elaine. *A Taste of Power: A Black Woman's Story*. New York: Pantheon Books, 1992.

Brown, Scot. *Fighting for US: Maulana Karenga, the US Organization, and Black Cultural Nationalism*. New York: New York University Press, 2003.

Buhle, Paul. *C.L.R. James: The Artist as Revolutionary*. London: Verso, 1988.

————. *Marxism in the United States: Remapping the History of the American Left.* London: Verso, 1987.

Bush, Rod. *We Are Not What We Seem: Black Nationalism and Class Struggle in the American Century.* New York: New York University Press, 1999.

Cade, Toni, ed. *The Black Woman: An Anthology.* New York: New American Library, 1970.

Campbell, James. *Talking at the Gates: A Life of James Baldwin.* London: Faber and Faber, 1991.

Carby, Hazel. *Race Men.* Cambridge: Harvard University Press, 1998.

Carew, Jan. *Ghosts in Our Blood: With Malcolm X in Africa, England, and the Caribbean.* Chicago: Lawrence Hill Books, 1994.

Carmichael, Stokely. *Stokely Speaks: Black Power Back to Pan-Africanism.* New York: Vintage Books, 1971.

Carmichael, Stokely, and Charles Hamilton. *Black Power: The Politics of Liberation in America.* New York: Random House, 1967.

Carmichael, Stokely, with Ekwueme Michael Thelwell. *Ready for Revolution: The Life and Struggles of Stokely Carmichael (Kwame Ture).* New York: Scribner, 2003.

Caro, Robert A. *The Power Broker: Robert Moses and the Fall of New York.* New York: Vintage Books, 1975.

————. *The Years of Lyndon Johnson: Master of the Senate.* New York: Knopf, 2002.

Carson, Clayborne. *In Struggle: SNCC and the Black Awakening of the 1960s.* Cambridge: Harvard University Press, 1981.

————. *Malcolm X: The FBI File.* New York: Carroll & Graf, 1991.

Chafe, William H. *Civilities and Civil Rights: Greensboro, North Carolina, and the Black Struggle for Freedom.* New York: Oxford University Press, 1981.

————. *The Unfinished Journey: America Since World War II.* New York: Oxford University Press, 1991.

Chester, Lewis, Godfrey Hodgson, and Bruce Page. *An American Melodrama: The Presidential Campaign of 1968.* New York: Viking, 1969.

Churchill, Ward, and Jim Vander Wall. *Agents of Repression: The FBI's Secret Wars Against the Black Panther Party and the American Indian Movement.* Boston: South End Press, 1988.

Clarke, John Henrik, ed. *Malcolm X: The Man and His Times.* New York: Macmillan, 1970.

Cleaver, Eldridge. *Post-Prison Writings and Speeches.* Ed. Robert Scheer. New York: Random House, 1970.

————. *Soul on Fire.* Waco: Word Books, 1978.

————. *Soul on Ice.* New York: Dell Books, 1968.

Cleaver, Kathleen, and George Katsiaficas, eds. *Liberation, Imagination, and the Black Panther Party: A New Look at the Panthers and Their Legacy.* New York: Routledge, 2001.

Clegg, Claude Andrew, III. *An Original Man: The Life and Times of Elijah Muhammad.* New York: St. Martin's Press, 1997.

Cobb, William Jelani, ed. *The Essential Harold Cruse: A Reader.* New York: Palgrave, 2002.

Collier-Thomas, Bettye, and V. P. Franklin, eds. *Sisters in the Struggle: African American Women in the Civil Rights–Black Power Movement.* New York: New York University Press, 2001.

Collins, Patricia Hill. *Black Feminist Thought: Knowledge, Consciousness, and the Politics of Empowerment.* New York: Routledge, 1990.

Countryman, Matthew. *Up South: Civil Rights and Black Power in Philadelphia.* Philadelphia: University of Pennsylvania Press, 2006.

Cox, Oliver C. *Race Relations: Elements and Social Dynamics.* Detroit: Wayne State University Press, 1976.

Cruse, Harold. *The Crisis of the Negro Intellectual: A Historical Analysis of the Failure of Black Leadership.* New York: Quill, 1984.

———. *Rebellion or Revolution?* New York: William Morrow, 1968.

Cummins, Eric. *The Rise and Fall of California's Radical Prison Movement.* Stanford: Stanford University Press, 1994.

Davis, Angela. *An Autobiography.* New York: International Publishers, 1988.

———, et al. *If They Come in the Morning.* New York: Signet, 1971.

Dawson, Michael C. *Black Visions: The Roots of Contemporary African-American Political Ideologies.* Chicago: University of Chicago Press, 2001.

De Caro, Louis A. Jr. *Malcolm and the Cross: The Nation of Islam, Malcolm X and Christianity.* New York: New York University Press, 1998.

Denning, Michael. *Cultural Front: The Laboring of American Culture in the Twentieth Century.* London: Verso, 1997.

Dent, Gina, ed. *Black Popular Culture.* New York: New Press, 1998.

De Veaux, Alexis. *Warrior Poet: A Biography of Audre Lorde.* New York: Norton, 2004.

Dittmer, John. *Local People: The Struggle for Civil Rights in Mississippi.* Urbana: University of Illinois Press, 1995.

Dougherty, Jack. *More Than One Struggle: The Evolution of Black School Reform in Milwaukee.* Chapel Hill: University of North Carolina Press, 2004.

Du Bois, W. E. B. *Black Reconstruction: An Essay Toward a History of the Part Which Black Folk Played in the Attempt to Reconstruct Democracy in America, 1860–1880.* New York: Harcourt, Brace, 1935.

———. *Color and Democracy: Colonies and Peace.* New York: Harcourt, Brace, 1945.

Dudziak, Mary L. *Cold War Civil Rights: Race and the Image of American Democracy.* Princeton: Princeton University Press, 2000.

Durden-Smith, Jo. *Who Killed George Jackson?* New York: Knopf, 1976.

Dyson, Michael Eric. *I May Not Get There with You: The True Martin Luther King, Jr.* New York: Basic Books, 2000.

———. *Making Malcolm: The Myth and Meaning of Malcolm X.* New York: Oxford University Press, 1995.

Elbaum, Max. *Revolution in the Air: Sixties Radicals Turn to Lenin, Mao, and Che.* London: Verso, 2002.

Ellison, Ralph. *Invisible Man.* New York: Random House, 1952.

Epps, Archie, ed. *Malcolm X Speeches at Harvard.* New York: Paragon House, 1991.

Eskew, Glen T. *But for Birmingham: The Local and National Movements in the Civil Rights Struggle.* Chapel Hill: University of North Carolina Press, 1997.

Evans, Sara. *Personal Politics: The Roots of Women's Liberation in the Civil Rights Movement and the New Left.* New York: Knopf, 1979.

Evanzz, Karl. *The Messenger: The Rise and Fall of Elijah Muhammad.* New York: Vintage Books, 2001.

Evers-Williams, Myrli. *Watch Me Fly: What I Learned on the Way to Becoming the Woman I Was Meant to Be.* New York: Little, Brown, 1999.

Fairclough, Adam. *Better Day Coming: Blacks and Equality, 1890–2000.* New York: Penguin Books, 2001.

———. *To Redeem the Soul of America: The Southern Christian Leadership Conference and Martin Luther King, Jr.* Athens: University of Georgia Press, 2001.

Farber, David. *Chicago '68.* Chicago: University of Chicago Press, 1988.

Fanon, Frantz. *Black Skin, White Masks.* New York: Grove Press, 1967.

———. *Toward the African Revolution.* New York: Monthly Review Press, 1967.

———. *The Wretched of the Earth.* New York: Grove Press, 1967.

Farmer, James. *Lay Bare the Heart: An Autobiography of the Civil Rights Movement.* Fort Worth: Texas Christian University Press, 1998.

Fleming, Cynthia Griggs. *Soon We Will Not Cry: The Liberation of Ruby Doris Smith Robinson.* Lanham: Rowman & Littlefield, 1998.

Foner, Philip S. *The Black Panthers Speak.* New York: Da Capo Press, 2002.

Forman, James. *The Making of Black Revolutionaries.* Washington: Open Hand, 1985.

Franklin, V. P. *Living Our Stories, Telling Our Truths: Autobiography and the Making of the African American Intellectual Tradition.* New York: Oxford University Press, 1995.

Freed, Donald. *Agony in New Haven: The Trial of Bobby Seale, Ericka Huggins and the Black Panther Party.* New York: Simon and Schuster, 1973.

Gallen, David, ed. *Malcolm X: As They Knew Him.* New York: Carroll & Graf, 1992.

Garrow, David. *Bearing the Cross: Martin Luther King Jr. and the Southern Christian Leadership Conference.* New York: Harper Perennial, 1999.

———. *The FBI and Martin Luther King, Jr.* New York: Penguin Books, 1983.

Garry, Charles, and Art Goldberg. *Streetfighter in the Courtroom: The People's Advocate.* New York: Dutton, 1977.

Gayle, Addison, ed. *The Black Aesthetic.* New York: Doubleday, 1971.

———, ed. *Black Expression.* New York: Weybright and Talley, 1969.

Georgakas, Dan, and Marvin Surkin. *Detroit: I Do Mind Dying.* Boston: South End Press, 1998.

Giddings, Paula. *When and Where I Enter: The Impact of Black Women on Race and Sex in America.* New York: Bantam Books, 1984.

Gilroy, Paul. *The Black Atlantic: Modernity and Double Consciousness.* Cambridge: Harvard University Press, 1993.

Gitlin, Todd. *The Sixties: Years of Hope, Days of Rage.* New York: Bantam Books, 1989.

———. *The Whole World Is Watching: Mass Media in the Making and Unmaking of the New Left.* Berkeley: University of California Press, 1980.

Glaude, Eddie S., Jr., ed. *Is It Nation Time? Contemporary Essays on Black Power and Black Nationalism.* Chicago: University of Chicago Press, 2002.

Gleijeses, Piero. *Conflicting Missions: Havana, Washington, and Africa, 1959–1976.* Chapel Hill: University of North Carolina Press, 2002.

Goldberg, David Theo, *Racist Culture.* London: Basil Blackwell, 1993.

———, ed. *Anatomy of Race.* Minneapolis: University of Minnesota Press, 1990.

Goldman, Peter. *The Death and Life of Malcolm X.* New York: Harper & Row, 1973.

Gordon, Jane Anna. *Why They Couldn't Wait: A Critique of the Black-Jewish Conflict over Community Control in Ocean Hill–Brownsville, 1967–1971.* New York: Routledge-Falmer, 2001.

Gordon, Lewis R. *Bad Faith and Antiblack Racism.* Amherst, N.Y.: Humanity Books, 1995.

———. *Existence in Black: An Anthology of Black Existential Philosophy.* New York: Routledge, 1996.

———. *Fanon and the Crisis of European Man: An Essay on Philosophy and the Human Sciences.* New York: Routledge, 1995.

————. *Her Majesty's Other Children: Sketches of Racism from a Neocolonial Age.* Lanham: Rowman and Littlefield, 1997.

Gordon, Lewis R., et al., eds. *Fanon: A Critical Reader.* London: Blackwell, 1995.

Gosse, Van. *Where the Boys Are: Cuba, Cold War America and the Making of a New Left.* London: Verso, 1993.

Greenberg, Cheryl Lynn, ed. *A Circle of Trust: Remembering SNCC.* New Brunswick: Rutgers University Press, 1998.

Griffin, Farah Jasmine. *If You Can't Be Free, Be a Mystery: In Search of Billie Holiday.* New York: Free Press, 2001.

————. *"Who Set You Flowin?": The African-American Migration Narrative.* New York: Oxford University Press, 1995.

Guevara, Ernesto. *The African Dream: The Diaries of the Revolutionary War in the Congo.* New York: Grove Press, 2000.

Hacker, Andrew. *Two Nations: Black and White, Separate, Hostile, and Unequal.* New York: Scribner, 1992.

Halberstam, David. *The Children.* New York: Fawcett Books, 1998.

Haley, Alex. *The Autobiography of Malcolm X.* New York: Ballantine Books, 1998.

Hall, Simon. *Peace and Freedom: The Civil Rights and Antiwar Movements in the 1960s.* Philadelphia: University of Pennsylvania Press, 2005.

Hampton, Henry, and Stephen Fayer, eds. *Voices of Freedom: An Oral History of the Civil Rights Movement from the 1950s through the 1980s.* New York: Bantam Books, 1991.

Hansberry, Lorraine. *A Raisin in the Sun.* New York: Modern Library, 1995.

Harding, Vincent. *Martin Luther King: Inconvenient Hero.* New York: Orbis Books, 1991.

————. *There Is a River: The Black Struggle for Freedom in America.* New York: Harcourt Brace Jovanovich, 1981.

Harris, William J., ed. *The LeRoi Jones/Amiri Baraka Reader.* New York: Thunder's Mouth Press, 1995.

Hayden, Tom. *Rebellion in Newark: Official Violence and Ghetto Response.* New York: Vintage Books, 1967.

————. *Reunion: A Memoir.* New York: Random House, 1988.

————. *Trial.* New York: Holt, Rinehart, and Winston, 1970.

Haywood, Harry. *Black Bolshevik: Autobiography of an Afro-American Communist.* Chicago: Liberator Press, 1978.

Henry, Paget. *Caliban's Reason: Introducing Afro-Caribbean Philosophy.* New York: Routledge, 2000.

Hill, Lance. *The Deacons for Defense: Armed Resistance and the Civil Rights Movement.* Chapel Hill: University of North Carolina Press, 2004.

Hilliard, David, and Lewis Cole. *This Side of Glory: The Autobiography of David Hilliard and the Story of the Black Panther Party.* New York: Little, Brown, 1993.

Hilliard, David, and Donald Weise, eds. *The Huey P. Newton Reader.* New York: Seven Stories Press, 2002.

Hoare, Quinton, and Geoffrey Nowell Smith, eds. *Selections from the Prison Notebooks of Antonio Gramsci.* New York: International Publishers, 1971.

Hodgson, Godfrey. *America in Our Time: From World War II to Nixon: What Happened and Why.* New York: Vintage Books, 1978.

Horne, Gerald. *Black and Red: W.E.B. Du Bois and the African-American Response to the Cold War, 1944–1963.* Albany: State University of New York Press, 1986.

———. *Black Liberation and Red Scare: Ben Davis and the Communist Party.* Newark: University of Delaware Press, 1994.

———. *Communist Front?: The Civil Rights Congress, 1946–1956.* Rutherford: Fairleigh Dickinson University Press, 1988.

———. *The Fire This Time: The Watts Uprising and the 1960s.* New York: Da Capo Press, 1997.

———. *Race Woman: The Lives of Shirley Graham Du Bois.* New York: New York University Press, 2000.

Houser, George M. *No One Can Stop the Rain: Glimpses of Africa's Liberation Struggle.* New York: Pilgrim Press, 1989.

Isserman, Maurice, and Michael Kazin. *America Divided: The Civil War of the 1960s.* New York: Oxford University Press, 2000.

Jackson, Esther Cooper, ed. *Freedomways Reader: Prophets in Their Own Country.* Boulder: Westview Press, 2000.

Jackson, George. *Blood in My Eye.* Baltimore: Black Classic Press, 1990.

———. *Soledad Brother: The Prison Letters of George Jackson.* Chicago: Lawrence Hill Books, 1994.

Jackson, Lawrence. *Ralph Ellison: Emergence of Genius.* New York: Wiley, 2002.

Jamal, Hakim A. *From the Dead Level: Malcolm X and Me.* New York: Warner Books, 1973.

James, Joy. *Shadowboxing: Representations of Black Feminist Politics.* New York: St. Martin's Press, 1999.

———. *Transcending the Talented Tenth: Black Leaders and American Intellectuals.* New York: Routledge, 1997.

———, ed. *Angela Davis: A Reader.* London: Basil Blackwell, 1999.

James, Winston. *Holding Aloft the Banner of Ethiopia: Caribbean Radicalism in Early Twentieth-Century America.* London: Verso, 1998.

Jeffries, Judson, L. *Huey P. Newton: The Radical Theorist.* Jackson: University of Mississippi Press, 2002.

Jennings, James. *The Politics of Black Empowerment: The Transformation of Black Activism in Urban America.* Detroit: Wayne State University Press, 1992.

———, ed. *Race and Politics.* London: Verso, 1998.

Jones, Charles, ed. *The Black Panther Party Reconsidered.* Baltimore: Black Classic Press, 1998.

Joseph, Peniel E., ed. *The Black Power Movement: Rethinking the Civil Rights–Black Power Era.* New York: Routledge, 2006.

Jules-Rosette, Bennetta. *Black Paris: The African Writers Landscape.* Urbana: University of Illinois Press, 1998.

Kadalie, Modibo M. *Internationalism, Pan-Africanism and the Struggle of Social Classes: Raw Writings from the Notebook of an Early Nineteen-Seventies African-American Radical Activist.* Savannah: One Quest Press, 2000.

Karim, Benjamin, ed. *The End of White World Supremacy: Four Speeches by Malcolm X.* New York: Arcade Publishing, 1971.

Karim, Benjamin, with Peter Skutches and David Gallen. *Remembering Malcolm.* New York: One World, 1992.

Katsiaficas, George. *The Imagination of the New Left: A Global Analysis of 1968.* Boston: South End Press, 1987.

Katz, Michael B., ed. *The Underclass Debate: Views from History.* Princeton: Princeton University Press, 1993.

Keating, Edward M. *Free Huey!* Berkeley: Ramparts, 1971.

Kelley, Robin, D. G. *Freedom Dreams: The Black Radical Imagination.* Boston: Beacon Press, 2002.

———. *Hammer and Hoe: Alabama Communists During the Great Depression.* Chapel Hill: University of North Carolina Press, 1990.

———. *Race Rebels: Culture, Politics, and the Black Working Class.* New York: Free Press, 1994.

———. *Yo' Mama's Dysfunktional!: Fighting the Culture Wars in Urban America.* Boston: Beacon Press, 1997.

Kempton, Murray. *The Briar Patch: The People of the State of New York v. Lumumba Shakur et al.* New York: Dutton, 1973.

Keppel, Ben. *The Work of Democracy: Ralph Bunche, Kenneth B. Clark, Lorraine Hansberry, and the Cultural Politics of Race.* Cambridge: Harvard University Press, 1995.

Kerner Commission. *Report of the National Advisory Commission on Civil Disorders.* New York: Bantam Books, 1968.

King, Martin Luther, Jr. *Where Do We Go from Here: Chaos or Community?* New York: Penguin Books, 1968.

———. *Why We Can't Wait.* New York: Signet, 1964.

Klinkner, Philip A., with Rogers M. Smith. *The Unsteady March: The Rise and Decline of Racial Equality in America.* Chicago: University of Chicago Press, 2002.

Kornweibel, Theodore. *"Seeing Red": Federal Campaigns Against Black Militancy, 1919–1925.* Bloomington: Indiana University Press, 1999.

Kotz, Nick. *Judgment Days: Lyndon Baines Johnson, Martin Luther King Jr., and the Laws That Changed America.* New York: Houghton Mifflin, 2005.

Kurlansky, Mark. *1968: The Year That Rocked the World.* New York: Ballantine Books, 2004.

Lacy, Leslie Alexander. *The Rise and Fall of a Proper Negro: An Autobiography.* New York: Macmillan, 1970.

Lawson, Steven F., and Charles Payne. *Debating the Civil Rights Movement, 1945–1968.* Lanham: Rowman and Littlefield, 1998.

Layton, Azza Salama. *International Politics and Civil Rights Policies in the United States, 1941–1960.* Cambridge: Cambridge University Press, 2000.

Lee, Chana Kai. *For Freedom's Sake: The Life of Fannie Lou Hamer.* Urbana: University of Illinois Press, 1999.

Lemelle, Sidney, and Robin D. G. Kelley, eds. *Imagining Home: Class, Culture and Nationalism in the African Diaspora.* London: Verso, 1994.

Lerner, Gerda, ed. *Black Women in White America: A Documentary History.* New York: Pantheon, 1972.

Lester, Julius, *All Is Well.* New York: William Morrow, 1976.

———. *Look Out Whitey! Black Power's Gon' Get Your Mama.* New York: Dial Press, 1968.

———. *Revolutionary Notes.* New York: Grove Press, 1969.

Levy, Peter B. *Civil War on Race Street: The Civil Rights Movement in Cambridge, Maryland.* Gainesville: University Press of Florida, 2003.

Lewis, David Levering. *King: A Biography.* Urbana: University of Illinois Press, 1978.

———. *W.E.B. Du Bois: Biography of a Race, 1868–1919.* New York: Henry Holt, 1994.

———. *W.E.B. Du Bois: The Fight for Equality and the American Century, 1919–1963.* New York: Henry Holt, 2000.

———. *When Harlem Was in Vogue*. New York: Penguin Books, 1997.

Lewis, John, with Michael D'Orso. *Walking with the Wind: A Memoir of the Movement*. New York: Simon and Schuster, 1998.

Lockwood, Lee. *Conversations with Eldridge Cleaver: Algiers*. New York: McGraw-Hill, 1970.

Lomax, Louis E. *To Kill a Black Man*. Los Angeles: Holloway House, 1968.

———. *When the Word Is Given: A Report on Elijah Muhammad, Malcolm X, and the Black Muslim World*. Toronto: Signet Books, 1963.

Lusane, Clarence. *Race in the Global Era: African Americans at the Millennium*. Boston: South End Press, 1998.

Major, Reginald. *A Panther Is a Black Cat*. New York: William Morrow, 1971.

Makeba, Miriam, with James Hall. *Makeba: My Story*. New York: New American Library, 1987.

Marable, Manning. *Black American Politics: From the Washington Marches to Jesse Jackson*. London: Verso, 1985.

———. *Black Leadership*. New York: Columbia University Press, 1998.

———. *Blackwater: Historical Studies in Race, Class Consciousness, and Revolution*. Boulder: University Press of Colorado, 1993.

———. *Beyond Black and White: Transforming African-American Politics*. London: Verso, 1995.

———. *From the Grassroots: Essays Toward Afro-American Liberation*. Boston: South End Press, 1980.

———. *Race, Reform, and Rebellion: The Second Reconstruction in Black America, 1945–1990*. Jackson: University Press of Mississippi, 1990.

———. *Speaking Truth to Power: Essays on Race, Resistance, and Radicalism*. Boulder: Westview Press, 1996.

Marqusee, Mike. *Redemption Song: Muhammad Ali and the Spirit of the Sixties*. London: Verso, 1999.

Mayfield, Julian. *The Hit and the Long Night*. Boston: Northeastern University Press, 1989.

McCartney, John T. *Black Power Ideologies: An Essay in African-American Political Thought*. Philadelphia: Temple University Press, 1993.

McMillian, John, and Paul Buhle, eds. *The New Left Revisited*. Philadelphia: Temple University Press, 2003.

McWhorter, Diane. *Carry Me Home: Birmingham, Alabama: The Climactic Battle of the Civil Rights Revolution*. New York: Touchstone, 2002.

Mealy, Rosemari. *Fidel and Malcolm X: Memories of a Meeting*. Melbourne, Australia: Ocean Press, 1993.

Meier, August, and Elliot Rudwick. *CORE: A Study in the Civil Rights Movement, 1942–1968*. New York: Oxford University Press, 1973.

Meriwether, James H. *Proudly We Can Be Called Africans: Black Americans and Africa, 1935–1961*. Chapel Hill: University of North Carolina Press, 2002.

Miller, James. *Democracy Is in the Streets: From Port Huron to the Siege of Chicago*. Cambridge: Harvard University Press, 1995.

Milne, Jules. *Kwame Nkrumah: A Biography*. London: Panaf Books, 2000.

———, ed. *Kwame Nkrumah: The Conakry Years: His Life and Letters*. London: Panaf Books, 1990.

Moore, Gilbert. *A Special Rage*. New York: Harper & Row, 1971.

Moore, Leonard N. *Carl B. Stokes and the Rise of Black Political Power*. Urbana: University of Illinois Press, 2003.

Morris, Aldon. *The Origins of the Civil Rights Movement: Black Communities Organizing for Change.* New York: Free Press, 1984.

Moses, Wilson J., ed. *Classical Black Nationalism: From the American Revolution to Marcus Garvey.* New York: New York University Press, 1996.

———. *The Golden Age of Black Nationalism, 1850–1925.* New York: Oxford University Press, 1988.

Naison, Mark, *Communists in Harlem During the Depression.* Urbana: University of Illinois Press, 1983.

Neal, Mark Anthony. *What the Music Said: Black Popular Music and Black Public Culture.* New York: Routledge, 1998.

Newton, Huey, P. *Revolutionary Suicide.* New York: Ballantine Books, 1974.

———. *To Die for the People.* New York: Writers and Readers, 1995.

Newton, Huey P., and Erik H. Erikson. *In Search of Common Ground.* New York: Norton, 1973.

Nixon, Richard M. *The Memoirs of Richard Nixon.* New York: Grosset & Dunlap, 1978.

Oates, Stephen B. *Let the Trumpet Sound: A Life of Martin Luther King, Jr.* New York: Harper Perennial, 1994.

Ogbar, Jeffrey O. G. *Black Power: Radical Politics and African American Identity.* Baltimore: Johns Hopkins University Press, 2004.

Olsen, Jack. *Last Man Standing: The Tragedy and Triumph of Geronimo Pratt.* New York: Doubleday, 2000.

Omi, Michael, and Howard Winant. *Racial Formation in the United States: From the 1960s to the 1990s.* New York: Routledge, 1994.

O'Reilly, Kenneth. *Nixon's Piano: Presidents and Racial Politics, from Washington to Clinton.* New York: Free Press, 1995.

Padmore, George. *Pan-Africanism or Communism?* London: Dennis Dobson, 1956.

Payne, Charles. *I've Got the Light of Freedom: The Organizing Tradition and the Mississippi Freedom Struggle.* Berkeley: University of California Press, 1995.

Pearson, Hugh. *The Shadow of the Panther: Huey Newton and the Price of Black Power in America.* Reading, Mass.: Addison Wesley, 1994.

Perry, Bruce. *Malcolm X: The Life of a Man Who Changed Black America.* Barrytown, N.Y.: Station Hill Press, 1992.

Pinckney, Alphonso. *Red, Black and Green: Black Nationalism in the United States.* Cambridge, U.K.: Cambridge University Press, 1976.

Plummer, Brenda Gayle. *Rising Wind: Black Americans and U.S. Foreign Affairs, 1935–1960.* Chapel Hill: University of North Carolina Press, 1996.

———, ed. *Window on Freedom: Race, Civil Rights, and Foreign Affairs, 1945–1988.* Chapel Hill: University of North Carolina Press, 2003.

Polsgrove, Carol. *Divided Minds: Intellectuals and the Civil Rights Movement.* New York: Norton, 2001.

Porter, Eric. *What Is This Thing Called Jazz?: African American Musicians as Artists, Critics, and Activists.* Berkeley: University of California Press, 2002.

Powers, Richard. *Secrecy and Power: The Life of J. Edgar Hoover.* New York: Free Press, 1987.

Ransby, Barbara. *Ella Baker and the Black Freedom Movement: A Radical Democratic Vision.* Chapel Hill: University of North Carolina Press, 2003.

Reed, Adolph L., Jr. *The Jesse Jackson Phenomenon: The Crisis of Purpose in Afro-American Politics.* New Haven: Yale University Press, 1986.

————. *Stirrings in the Jug: Black Politics in the Post-Segregation Era.* Minneapolis: University of Minnesota Press, 1999.

————, ed. *Race, Politics, and Culture: Critical Essays on the Radicalism of the 1960s.* New York: Greenwood Press, 1986.

Reitan, Ruth. *The Rise and Decline of an Alliance: Cuba and African American Leaders in the 1960s.* East Lansing: Michigan State University Press, 1999.

Robeson, Paul. *Here I Stand.* Boston: Beacon Press, 1988.

Robinson, Armstead L., and Patricia Sullivan, eds. *New Directions in Civil Rights Studies.* Charlottesville: University Press of Virginia, 1991.

Robinson, Cedric. *Black Marxism: The Making of the Black Radical Tradition.* Chapel Hill: University of North Carolina Press, 2000.

Robinson, Dean E. *Black Nationalism in American Politics and Thought.* Cambridge, U.K.: Cambridge University Press, 2001.

Robnett, Belinda. *How Long? How Long?: African-American Women in the Struggle for Civil Rights.* New York: Oxford University Press, 1997.

Roediger, David, ed. *Black on White: Black Writers on What It Means to Be White.* New York: Schocken Books, 1998.

————. *The Wages of Whiteness: Race and the Making of the American Working Class.* London: Verso, 1991.

Said, Edward. *Culture and Imperialism.* New York: Knopf, 1993.

Sales, William, Jr. *From Civil Rights to Black Liberation: Malcolm X and the Organization of Afro-American Unity.* Boston: South End Press, 1994.

Sanchez, Sonia. *Homecoming.* Detroit: Broadside Press, 1971.

Saul, Scott. *Freedom Is, Freedom Ain't: Jazz and the Making of the Sixties.* Cambridge: Harvard University Press, 2003.

Seale, Bobby. *A Lonely Rage: The Autobiography of Bobby Seale.* New York: Times Books, 1978.

————. *Seize the Time: The Story of the Black Panther Party and Huey P. Newton.* New York: Random House, 1970.

Self, Robert O. *American Babylon: Race and the Struggle for Postwar Oakland.* Princeton: Princeton University Press, 2003.

Sellers, Cleveland. *The River of No Return: The Autobiography of a Black Militant and the Life and Death of SNCC.* New York: William Morrow, 1973.

Shakur, Assata. *Assata: An Autobiography.* Westport, Conn.: Lawrence Hill, 1987.

Simanga, Michael. *In the Shadow of the Son: A Novel.* Chicago: Third World Press, 2000.

Simone, Nina. *I Put a Spell on You: The Autobiography of Nina Simone.* New York: Da Capo Press, 2003.

Singh, Nikhil Pal. *Black Is a Country: Race and the Unfinished Struggle for Democracy.* Cambridge: Harvard University Press, 2004.

Sitkoff, Harvard. *A New Deal For Blacks: The Emergence of Civil Rights as a National Issue.* New York: Oxford University Press, 1978.

————. *The Struggle for Black Equality, 1954–1992.* New York: Hill and Wang, 1993.

Smethurst, James Edward. *The Black Arts Movement: Literary Nationalism in the 1960s and 1970s.* Chapel Hill: University of North Carolina Press, 2005.

Smith, Barbara, ed. *Home Girls: A Black Feminist Anthology.* New York: Kitchen Table Press, 1983.

Smith, Robert C. *We Have No Leaders: African-Americans in the Post–Civil Rights Era.* New York: SUNY Press, 1996.

Smith, Suzanne. *Dancing in the Street: Motown and the Cultural Politics of Detroit.* Cambridge: Harvard University Press, 1999.

Solomon, Mark. *The Cry Was Unity: Communists and African Americans, 1917–1936.* Jackson: University Press of Mississippi, 1998.

Springer, Kimberly, ed. *Still Lifting, Still Climbing: African American Women's Contemporary Activism.* New York: New York University Press, 1999.

Staniland, Martin. *American Intellectuals and African Nationalists, 1955–1970.* New Haven: Yale University Press, 1991.

Steinberg, Stephen. *Turning Back: The Liberal Retreat from Racial Justice in American Thought and Policy.* Boston: Beacon Press, 1995.

Strain, Christopher B. *Pure Fire: Self-Defense as Activism in the Civil Rights Era.* Athens: University of Georgia Press, 2005.

Sugrue, Thomas J. *The Origins of the Urban Crisis: Race and Inequality in Postwar Detroit.* Princeton: Princeton University Press, 1996.

Taylor, Clarence. *Knocking at Our Own Door: Milton A. Galamison and the Struggle to Integrate New York City Schools.* New York: Columbia University Press, 1997.

Theoharis, Jeanne F., and Komozi Woodard, eds. *Freedom North: Black Freedom Struggles Outside the South, 1940–1980.* New York: Palgrave Macmillan, 2003.

———. *Groundwork: Local Black Freedom Movements in America.* New York: New York University Press, 2005.

Trouillot, Michel-Rolph. *Silencing the Past: Power and the Production of History.* New York: Beacon Press, 1995.

Tyson, Timothy B. *Radio Free Dixie: Robert F. Williams and the Roots of Black Power.* Chapel Hill: University of North Carolina Press, 1999.

Van Deburg, William. *New Day in Babylon: The Black Power Movement and American Culture, 1965–1975.* Chicago: University of Chicago Press, 1992.

Varon, Jeremy. *Bringing the War Home: The Weather Underground, the Red Army Faction, and Revolutionary Violence in the Sixties and Seventies.* Berkeley: University of California Press, 2004.

Von Eschen, Penny. *Race Against Empire: Black Americans and Anticolonialism, 1937–1957.* Ithaca: Cornell University Press, 1997.

———. *Satchmo Blows Up the World: Jazz Ambassadors Play the Cold War.* Cambridge: Harvard University Press, 2005.

Walters, Ronald W. *Pan-Africanism in the African Diaspora: An Analysis of Modern Afrocentric Political Movements.* Detroit: Wayne State University Press, 1997.

Ward, Hiley H. *Prophet of the Black Nation.* Philadelphia: Pilgrim Press, 1969.

Washington, James, ed. *Testament of Hope: The Essential Writings and Speeches of Martin Luther King, Jr.* New York: HarperCollins, 1986.

Watts, Jerry Gafio. *Amiri Baraka: The Politics and Art of a Black Intellectual.* New York: New York University Press, 2001.

Weiner, Mark S. *Black Trials: Citizenship from the Beginnings of Slavery to the End of Caste.* New York: Knopf, 2004.

Werner, Craig. *A Change Is Gonna Come: Music, Race and the Soul of America.* Edinburgh: Payback Press, 1998.

West, Cornel. *Race Matters.* Boston: Beacon Press, 1993.

White, Deborah Gray. *Too Heavy a Load: Black Women in Defense of Themselves, 1894–1994.* New York: Norton, 1999.

White, E. Francis. *Dark Continent of Our Bodies: Black Feminism and the Politics of Respectability.* Philadelphia: Temple University Press, 2001.

Williams, Rhonda Y. *The Politics of Public Housing: Black Women's Struggles Against Urban Inequality.* New York: Oxford University Press, 2004.

Williams, Robert F. *Negroes with Guns.* New York: Marzani and Munsell, 1962.

Wilkins, Roger. *A Man's Life: An Autobiography.* New York: Touchstone, 1984.

Williams, Yohuru. *Black Politics/White Power: Civil Rights, Black Power, and the Black Panthers in New Haven.* New York: Brandywine Press, 2000.

Wolfe, Tom. *Radical Chic and Mau-Mauing the Flak Catchers.* New York: Farrar, Straus and Giroux, 1970.

Wood, Joe, ed. *Malcolm X: In Our Own Image.* New York: St. Martin's Press, 1992.

Woodard, Komozi. *A Nation Within a Nation: Amiri Baraka (LeRoi Jones) and Black Power Politics.* Chapel Hill: University of North Carolina Press, 1999.

Wright, Richard. *Black Power: A Record of Reactions in a Land of Pathos.* New York: Harper & Brothers, 1954.

———. *The Color Curtain: A Report on the Bandung Conference.* Cleveland: World Publishing Company, 1956.

———. *White Man, Listen!* New York: Anchor Books, 1957.

Zimroth, Peter L. *Perversions of Justice: The Prosecution and Acquittal of the Panther 21.* New York: Viking Press, 1974.

ACKNOWLEDGMENTS

This book is the result of numerous instances of love, understanding, compassion, and generosity. An undertaking as ambitious as *Waiting 'Til the Midnight Hour* would have been impossible without the aid of countless intellectuals, archivists, friends, colleagues, and family members. Although I cannot possibly thank each and every person whose assistance and encouragement has helped me over the years, I am going to try.

Sonia Sanchez, whose art and activism grace some of these pages, has been generous with her time, wisdom, and resources. For over a decade, she has provided me with the mentoring and friendship without which this project would never have been completed.

A resident fellowship at the Woodrow Wilson International Center for Scholars during the 2002–2003 academic year allowed me the time to write much of the first draft of this book. The center's fellows and staff created a stimulating, responsive environment. I am also grateful for the work that my research assistants, Jon White and Leneise Smith, performed during my tenure at the Wilson. Thanks go to Lee Hamilton, Rosemari Lyon, Arlyn Charles, Philippa Strum, Kimberly Conner,

Janet Spikes, Dagne Gizaw, Michelle Kamalich, Sean McQuitty, Carolina Fernandez, and Joseph Tulchin for making my time at the center enjoyable and productive. Thanks, as well, to 2002–2003 fellows Sharon Harley, Stephen King, and Mary Osirim, who made time away from the computer fun and informative. In Washington, I was fortunate enough to meet Delma and Alice Robinson, whose knowledge, enthusiasm, and passion for black history buoyed my spirits. Special thanks to Theo Abbott for his friendship and support during my time in D.C. and after.

The Ford Foundation fellowship for minorities provided vital support for the completion of this project. As a Ford fellow during the summers of 2002 and 2003, I accomplished important research goals and drafted early chapters of this book. Since its inception, the fellowship has facilitated higher education's post–Black Power aim of diversity and multiculturalism by offering opportunities to minority scholars. Through annual meetings of Ford fellows, I have met supportive colleagues and made lasting friendships. I am proud and grateful to be part of the Ford family of fellows. Thanks especially to Christina O'Brien, Jovett Solomon, Peggy Petrochenkov, and Vicki Rahamalati. Thanks to the new Ford fellows who showed support and enthusiasm for this project: you are the future.

The University of Rhode Island, my former employer, especially the history department and Afro-American studies program, stood firmly behind my work. Thanks go to Rae Ferguson, Marie Schwartz, Rod Mather, Tim George, Eve Sterne, Michael Honhart, and Sharon Strom. My former office mates, Bob Weisbord and Joel Cohen, imparted wisdom and humor in equal doses. Thanks, as well, to Fran Cohen, Maureen Moakley, Marc Genest, Scot Molloy, Al Killilea, Tim Hennessey, Art Stein, Donald Cunnigan, Gerry Tyler, Norman Zucker, and Abu Bakr for their support and good humor.

A summer's research and writing during 2001 and 2004 was facilitated by URI's Council of Research. Dean Winifred Brownell allowed me leave time to finish this project and showed genuine interest in its successful completion. Thanks, as well, to associate deans Bob Bullock and Will Dvorak.

My students at URI did much to shape this project through their enthusiasm, critical questions, and support. My time there has only deepened my respect for and commitment to the pivotal role of America's public universities. Cynthia Hamilton, chair of Afro-American studies at URI, and Melvin Wade, director of the Multicultural Center, have been great friends, colleagues, and enthusiastic supporters.

Special thanks to Sal and Jess Mena for their friendship over the years. Sal was one of the first people that I met when I moved to Providence, and the encounter proved serendipitous. A fellow New Yorker transplanted to Rhode Island, Sal provided stimulating conversation and debate over a number of social, political, and philosophical issues. Over the years we have come to regard each other more as brothers than as friends.

I first encountered Lewis Gordon's writings—on race, philosophy, and the human sciences—at a bookstore while a graduate student in Philadelphia. The memory lingers because his work remains extraordinarily compelling. His groundbreaking research-scholarship on Frantz Fanon opened up new worlds. Lewis's inimitable intellect and prodigious scholarship are matched only by his generous friendship and warm hospitality, which were facilitated by the presence of Jane, Mathieu, Jenny, Sula, and Elijah Gordon.

Robin D. G. Kelley has been a guide, mentor, and friend for over a decade. Along with countless others, I find myself amazed by his warmth, generosity, and towering intellect. Robin's work on African American history and radicalism continues to shape my approach to this subject. The enthusiasm and selflessness that he has displayed provides a model for scholars in the American academy.

My colleagues in SUNY–Stony Brook's Africana Studies Department have supported this project with praise, encouragement, and enthusiasm. Thanks go to Les Owens, Tony Hurley, Floris Cash, Tracey Walters, Georges Fouron, David Ferguson, and Femi Vaughan. Les has been a fine example as a scholar and teacher for many years, and Femi and Rosemary's support and encouragement have been especially appreciated. Thanks, as well, to all my students, both undergraduate and graduate, who have encouraged me during the final stages of the work.

Dean James Staros has welcomed me to the Stony Brook University family and has shown interest in the project.

A Robert Woodruff Special Collections library grant allowed me to spend a week in Atlanta during the summers of 2001 and 2002. I want to thank Randall Burkett and his staff for their professionalism. Archives and historical repositories were key to completing this book. Andre Elizée and Diana Latchatanare at the Schomburg Center for Research in Black Culture have provided much-needed information and support. Margaret Jerrido at Temple University's Urban Archives has been a font of knowledge since my first year in graduate school. Thanks as well to Brenda Galloway-Wright. My research trips to Stanford University were greatly facilitated by Polly Armstrong in the Department of Special Collections. Special thanks to Clayborne Carson, director of the King Center, and his staff for making materials available to me, and kudos to Louis Nicholas Jackson for his research assistance at a pivotal moment. Ida Jones, Joellen El-Bashir, and the rest of the staff at Howard University's Moorland-Spingarn Research Center made the archives easier to navigate. Special thanks to Peggy Appleman, formerly of Washington's Martin Luther King Public Library, and Mark Greek, the current photo archivist of the King Library. Many thanks to Roz Payne for use of her powerful photos. Thanks to Octavio Olvera for facilitating photos from UCLA's special collections and Mary Wallace for help with the striking Albert Cleage photo.

The following archives were also crucial to this book's completion. In New York: the Tamiment Library. In Washington: Martin Luther King Public Library; the FBI Reading Room; Howard University's Moorland-Spingarn Center, Bethune-Cookman Archives. In California: Stanford University's Hoover Collection; the Southern California Library for Social Studies and Research; KPFA Pacifica Radio Archives; UCLA Special Collections; Los Angeles Public Library. In Atlanta: Auburn Avenue Research Library; Atlanta University Center Archive. In Michigan: Walter Reuther Library, Wayne State University; Bentley Library, University of Michigan. In Madison, Wisconsin: State Historical Society. Many thanks to those in the record dissemination section of the FBI, especially Gloria Ralph-McKissick and Deanna Staley.

An undertaking this ambitious has given me a new perspective on and an appreciation for the educational opportunities that have been afforded to me since birth. Dedicated teachers at elementary, secondary, and high schools in Queens, New York, encouraged my rambunctious love of reading, writing, and debating. My enthusiasm for these pursuits intensified at SUNY–Stony Brook. Amiri Baraka, one of this book's characters, was a faculty member in Stony Brook's Africana Studies Department when I was a student. Although I never took one of Baraka's classes, I had the opportunity to engage with him in conversations that piqued my interest in Black Power. I remain grateful for his presence and his willingness to talk to me over the ensuing years. Thanks, as well, to Louis Reyes Rivera for his brilliant poetry, prose, and political insights. Kathleen Wilson's lectures on British imperialism made a lasting impression on a budding young historian.

At Temple University, I discovered the extraordinary nuances of African American history. I would like to thank Kenneth Kusmer, Wilbert Jenkins, and Teshale Tibebu for their guidance during graduate school. Five years of living in Philadelphia exposed me to worlds of intellectual inquiry, social and cultural activism, and political insight. Special thanks to Mark and Orion Barnes. Mark, an intellectual in his own right and a loyal and generous colleague, provided pivotal aid during this book's completion and continues to be a good friend and brother.

I have been fortunate to encounter numerous scholars who have encouraged me during the research and writing of this work. Juan and Stacey Floyd-Thomas have been excellent friends and gracious hosts. Rhonda Y. Williams has been an invaluable colleague, friend, and constructive critic. Rhonda enthusiastically read the entire manuscript, offering suggestions and pointed questions that made the final product stronger, aesthetically and conceptually.

A group of scholars (many have gone prematurely gray or bald conducting research) working on the Black Power movement have provided friendship and collegiality over the years. Yohuru Williams is a brilliant scholar, colleague, and author whose work has provided inspiration. Komozi Woodard's scholarship on the Black Power era has broken new ground, and he has been a generous colleague as well. Stephen Ward's enthusiasm for the study of black radicalism is infectious. Robert Self's scholarship on Oakland, a deft combination of urban, social, and political history, accorded complexity to the Black Power era that remains infrequent among historians. I would like to thank Robert Chrisman for allowing me a forum, in *The Black Scholar*, to express some of my early thoughts.

In the course of writing this book, various conferences became not only spaces to present work but intellectual havens to discuss history with a diverse group of colleagues. Numerous individuals have supported me through the years with words of encouragement that emboldened me to continue this project. On this score, thanks goes to Van Gosse, Sundiata Cha-Jua, David Roediger, Fanon Wilkins, Jeff Ogbar, Will Jones, V. P. Franklin, John McMillian, Ben Vinson, Kimberly Springer, Kwame Alford, Frank Wilson, Nathaniel Norment, Brian Purnell, Scot Brown, James Smethurst, T. J. Davis, Geneva Smitherman, Rod Bush, Manning Marable, Ron Walters, Farah Jasmine Griffin, Jeanne Theoharis, Craig Werner, Hasan Jeffries, Gabrielle Foreman, Keith Mayes, Lucius Outlaw, David Theo Goldberg, Joy James, Craig Wilder, Brenda Gayle Plummer, Abdul Alkalimat, David Canton, Madhu Dubey, and Charles Jones.

Niani Kilkenney has been a mentor and friend since a summer internship at the Smithsonian. Niani's passion for the dissemination of African American history continues to be nothing short of inspirational.

Ernest Allen Jr. has been a selfless mentor over the years. Always probing and interested in getting the story right, Ernie read parts of the manuscript, shared valuable information, and provided cheerful encouragement along the way. Thanks to Paget Henry, Tony Bogues, Anani Dzidzienyo, Sheila Grant, and Donna Mitchell for their scholarly example and collegial support.

Timothy Tyson provided advice, good cheer, and a place to stay at a critical stage of this project. Gerald Horne's words of encouragement proved pivotal. Gerald's prodigious scholarship on black radicalism during the Cold War also served as a bellwether during much of its writing.

I would like to thank all of those who agreed to be interviewed, especially Amiri Baraka, Askia Muhammad Touré, Michael Thelwell, Kathleen Cleaver, William Strickland, Muhammad Ahmed, Louis Reyes Rivera, James Garrett, Howard Fuller, John Bracey Jr., Ethelbert Miller, Gwen Patton, and Frances Beal.

Thanks go to Larry Hughes, Zook, Pep, Donald Tibbs, Tim Walton and family, and Mike and Natalie Williams, for their friendship throughout this process. Darryl Toler has been a great friend for almost twenty years. Our long-running dialogue (another much-discussed book project) over race, politics, and culture has found its way into the best parts of this volume. Derrick "Priest" Myers has been a true friend through the ups and downs of this project. Chris, Ina, Savio, and Djuna Pisani provided great company and fine wine during research trips to California that included luxurious weekends in the picturesque Napa Valley.

Many thanks to Sonia Sanchez for introducing me to Gloria Loomis. I had no idea that Gloria was not only the best literary agent in the business but a wonderful person to boot. Gloria's daunting list of talented clients was enough to make the most confident first-time author blush, but she expressed belief in me and this project from the beginning, and for that I am grateful.

My editor, Vanessa Mobley, and I clicked from our first meeting, and the intellectual chemistry never flagged. Vanessa's dazzling editorial skills, subtle interventions, and breathtaking intelligence have made this experience the best kind of intellectual adventure. Her meticulous eye and feel for tone, narrative, and structure have immeasurably enhanced the final product. I would also like to thank the entire Henry Holt family, especially John Sterling, Jennifer Barth, Daniel Reid, Sadie Stein, Christopher O'Connell, Victoria Hartman, and Susan C. Joseph.

Family has been a source of strength while I finished this book. Conversations with my brother, Kerith, a medical doctor who reads thick works of narrative history and literature in his spare time, helped me sharpen my ideas. Thanks to Kerith, Dawn, and Caitlin Joseph for their love, moral support, and much-needed downtime during trips to Maryland. Thanks, as well, to extended family members: Matilde and

Gilberto da Silva and Paulo, Jackie, Sandra, Mike, and Michael Robert, and a special shout-out to Anecia.

Giving thanks to the "black community" may seem, at first blush, gratuitous. But throughout the writing and researching of this work, I have had the chance to discuss the book with a broad range of black folk (Caribbean, native-born, Africans, and those from far-flung parts of the world): on planes and buses, in archives and bookstores, in coffee shops and lounges, in churches and community centers, and on street corners and subways. I almost always received generous support from the countless men, women, and young people that I met along my journey. There was pride that I was a young black man with a Ph.D. writing a book; fascination with my choice of topic; and a deep, abiding respect for the fact that I was writing about a group of people who (love them or hate them) had stood up for what they believed in. Thanks for all those who provided words of encouragement, praise, and support.

This book's first dedication is a small gesture of love to my mother, Germaine Joseph. Through steadfast determination, Mom bequeathed to her children a historical legacy that stretched from Haiti to Queens, New York, and beyond. A single black woman who raised two boys into manhood in inner-city New York, my mom has a story that is nothing less than heroic. As a hospital worker and union member for forty years, she marched on picket lines, confronted economic calamities, and endured personal crises that would have felled the less resilient; and all the while providing a running conversation about history, politics, philosophy, and social movements that I am privileged to be a part of. Open-minded and curious, my mother draws a line in the sand when it comes to social, political, and racial injustice. Mom's nonnegotiable quest for justice, thirst for a better world, and energy to manifest these dreams in her children is miraculous. She is the single most influential person in my life, and it is her love, discipline, intellect, and passion for social and political justice that is contained in these pages.

Catarina Alexandra da Silva deserves a special dedication. Catarina met me when this project was just beginning to take shape and has endured through both the good times and the rocky patches that ensued. She made me think about the practical connections between black and African liberation struggles in new ways. While I was writing this book, she took time away from her doctoral studies to provide criticism, personal companionship, and unconditional love. Throughout, she has remained my biggest champion: a relentless optimist who provided perspective and coordination every step of the way. Catarina's strength of character and commitment to educating a generation of urban schoolchildren virtually written off by society makes me not only proud to know her but fortunate as well.

INDEX

ABOUT THE AUTHOR

PENIEL E. JOSEPH teaches in the Department of Africana Studies at SUNY–Stony Brook. He is the editor of *The Black Power Movement: Rethinking the Civil Rights–Black Power Era*. He has received fellowships from the Ford Foundation and the Woodrow Wilson International Center for Scholars. A native New Yorker, he lives in Brooklyn.